Television and Radio Announcing

NINTH EDITION

Television and Radio Announcing

NINTH EDITION

STUART HYDE

San Francisco State University

HOUGHTON MIFFLIN COMPANY Boston   New York

Once again,
to my wife, Allie, and to our children,
Stuart Jr.,
John Christian, and
Allison Elizabeth Ann

Sponsoring Editor: Adam P. Forrand

Associate Editor: Jennifer Wall

Editorial Assistant: Brigitte Maser

Associate Project Editor: Patricia English

Editorial Assistant: Cecilia Molinari

Senior Production/Design Coordinator: Sarah L. Ambrose

Senior Manufacturing Coordinator: Priscilla J. Bailey

Marketing Manager: Stephanie Jones

Credits for reprinted material appear beginning on page 500.

Printed in the U.S.A.

Library of Congress Catalog Card Number: 00-103225

ISBN: 0-618-04243-1

123456789-QF-04-03-02-01-00

CONTENTS

3   Voice Analysis and Improvement   61

4   Pronunciation and Articulation   91

5   Audio Performance   123

6   Video Performance   145

7   Commercials and Public-Service Announcements   175

8   Interview and Talk Programs   209

9 Radio News   247

13 Starting Your Announcing Career   367

Appendixes References for Broadcast Performers   403

PREFACE

The first edition of *Television and Radio Announcing* was published in 1959 and remained in print until a second edition was published twelve years later. Changes in broadcast practices and equipment were few during those years, so it took more than a decade to justify a new edition.

But, stability in this dynamic field of broadcasting soon was lost as innovations in programming, technology, government regulation, and business practices made frequent revision necessary. In the three years since the Eighth Edition appeared in 1998 far more changes have occurred in the broad field of electronic communication than in any similar span of years since publication of the initial edition.

When I wrote the First Edition of this text, television was in its infancy, and radio was the most prevalent medium of communication in the world. Here are a few examples of how remote those days were from today's reality. One feature of the First Edition was a description of how baseball games were "re-created" by taking the scanty information sent by Western Union ("FOUL LINER TO LEFT FIELD, S1. FB IN NET, S2. B1 LOW WIDE") and turning it into a full-scale audio production, complete with recorded crowd sounds, the crack of a mallet on a suspended bat or catcher's mitt, and the narration of an imaginative sports announcer.[1]

To mention a few other outdated items, in 1959 nearly all announcers needed to earn a first-class radiotelephone operator license—a "first phone." A public-service announcement promoted the Ground Observer Corps, asking for volunteers to become "skywatchers" to help thwart an enemy bomber attack. A section of the chapter on interviewing gave tips on interviewing "for the women's audience," and the text often used the masculine gender to mean everyone, as in "Who is your listener? Can you visualize him?" A commercial by a

---

[1]Announcer: "The pitch to Kaline. He swings, (CRACK OF BAT, CROWD SOUNDS UP) he rips it to left field . . . just a few feet foul. (NOISE OF CROWD) The pitch. (CRACK OF BAT ON BALL) Another foul, this time into the net. It's 0 and two on Kaline. Donovan into the wind up. Ball one, outside."

national advertiser presented a "humorous" stereotype of an Asian infant in an insensitive manner that wouldn't be tolerated today.

Following the appearance of each edition, I found myself eager to begin working on the next to keep pace with changes that were taking place at an accelerating rate! And so it went, from year to year, and edition to edition.

The electronic media will always be in the process of evolution, and production methods, economics, and audience preferences will sooner or later make any text on media performance obsolete in certain ways. The very title of this text is, in a literal sense, obsolete. A more accurate name would be "Communicating Through the Electronic Media," and I'd make that change were the present title not established so firmly.

In this edition, as in previous ones, I've attempted to satisfy two major criteria: To present information that's timeless and forever relevant, and to provide information on the most important practices in the broad field of electronic communication.

The thirteen chapters and five appendixes of *Radio and Television Announcing,* Ninth Edition, divide into two categories. The first presents material that's unchanging (or nearly so), such as interpretation of copy, ad-lib announcing, voice analysis and improvement, interviewing techniques, and pronunciation and articulation, with many exercises for speech improvement. The second category addresses that which undergoes rapid and sometimes drastic change, such as descriptions of production practices, distribution methods, and styles in news, narration, music, and sports performance.

Because this is a book about *performance,* I've reduced the space given to discussions of equipment. Electronic communication technology advances so rapidly as to make much of what's written about it obsolete within years and even months! Additionally, automation and computerization have simplified technical operations, making manipulative skills required for most announcing specializations easy to acquire.

Some parts of this text will serve you well for many years, while others will not. But, that's the nature of this fascinating field we love: certain change, but unchanging relevance. Those who use the public airwaves are expected to entertain, challenge, and enlighten, and this has always been so. While this text may be described accurately as a guidebook for success in announcing, its real focus is on you: its overriding goal is to help you become an effective and responsible communicator. That's what this text is really all about.

New to This Edition

One of the most helpful additions to the Ninth Edition are boxed features that point to materials that may be accessed through the Internet by anyone with a computer, a modem, and a service provider. URLs (Universal Resource Locators) are given that will allow you to access such resources as up-to-the-minute news copy, as well as scripts of sitcoms, dramas, analyses and commentaries, and commercial copy.

In addition, the URLs will allow you to access information about student memberships in national organizations, as well as access biographies of professional announcers, information on job opportunities, and much, much more.

Moving from printed to spoken words, URLs are given for finding, recording, and studying voiced material, including audition recordings made by professional voice-over announcers. If you want more information on URLs, use a New Web Browser to access this URL:

www.netspace.org/users/dwb/url-guide.html

Other changes and additions to the Ninth Edition are many. New Spotlights include "Feature Reporting As Storytelling," which details the practices of one of television's most honored feature reporters, Wayne Freedman. This Spotlight reveals how Freedman regards himself and his work. It follows Freedman through a day in his life as a writer, producer, and performer, and includes his advice to those who want to excel in the demanding specialization of feature reporting.

Longtime sports reporter and analyst Glenn Dickey presents "A Plea to Radio Sportscasters: Give Us the Details," in which he criticizes play-by-play announcers who seemingly forget that their radio listeners can't see the action, as when the game is on television. Dedicated play-by-play radio announcers are responsible for reporting every relevant detail of the game they cover, because their accounts are the sole means by which the audience experiences the event.

Cosmo Rose, veteran DJ and host of Almost Radio, a web site on show preparation for music radio hosts, contributes "Showprep Is Everything and Everything Is Showprep." In this insightful editorial, Cosmo reveals his own work regimen, and includes many suggestions that can be applied by students who plan to become DJs.

Aside from changes in content, I've also worked to make this edition more "readable" than ever. It's always been my goal to write in a straightforward, easily understood manner, and I believe I've been successful in that. I'm excited about our field—electronic human communication—and believe that words written about it should be direct, spirited, fresh in outlook, and convey honest enthusiasm. I hope I've succeeded in achieving this goal.

I wish you a great, productive, and constructive career as a communicator!

Acknowledgments

Revising a textbook in the field of electronic communication is a formidable challenge. Topics covered include such diverse specializations as voice analysis and improvement, interviewing, voice-over announcing, radio and television news, sports, DJ announcing, job seeking, and much more. No one person can be an authority on every detail of this increasingly complex field.

In preparing the Ninth Edition of *Television and Radio Announcing,* I consulted with professional broadcasters, colleagues, instructors, career guidance experts, and advertising agency personnel. A great many people contributed information to this text, and it's important that their contributions be acknowledged.

Among my colleagues who provided special help are Dr. Stanley T. Donner, professor emeritus of the University of Texas at Austin, and Ernie Kreiling, professor of telecommunications and syndicated television columnist. Herbert L. Zettl helped me update television production techniques, and Rick Houlberg once again gave permission for the inclusion of his study on audience rapport. I am grateful to my colleague, the late Professor Paul C. Smith, long-time audio coordinator for the Broadcast Communication Arts Department at San Francisco State University. Paul is responsible for much of what I know about audio. Professor Emeritus Arthur S. Hough, Jr. granted permission for the inclusion of his insightful article "The Art of Interviewing."

Manuscript for this revision was read and commented upon by professionals from radio and television stations and professors of broadcasting. Their comments, suggestions, and questions were extremely helpful to me. I am grateful to these individuals:

Mark Raduziner, *Johnson County Community College, Overland Park, Kansas*

Paul Philips, *Navarro College, Corsicana, Texas*

Darrell Kitchell, *Fullerton College, Fullerton, California*

I am also indebted to Sponsoring Editor Adam P. Forrand, Associate Editor Jennifer Wall, Editorial Assistant Brigitte Maser, Associate Project Editor Patricia English, and Editorial Assistant Cecilia Molinari of Houghton Mifflin Company for their support, encouragement, and guidance.

Special thanks go to feature reporter Wayne Freedman for tolerating my presence as he and his associates, editor James "Suds" Sudweeks and camera operator John L. Griffen, worked during a nine-hour period to produce two reports, each about five minutes in length. The work of this team is described in the Spotlight for Chapter 6, "Video Performance."

Several performers at KGO-TV, San Francisco, California, permitted me to photograph them at work. These include anchor–reporters Dan Noyes and Cheryl Jennings and general assignment reporter Carolyn Tyler, as well as consumer reporter Michael Finney and medical reporter Dr. Dean Edell.

I also thank Chet Casselman, for once again allowing me to use his excellent suggestions for writing news copy, and media critic Ernie Kreiling, for his suggestions on interviewing. Veteran news anchor Al Hart spoke with me about his practice of "woodshedding" copy and demonstrated his techniques in marking a commercial for delivery. Special assignment reporter Mike Sugerman of KCBS, San Francisco, California, shared with me his techniques for producing radio news packages.

Hal Ramey, sports reporter and director, also of KCBS, explained and demonstrated how he obtains, edits, and produces actualities for his daily sports reports. Other professionals in sports broadcasting who were helpful include Steve Bitker, sports reporter for KCBS, and Fred Inglis, sports reporter for KTVU-TV, Oakland, California. San Francisco Giants play-by-play announcer Ted Robinson was generous with his time and patience, as I observed him calling several Giants baseball games. Lee Jones, San Francisco Giants radio producer–engineer, demonstrated for me his recording, editing, and playback techniques using a tapeless Short/Cut Unit produced by 360 Systems.

Sports reporter Joan Ryan contributed the essay "Our Weird Fascination With Colossal Failure," which is reprinted through permission of the *San Francisco Chronicle*.

Broadcast personnel from KTVU who made special contributions include news director Andrew Finlayson and anchor–reporters Frank Somerville and Tori Campbell. Bob Hirschfeld, senior producer of Cox Interactive Media, also made special contributions. Floor director Charlene Johnson posed as I photographed her showing the hand signals used during newscasts. Station engineering director Ed Cosci was generous with his time in explaining complex technical operations. Field reporter Thuy Vu gave permission for me to follow and photograph her as she reported live from the field. Feature reporter Bob MacKenzie demonstrated his procedures in taking recorded video material furnished by a nonprofit organization and editing it into a story about that organization's work.

Afternoon drive-time radio news anchors Rosie Allen and Ed Baxter and traffic reporter Stan Burford of KGO-AM, San Francisco, California, shared information about their daily preparation and performance, while allowing me to photograph them at work. I thank Kristi Orcutt, community relations director, for making those arrangements.

Veteran DJ Carter B. Smith, and Ron Rodrigues of *Radio & Records (R & R)*, provided information that helped update the data on popular music broadcasting. The Spotlight, "Learning to Sound Local," by Dan O'Day, is reprinted here through the courtesy of Erica Farber, publisher and chief executive officer of *Radio & Records (R & R)*.

Al Covaia, producer–host for Classical-music station KKHI-AM/FM, Corte Madera, California, discussed his methods of preparing a weekly music program and permitted me to photograph him as he performed. Lauraine Bacon, freelance voice-over performer, granted permission to be photographed during a recording session. Gian Voglino of KABA Audio Research and Development, Novato, California, arranged for this session.

Cosmo Rose, popular morning drive-time host on "Classy 100 FM," WXKC, Erie, Pennsylvania, shared his thoughts on "personality-intensive" popular-music performance and made available to me his weekly newsletter "Almost Radio," from which I've gathered much inside knowledge of his field. One of his many editorials, "Showprep Is Everything and Everything Is Showprep," became the Spotlight for Chapter 11, "Music Announcing."

Steve Walker, operations manager and morning show host on "The Mountain96.5," WMTZ-FM, Johnstown, Pennsylvania, contributed valuable information about audience rapport and discussed his feelings about the future of music radio.

DJs Chuy Gomez of KMEL, San Francisco, California, and Ray White of KKSF, San Francisco, California, allowed me to observe them at work and to photograph them as they opened their mics to tease upcoming selections and to back-announce music sweeps.

Broadcasting students Jennie Jones and Doug Brown explained the operations of their campus radio station KSFS while I shot photos of them as they performed in an on-air studio at San Francisco State University.

Barbara Lazear Ascher, author of the Chapter 3 Spotlight, "Improving Your Voice Personality," gave her permission to include this valuable article. Two former students Ayrien Houchin and Midei Toriyama contributed the essays "Talk Show Trash" and "About the Rooms," respectively, both of which are included in Appendix A as material for student practice.

Award-winning commercials were provided by their creators, Eric Poole, head of Splash Radio, and Donn Resnick, of Donn Resnick Advertising. Outstanding public-service announcements were provided by the Advertising Council, and my thanks go to Sarah Moser, Stacy Brown, and David Lowe for making these spots available.

I am also appreciative of the help given by Samantha Paris, Fred La-Cosse, and Denny Delk, who provided valuable information on media performance and job seeking.

I also want to thank the following performers for permitting me to photograph them at work: DJ Tom Plant of KZST, Santa Rosa, California; jazz program host Bob Parlocha; talk-show host Ronn Owens of KGO Radio, San Francisco, California; Amaury Pi-Gonzalez, Spanish-language announcer for the San Francisco Giants; Roger Brulotte and Denis Casavant of the Montreal Expos; the late Harry Caray of the Chicago Cubs; Sherry Davis of the San Francisco Giants; and Al Hart, Ron Reynolds, and Bob Price of KCBS radio, San Francisco, California.

Stuart Hyde

CHAPTER 1

Announcing for the Electronic Media

CHAPTER OUTLINE

- The Announcer for the Electronic Media
- Employment as an Announcer
- Education and Training
  Coursework Considerations
- The Announcer's Responsibility
- SPOTLIGHT: Broadcast Ethics and the Announcer's Responsibility

THIS BOOK IS ABOUT HUMAN COMMUNICATION, WITH A FOCUS ON THE electronic media. Its purpose is to help you improve your communication skills. Studying to improve your communication abilities can be of lasting benefit, whether or not you intend to become a performer on radio or television. Confident, effective expression has always been an invaluable tool. The ever-increasing significance of electronic media means that competent communication skills may become nearly as important as literacy was a century ago.

In one sense, then, this book is about the electronic media, including television and radio. It discusses announcing as a profession, treats both the theoretical and performance aspects of the field, describes major areas of specialization within the field, provides copy for practicing performance skills, and offers job-seeking information and suggestions.

In a broader sense this book is about *communication.* If you apply yourself, you can look forward to noticeable improvement in your ability to (1) make pleasant speech sounds; (2) clearly articulate the sounds of the English language; (3) vary pitch and volume effectively; (4) pronounce words according to accepted standards; (5) select and use words, phrases, similes, and metaphors effectively; (6) express yourself confidently; (7) interpret copy; (8) speak ad lib or impromptu; and (9) communicate ideas clearly, both orally and nonverbally. Aside from such specifics, your development as an effective communicator will enhance your rapport—your affinity—with others.

Figure1.1

Like most music announcers on radio, veteran jazz announcer Bob Parlocha operates his audio console and all other units of broadcast equipment. He ad-libs comments based on album notes and his own encyclopedic knowledge of jazz music. *Courtesy of Bob Parlocha.*

The Announcer for the Electronic Media

Media performers are products of the electronic age, but several related professions preceded them by centuries. Preliterate storytellers, troubadours, singers of psalms, town criers, and early newspaper journalists were all forerunners of modern announcers. Each provided a service to a public. With some, the emphasis was on the delivery of information; with others it was on entertainment. **Announcers** are like storytellers in that they speak directly to their audiences. Radio announcers also resemble writers for the print media in that they describe events their audiences can't see. Television reporters and news anchors frequently describe events that are simultaneously being viewed by their audiences.

Imagine a range of newsworthy events—a hurricane, election returns, even war—and then try to imagine the coverage of these events without the comments and explanations of on-the-scene reporters. In the late 1990s, for example, radio and television kept millions of viewers informed of armed conflicts as they occurred in Iraq, Somalia, and Kosovo. For **live coverage** of significant occurrences, there's simply no model from earlier times to parallel the television announcer commenting on events as they happen.

Despite the similarities that announcing shares with earlier professions, there are some important differences. Both radio and television reach vast audiences scattered over thousands of miles. And, both possess instantaneousness. Radio made it possible for the first time in history to describe to millions of people events as they were occurring. Because radio presented "real time" communication over great distances and because radio is a "blind" medium, announcers became indispensable. Radio couldn't function without those who provided direct oral communication by describing events, reporting the news, introducing speakers and entertainers, and alerting audiences to tornado, hurricane, or flood dangers.

The radio announcer is the clarifying link between listeners and what would otherwise be a jumble of sound, noise, or silence. On television the announcer is the presenter, the communicator, and the interpreter. Without such performers neither radio nor television as we know them would be possible. Announcers are important to many types of programs, and through many electronic distribution systems. Their responsibility is substantial, and because announcers usually make direct presentations to their audiences, they also are efficient and economical. No other means of disseminating information is so direct and swift as the word spoken directly to the listener. Small wonder, then, that radio or television announcers must possess native talent, acquire a broad educational background, and then undergo intensive training and consistent practice as they develop professional competencies.

Many broadcast performers don't like to be called "announcers," preferring instead to be known by their area of specialization: *anchor, talent, DJ (disc jockey), host, narrator, voice-over performer, sportscaster,* or *reporter.* Precise terminology should be used when appropriate, but the term *announcer* is used throughout this book for simplicity whenever the profession is discussed in general terms.

As used in this book, an **announcer** is *anyone who communicates over the public airwaves, as on radio or television broadcasts; through cable channels into homes, schools, offices, etc.; or over closed-circuit audio or video distribution by electronic amplification, as in an auditorium, stadium, arena, or theater.* Singers, actors, and actresses are considered announcers only when they perform that specific function: in commercial presentations, for example. Announcing includes many areas of specialization:

Broadcast Journalism

    Anchors, or news readers

    Field reporters—special assignment or general assignment

    Feature reporters (who often take a humorous or satiric view of a current event)

    Analysts

Commentators
Weather reporters
Consumer affairs reporters
Environmental reporters
Science reporters
Entertainment reporters
Farm news reporters
Business news reporters
Medical reporters (frequently doctors)
Traffic reporters

Sports Coverage on Radio and Television

Play-by-play announcers
Play and game analysts
Sports reporters
Sports news program hosts

Music

Announcers on popular music stations (referred to variously as DJs, deejays, or jocks)[1]
Music video jockeys (VJs or veejays)
Classical music announcers (for both live and recorded performances)

Public Affairs

Interviewers
Panel Moderators

Commercials

Voice-over announcers (radio and television)
Demonstration and commercial announcers (television)

---

[1]The term *disc jockey* was coined many years ago, and was a slangy but useful term until recent times. Popular music announcers once handled phonograph records, selecting, cueing, and introducing them on the air, and then playing them. So they did "jockey" the records in the sense of manipulating them. Now that most announcers work with music stored on hard drives, the term has lost its literal meaning. A survey of a number of successful announcers who perform this function found that nearly all prefer the term *DJ,* or *deeJay.*

"Infomercial" announcers (television)—those who present lengthy commercials showing and demonstrating products

Salespersons on the Home Shopping Network or QVC

Narration

Narrators of documentaries, such as *National Geographic* specials, A&E's *Biography,* and most of the documentaries shown on The History Channel

Readers of scripts for industrial or corporate presentations

Readers of essays, editorials, feature reports, and "impressions" for both radio and television. Such readers almost always write the pieces they read on the air.

Hosting Special Programs

Talk shows

Interview and phone-in shows (television and radio)

Magazine shows such as *Entertainment Tonight, Hard Copy, Frontline,* and *Talk of the Nation* (television), and *All Things Considered* and *Science Friday* (radio)

Food, gardening, home repair, and similar specialty shows

Dance and popular music shows (television)

Children's programs

Game shows

Introducers of feature films on television

Single-subject specialists also appear regularly on talk shows or newscasts on topics such as gardening, cooking, exercise, consumerism, science, art, and health. These specialists sometimes perform "solo" on brief segments of one to five minutes; others work with station staff announcers who serve as hosts. During televised parades (Macy's Thanksgiving Day Parade, the Rose Bowl Parade), announcing teams identify participants, explain float construction, and provide color.[2]

---

[2]*Color* was coined for radio to mean the description of things of interest that couldn't be seen by the listeners. Today, in both television and radio usage, color announcers are those who provide anecdotes of an informative, amusing, or offbeat nature.

Employment As an Announcer

According to the *Occupational Outlook Handbook*, published by the U.S. Department of Labor, approximately fifty-seven thousand men and women are currently employed as announcers.[3] Most are full-time employees of radio and television stations, cable operations, and broadcast networks. Some are full- or part-time freelance announcers who perform as DJs under contract. Other freelance announcers narrate for documentaries and instructional recordings, or serve as both on-camera and off-camera voice-over performers of commercials.

 National employment and wage estimates for announcers in cable and broadcasting, may be found on the Internet. Choose "New Web Browser." The URL is[4]:

stats.bls.gov/oes/national/oes34017.htm

This site is maintained by the U.S. Bureau of Labor Statistics. For a complete, updated list of URLs for this textbook, please see the text home site available at *www.hmco.com/college.*

The rapid expansion of cable television services has created additional openings for announcers. In 1975, most citizens of the United States and Canada could receive between seven and fifteen television channels. These included network affiliates, public broadcasting and other noncommercial stations, and independent commercial stations. As cable entered the picture and began to grow, options for viewers multiplied. By the early 2000s, as many as a hundred cable channels will be available to home subscribers. With this dramatic expansion of cable channels will come new opportunities for announcers.

---

[3]*Occupational Outlook Handbook*, U.S. Department of Labor, January, 1996. *The Encyclopedia of Careers and Vocational Guidance,* ninth edition, estimates the number of announcers and newscasters at "about fifty-seven thousand."

[4]The Internet is changing constantly as new web sites are added and old web sites are abandoned. The URL listings in this textbook should be regarded as samples of the kinds of material available rather than as a stable index. If you seek a web site using one of these URLs and cannot connect, enter the key words for the topic into a search engine to find a site that may provide the information you want.

Figure 1.2

Consumer reporter Michael Finney hosts a daily feature, "Seven on Your Side," a service that acts on behalf of viewers who believe they've been treated unfairly by a business or governmental agency. Michael's path to his present major market position began as a television reporter in Pocatello, Idaho, followed by reporting and anchoring in Idaho Falls, Idaho; Bakersfield, California; San Diego, California; and finally at KGO-TV in San Francisco, California. Michael earned his bachelor's degree in communications from California State University, Chico. You can find his biography at URL: *www.kgoam810.com/*.
Courtesy of Michael Finney and KGO-TV, San Francisco, California.

Cable television began as *community antenna services* (CATV), originally devised to collect broadcast signals and feed them by wire to homes in which television reception was poor. By the mid-1960s, enterprising CATV operators saw opportunities beyond the distribution of signals from existing stations. Equipment was developed and installed that permitted CATV systems to receive transmissions from far-off stations and to add their programs to those of stations in their immediate areas. By the early 1970s, cable capacity was increased to more than 100 channels. So-called superstations were created, and their programming was sent to all parts of the country.[5] Companies devoted to creating or bringing back programs of the past, soon followed. Cable television, as we now know it, was born.

---

[5]WTBS, the Atlanta station owned by Turner Broadcasting, was the first to go "national" by way of cable TV.

Today, cable companies continue to offer programming from both local and distant on-air stations, but they offer, as well, such nonbroadcast services as the Discovery Channel, Comedy Central, Cable News Network (CNN), Entertainment and Sports Programming Network (ESPN and ESPN2), American Movie Classics (AMC), Lifetime, Nickelodeon, Arts and Entertainment (A&E), Sundance Channel, Turner Classic Movies, Chinese Television Network (CTN), Black Entertainment Television, MTV, and shopping channels. So-called premium channels—channels for which subscribers pay fees beyond the basic rate for cable service—include Home Box Office (HBO), Showtime, The Movie Channel, Bravo, Cinemax, the Disney Channel, as well as regional sports channels. Most cable systems also offer pay-per-view programming, usually featuring recent motion pictures and prime sports events.

With the availability of dozens of new channels through "digitally compressed" cable and satellite downlinks, cable companies are planning even more comprehensive **narrowcasting** or **microcasting** than now exists. Under consideration (and already available in some areas) are channels devoted to such narrowly focused interests as golf, tennis, gardening, gymnastics, health, war movies and documentaries, western movies and television dramas, detective dramas, cooking shows, game shows, specialized music channels, and daytime serials. Some predict there will be television channels for all major political parties, seniors, automobile enthusiasts, small business owners, and so on. And—one hopes—all this in addition to a considerable growth in self-improvement and instructional programs.

While much of the programming no doubt will be recycled material—movies, syndicated television packages, classic sports events, and television miniseries—it's safe to predict an increased demand for on-camera and voice-over announcers.

To prepare for this revolution in television, you should develop the skills discussed in this text; you also should plan an educational program that will help you become an expert in at least some of the categories of programming now in use or on the horizon. Regardless of the number of job openings, competition for them will continue to be keen.

A growing number of men and women work in **industrials**, also called **corporate media**. Audio and video presentations are made for employee training, introduction of new products, providing information to distant branches, and in-house communication. The term **industrial media** is a loose one, because it applies to media used by hospitals, government agencies, schools, prisons, and the military, as well as businesses. Few media departments can afford the services of a full-time announcer, so, if this work appeals to you, you should prepare for media writing and producing as well as announcing. (Chapter 13, "Starting Your Announcing Career," provides specific information on job seeking.)

The chapters that follow this introductory overview describe working conditions and the kinds of abilities you'll need to succeed in each of the major announcing specializations. You should work on every facet of announcing while emphasizing the area in which you hope to specialize.

Local television stations provide multiprogram service, but aside from newscasts and interview/talk shows, they employ few announcers. But most local television stations *do* produce commercials. Even the smallest community with a commercial television station may offer some work for announcers. If this field interests you, call a station's sales or promotion department for specific information about how they hire announcers.

Several lists of talent agencies may be found on the Internet. Choose "New Web Browser" and click "Open." Here are some URLs:

www.cybershowbiz.com/ncopm/member_1.html

www.pozproductions.com/agtmainp.htm

For a complete updated list of URLs for this textbook, please see the text home site available at *www.hmco.com/college.*

Education and Training

Broadcast stations and cable networks spend their hours of operation distributing a broad range of programming, including news, weather, music, sports, political discussion, and drama. Assuming that you're majoring in "electronic communication" (or whatever term is used at your school), you should consider enrolling in one or more minor programs in such content areas as history, political science, urban studies, literature, sociology, economics, or geography. Career-oriented courses of study also should be considered, including journalism, sports history, and meteorology.

Information about academic programs in communication is available on the Internet. Select "New Web Browser," click "Open," and enter this URL:

www.beaweb.org/inst1.html

You'll find a list of U.S. and Canadian institutional members of the Broadcast Education Association. Click on those you want to examine for information, including faculty, courses taught, entrance and degree requirements, and fees.

For a complete, updated list of URLs for this textbook, please see the text home site available at *www.hmco.com/college.*

Figure 1.3

General assignment reporter Carolyn Tyler has earned many awards, including citations from the National Association of Black Journalists, the Black Media Coalition, and American Women in Radio and Television. Carolyn received her bachelor's degree in broadcasting from the University of Wyoming. Prior to her current employment, Carolyn worked as a reporter in Minneapolis and Philadelphia. *Courtesy of Carolyn Tyler and KGO-TV, San Francisco, California.*

Informational media are reaching millions of people with more and more messages of critical importance to their future, and there is little room for narrowly educated announcers. For one thing, the influence—for good or ill—of radio and television performers is immense and mustn't be underestimated. Announcers are addressing and being evaluated by increasingly sophisticated listeners. Americans are better informed today than ever before, and they are quick to spot shallowness or ignorance.

The dramatic explosion of knowledge in the past several years will make announcers who don't grow with the times inadequate in the twenty-first century. Dictionaries have been adding new entries at an unprecedented pace; each represents to an announcer or reporter not only a new word to pronounce but a new concept, a new technological breakthrough, a newly perceived human condition, or a new phenomenon to understand.

The number of program hours on radio and television devoted to unscripted presentations has increased considerably during the past dozen years. Television program hosts, DJs, interviewers, announcers covering sports and special events, and talk-show personalities use written material only occasionally; most of the time they're on their own. Radio and television field reporters covering breaking stories as they unfold never work from scripts; they ad-lib their reports from hastily scribbled notes that are limited to basic information. The opportunity to frame your personal thoughts in words of your own choosing carries with it the responsibility to have much information at hand to share with your audience.

Coursework Considerations

Your career goals should determine your choice of courses outside your major, but you should also be aware of the expectations of future employers. Nearly all look for well-educated people who possess certain basic skills: good writing ability, outstanding proficiency in spoken communication, computational skills (basic math), and critical thinking. They also look for people who are hardworking, self-motivated, and pleasant to be around.

In studying to be a broadcast announcer, obviously you should pursue *subjects that prepare you for your first announcing job*. You also should select *courses that qualify you for one or more specializations beyond straight announcing*. You must obtain a *broad background in the liberal arts and sciences*. If you're serious about an announcing career, your education must have breadth. You probably won't be able to study all areas mentioned in the checklist on page 13, but you should at least discuss them with an adviser.

Control-room operations should include practice with **audio consoles** and storage devices, such as compact disc (CD) players, digital audiotape (DAT) players, and disk drives. Take courses in video production and editing because many television stations expect reporters to record and edit their news stories. Anchors and reporters must learn to write news copy. Most stations in medium-to-small markets expect announcers to write commercial copy and station promotional pieces as well.

Expand your ability to pronounce names and words in the most commonly used languages. Many departments of music offer a course in lyric diction, which teaches principles of pronunciation of French, German, Italian, and, occasionally, Russian or Spanish.

 The web site for this textbook provides extensive information on rules of pronunciation for French, German Spanish, and Italian, with a less extensive discussion of Chinese pronunciation. The web site may be accessed with the following URL:

www.hmco.com/college

Many of the general education courses you'll take are required for a liberal arts degree, including English composition. Note, however, that it isn't enough to study and practice writing for the media. Departments of English offer courses in expository writing, essay writing, creative writing, and dramatic writing. It's impossible to get too much writing experience!

One area of preparation is important enough to warrant separate mention. Broadcast stations rely heavily on the use of **computerized information systems.**[6] Computers are central to video editing systems, character generators, word processors, graphics systems, scheduling and billing systems, and data-retrieval systems. Computers are used

---

[6]Preparation for work at a highly sophisticated radio station is the subject of a detailed discussion in Chapter 11, "Music Announcing."

CHECKLIST

COURSES TO
BUILD YOUR
CAREER

BASIC PREPARATION FOR ANNOUNCING

Take courses that focus on the following subjects:
- Interpretation
- Articulation
- Phonation
- Phonetic transcription
- Microphone use
- Camera presence
- Ad-libbing
- Script reading
- Adapting one's personality to the broadcast media
- Foreign language pronunciation
- Control room operations
- Small-format video production and editing
- Writing for radio and television.

Specialized Courses to Prepare You for Specific Duties
- **Broadcast journalism**—courses in journalism, international relations, political science, economics, history, and geography
- **Broadcast sales and advertising**—courses in business, marketing, accounting, sales techniques, sales promotion, and audience research
- **Sports, including play-by-play announcing**—courses in the history of sports, sports officiating, and sociology of sport
- **Weather reporting**—courses in meteorology, weather analysis, weather forecasting, and geography

Courses to Further Your General Education
- Social, ethical, aesthetic, and historical perspectives on **electronic communication**
- **The arts**—music, theater, literature, or painting and sculpture
- **Social and behavioral sciences**—psychology, sociology, urban studies, and ethnic studies
- **Quantitative reasoning**—essentially math and computation
- **Critical thinking**—skills crucial to clear and constructive thought
- **Media law and regulation**
- **Writing, writing, writing**

almost exclusively in newsrooms in the writing and editing of news copy. Familiarity with information systems is highly desirable, and the ability to type well is mandatory. Courses in "information science" may or may not be appropriate and should be selected with care. Most aren't geared toward their use in electronic communication. For most students of announcing, basic courses in the use of both Macintosh- and PC-compatible computers may be sufficient for your needs.

Evaluate these suggestions in light of your own aptitudes, interests, and career plans. College counselors can help you determine the appropriateness of the courses available to you. The important point is that only you can apply your growing knowledge to your announcing practice.

Most community colleges require sixty semester hours for an associate in arts or associate in science degree. Four-year colleges or universities require about one hundred and twenty-five semester hours for a bachelor's degree. Whether you're enrolled in a two- or four-year program, it's unlikely that you'll be offered more than six semester hours of performance courses. You should, therefore, look for performance opportunities wherever they present themselves—on a campus radio station, in television directing and producing classes, or on public access cable stations. Remember, though, that you'll spend most of your broadcasting class hours in nonperformance courses, all of which are important to your development as a well-rounded broadcaster.

Clearly, announcing encompasses a wide range of activities. Most modern liberal arts colleges and their broadcasting departments are well equipped to help you begin the process of becoming a competent and versatile communicator—which is what you must become if you're to manage challenges such as these:

- You're a staff announcer. You are to read a commercial for a local restaurant featuring international cuisine. You must pronounce correctly *vichyssoise, coq au vin, paella, sukiyaki, saltimbocca alla Romana,* and *hasenpfeffer.*
- You're a staff announcer and must read news headlines containing the place names *Sault Sainte Marie, Pristina, Schleswig-Holstein, Bosnia-Herzegovina, Santa Rosa de Copán, São Paulo,* and *Leicester.*
- You're the announcer on a classical music program, and you need to know the meaning and correct pronunciation of *scherzo, andante cantabile, Götterdämmerung,* and *L'Après-midi d'un faune.*
- You're a commercial announcer, and the copy for a pharmaceutical company demands that you correctly pronounce *isoflavones, ipratropium bromide, gingivitis, fungicide,* and *ketoconazole.*

Figure 1.4

Sports director and reporter Hal Ramey reviews and edits audiotaped interviews. Ramey attends numerous sporting events and tapes brief interviews with athletes, coaches, managers, and front-office personnel for later inclusion as actualities on his twice-hourly sports reports. Hal received his bachelor's degree in telecommunications from San Jose State University. *Courtesy of Hal Ramey and KCBS, San Francisco, California.*

- You're a play analyst on a sports broadcast, and you need to obtain extensive historical and statistical information on football in order to fill the inevitable moments of inactivity.

- You're the play-by-play announcer for a semipro baseball team, and you must pronounce such "American" names as Martineau, Buchignani, Kuyumjian, Yturri, Ulloa, Sockolow, Watanabe, Engebrect, and MacLeod.

- You've been assigned to interview a Nobel Prize winner in astrophysics, and you must obtain basic information about the field as well as biographical data on the winner—and do so under extreme time limitations.

- You're narrating a documentary, and you must analyze the intent and content of the program to determine the mood, rhythm, structure, and interrelationship of sound, picture, and script.

- You're covering a crowd scene that could deteriorate into a riot. You're expected to assess responsibly the human dynamics of the scene, while carefully avoiding comments or activities that could precipitate violence in this already dangerous situation.

- You're a DJ, and you're on duty when word is received of the unexpected death of a great American (a politician, an entertainer, or a scientist). Until the news department can take over, you must ad-lib appropriately.

It's obvious that no one type of course will completely educate you as an announcer.

In addition to your academic studies, you may benefit from becoming a member of one or more organizations that are open to students. Through such organizations, you may attend meetings and conventions and receive news and information over the Internet. You also may make connections that may some day pay off. Join broadcast-related organizations such as College Students in Broadcasting, the Association for Women in Communication, Inc. (AWC), the International Radio and Television Society–Alpha Epsilon Rho, and the National Black Media Coalition. Students with a broadcast journalism emphasis may become members of the Radio-Television Journalism division of the Association for Education in Journalism and Mass Communication. Membership in the student category of the Radio and Television News Directors Association (RTNDA) is also available to you.

 For information about joining these organizations, use these URLs:

Association for Women in Communication, Inc.:

www.womcom.org/

International Radio and Television Society–Alpha Epsilon Rho:

www.onu.edu/org/nbs/

Radio and Television News Directors Association:

www.rtnda.org/join/index.htm

National Black Media Coalition:

www.nbmc.org/index.html

The Radio-Television Journalism Division (RTVJ) of the Association for Education in Journalism and Mass Communication sponsors a list for broadcast professionals, academics, and students. The list is a vehicle for a lively discussion forum for broadcast news issues. Much information and opinion is sent daily to those on the list, and an opportunity is offered for any member to add or reply to the discussions. To subscribe to the RTVJ list, select the Alta Vista browser, click "OPEN," and enter this URL:

www2.drury.edu/rtvj/rtvj1.html

You'll receive detailed information about the list and instructions for becoming a member. Be sure to indicate the e-mail address at which you wish to receive messages.

For a complete updated list of URLs for this textbook, please see the text home site available at *www.hmco.com/college.*

The Announcer's Responsibility

Before committing yourself to a career as an announcer, you should recognize that, along with the undeniable privileges and rewards that come to people working in this field, there are several areas of responsibility as well. First is the obligation all performers owe their audiences: to be informative, objective, fair, accurate, and entertaining. Announcers who are sloppy, unprepared, given to poor usage, or just plain boring usually get what they deserve—two weeks' notice.

There are, as you undoubtedly know, announcers who work hard and possess talent, but, who, at the same time, pollute the public air, chiefly on radio and television talk and interview shows.[7] A number of radio and television performers are willing to say almost anything, however outrageous or hurtful to others, in order to attract and hold an audience. In our free society such announcers are protected by the First Amendment to the Constitution; the only protection the audience has resides in the integrity of each announcer. Most departments of broadcasting offer courses in ethics and social responsibility. A grounding in

---

[7]For additional discussion of irresponsible behavior, see the opening section of Chapter 8, "Interview and Talk Programs."

this subject, together with serious consideration of the effects of mass communication, should be understood as vitally important to your development as a public communicator.

Social responsibility goes beyond the normal obligation of performer to audience. Nearly all announcers, whether they realize it or not, have influence because of their visibility and prestige. Years ago, Paul F. Lazarsfeld and Robert K. Merton perceived and described what they called the **status-conferral function** of the mass media. In essence, they said the general public attaches prestige to people who appear in the mass media, and that the average person is more readily influenced by prestigious people than by equals. The public's reasoning is circular: "If you really matter, you will be at the focus of attention, and if you are at the focus of mass attention, then you must really matter." A newscaster, then, is not simply an efficient conveyer of information; as a radio or television star, he or she is trusted and believed as a qualified authority. Even an entertainment show announcer or a DJ has automatic, though sometimes unwarranted, authority. As an announcer for any of the electronic media, you should be aware of your status and measure up to it.

Announcers must demonstrate a sense of social commitment. Be aware of opportunities you may have to either enlighten or confuse the public. As a nation we've been slow to perceive and attack the serious problems of urban deterioration, increasing crime, environmental pollution, racial inequities, world hunger, poverty, homelessness, AIDS, the rise of antidemocratic action groups, and increased drug use. If you're committed to using the mass media to help build a better society, you're already socially responsible and potentially important as the kind of communicator demanded by our times.

Another area of responsibility for announcers is that of emergency notification. When floods, hurricanes, earthquakes, tornadoes, and other disasters occur, broadcast announcers are in a position to save lives through early warnings and post-disaster information. The U.S. government has established the **Emergency Alert System (EAS)** to replace the long-established **Emergency Broadcast System (EBS)**. The alert system requires broadcast licensees to disseminate disaster information. It's imperative that all broadcast announcers study the disaster manual (found at all stations) and be prepared to act swiftly and appropriately in emergencies.[8]

---

[8]Automated stations classified as "unattended operations," must opt out of the EAS system; during emergencies, their programming is terminated, and emergency broadcast duties are taken over by other stations.

Broadcast Ethics and the Announcer's Responsibility

Beyond textbook theory, ethics includes a broad range of decisions you'll have to make on your job. Here are some hypothetical situations in which you could find yourself as a radio or television announcer:

- You're a music director on a radio station where you select all songs to be played on the air. A friend offers you one thousand dollars to play a song he's produced. Because you think the music is quite good, you accept the one thousand dollars and schedule the record at least once during each of the daily air shifts. You justify your action on the grounds that you would have programmed the piece without the gift of money.

- You're a television reporter, and you've been told by a reliable witness that some children at the scene of a disturbance threw rocks at a police car before you arrived. You pay the children five dollars each to throw rocks again, while you record the action. Your position is that you recorded an event that actually occurred, and you brought back to the station some high-impact footage for the nightly news.

- You're a talk-show host on an early evening radio show. Your guest is an outspoken advocate of free speech on radio, arguing that there should be no language restrictions whatever. During your interview, you speak a number of words that are generally considered indecent in order to determine whether your guest is sincere in her (to you) extremist position. You maintain that only by saying the words on the air can you test her conviction.

- Your morning drive-time partner takes a two-week vacation. In order to stir up a little audience interest, you announce that he's been kidnapped. For most of the two-week period, you broadcast regular "flashes" on the status of the "event." Audience ratings skyrocket as you report on phony ransom notes, police chases, and so on. You feel that your reputation as an on-air jokester justifies this hoax.

- You're host on a television talk show, and you're insulted and angered by the behavior of a hostile guest. The next day you launch an attack on that person, questioning his integrity, honesty, and character. The reactions of your viewers are very supportive of your attack, and you feel that, having had your revenge, you can let the matter drop.

- As the business reporter for a talk radio station, you decide to mention with favor a company in which you own stock. The interest you generate causes listeners to invest in the company, and the value of its stock rises. You feel justified in the favorable comments you made, because you didn't receive payment from the company in return.

- As a television reporter, you're given some highly sensitive information about the misdeeds of an important local politician. You report the details as accurately as you can, but in order to protect the person who gave you the information, you invent a fictitious informant.

What all of these scenarios have in common is that each violates a law, a regulation, or a provision of a professional code of ethics. As an announcer, your words reach and influence vast numbers of people; because of the potential for wrongdoing, your freedoms to speak and act are restricted. Freedom of speech, as guaranteed by the First Amendment to the Constitution, doesn't always apply to those using the public airwaves. Areas of restriction are obscenity, fraud, defamation (making libelous statements), plagiarism, inciting insurrection, and invasion of privacy.

Generally speaking, laws regarding obscenity, indecency, and profanity are governed by the United States Criminal Code. *Obscene* may be defined as "offensive to accepted standards of decency or modesty." *Indecency* is defined as that which is "offensive to public moral values." *Profanity* is defined as "abusive, vulgar, or irreverent language."[9]

Payola and **drugola** refer to the acceptance of money, drugs, or other inducements in return for the playing of specific recordings on the air. **Plugola** refers to the favorable mention of a product, company, or service in which the announcer has a financial interest. The acceptance of any sort of bribe in return for favors is prohibited by the Federal Communications Commission (FCC).

The Code of Broadcast News Ethics of the Radio and Television News Directors Association specifically labels as irresponsible and unethical such practices as staging news events, misrepresenting the source of a news story, sensationalizing the news, and invading the privacy of those with whom the news deals.

The FCC is the chief regulatory agency for broadcasters. Its *personal attack rule* requires that persons who are attacked on the air be furnished with a transcript of the attack within a specified period of time and that provision be made for the attacked person to reply on the air.

The radio and television codes of the National Association of Broadcasters were invalidated by a 1980s court decision, but many broadcasters continue to use the ethics portions of those codes as models for professional and ethical behavior. Among

---

[9]*The American Heritage Dictionary of the English Language,* 3rd edition. Boston: Houghton Mifflin Company, 1992.

the provisions still widely honored are those prohibiting the broadcasting of any mat-ter that is deemed fraudulent, and the provision that requires clear identification of sponsored or paid-for material.

Most libelous statements aren't *criminally* illegal; most are civil offenses, in which the person offended can sue another person—such as an announcer—and in which the government acts as arbiter. Laws regarding libel vary from state to state, but in no state is an announcer given total freedom to make accusations against others.

As an announcer, you must be thoroughly aware of the realities of broadcast law and ethics. Only by having in-depth knowledge of the applicable laws and codes can you routinely avoid violating them in your behavior or words.

Talk-show host Ronn Owens is highly respected for his breadth of knowledge and his even-handed treatment of studio guests and call-in listeners. With a format that explores everything from politics to popular culture, Owens conducts his program as an electronic town meeting. He tackles sensitive issues, but avoids sensationalism. His top-rated weekday morning program draws nearly half a million listeners each week. Ronn is up before most of his listeners, at 4:00 A.M., to prepare for the show, and spends several hours after a show getting ready for the next day. You can access his brief biographical section at this URL: *www.kgoam180.com/*. *Courtesy of Ronn Owens and KGO Newstalk Radio, San Francisco, California.*

Use the Internet to find and print copies of codes that pertain to announcers, such as the Radio and Television News Directors Association (RTNDA)

www.rtnda.org/rtnda/index.htm

and the Statement of Principles of the American Society of Newspaper Editors (ASNE)

www.asne.org/kiosk/archive/principl.htm

For a complete, updated list of URLs for this textbook, please see the text home site available at *www.hmco.com/college.*

PRACTICE

Practicing with Equipment

The regular use of audio and video recorders can be of immense help in your development as a broadcast performer. After hearing and seeing yourself perform over a period of several weeks, you should begin to note and correct annoying mannerisms, faulty speech habits, and voice deficiencies that displease you. Ask others to comment on your performances, because you may fail to detect some of your shortcomings. As you make adjustments and improve, you'll gain confidence; this, in turn, should guarantee further improvement.

You can also work on speech improvement without equipment of any kind. You speak with others for a considerable amount of time each day. Without sounding affected you can practice speaking clearly in ordinary conversations. Many college students tend to slur words as they speak. Make note of the number of times each day someone asks you to repeat what you've just said, often by uttering a monosyllabic "Huh?" Frequent requests of this kind are an indication that you're not speaking clearly enough for broadcast work.

For improvement of nonverbal communication skills, you can practice in front of a mirror. Note the degree—too pronounced, just right, or too weak—of your facial expressions and head movements. Watch for physical mannerisms that may be annoying or that interfere with clear communication. Through practice you can improve your performance abilities significantly, even without the use of recording equipment.

Closely related to performance ability is **ear training.** It's doubtful that anyone who doesn't hear well can speak well. Develop a critical ear as you listen to television and radio performers. Listen for vowel variations, mispronunciations, poor interpretation, and other qualities of spoken English that may interfere with good communication. Listen, as well, for those who articulate clearly, who have a pleasant voice quality, and who are effective in communicating thoughts and ideas. Decide who impresses you as an outstanding user of spoken language. Identify speakers who make you pay attention, as well as those who cause you to tune out. Try to determine the positive and negative characteristics and qualities of speakers, and apply what you learn to your own work. (Speech diagnosis, speech problems, and suggestions for improvement are covered in Chapter 3, "Voice Analysis and Improvement," and Chapter 4, "Pronunciation and Articulation.")

Backgrounds of Successful Announcers

Many radio and television stations maintain web sites, and most include brief biographies of on-air performers. Using these as your source, compile information about several announcers whose work you admire. You may want to look for these information items: Where did they attend school? In what academic area did they major? Where did they begin their announcing careers?

For a complete updated list of URLs for this textbook, please see the text home site available at *www.hmco.com/college.*

CHAPTER 2

The Announcer As Communicator

RADIO AND TELEVISION ANNOUNCERS HAVE ONE OVERRIDING PURPOSE: *to effectively communicate ideas and feelings to others.* This deceptively simple statement is the key to success in announcing. Understanding that effective communication ought to be your goal is by no means the same thing as achieving it. This chapter discusses the communicative process, and offers specific advice on interpreting copy, as well as suggestions for ad-lib announcing.

Unfortunately, some students of announcing believe they've become successful announcers when they develop the ability to "sound like an announcer." They suffer from the most common shortcoming of ineffective announcers: they've put aside their own personalities and developed the ability to act the part of an announcer. They've become competent imitators.

Good announcing isn't *imitation*—it's *communication.* Top announcers retain their individuality as they concentrate on conveying their messages. True communication as an announcer begins when you learn *who you are, reflect yourself in your delivery, and realize that you are speaking to individuals, not to a crowd.* It's important for you to improve your voice quality, further develop articulation and pronunciation, and expand your vocabulary, but these alone won't guarantee that you'll become an effective communicator. You must also employ two other aspects of successful oral communication: reflecting your personality, and conveying to your audience the ideas and feelings inherent in the words you speak.[1]

Announcers must be skilled in several kinds of performance: ad-libbing, ad-libbing from notes, impromptu speaking, script reading with preparation, and script reading from cold copy (material not seen until the very moment of delivery). Ad-lib announcers—those who have thought through what they're going to say but have no script to work from—include field reporters, weather and traffic reporters, and popular music personalities. Impromptu announcers—those with no opportunity to plan their comments in advance—include television talk-show hosts, radio and television phone-in hosts, and sports play-by-play announcers. News anchors often see some of their copy for the first time when it appears on a prompter. At the other extreme are documentary narrators and readers of recorded commercials. Hours—and sometimes days—are required for them to deliver the performance demanded by a producer. You should practice all of these modes of performance until you're comfortable with each.

One of your toughest challenges as an announcer is to be effective when reading copy written by someone else. You're the middle link in a chain that begins with a writer and ends with a listener or viewer. It's your responsibility to ensure that the writer's ideas are transmitted faithfully to the minds of your listeners.

Principles of Effective Communication

Copy begins not as a *script* but as *ideas* in the mind of a writer—an ad agency copywriter, a newswriter, a documentary scriptwriter, a station sales representative, or some other specialist in broadcast writing. Having conceived the idea, the writer next casts it into words (and, in television, pictures). The ability to conceive compelling messages and to select fresh, meaningful words and arrange them effectively is the art of broadcast writing. The ability to communicate these words effectively is the art of announcing.

---

[1]See the discussions of "audience rapport" at the opening of Chapters 5 and 6.

Radio communicates by spoken and sung language, instrumental music, and sound effects. Television has a vital visual component. The audio aspects of television are also important in conveying messages. As a professional announcer, you can make messages more effective than they would be if communicated only in writing. Beyond the basic level of accurate reading and pronunciation, you can convey an emotion appropriate to your copy—enthusiasm, seriousness, or humor—and in doing so provide meaning for your listeners. You can clarify a message's meaning by communicating the relative importance of its various parts. In short, you can present the material in its most persuasive and readily understandable form.

Oral communication, however, loses its effect when announcers fail to present their material clearly and with conviction. Too many professional announcers merely read the words before them, and consider themselves successful if they don't stumble over the words. A word is a symbol of an idea. If the idea isn't clear to an announcer, or if it isn't read compellingly, the chances are slight that the announcer will transmit the idea clearly to his or her listeners. Announcers are paid to be effective. To do this they must develop oral reading skills that are more than just adequate.

Make a point of listening to announcers, such as music station radio personalities, radio and television newscasters, and radio and television documentary narrators. Study the announcers' deliveries and decide for yourself which announcers are true communicators. You'll discover that you listen closely to those who communicate well, and mentally tune out those who do not. Few people think consciously about the communicative ability of announcers, but we're all certainly affected by it. We find ourselves listening to those announcers who are best able to help us receive and assimilate ideas.

Radio announcers who believe that only their voices matter may attempt to project vitality without using gestures. Such play-acting isn't likely to be convincing. Learn to announce for radio and television as though your listener were sitting nearby. Use your face, hands, and body just as you do in ordinary conversation. Integrating all of the tools of communication—verbal and nonverbal—will help you clarify and intensify your message, even though radio listeners can't see you. Appropriate gesturing for both radio and television is marked by two considerations: honest motivation, and harmony with the importance and the mood of the ideas expressed. Energy is easy to simulate, but unless a speaker is genuinely motivated by the content and purpose of a message, energy usually comes across as phony. Uncalled-for enthusiasm hinders communication. Oversized grins, frowns, and grimaces and sweeping arm movements are seldom appropriate to these intimate media. Good

Figure 2.1

Afternoon drive-time news anchors Ed Baxter and Rosie Allen are a popular and exceedingly compatible announcing team. They combine straight news delivery with human-interest sidelights. *Courtesy of KGO NewsTalk Radio, San Francisco, California.*

communication occurs when the listener or viewer receives an undistorted and meaningful impression of the ideas of the writer with appropriate verbal and nonverbal emphasis given to each part of the message.

 Audition performances by professional announcers may be found on the Internet and played through your computer's speakers. To receive these voiced auditions, you will need the software program *RealAudio.* Begin by choosing "New Web Browser." Enter URL[2]

www.provoice.com

and click on "Search." Click on "Union Professionals." Enter information as to gender, voice range, and so on. Click on "Search." Choose a name, and click on "Listen to My Demo."

For a complete, updated list of URLs for this textbook, please see the text home site available at *www.hmco.com/college*.

---

[2]The Internet is changing constantly as new web sites are added and old web sites are abandoned. The URL listings in this textbook should be regarded as samples of the kinds of material available rather than as a stable index. If you seek a web site using one of these URLs and cannot connect, enter the key words for the topic into a search engine to find a site that may provide the information you want.

Interpreting Copy

Superior interpretation of a script demands a clear understanding of the writer's intention. Announcers who speak words written by others are *interpretive artists*. Those who read scripts on the air are links between the script creator (writer) and the audience. No matter how beautiful your voice is and how rapidly and accurately you read copy, you're not truly a good announcer unless you're able to communicate the writer's ideas and values as he or she conceived them originally.

News anchors read some stories without preparation, as when they're given new or revised stories after they've gone on the air. News anchors are able to work effectively with new or revised copy because at the start of their careers they engaged in copy analysis and methodical practice. The best time to establish a solid foundation in copy analysis is before your career depends upon it.

Stanley T. Donner, professor emeritus of the University of Texas at Austin, has prepared an excellent approach to analyzing copy. He suggests that you work on the points in the checklist "Analyzing Broadcast Copy" when approaching a new script. If you use this checklist for serious analysis of many different types of copy, you should develop the ability to size up a new script almost unconsciously.[3]

CHECKLIST
ANALYZING BROADCAST COPY[4]

1. Read the copy as often as necessary to get the general meaning. If the message is brief and written clearly, perhaps one reading is enough. For a longer or more complex script, you may need to read it two or more times to ferret out its meaning.
2. Determine the objective of the message. State the specific purpose of the copy in one brief sentence.
3. Identify the general mood of the copy. Most short messages have one overriding mood. Longer scripts frequently have shifts in mood.

(Cont.)

---

[3]From a class handout prepared by Stanley T. Donner for his course in Radio and Television Announcing.

[4]As noted elsewhere, news scripts are written to tight deadlines with little time for preparation by news anchors, so careful analysis usually isn't possible. However, the points in this list *are* important for you to know and practice as you prepare for a career as a news anchor. At a later date, when you're asked to read news stories handed to you just before airtime, the hours of practice you engage in now reading and analyzing news copy will pay off.

(Cont.)

4. After determining the general mood, locate any shifts in mood.
5. Determine the copy's structure and its parts. Find and mark the beginning and the end of each part.
6. Analyze punctuation to see what help the punctuation provides in understanding the copy.
7. Note any words you don't fully understand or can't pronounce. It's good practice to underline, for later research, any words that are unclear or new to you.
8. Read the copy aloud.
9. Think about how you can convey interest in the copy's subject matter.
10. Visualize your listener. Establish a mental rapport, and imagine you're actually talking to that person.
11. Decide if there's anything you should know about the origin and background of the copy.
12. Decide if any characterization is needed.

Because this list of considerations suggests much more than might seem obvious in the first reading, elaborations of Donner's twelve points follow.

Identifying the General Meaning

Too much concentration on pronunciation or timing may obscure a script's overall meaning and purpose. Form an impression of the entire piece by silently reading through it at least twice—more, if necessary—before undertaking any of the more detailed work of preparation. Remember that after you read the piece silently to determine the meaning and purpose, *all of your subsequent readings should be performed aloud.*

Stating the Specific Purpose

Stating the specific purpose is the most important point in Donner's checklist. Just as it's pointless to begin a trip without deciding where you're going, it's foolish to begin to interpret copy without first knowing the copy's goal. Sentences can be read in different ways depending on their context or purpose. Raising questions about the purpose of the copy will help you determine the most appropriate delivery.

Here's a recent example of an announcer failing to communicate the writer's intent. In reading "Most of us want to succeed, not just get by," the announcer stressed *want*. The writer, however, wanted to contrast two outlooks on life—*succeeding* and *getting by*. The sentence, when performed, was read "Most of us *want* to succeed, not just get by," rather than "Most of us want to *succeed*, not just *get by*." This may seem to be a small point, but announcers who earn their living delivering messages risk their careers by such carelessness. Read this fifteen-second commercial and decide on its specific purpose:

ANNCR:

See the all-new Jupiter, on display at Montoya's Motorcar Center, 16th and Grand. You'll love its all-leather interior, high-tech styling, and out-of-this-world performance. If you want luxury in an automobile, come meet the Jupiter. America's answer to imports!

If you decided that the purpose of this copy is to awaken curiosity and interest in the new Jupiter, you analyzed the copy correctly. If you decided that its purpose is to promote the name and address of the sponsor, you analyzed it incorrectly. The phrase "at Montoya's Motorcar Center, 16th and Grand" is subordinate to the idea of "the all-new Jupiter." Although it's unusual to subordinate a sponsor's name and address, in this instance the copy indicates clearly that the name and address should be subordinated. Perhaps the sponsor's identification has been built up over time through other commercials. The moral in this instance is that it's unsafe to assume that the sponsor's name and address are to be stressed in all commercial copy.

Now read this commercial for the same sponsor:

ANNCR:

See the all-new Jupiter at Montoya's Motorcar Center. Serving you since 1933, we offer total service and complete

repair and parts departments. Credit cards gladly accepted.
No appointment necessary. That's Montoya's Motorcar
Center, 16th and Grand.

This commercial uses phrases from the first commercial we read, but it's obvious that in this commercial the name of the automobile is subordinate to the name of the sponsor. If, in analyzing this copy, you decided that the copy's chief purpose is to impress upon the audience the dealer's name, address, and reliability, you were correct.

Identifying the General Mood

Once you determine the purpose of the copy, next you should identify the copy's **mood,** because this will influence your **attitude** as you read the copy. To some extent the number of words in the copy will limit your control of mood, especially with commercial copy. Many commercials, particularly those written for clients who want to send a fast-paced, high energy message, may require you to read at your top rate of speed, and this will lock you automatically into the mood desired by the sponsor. In contrast, the commercials for Montoya's Motorcar Center require you to read about forty-four words in fifteen seconds, or one hundred seventy-six words a minute. This is a slower, comfortable rate for oral delivery, and should give you an opportunity to communicate a mood of interest, as well as enthusiasm.

At a greater contrast, the commercial in Chapter 3, page 86, for Dairyland Longhorn Cheese uses only seventy-eight words for a thirty-second spot. You should be able to "milk" this commercial as you gently evoke warm feelings about the product, nostalgia for the "good old days," and (perhaps) hunger for Longhorn Cheese. Excluding commercial announcements, which are written with inflexible time limits, copy for radio and television may be shortened or lengthened to allow for a rate of delivery geared to a particular mood.

Because the mood of a piece of copy will determine your attitude, it's helpful to attach an adjective to your script. Attitudes are described as *ironic, jocular, serious, somber, urgent, sad, light, gloomy,* and *sarcastic.* Read the following items aloud, communicating the indicated attitude of each. The mood of each item, except the tornado reports, is to be conveyed with only a hint of the emotion mentioned.

Urgent

> **(Chicago)** The National Weather Service has issued tornado warnings for the entire upper Midwest. Small-craft warnings have been raised for Lake Michigan, and boat owners are urged to secure their craft against the expected heavy weather.

Somewhat Angry

> **(Miami)** A civilian pilot has reported sighting two more oil slicks off the coast of Florida near Fort Lauderdale and Palm Beach. Clean-up crews are still at work on a massive oil slick that spread one week ago.

Slight Note of Victory—Winning One for the People

> **(Washington)** The Federal Election Commission has voted to halt secret congressional "slush funds," a practice in which lawmakers use private donations to pay personal and office expenses.

Very Urgent

> **(Minnesota)** I've just been given a bulletin that says a tornado has been spotted about twenty miles from Duluth. There are no additional details at this time, but we'll give you more details as we receive them.

Straightforward

> **(Washington)** The government said yesterday that people are taking better care of themselves now than ever before and that the problem now is to find ways to care for the

Figure 2.2

No news announcer should go on the air without studying the script to establish the pace, tone, and mood of each item. Bessie Moses, the radio announcer shown here, must do more than analyze the news: she must also translate it into the Inupiaq Eskimo language. *Courtesy of Bessie Moses and KICY Radio, Nome, Alaska.*

large number of people who live longer as a result. Our nation's success in keeping people healthy and helping them to live longer is placing great stress on the nation's health care resources.

Light, Slightly Humorous

(Montpelier, Vermont) It took eighteen days, but searchers have finally tranquilized one of the baby elephants lost in the woods. The manager of the Carson and Barnes Circus says the elephant will be tied to a tree in an effort to lure the other lost baby elephant out of the woods.

Determining Changes in Mood

A long piece of copy may contain several moods, even if the dominant mood remains constant. In commercial copy, a familiar construction calls for a change from concern to joy as the announcer first describes a common problem and then tells how Product X can solve it. Spot such changes in mood as you read copy initially and note the changes in mood on your script. Unless the script calls for a mock-serious delivery, be careful not to exaggerate the moods.

In a lengthy television documentary or a thirty- or sixty-minute radio or television newscast, changes of mood come more often and should be reflected in your delivery. When you monitor newscasts, make it a point to notice such changes and how speakers reflect the shifting moods. Effective use of variations in mood adds much to the flow, unity, and overall meaning of a presentation. There are techniques to help smooth your change in mood from one item to another. As you practice, try to find transitional words or phrases to shift mood: *meanwhile, locally, in other news,* or *on a lighter note* are examples of this.

In newscasting, changes in mood take place usually between the end of one story and the opening lines of the next. In addition, many newscasts begin with brief headlines that call for abrupt changes in mood within a short span of time. Read these headlines and determine the mood of each:

Here is the latest news: More than eight inches of rain has fallen on eastern Iowa in the last twenty-four hours, and there are reports of widespread damage and some deaths.

A Chicago woman who claimed she killed her husband in self-defense after ten years of beatings has been acquitted by an all-male jury.

A fourteen-year-old Milwaukee boy has been awarded the city's heroism medal for rescuing an infant from a swimming pool.

And, there's joy at the zoo tonight because of the birth of a litter of ligers—or is it tigons? Anyway, the father is a lion, and the mother is a tiger.

The range of emotions inherent in these stories requires rapid changes of mood—a challenge that faces newscasters daily.

News scripts for realistic and up-to-date practice sessions may be obtained by opening Yahoo, and clicking on "full coverage" under "News and Media."

You'll obtain many news stories from this web site that can be selected for practicing reading on camera or into an audio recorder.

For a complete, updated list of URLs for this textbook, please see the text home site available at *www.hmco.com/college.*

Determining Parts and Structure

Almost any example of well-written copy shows clearly defined parts. On the most basic level, copy may be broken down into a beginning, a middle, and an end. The beginning is the introduction, and customarily is used to gain attention. The middle, or body, contains most of the information. In commercials, the middle often states the advantages of one product over its competitors, while in news stories, the middle states most of the information. The end summarizes the most important points.

In most copy these three parts may be subdivided further. Commercial copy that attempts to offer rational reasons for purchasing a particular product frequently employs the following organization or outline.

1. Grab the listener's or viewer's attention.
2. Offer a concrete reason for further interest and attention.
3. Explain why the particular product or service is superior.
4. Mention or imply a price lower than the listener has been led to expect.
5. Repeat some of the selling points.
6. Repeat the name and address or phone number of the commercial's sponsor.

The following is an example of a commercial written according to this organization. The commercial isn't particularly creative, but it represents a type of commercial that's heard often on radio. Notice how it conforms to the six-part outline. (Note: SFX is short for *sound effects*.)

AGENCY: Reist Advertising, Inc.
CLIENT: Mertel's Coffee Mills
LENGTH: 60 Seconds

ANNCR: Are you a coffee lover? Most Americans are. Would you like to enter the world of gourmet coffees? Mertel's can help.

SFX: SOUND OF COFFEE BEING POURED INTO CUP

ANNCR: Gourmet coffee begins with whole beans, carefully selected, freshly roasted.

SFX: SOUND OF COFFEE BEANS BEING GROUND

ANNCR: Gourmet coffee is ground at home, just before brewing. Choose your coffee according to your taste and time of day. A rich but mild Mocha Java for breakfast. A hearty French Roast for that midday pickup. A nutty Arabian with dinner. And a Colombian decaf before bed. Sound inviting? You bet. Sound expensive? Not so. Mertel's Coffee Mills feature forty types of coffee beans from around the world, and some are only pennies more per pound than canned coffees. And there's always a weekly special. This week, it's Celebes Kalossi, at just $6.99 a pound! Remember—if you want gourmet coffee, begin with whole beans, and grind them just before brewing. So, come to Mertel's Coffee Mills, and move into the world of gourmet coffee! We're located at the Eastside Mall, and on Fifth Street in downtown Dickinson. Mertel's Coffee Mills.

Outstanding commercials are both subtle and complex. Special consideration is given to the analysis of superior commercials in Chapter 7.

Analyzing Punctuation Marks Used in Scripts

In addition to the symbols of ideas we call words, writers use punctuation marks. Punctuation is helpful to an announcer because it shows the author's intentions regarding mood and meaning. However, although you should pay attention to the punctuation in your copy, you needn't be a slave to it. The copy was punctuated by a writer who thought it should be interpreted in a particular way. When you perform it, you need to make the copy your own—true to your particular personality. Therefore, repunctuate as appropriate.[5]

Punctuation marks, like the diacritical marks used to indicate pronunciation, are so small and differ so subtly that they may cause occasional difficulties for an announcer—especially when there is little or no time to study a script. Announcers working with written material need near-perfect eyesight. Some announcers wear reading glasses during their air shifts or recording sessions even though they don't wear reading glasses at other times. Whenever possible, review your copy prior to airtime and, if you find it helpful or necessary, add to and enlarge punctuation marks. (Some suggestions for the use of emphatic punctuation marks are found on page 42.)

 The Internet is a source of near-instantaneous information on usage and grammar, including specific rules for punctuation. With a New Web Browser, enter this URL:

www.yourdictionary.com/

For a complete, updated list of URLs for this textbook, please see the text home site available at *www.hmco.com/college.*

You probably have a good grasp of punctuation, so the review that follows discusses only a few specific punctuation marks as they relate to

---

[5]In a recording session supervised by a producer or director, you'll most likely repunctuate the copy according to the interpretation preferred by your supervisor.

broadcast copy. It doesn't consider every use of each punctuation mark, but comments on those uses that relate specifically to writing and interpreting copy.

The Period. In written copy, abbreviations such as *FBI* and *AFL-CIO* appear without periods. *Ms.* and *Mr.* may appear with or without concluding periods. An acronym such as *SCSCI* (pronounced "scuzzy") should have no periods. If there's doubt about the pronunciation of an acronym, a script should include a phonetic transcription in parentheses.

The Comma. The comma usually marks a slight pause in broadcast speech, which gives you an opportunity to breathe. Good writing for oral delivery uses commas with precision and frequency. You may find it appropriate to use many commas when writing broadcast copy, and fewer when writing papers and essays for nonbroadcast instructors, such as English composition teachers, who tend to favor long, complex sentences.

The Question Mark. In written English the question mark appears at the end of a sentence that asks a question. Because the question mark comes at the *end* of the sentence, you may find it helpful to follow the Spanish practice of placing an upside-down question mark (¿) at the beginning. This way, as you begin to read the sentence, you will know it is an interrogative.

Quotation Marks. Quotation marks are used in broadcast copy for two different purposes: to indicate that words between the marks are a word-for-word quotation, and to substitute for italics. The first use of quotation marks is found extensively in news copy:

> . . . he said an anonymous male caller told him to "get out of the case or else."

In reading this sentence, you can indicate the presence of a quotation by the inflection of your voice, or you can add words of your own to make it clear that it's a direct quotation:

> . . . he said an anonymous male caller told him to, and this is a quotation (or and I quote), "get out of the case or else."

Don't say "unquote" at the end of a quotation, because you can't cancel a quotation you've just given.

Quotation marks are sometimes used in news copy in place of italics, although this practice most likely will disappear because computers, unlike typewriters, can italicize words easily:

> ... her new book, "Reading for Fun," has been on the "Times'"
> best-seller list for three months.

Parentheses. Although parenthetical remarks—remarks that are important but not necessary for the sentence to make sense—are used occasionally in radio and television copy, the same result is usually achieved with dashes, as shown in this sentence. Parentheses are used in radio and television copy to set apart instructions to the audio operator, to indicate music cues, and to contain instructions or interpretations for the announcer or the performer:

(SFX: OFFICE SOUNDS)

(MUSIC UP AND UNDER)[6]

(SLIGHT PAUSE)

(MOVE TO SOFA)

Words and sentences within a parentheses are not to be read aloud by announcers.

Parenthetical remarks sometimes are added to newspaper copy, usually for purposes of clarification, as in this example:

> Mayor Bacic said that he called the widow to demand that
> she "return my (love) letters immediately."

A person who reads this sentence in a newspaper can see that "(love)" has been added by a reporter or editor. If this copy were used on the air and the announcer did not indicate that "(love)" had been added by an editor or a writer, the Mayor's statement could be misrepresented.

---

[6]"MUSIC UP AND UNDER" means to begin with music at full volume and then to fade music to a lower volume.

Ellipses. An ellipsis, a sequence of three or four dots, indicates an omission of words within a sentence or between sentences. Ellipses are used rarely in broadcast copy but may be used more often in newspaper copy, as in the following example:

> Senator Meyer stated yesterday, "I do not care what the opposition may think, I . . . want only what is best for my country."

In this example, the points of ellipsis have been used to indicate that one or several words have been omitted from the original quotation. There is no way to indicate the omission on the air. Thus, quotations with omissions should not be used in broadcast copy.

Newswriters often use ellipses to mark the ends of sentences and to substitute for commas, dashes, semicolons, and colons. Here's an example:

> The mayor was late to his swearing-in ceremony today . . . He told those who had gathered for the ceremony . . . some two hundred supporters . . . that he had been held up in traffic.

This practice is regrettable but so widespread that you can expect to be asked at some time to work from copy so punctuated. Should you become a newswriter, you may be expected to write copy in this style. Obviously, such punctuation is workable. The problem is that ellipses cannot indicate the shades of meaning conveyed by the six other more specific punctuation marks.

Marking Copy

Because punctuation marks are quite small, when time permits many announcers add punctuation marks to copy that are much larger and therefore more readily seen. These are far from standard, but the following are a few of the ones used more commonly:

- A slanted line (/), called a *virgule,* is placed between words to approximate the comma.
- Two virgules (/ /) are placed between sentences or between words to indicate a longer pause.

Figure 2.3

Al Hart marks copy prior to airtime. Although he's had years of professional experience as a news anchor and voice-over announcer, he takes nothing for granted. He continues to prepare thoroughly for each air shift and commercial assignment. Figure 2.4 is a commercial marked by Al Hart before it was recorded. *Courtesy of Al Hart and KCBS, San Francisco, California.*

- Words to be stressed are underlined. Some announcers mark copy with a colored highlighter to indicate words, phrases, and sentences to be stressed. A highlighter, however, is useful only when working with *printed* scripts—as when recording voice tracks for commercials or documentaries. Highlighting can't be used when reading from a prompter or a computer screen.
- Question marks and exclamation marks are enlarged.
- An upside-down question mark (¿) is placed at the beginning of any sentence that is a question.
- An upside-down exclamation point (¡) is placed at the beginning of any exclamatory sentence.
- **Crescendo** (∧) and **decrescendo** (∨) marks are placed in any passage that is to receive an increase or a decrease in stress.

Verifying Meaning and Pronunciation

It's obvious that when you interpret copy you must understand the meaning of the words used. Most copy uses familiar words, so it's not often that you need to question the meaning or the pronunciation of words in your script. However, some scripts are written for narrow target audiences, and unfamiliar words may cause problems in interpretation or

Figure 2.4

A commercial marked by
Al Hart before being
recorded.

GALLO SALAME, INC.   Edward J. McElroy, Inc.

60 SECONDS

In this day and age when everybody seems to be in a hurry, maybe you'd like to hear about a food that takes its <u>own sweet time</u>. That food is/Gallo Italian Dry Salame. Gallo is made the fine old Italian way, with no spices or herbs added. It starts with superb beef and pork (<u>mixed together,</u>) then slowly and patiently aged/to develop its unique, tantalizing flavor . . . a flavor you simply can't get in a hurry. Maybe that's why Gallo Italian Dry Salame is the choice of people who take the time to appreciate/the finer things in life. Maybe that's why Gallo Italian Dry Salame adds so much <u>pleasure</u> to that "quiet hour" before dinner. Tomorrow night, serve a tray of thin Gallo Italian Dry Salame slices with your favorite beverage. It's a beautiful Italian way to relax/and unwind. Gallo Italian Dry Salame is waiting in the deli case . . . waiting <u>patiently</u> for you . . . <u>very</u> patiently.

---

pronunciation. You should cultivate the habit of looking up all unfamiliar words in an authoritative dictionary. Develop a healthy skepticism about your own vocabulary. Through years of silent reading you've probably learned to settle for an approximate pronunciation and meaning of many words. As a quick test, how many of the following words can you define and use correctly?

voilà (French)	fulsome
impassible	rhetoric
burlesque	capricious
ordnance	catholic (uncapitalized)

Check the definitions of these words in any standard dictionary. Some of them are seen and heard frequently, whereas others only sound or look familiar.

TABLE 2.1	CORRECT PRONUNCIATION OF SOME TRICKY WORDS		
Word	IPA	Diacritics	Wire–Service System
drought	[draut]	/drout/	(DROWHT)
forehead	[ˈfɔrɪd]	/fôr′ ĭd/	(FOR-ihd)
toward	[tɔrd]	/tôrd/	(TAWRD)
diphtheria	[difˈθiria]	/dĭf-thîr-ē-ə/	(diff-THIR-ee-uh)
accessories	[ækˈses ə riz]	/ăk-sĕs′-ə-rēz/	(ak-SESS-uh-reez)
quay	[ki]	/kē/	(KEE)
pestle	[pes əl]	/pĕs′-əl/	(PESS-uhl)
worsted	[ˈwʊstid]	/wŏ͝os′tĭd/	(WUHS-tid)

Correct pronunciation is as important as accurate understanding. You should, therefore, be skeptical about your ability to pronounce words correctly. Check your pronunciation of each word in Table 2.1 against the correct pronunciation, which is shown in the table with three different systems of phonetic transcription.

In addition to using and pronouncing words correctly, you must understand allusions that appear in your copy. An **allusion** is an indirect but pointed or meaningful reference. Writers sometimes use phrases from the Bible, mythology, Shakespeare, and other sources from the past. Explanations of the four phrases that follow can be found in dictionaries, encyclopedias, and published collections of well-known myths. The following allusions aren't common but any one of them could appear in your copy. If you don't know the origins of the following allusions, search them out. (All four may be found in the *American Heritage Dictionary*.)

He was considered a quisling.
She was given to malapropisms.
He added his John Hancock.
He suffered as painfully as Job.

You can't expect to be familiar with all of the allusions contained in the copy you receive. During your career you may read copy written by hundreds of people, each drawing on a separate fund of knowledge. You can, though, cultivate the habit of tracking down allusions that are not familiar to you. Self-discipline is required, however, because it's easy to convince yourself that the context of the copy you are reading will make an allusion clear to the audience even if you don't understand it.

Reading Aloud

Because you'll perform *aloud*, you should practice *reading aloud*. Copy written for radio or television differs from copy written for newspapers, magazines, and books. Good broadcast copy usually makes poor silent reading. Short, incomplete, or ungrammatical sentences are often found in perfectly acceptable radio and television scripts. Consider the following example:

ANNCR:

Been extra tired lately? You know. Sorta logy and dull? Tired and weary—maybe a little cranky, too? Common enough, this time of year. The time of year when colds are going around. And when we have to be careful to get the nutrition we need. Vitamin deficiency can be the cause of that "down-and-out" feeling. And Supertabs, the multiple vitamin, can be the answer . . .

This is quite different from the copy an agency would write to advertise the same product in a newspaper. Giving this copy the conversational quality it needs requires a kind of skill developed most rapidly by practicing aloud.

Reading Ahead

Reading a long script aloud can be difficult. You can't afford to make even the minor errors the silent reader may make, such as skipping over words or sentences, passing over difficult material or unfamiliar words, and resting your eyes when they become tired. If you're asked to read a lengthy script, you'll need to read for extended periods of time, read everything before you, read it accurately and with appropriate expression, and do all of this with little opportunity to rest your eyes. As your eyes tire, you're more and more likely to make mistakes.

One way of giving your eyes the rest they need is by reading ahead. Reading ahead means that your eyes are several words ahead of your voice as you read the copy. In this sentence, when your voice is at about *this point,* your eyes should be about *here.* When your eyes have reached the end of the sentence, you should be able to glance away from your

Figure 2.5

News anchors Cheryl Jennings and Dan Noyes prepare for a return from a commercial break. They read their news copy into robotic cameras and are cued to the cameras by the only other person in the studio, the floor director. *Courtesy of Cheryl Jennings and Dan Noyes, and KGO-TV, San Francisco, California.*

script while you finish speaking the words. Practice this technique and you should be able to read even lengthy scripts without excessive eyestrain. But, as you practice, make certain you don't fall into the irritating habit of many announcers—using a monotonous, decelerating speech pattern at the end of every sentence. Unless you guard against it, you may be unconsciously relaxing your interpretation as you rest your eyes.

Conveying Interest in Your Material

Whatever the purpose or nature of the copy to be read, you must show interest in it if you're to communicate it effectively. Most of the time, you'll have a genuine interest in the subject, as when delivering the news or narrating a documentary. At other times—for example, when reading a commercial for a product you don't use or perhaps even dislike—it may be difficult for you to feel genuine interest. As a professional, you can't afford to show disinterest in or disrespect for the copy you're paid to read. You must try to put your biases aside. You're an intermediary between people who provide information and those who receive it. You act as a magnifying glass: it's your job to enhance perceptions with the least possible distortion. Of course, if you're asked to perform a commercial for a product you know to be shoddy or misrepresented, then your conscience should take over. And, if you find yourself reading copy that's offensive to you, find out if it's possible to have it changed.

Even when working with good copy for reputable advertisers, it's impossible to develop a belief in every product. At many stations, announcers work shifts in a small control room, recording and editing copy for many products and services. Here are two suggestions that may help you:

1. When you must read a number of commercials, and you find it's impossible to develop honest enthusiasm for all of them, your best option is to read each with as much effectiveness and interpretive skill as possible.

2. When you're in the enviable position of being the exclusive speaker for a product or have had a long personal relationship with a sponsor, you should gain firsthand knowledge of the product and communicate your honest belief in it.

Assuming that your announcing copy deserves genuine interest, how can you reflect it in your interpretation? Honest enthusiasm is seldom noisy or obtrusive. It manifests itself in inner vitality and quiet conviction. As a radio or television commercial announcer, you won't be dealing with life-or-death matters, and you'll be speaking, in effect, to individuals or small groups of people who are only a few feet away. In a sense you're their guest. Your conviction is revealed through a steady focus on your listeners and through your earnestness and your personality. These suggestions don't rule out the possibility of a humorous commercial or introduction. Being sincere doesn't mean being somber!

 SPOTLIGHT

Learning to Sound Local

by Dan O'Day

As a transplanted DJ, new to an unfamiliar market, one of your most urgent requirements is to learn about your new community as quickly as possible. Listeners will "turn off" in short order if you mispronounce local place names or call such diverse things as activities or foods by names not used by locals. To learn how to "sound local," leave the station and enlist the aid of others—friends, landlords, strangers, shopkeepers, taxi drivers—to get answers to basic questions about your new hometown.

Don't accept one person's answer as correct, though; look for a consensus. Here are some particularly important areas to research.

Lingo

In the North, people "go to the movies." In the Deep South, folks "go to the show." Similarly, New Englanders have a "cookout," while Westerners have a "barbecue."

What words will brand you as an outsider if you pronounce them the "wrong" way? For instance, do locals pronounce the word *route* as *root* or *rowt?* Pay special attention to people or places that outsiders are known to mangle. South Florida has a town named Riviera Beach. Obviously the first word is pronounced *riv-ee-air-uh,* right? Not if you're a local. Only a tourist enunciates all four syllables. Locals say *Rivera*—as in Geraldo.

What local cultural quirks affect the language? I was raised in a big city, but my first radio job was in rural Virginia. When I read a live spot for farm equipment, I pronounced *Deere*—as in *John Deere—Deerie.* It wasn't difficult for the average listener to detect I was a foreigner. Make a list of twenty difficult-to-pronounce names of streets, parks, or prominent citizens.

Government

Does your community have a mayor, city manager, or both? Who really runs things? Is there a city council or a board of supervisors? Are these officials elected in general or district elections? How long are the terms of office?

Find out which politicians have been on the scene forever. Ask how long the mayor has been in office. Talk to people about current political controversies. What's the best-known political scandal of the past ten years? What about the police department? Does the police chief get along with the mayor? What was the last big police department controversy?

Education

Find out what the hottest issue is in the public school system. Learn which schools are considered the best academically, and which the worst. How do the schools compare with other schools in other regions of the country? Which schools are the best in sports?

Sports

Speaking of sports, what are the local high school dynasties, rivalries, mascots, and so on? Who are the leading coaches?

Connecticut has duckpin bowling. Florida has jai-alai. What sports are played in your region but unknown to many others?

Food Facts

In Philadelphia, you order a "hoagie." To get the same thing in New York, you ask for a "hero." In some places it's a "submarine," and in others, a "grinder."

Local dishes may sound odd to out-of-towners but may be sources of pride to the community. What are they? And what about the bread served in local restaurants? San Francisco's big on sourdough; Los Angeles restaurants often serve multigrain. And don't think these little details are unimportant.

Are people very health conscious—or do they think a bran muffin is some sort of Danish? What are the most common ethnic restaurants? What are the most expensive, romantic, or famous restaurants? Which restaurants are known for their bad food?

Heroes

There are bound to be local heroes. Find out who they are; you'd better not make fun of them. Who are the high school, college, and professional sports legends? Which celebrities were born or raised in the community?

Working World

What are the top ten industries or biggest employers? Which companies are popular or unpopular? What's the local unemployment rate—and how does it compare to the rest of the region? What is the starting salary of a policeman? Of a teacher?

Getting Around

Some places have subways; some have buses; some have both. What's the mass transit system, how much does it cost, and who uses it? What is its reputation for safety, cleanliness, comfort, reliability, and convenience?

What cars dominate the streets and highways? Toyotas and Nissans are ubiquitous in Southern California but are rare—and sometimes reviled—in Michigan. What models are the most popular—subcompacts, luxury sedans, station wagons, cars with four-wheel drive? Do people have car phones or CB radios?

What are the most dangerous intersections? Where will you be stuck the longest at a red light? Which freeways (or section of freeways) are most congested at what times?

Neighborhoods

What are the names of various ethnic neighborhoods? Where are they located? Is there a gay section? What's the most expensive area? Which neighborhoods are the most crime ridden?

Lifestyles

What are the favorite weekend activities? Where are the hot spots for singles? Where do teens, yuppies, seniors, and other groups hang out? Where is the local lovers' lane? When do people eat dinner—5:30 P.M., 9:00 P.M.?

One local newspaper is probably read more than the others. Certain movies do better than others. And the community is bound to have particular political and social leanings. Find out what they are. Are there any seemingly mundane subjects that can lead to controversy? What are the worst bugs or pests? What do the locals think of their drinking water? Is there one tragedy in the community's history you should never joke about?

Finally, discover the local tourist attractions and what people think of them.

Talking to the Listener

Several suggestions for communicating effectively with a listener have been mentioned already, but one more point should be made. Most of this chapter has emphasized the problems of *reading* scripts. It might be better if you considered your job to be one of *talking* scripts. Even though you work from a script and your listeners know it, they appreciate it when you sound as though you're not reading aloud. The best way to achieve a conversational style is to visualize the person to whom you're speaking and "talk" your message to him or her. Of course, some scripts lend themselves more readily to intimate delivery than others.

When asked to interpret a piece of copy, you should ask yourself several questions:

Who am I as I read this piece?

To whom am I talking?

To how many people am I talking?

How old is the person to whom I'm speaking?

Where am I as I speak?[7]

See also the section "Achieving a Conversational Style" in Chapter 5, "Audio Performance."

---

[7]This list of questions is applicable to some kinds of copy, especially to commercials, documentary narratives, essays, and public-service announcements (PSAs). The questions aren't relevant to the reading of news reports, because time doesn't permit prolonged study of them.

Getting Background About Authors and Copy

Unlike brief commercials, which tend to be self-explanatory, longer and more complex pieces of copy will be better interpreted if you know something about the writer and understand the author's intentions.

Think about what you should find out before narrating the following pieces:

A miniseries of television packages on the problems of the inner cities

A feature report on migrant farm workers

A documentary on the works of a great painter

An instructional piece on the use of a particular personal computer

Each of these topics requires some specialized knowledge and an understanding of the author's intentions. Commercials are designed quite obviously to sell products or services, but what are the purposes of programs such as those listed above? One good way to find out is by talking to writers, producers, and directors. On a basic level, you'll learn whether the program is intended to be objective and factual or to be a position statement. You may discover also the mood the writer intends to convey. You can question passages that puzzle you, suggest improvements (when appropriate), check on the pronunciation of names or words, and ultimately do a better job of interpretation.

Employing Characterization

You may be asked at times to read copy calling for characterization. Courses in acting and participation in plays (both stage and television plays) will help you learn character interpretation. Some commercials call for no real characterization but demand a foreign accent or a regional dialect. Before starting to practice copy with a dialect, accent, or character voice, determine the purpose of the copy, the mood of the copy, the person or persons to whom you are speaking, and so on. Characterization alone is insufficient to make a piece of copy effective. First get the interpretation down and then work on the character voice. Make sure that when you read copy that calls for a regional dialect or foreign accent you don't project an offensive stereotype. Some commercials have been taken off the air because they offended an ethnic group. In today's world of broadcasting, there's no room for messages that are demeaning to any segment of society. The Spotlight, "Tips From a Voice-over Pro," in Chapter 7, offers many suggestions on interpreting copy.

You can't apply every one of the points discussed here each time you pick up a piece of copy. In time, however, you should develop a conditioned reflex that allows you to size up a script and interpret it effectively without relying on a checklist. In the meantime, the suggestions given here may help you spot your weaknesses and measure your progress.

The web site for this textbook includes several exercises for practicing accents, dialects, and character voices.

www.hmco.com/college

PRACTICE

Analyzing the Delivery of Professional Announcers

Make an audio recording of a radio or television newscast or a talk show and listen to it as often as necessary to analyze each of these factors:

Voice quality of announcers

Good or bad articulation

Too much or too little vitality

Absence or presence of predictable pitch patterns

Ability to convey a point

Ability to hold attention

Ability to communicate appropriate emotions

PRACTICE

Effecting Mood Changes

Make an audio recording of a news anchor delivering three different stories, each calling for a different mood. Determine the techniques the news anchor uses to change from one mood to another.

PRACTICE

Talking a Script

The following two scripts may be used for practice in talking scripts. The Blue Cross script should be delivered in a straightforward, matter-of-fact manner. The Six Flags commercial is marvelous for practicing changes in rate of delivery, pitch, and volume, as well as for practicing conversational style. Both commercials defy conventional rules of structure, and both benefit from their originality. Sound effects enhance both commercials.

AGENCY: Allen and Dorward
CLIENT: Blue Cross of Northern California
LENGTH: 60 seconds

MUSIC: LOUD MUSIC

MOM: Annie . . . would you turn that down, please?

MUSIC: MUSIC DOWN AND UNDER

MOM: Thank you, dear. I'm a working mother with two teenage girls. Sometimes, it seems that they're at that difficult age. Sometimes, it seems they've been there for years. I've got my own business and we're all healthy. When I opened my shop, I signed up for Blue Cross protection. I looked at other health plans, but it was obvious that the Blue Cross Concept One Hundred Plan had everything we needed . . . and, I can afford it! Last spring, Cindy was in the hospital for a few days. Nothing serious . . . but I know how much it would have cost me. Believe me. Plenty!

START
FADE: I just couldn't handle a bill like that alone.

ANNCR: There's no reason for you to handle it alone. Our Blue Cross Concept One Hundred Plan offers a full range of benefits for your growing family. See our ad in this Sunday's magazine section or *TV Guide* or call eight hundred . . . five, five, five . . . forty-eight hundred. Blue Cross.

MOM: As a single parent, I've made a lot of decisions. Blue Cross was one of the best.

AGENCY: McDonald & Little Advertising
CLIENT: Six Flags
LENGTH: 60 seconds

TITLE: It Starts Off Slowly

ANNCR: It starts off slowly at first, climbing upward at maybe two miles an hour. Then it hits the crest, picks up speed, and before you know it, it happens. The ground is gone. The world is a blur far below; look down if you dare. And don't think about the fact that you're moving at almost a mile a minute and headed straight down into a lake. Or that you're screaming and laughing at the same time. It's all in good fun. Here on the biggest, fastest, highest roller coaster in the world. The Great American Scream

Machine. Just one of the many, many new experiences now at the new Six Flags Over Georgia. There's a whole lot new to do this year at Six Flags. Things you'll never forget. Because good times here are not forgotten.

Ad-lib Announcing

The term **ad lib** is short for the Latin *ad libitum,* meaning performed with freedom; freely, spontaneously. In broadcasting, to ad-lib is to improvise and deliver extemporaneously. Related adjectives are *impromptu,* meaning speaking on the spur of the moment with no prior preparation, and *extemporaneous,* meaning prepared in advance but delivered without notes or a script.

As an announcer, you'll often work without a script. All of your acquired skills of phonation, articulation, and interpretation can't guarantee

Figure 2.6

News anchor and reporter Cheryl Jennings writes lead-ins to stories she'll report on the 5:00 P.M. news. Cheryl has been awarded three Emmys, as well as awards and citations from the Radio and Television News Directors Association, Mothers Against Drunk Driving, American Women in Radio and Television, National Commission on the Status of Women, and Veterans of Foreign Wars. Cheryl attended San Francisco State University, and started her career as an intern. *Courtesy of Cheryl Jennings and KGO-TV, San Francisco, California.*

Figure 2.7

Frank Somerville and Tori Campbell, co-anchors of the News at Noon, make last-minute preparations while waiting for a cue to open the show. *Courtesy of Frank Somerville and Tori Campbell, and KTVU, Oakland, California.*

effective communication. When you're on your own as an announcer without a script, only your ability as a compelling communicator will earn you listeners. Much of the broadcast day consists of unscripted shows. Disc jockeys, field reporters, telephone talk-show hosts, interviewers, game-show hosts, and panel moderators are among those who seldom see a script and who must conduct their programs spontaneously. Field reporters often work from notes, but they work with a complete script only when they return to the station to prepare a "package."

Ad-lib announcing can be practiced but it probably can't be taught. The formula for success is easy to state but difficult to achieve: *Know what you're talking about, be interested in what you're saying, be eager to communicate with your listener, and try to develop an attractive personality. In interviews, show a genuine interest in your subjects and their views.*

Announcers working without scripts can be more spontaneous than script readers. At the same time, they run a greater risk of boring their listeners. Scripts are usually tightly written. An ad-lib or impromptu announcer can wander from point to point. Scripts have specific objectives. Ad-lib announcers are free to ramble without a clear intent. Scripts are often polished and tightened during recording sessions. The impromptu comments of an announcer can't be taken back once they're spoken.

Despite all of these potential pitfalls, ad-lib, impromptu, and extemporaneous announcing are crafts that must be practiced and perfected by anyone who wants to become a professional announcer. Keeping this in mind, practice unscripted announcing at every opportunity, using a tape recorder for self-evaluation. The following tips should be helpful.

Know What You're Talking About

We expect a sportscaster to have a thorough knowledge of sports, and a DJ to know music. But problems arise when an announcer has to speak on an unfamiliar topic. As a special-assignment reporter, for instance, after delivering a live report from the scene of a breaking story, you'll often be asked by an anchor to elaborate on specific details. Or you may be assigned to an interview with a person about whom you know little and about whose special interests you know nothing at all. Suppose, for example, you're to interview a medical researcher about an important discovery. How would you prepare? Most news and talk-radio stations and nearly all major-market television stations maintain computers linked to information banks. Online inquiries quickly provide reams of information on almost any topic or famous person.

To be a competent talk-show host, you wouldn't rely entirely on computer data banks. You'd be a voracious reader of newspapers, newsmagazines, current fiction and nonfiction bestsellers, and general-interest periodicals. At a large station you'd have the help of a research assistant who'd gather information about a particular guest or topic. (Chapter 8 discusses the role of radio and television talk-show hosts.)

Be Interested in What You're Saying

If you listen carefully to radio or television announcers, you can't help but notice that some seem to have little or no interest in what they're saying. Among the guilty are certain weather, traffic, and business reporters, usually on radio, who make frequent reports throughout the day. It's easy to fall into a routine delivery pattern, to speak too rapidly, and to show no interest in what you are saying.

Be Eager to Communicate with Your Listener

Only if you really want to communicate to others should you consider announcing in the first place. If you want to speak merely for and to yourself, buy a tape recorder and have fun "doing your own thing."

Develop an Attractive Personality

Very little advice can be offered on developing an attractive personality. Most people who are found attractive by others have learned to be truly themselves, are eager to show their interest in others, and have wide intellectual curiosity. Wit, wisdom, and charm are also characteristics of those with appeal. These qualities are greatly appreciated but hard to come by.

PRACTICE

Ad-lib Announcing

The exercises that follow require an audio recorder. Most exercises can be adapted to video recording and can be taped with a tripod-mounted camcorder.

Don't look at the topics that follow until you're fully prepared to begin practicing. To prepare, get a stopwatch or a clock or watch with a sweep second hand and find an isolated area that's free from distractions. Cue a tape on an audio recorder. Then choose a number from one to twenty. Without looking at any other topics, read the item corresponding to the number you've chosen. Start your stopwatch. Give yourself exactly one minute to formulate your thoughts. Make notes, if desired. When the minute is up, reset the stopwatch and start it and the tape recorder simultaneously. Begin your ad-lib performance and try to speak fluently on your topic for a predetermined time—one minute for your first few efforts and two minutes after you've gained experience. Decide on the length of your performance before you look at your topic. Eliminate the number of each topic when you use it so that you'll have a fresh challenge each time you practice.

As you form your thoughts, try to think of (1) an appropriate opening, (2) material for the body of your remarks, and (3) a closing statement. Don't stop your commentary because of stumbles, hesitancies, or other problems. Don't put your recorder on pause while you collect your thoughts. This exercise is valueless unless you work your way through your ad-libs in "real time." In order to improve, you must have firsthand knowledge of your shortcomings. The only way to gather this knowledge is to follow these instructions to the letter, regardless of initial failures. Keep all of your taped performances so you can review them and measure your progress.

Some of the ad-lib topics that follow suggest a humorous approach; others demand a more sober delivery. All topics are general, and anyone should be able to find something to say about each. These topics serve well for initial practice, but eventually you must graduate to more current and realistic topics. As a broadcast announcer you'll be asked to speak on current events as reflected in newscasts and newspapers. To truly test your ad-libbing abilities with important topics, make a list of the week's headlines. A typical week will yield topics as diverse as Third World indebtedness, hunger in some parts of the planet, labor negotiations in your community or area, breakthroughs in medicine, important Supreme Court decisions, newly proposed legislation on various issues, election results and their implications, speedups or slowdowns of the economy, and news on the greenhouse effect. List each topic on a separate slip of paper and follow the same instructions for ad-libbing, but don't limit yourself to arbitrary time constraints.

1. Give reasons for agreeing or disagreeing with this proposal: "Upon graduating from high school, all students should be required to serve for one year in the Peace Corps or perform some type of community service."
2. Discuss the most influential book you've ever read.
3. Describe your memories of some important holiday during your childhood.
4. Name the most important college course you've taken and give reasons for your choice.
5. Describe your most influential relative.
6. Describe your most embarrassing experience.
7. If you could change one law, what would it be, how would you change it, and why?
8. Tell about your first memories of school.
9. What do you hope to be doing in ten years?
10. Describe your most memorable vacation.
11. Tell about your most memorable pet.
12. Attack or defend this statement: "Final examinations should be abolished in favor of several quizzes and a term paper."
13. What turns you on?
14. What turns you off?
15. Tell about your recurring nightmares.
16. How should the government deal with terrorists?
17. What should the government do to be more effective in combating illegal drugs?
18. Tell how you feel about graffiti on buses and public buildings. If you disapprove, describe what you think should be done.
19. Describe the characteristics or qualities of a broadcast announcer whose work you admire.
20. What are your strengths and weaknesses?

CHECKLIST

IMPROVING
AD-LIB
ANNOUNCING
SKILLS

1. Know what you're talking about, research specific topics; read widely to be knowledgeable about a range of current topics.
2. Be interested in what you're saying: keep the material fresh every time you report.
3. Be eager to communicate with your listeners: your announcing must reach real people on the other end.
4. Develop an attractive personality: be yourself and be genuinely interested in others.

CHAPTER 3

Voice Analysis and Improvement

YOUR VOICE IS THE MOST IMPORTANT INSTRUMENT OF COMMUNICATION you possess. You'll use your voice daily for the rest of your life, so you should make every effort to polish your speaking voice, to eliminate harsh or shrill sounds, and to articulate words clearly—in short, to develop the most pleasant and effective speaking voice you're capable of producing.

The Importance of Voice Improvement

It's impossible to overemphasize the importance of voice training for those who intend to spend a career speaking to others through the electronic media of audio and video. Announcers often are *unseen* (as in radio and in television voice-overs), but they always are *heard*. Few of us reach adulthood with voices that are developed to their full potential. The sound—the tonal quality, the resonance, the "music"—of an announcer's voice requires training and practice. This text offers many suggestions for analyzing voice quality and thereby pinpointing what needs work. It also provides many readings designed to help you improve your voice quality. No one but you can improve your voice; teachers and voice coaches can, of course, provide assistance and encouragement, but they have no magic wand to wave. They can't "confer" voice improvement on you. Only by taking seriously the challenge of improving your voice and by practicing regularly can you develop your vocal instrument into one that reaches its full potential. If you want to succeed in a career that is basically the art of talking to others, a serious and thorough analysis and many hours of subsequent practice are mandatory.

This chapter will help you identify problems of voice quality and provide you with exercises for overall speech improvement. Chapter 4 is devoted to the analysis and improvement of pronunciation and articulation. Please understand that neither chapter is a substitute for speech therapy where significant problems exist.

In discussing speech sounds of American English, the symbols of wire-service transcription, diacritical marks, and the International Phonetic Alphabet (IPA) are used. However, these chapters (and, indeed, the entire book) can be studied without knowledge of any system of phonetic transcription.

Even if yours is a naturally pleasant voice, you can improve its quality. Just as some people exercise to strengthen their biceps or thigh muscles, you can exercise to strengthen your voice. Most authorities on voice improvement suggest that students read nearly everything— newspapers, magazines, textbooks—aloud. As you exercise your voice in this way, you'll find that you're able to speak without strain for long periods of time. Some on-air shifts are four or more hours in duration, and sports play-by-play announcers call games that sometimes last even longer! Regular exercise will also increase your pitch range by at least half an octave.

Most professional announcers have excellent voices. Both male and female announcers tend to have moderately low, resonant voices. They speak at an ideal rate of speed for easy comprehension, and they articulate words and phrases with clarity and precision. Some sports announcers, many of those who do cartoon voice-overs, and all commercial pitch "artists" (announcers of commercials who speak at a rate in excess of 200 words a minute) are exceptions. But news anchors and reporters, documentary narrators, talk-show hosts, interviewers, and announcers on classical and popular music stations must have pleasant voices and speak at a comfortable and easily understood rate of delivery.

As a radio announcer, you'll rely totally on your voice for the communication of messages; on television, your voice is only slightly less important. It's essential that you protect this instrument. Smoking and yelling until hoarse at sports events are two ways of "losing" or seriously impairing your voice. In addition to affecting voice quality, smoking cigarettes will decrease your lung capacity, and this, in turn, will negatively affect your breathing. At worst, smoking can cause a permanently hoarse voice, a rasping cough, and, eventually, emphysema or lung cancer. If you have a smoking habit, yet want to succeed as a professional announcer, you should seriously reassess your priorities. Quitting smoking becomes more and more difficult as you grow older. There's never been a better time to quit than now!

Speech Personality

Your **speech personality** is the way you sound, and what makes you instantly recognizable when you speak to a friend on the telephone. A speech personality is made up of seven variables: (1) **pitch**, including pitch range and **inflection** patterns; (2) **volume** (degree of loudness); (3) **tempo**, or rate of delivery; (4) **vitality**, or energy; (5) **voice quality**, including resonance, timbre, and tone; (6) **pronunciation**; and (7) **articulation**, sometimes referred to as *diction* or *enunciation* (the movement of speech organs to make speech sounds). The overall sound of your voice is shaped by the first six of these variables.

In addition to vocal sounds, you have a distinctive manner of **articulation**—the way in which you break up both **phonated** tones (voiced consonants, diphthongs, and vowels) and **unphonated** sounds (the unvoiced consonants discussed in Chapter 4) into words and phrases. Pronunciation and articulation are closely linked and are examined in detail in Chapter 4. This chapter focuses on pitch, volume, tempo, vitality, and voice quality.

You can, to a degree, isolate each of these speech qualities and characteristics and work on them for speech improvement. Using appropriate

Figure 3.1

Radio talk-show host Michael Krasny gears his weekday two-hour programs to an audience interested in current events, developments in international affairs, scientific discoveries, and similar topics. Because his discussions with guests are intellectual by nature, he believes that his soft-spoken, conversational style of speech not only reflects his personality but also is conducive to discussions that are long on information and rational discourse. *Courtesy of Michael Krasny and KQED-FM, San Francisco, California.*

exercises, you can concentrate on your pitch, for example, without at the same time working on volume or tempo. Eventually, however, your efforts must come together if your speech is to avoid affectation and to blend successfully into the aural representation of the personality you want to project. You may not like some aspects of your speech personality, but one of the most positive results you can achieve through your study and practice of announcing is a considerable improvement in your speech.

Analyzing Your Speech

The two readings that follow are designed to help in evaluating your speaking voice. Every speech sound of American English appears in initial, medial, and final positions in each reading, unless a sound isn't used in one of those positions. The exercises are intended to meet four objectives: (1) to require you to manufacture all speech sounds to help detect possible speech problems, (2) to use the more difficult sounds several times, (3) to detect any problems of slurring over words, and (4) to make the reading as brief as possible. The passages may seem nonsensical, but you should read them as though they make a great deal of sense. Try to use your regular patterns of inflection and stress and your normal rate of delivery; only by doing so can voice or articulation problems be detected. It's highly recommended that you record your readings so that, after detecting specific problems, you can work on them and use your initial recording to measure progress.

Diagnostic Readings

William and His Friends

This is the story of a little boy named William. He lived in a small town called Marshville. Friends he had galore, if one may judge by the vast numbers of children who visited his abode (uh-BODE). Every day after school through the pathway leading to his house, the little boys and girls trudged along, singing as though in church. Out into the yard they came, a vision of juvenile (JOOV-uh-nuhl) happiness. But, joyous though they were, they served only to work little William up into a lather. For, although he assuaged (uh-SWAYDGD) his pain with comic books and the drinking of milk, William abhorred the daily routine. Even Zero, his dog, was aghast at the daily appearance of the running, singing, shuffling, open-mouthed fellows and girls. Beautiful though the sight may have been, William felt that they used the avenue leading to his abode as an awesome item of lush malfeasance (mal-FEEZ-unce). Their little oily voices only added fuel to the fire, for William hated music. "Oooo," he would say, "they mew like cats, baa like sheep, and moo like a cow. My nerves are raw." Then back into his menage (may-NAZH) the little joker would scamper, fast action earnestly being his desire.

Here's an alternate diagnostic reading:

The Battle of Atterbury

The big battle was on! Cannon thundered and machine guns chattered. The troops, weary after months of constant struggle, found themselves rejuvenated by a vision of triumph. Atterbury, the junction of three main roads, was on the horizon. Using whatever annoying tricks he could, Jacques (ZHOCK) Deatheridge, the former millionaire playboy, was much in charge as he eyed the oil capital of the feudal republic. Few would say that the Beige Berets had not cashed in on Jacques's flash of genius. Then the rather uncommon English fellow, a zany half-wit to many who now would writhe in agony, looked puzzled for a moment; the mob on top of Manhasset Hill was frantically throwing him a signal. He snatched the message from the courier. "My gracious," he muttered.

"Atterbury is our own capital!" Elated, nonetheless, he invited his overawed band to play in his honor. After a solo on the drums, Jacques spoke to the multitude. "Rejoice, my fellow citizens! All is not bad! At least our troops have won one victory!"

Voice Analysis

To describe the way a person speaks, we say the voice is of high or low **pitch**; that the speaker's **volume** is loud or quiet; that the speaker's **tempo** is fast or slow; that the speaker shows energy, or **vitality** or the lack of it; that the **voice quality** of the speaker is pleasing, grating, resonant, or "thin"; that words are, or are not, spoken according to established **pronunciation**; and that the speaker clearly enunciates or slurs words, which refers to **articulation**. In the sections that follow, pitch, volume, tempo, vitality, and voice quality are examined in some detail.

Figure 3.2

Vocal sounds are emitted through the vocal folds (cords), shown open and relaxed (upper right), and tensed and closed (lower right). Vocal folds are small bands of tissue that stretch across the larynx. When you begin to speak, larynx muscles pull on the vocal folds, narrowing the opening. Air emerging from the lungs vibrates against the tensed folds and forms the sounds you produce.

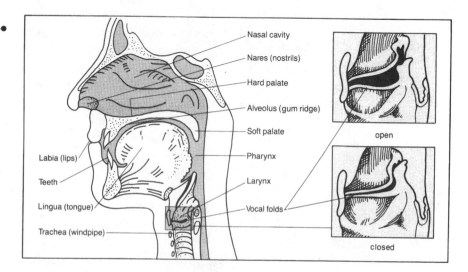

Pitch

In audio terminology, **pitch** is determined by the frequency of vibration of sound waves. Medium- to low-pitched voices are generally more pleasant than high-pitched voices. An exception occurs when a voice is pushed so far down the pitch scale as to sound guttural, unnatural, or even grotesque. You should speak near a pitch level that's comfortable and easy to vary for emphasis or variety and that doesn't strain your voice. Whatever your pitch range, make sure you don't consistently speak at your lowest level, because good speech demands variety in pitch (**inflection**). If you always speak at your lowest level, you have no way of lowering your pitch for selected words.

Pitch in human speech is determined by the rate of vibration of the vocal folds, sometimes referred to as the vocal cords; the faster they vibrate, the higher the pitch. The vocal folds of a mature woman generally vibrate about twice as fast as those of a mature man, so female voices are generally about an octave higher than male voices.

To make the best of your voice, find and develop your optimum pitch—the pitch at which you feel most comfortable and are able to produce your most pleasant sounds. Most of us sound best when we're speaking in the lower half of our available pitch range. Although careless speakers make little use of their available range, with practice nearly everyone can achieve a range of between one and two octaves.

You can determine your **optimum pitch** in one of several ways. One effective system is based on the theory that your optimum pitch is that level at which the greatest amount of resonance is produced. **Resonance** is the amplification of vocal tones during speech as the result of vibrations of the chief resonators: the bones of the chest and face, the **trachea** (windpipe), the **larynx** (connecting the trachea and the pharynx and containing the vocal folds), the **pharynx** (between the mouth and the nasal passages), the mouth, the nose, and the sinuses and cheekbones. When you resonate, you can feel these vibrations most noticeably alongside your nose. Place your palms on your cheekbones and your fingers on the sides of your nose. Now read a series of short sentences, each at a different pitch level. You should be able to feel it when you hit your optimum pitch. And, by recording and playing back the test sentences, you'll hear, without the distraction of bone-conducted sound, what you sound like when you're at or very near your optimum pitch.

Another useful method of determining optimum pitch involves a piano. Sitting at the piano, sing the scale as low and as high as you comfortably can, striking the note that corresponds with each sound. If your singing voice covers two octaves, your optimum speaking voice should be at about the midpoint in the lower of the two octaves. In other words, optimum pitch is very close to a quarter of the way up from your lowest to your highest pitch. Having found the note that corresponds to your optimum pitch, start reading a prose passage. When you reach a vowel sound that can be prolonged, hold the tone and strike the note that matches your optimum pitch. You can easily tell if you're consistently above, on, or below your optimum pitch level.

Because your vocal folds are actually two muscles, they're subject to contraction. In a taut, contracted state, they vibrate at a more rapid rate than when they're relaxed. The faster they vibrate, the higher the pitch. Because of this, your pitch may become more pleasant sounding if you can relax your vocal folds. To relax your throat muscles, however, you must simultaneously relax the rest of your body. Because announcing is a performing art, and because performing usually causes tension, it's important that you learn to relax. Professional announcers with several years of work experience behind them usually have no problem with nervousness. But students of announcing who perform before an instructor and fellow students or audition for that coveted first job can expect to be nervous. Some experience mic (microphone) fright or a raised pitch or stumble over words. (Chapter 5, "Audio Performance," discusses causes and cures of mic fright.)

Some radio and television announcers speak above their optimum pitch level. Many sports reporters apparently believe that a loud, frenetic, mile-a-minute delivery enhances the significance of their reports, and both the frenzy and the volume level tend to raise their pitch. On-the-scene reporters sending eyewitness stories to their stations amid high levels of ambient noise sometimes must raise their volume level—and with it, their pitch—to be heard. And some television performers unconsciously attempt to project their voices to a *camera* positioned several feet distant, rather than to the *lavaliere mic* that's only ten or twelve inches from their mouths. This habit raises both the volume level and the pitch. Use your medium: electronic communication doesn't usually require high volume. Speak softly, and the pitch of your voice will remain pleasingly low.

Inflection refers to the altering of the pitch or tone of the voice. Repetitious inflection makes some voices singsong, while lack of inflection causes others to speak in a monotone. Good speech avoids the extremes and reaches a happy medium. Untrained speakers often fail to use variations in pitch sufficiently, and the result is a boring performance. On the other hand, some few poorly advised speakers (who apparently were told at one time that they must avoid a monotone delivery) employ pitch patterns that regularly and repetitiously go up and down, without regard to the meaning of the words spoken. When practicing to increase pitch variety, avoid falling into predictable patterns in which you raise your pitch every so many words. Pitch should be altered to give emphasis to words that are important for understanding your message. Inflection should *always* be used to stress words that should be *underscored,* as indicated in *this* sentence by the use of *italics.*

You should be self-critical about the degree and style of your pitch variations. Listen intently to recordings of your speech. If you feel that improvement is needed, use the exercises at the end of this chapter. Always speak aloud, and tape, replay, and note your progress.

Volume

Volume level is seldom a problem in broadcast speech, except for laypersons who don't know how to use microphones and reporters or sportscasters covering events that produce high levels of **ambient noise.** In a studio or control room, sensitive microphones pick up and amplify all but the weakest of voices. An **audio console,** properly operated, ensures that the correct volume of speech goes through the board and on to the transmitter. Always remember that your listener is very close to you, so speak in a normal voice, as you would in a face-to-face conversation.

Outside the studio environment, volume level can be a problem. The noise from a parade, a political convention, or a sports event may make it necessary to use a louder voice. Under these circumstances you may achieve the best results by moving closer to the mic and actually reducing your volume level. On the other hand, if conveying the excitement of the event dictates an increased volume, back away from the mic and speak up. Your pitch may go up as you do so, but that might enhance the excitement of your report.

Most radio and television speech is at its best when it's delivered at a conversational level. Because this level remains relatively constant for all of us, there's an optimum distance from mouth to mic to achieve speech that's suited to the event. A weak voice, too distant from the microphone, will require an increase in the **gain** (volume level) of the console; this in turn will increase the volume of the ambient noise. Conversely, a strong voice too close to a microphone is likely to produce popping, excessive sibilance, or an unpleasant aspirate quality. **Sibi-**

lance is the hissing sound when speaking words that include the letters *s*, *sh*, and sometimes *z*. **Popping** is a blast of air when the plosive sounds *p*, *b*, *t*, *d*, *k*, and *g* are spoken. To **aspirate** is to release a puff of breath, as when saying the word *unhitch*. Aspirate sounds, like sibilance, are a part of our spoken language and are exaggerated by microphones. A *windscreen* or *pop filter*, as well as an audio device called a **de-esser**, will reduce popping and excessive sibilance, but any such device will also eliminate the higher frequencies.

Establishing your optimum volume level and microphone placement (distance from the mouth) should be one of your first priorities as a student of announcing. Because microphones vary in sensitivity, pickup pattern, and tonal reproduction, it's important to experiment with each type of microphone you're likely to use.

Tempo

Your tempo, or rate of delivery, is sometimes determined by the number of words to be read in a specified time, sometimes by the mood or nature of the occasion, and when **dubbing (looping)**, by the synchronization of speech with pictures on a monitor or projection screen. In general, newscasts and hard-sell commercials are read quite rapidly, whereas documentary narration, classical music copy, announcements on some popular music stations, and institutional commercials are spoken more slowly. When ad-libbing, you must judge what speed is appropriate to the mood of the event and adjust your rate of delivery accordingly.

There's no single correct rate at which to speak or read. When you have no time limit, gear your speed to the mood of the occasion or of your script. But keep in mind that most of us speak too rapidly much of the time. Speed is often the enemy of clear articulation. If read at too rapid a rate, the sentence "So give to the college of your choice" becomes "So give tuhthukallage uvyer choice." There's an absolute limit to the reading speed you can achieve without sacrificing good articulation. Few of us are good judges of our own speech; this is doubly true when it comes to judging tempo. Aside from requesting help from others, the best way to learn to achieve your optimum speaking or reading rate is by frequent use of an audio recorder. Isolate the one problem of tempo and work on it until a good rate of speed becomes automatic. If you detect slurring in your speech, the discussion and exercises in Chapter 4 should help you improve the clarity of your speech.

Aside from a good basic rate of delivery, you should also work for variety in speed. Speeding up for throwaway phrases and slowing down for emphatic words or phrases will help give more meaning to your message. Throwaway phrases include "member, FDIC," "substantial penalty for early withdrawal," and "your mileage may vary."

The diagnostic reading called "William and His Friends" (page 65) includes "speed traps" that may cause you to trip over your tongue. Other traps in the piece may lead you into slurring if you read too rapidly. Your challenge is to keep your reading moving while avoiding stumbles.

Vitality, Energy

Two speakers with nearly identical speech characteristics may sound quite different if they vary greatly in *vitality,* or *energy.*[1] Though a sense of vitality is easily communicated through rapid speaking or an increase of volume, it isn't necessary to rush your delivery or speak loudly to convey vitality. Many speakers are able to communicate feelings of energy or enthusiasm even when speaking slowly and softly; others may speak rapidly but use little energy and therefore come across as unenthusiastic. Many DJs and sports announcers speak with a fairly low volume level, but attain a feeling of vitality by speaking very rapidly.

Working toward two objectives should help you project vitality; first, use a degree of energy that's appropriate to your personality, and, second, gear the degree of vitality to the mood or significance of the event you're describing. Above all, don't push yourself up to a level of vitality that's forced, unnatural to you, or inappropriate for the occasion. Most announcers are at their best when they're being themselves. You may need years of study and practice to develop your latent speaking potential, but don't try to hasten the process by copying the speech personality of an announcer whose work you admire; you'll certainly waste your time if you try to substitute someone else's personality for your own.

Many beginning students of announcing are more subdued (and therefore show less energy) in performing assignments than they are in their normal, out-of-class speech exchanges with friends. When performing, your objective might well be to lift yourself up to your customary level of vitality when driving home a point in a spirited discussion. If, however, you're a "low-key" person, you may want to capitalize on your

---

[1]The terms *vitality, energy,* and *intensity* are used interchangeably in this discussion.

natural qualities, as you project vitality through *restrained urgency*. This is accomplished by using a relatively low volume—speaking almost with a hushed voice—and a measured delivery. In doing this, stress key words by prolonging them, or by pausing slightly before and after them, and by using whatever other means you possess to indicate that you're "holding back" your emotions.

Here are two readings that ask for differing degrees of energy. The first radio commercial demands a great deal of vitality. You should read and record this first with subdued volume but a high level of intensity, because this is what the author had in mind. You next may want to try it with all the stops pulled out: using as much volume, energy, and vocal pyrotechnics as you can muster. Then try it several more times, varying different elements of speech production with each reading. First use a fast pace; then use a slower pace. Try it with more inflection and then with a limited pitch range; finally, try it with *reduced* vitality and *increased* volume. Listening to and judging the results of each variation should help you gain an understanding of the ways your interpretation changes both the impression conveyed to listeners and the way you feel about your performance.

The second reading asks for a more restrained delivery. It's whimsical, slow-paced, and is to be read in a "tongue-in-cheek" manner. After recording it in the style indicated, try it in every variation of mood, rate, volume level, pitch, and degree of energy you can conjure.

Note that the first spot was created several years ago, before Eastern Airlines folded. It is revived here because it's an excellent illustration of a hard-hitting, staccato, and brash writing style that mirrors the brash qualities of the city it promotes. (Note: *SFX* is the standard abbreviation for *sound effects*.)

AGENCY: Young and Rubicam, Inc.
CLIENT: Eastern Airlines
LENGTH: 60 seconds

MUSIC: (UP-TEMPO FULL ORCHESTRA)

ANNCR: For sheer brass, nothing can touch it. Houston. The big rich. Brash. Confident. A brawler. That just opened the finest opera house in the Southwest. That calls itself one of the world's fashion centers. And is. Houston. It's oil. Hard cash. Enchiladas. It's a fast quip. A million-aire who rode before he could walk. The NASA space center. If ever there was a frontier, Houston is it. If ever there was a cosmopolitan city, call it Houston. But mostly, call it guts.

SFX: (SOUND OF JET TAKEOFF)

Houston . . . an Eastern address. Eastern Airlines has 3 nonstop jets going there every business day—throughout the business day. A lot of people want to get to Houston. We'd like to make it easier for every one of them. We want everyone to fly.

A much different mood is asked for in the next commercial. It, too, re-quires energy, because without energy a reading can be boring. The en-ergy asked for, though, is that born of conviction; to be successful in the performance of an announcement such as this, you need to project re-strained belief in the story you're telling, and the product you're selling.

AGENCY: Allen and Dorward
CLIENT: New Century Beverage Company
LENGTH: 60 seconds

ANNCR: Here is your one-minute gnu (NEW) training lesson for today. Gnu is spelled G-N-U. The first question most new trainers ask is, "What's gnu?" The gnu is part ox, part antelope, and part horse. This gives him a slight identity complex and makes him mean. He may charge, hook you with his horns, throw you down, and stomp on you. That's when you start the lesson. Remember, you can't teach an old gnu new tricks. Give the command, "Pay attention." If he hooks you and throws you and stomps you again . . . you have his attention. So stop the lesson and pour yourself a frosty, ice-cold Mug Old Fashioned Root Beer. Mug Root Beer is the ideal drink for gnu trainers and old gnu trainers. Mug Old Fashioned Root Beer. Regular or Diet. You haven't tasted root beer like this in years.

Voice Quality

Resonance Versus Thinness

A good voice for the electronic media is one with **resonance** (an intensification of vocal tones during articulation as a result of vibrations). A sensitive, top-quality microphone, such as a condenser mic, can enhance your natural resonance. But even the best equipment can work only with what you give it, and a voice that's thin or lacking in resonance can be significantly improved only by its owner.

The sound vibrations that originate with your vocal folds are weak and colorless. As described in the section on pitch, sound vibrations need resonators to strengthen and improve the quality of sound. The

Figure 3.3

Sports reporter Fred Inglis addresses the camera as he ad-libs a report on a breaking story from the newsroom. Fred received his master's degree in broadcast communication arts from San Francisco State University. *Courtesy of Fred Inglis and KTVU, Oakland, California.*

chief resonators are the bones of the chest and face, the windpipe (**trachea**), the **larynx** (connecting the trachea and the pharynx and containing the vocal folds), the **pharynx** (between the mouth and the nasal passages), the mouth, the nose, the cheekbones, and the sinuses.

In general, thinness of voice is caused by one or more of three factors: shallow, weak breathing; speaking at too high a pitch (usually the higher the pitch, the less the resonance); and inadequate use of the movable resonators (the pharynx, the larynx, and the tongue).

As with any other speech problem, the first step is diagnosing it. Do you have a thin voice? What causes it? What do you need to do about it? The following passage is provided for diagnostic purposes. Read it slowly, working for your most resonant quality. Record it, using a sensitive professional microphone and a high-quality recorder. If possible, ask help from a person qualified to assess both voice quality and the apparent causes of thinness. Begin this reading approximately five feet from the microphone, speaking at a volume level appropriate to that distance. At each number, move forward about six inches, until you're reading the final sentence about eight inches from the mic. Lower your volume as you move in. On playback, determine whether your resonance is significantly affected by distance and volume level. Unless other negative qualities interfere (excessive sibilance, popping, nasality), this test should help you find and use your optimum microphone position to bring out resonance.

1. Johnny has an IQ of 170, but he can't read. The words are jumbled, upside down. Mirrored.

2. He has dyslexia. A learning disability that affects one out of every ten children.

3. Johnny goes to school and faces frustration, humiliation, and ridicule.

4. It's a tragedy because the techniques are there to help the dyslexic child. He can learn to read and write. And survive in school.

5. He can even go to college. If—and only if—dyslexia is diagnosed early. And dealt with.

6. Today, there are over a dozen centers in Massachusetts that can diagnose dyslexia—even among
preschoolers.

7. To find out more, call 1-555-6880.

8. 1-555-6880.

9. One out of every ten kids has dyslexia.

10. And every one of them needs help.[2]

If yours is a thin, colorless voice, you should be able to increase resonance by following these suggestions:

- Practice deep breathing. Learn to breathe from the diaphragm.
Your **diaphragm** is a large muscle that separates your chest from
your stomach. Shallow breathing will result in a shallow or thin
voice. While you speak or read, consciously try to increase the
force of air coming from your lungs.

- Make sure you're moving your articulators. (Use the exercises in
Chapter 4 to work on an exaggerated use of jaw, tongue, and
lips.)

- Make sure that there's no blockage of your nasal passages.

- Try to lower your pitch. (See the suggestions given earlier in this
chapter.)

- Read passages that emphasize vowel sounds (nineteenth-century
British poetry is excellent for this). Prolong those sounds when
they occur and try to keep your throat as open as possible. The
suggested readings for this chapter list several standard speech-
improvement books that include exercises.

- Discover the best microphone for your voice, and establish your
optimum distance from it. (A ribbon mic will generally make
your voice sound more resonant than will a dynamic mic.)

---

[2]Courtesy of Ingalls Associates, Boston, Massachusetts.

A vast collection of the works of major British and American poets may be found on the Internet. Open a New Web Browser, enter this URL[3]:

etext.lib.virginia.edu/britpo.html

You'll be connected to the Alderman Center Library at the University of Virginia. The poems of Keats, Shelley, Wordsworth, Whitman, and many other poets may be opened and printed for practicing improved resonance.

For a complete, updated list of URLs for this textbook, please see the text home site available at *www.hmco.com/college.*

Breathing and Breathing Exercises

It's all but impossible to have a strong, resonant voice if you are given to poor posture and shallow breathing. Correct breathing requires that you maintain good posture, that your neck, shoulders, and face be relaxed, and that you breathe from the diaphragm. Good posture means sitting or standing with a straight spine and with your shoulders drawn back. It's impossible to breathe properly when you're hunched over. Check your posture frequently throughout the day, every day. Become aware of when you are slumping instead of standing or sitting erectly. When speaking or reading aloud, first check your posture and then eliminate any tension that may be present in your neck, shoulders, or face. In time, you should become so conditioned that good posture will be natural.

In the glory days of radio, those who announced, acted, sang, related stories, read the news, told jokes, or did play-by-play coverage of sports typically *stood* as they performed. Sound quality was even more vital then than now, because of the inferior fidelity of sending and receiving equipment. To gain every possible advantage of clear reception, announcers used every means to project strong and easily understood

---

[3]The Internet is changing constantly as new web sites are added and old web sites are abandoned. The URL listings in this textbook should be regarded as samples of the kinds of material available rather than as a stable index. If you seek a web site using one of these URLs and cannot connect, enter the key words for the topic into a search engine to find a site that may provide the information you want.

speech. Standing reduces pressure on the upper torso and the diaphragm and increases lung capacity. Even today, voice-over specialists stand as they rehearse and record commercials and documentary narrative. Most radio and television reporters stand as they record introductions, tags, and other bits of speech to be edited into "packages." Some sports announcers also stand as they describe football and other high-intensity games. Whenever possible and appropriate, stand as you perform announcing assignments: your voice quality and general effectiveness will be enhanced if you do so.

As described earlier, your diaphragm is a muscular membrane that separates your stomach from your chest cavity (lungs). Place your fingers just at the point where your upper abdomen meets your lowest ribs. When you breathe in, you should be able to feel outward movement, as air fills the lungs. When you speak, you should try to "push" your voice all the way up from your diaphragm. You simply can't have a strong, resonant voice if you're manufacturing speech sounds mainly in your mouth. Speech sounds other than sibilants and plosives are initiated by the vibration of the vocal folds. These sounds are then broken up into speech by the articulators. To produce a strong and healthy voice, the air stream that vibrates the vocal folds must be strong, which means that the stream should be forced up by the diaphragm.

To begin a regimen of breathing exercises, you need only to count aloud and see how many numbers you can say without effort. As you practice this exercise several times each day, you should soon find yourself able to count to thirty before beginning to run out of breath. Along with the counting exercise, begin to read aloud whenever you can. Work to strengthen your breathing by taking care to always push your voice up from your diaphragm.

Other exercises to develop good breathing habits may be found in a number of texts on speech improvement, including those mentioned as suggested readings in Appendix D.

 SPOTLIGHT

Improving Your Voice Personality

Your voice is the most important instrument of communication you possess. This is a strong statement, but it's by no means an exaggeration. Diagnostic exercises can help identify whatever problems you may have in voicing and articulating the words you use, and hours of practice can improve your speaking voice. However, there's another aspect to speech improvement, and that's the *unlearning of bad attitudes toward one-self* as those attitudes were developed in childhood.

Barbara Lazear Ascher has done an excellent job of identifying a variety of attitudes and physical postures that contribute to good and bad use of our vocal mechanism. Her essay is reprinted here in a slightly abridged form through her generous permission and that of *Self* magazine.[4]

Voice Lessons

The right voice can persuade a desperate person not to jump. It can extract a raise from your reluctant boss. It can calm a cranky pet. A dog trainer once told me: "Always speak in a low, quiet voice. You can yell and scream and it'll never work, but the minute you speak softly, you've got his attention." Could it be that what works on pups also works on people?

The voice I'm talking about flows from gentleness—a firm, adult *gentleness* not to be confused with *timidity*. Our voice conveys who we *are,* according to New York City acting coach Elizabeth Parrish. The problem is that too often it still carries inflections of who we *were.* We all know those voices that survive childhood. The don't-expect-too-much-of-me voice. The whiny life-is-unfair voice. To change your tone and your future, says Parrish, "you have to break a barrier as to who you think you are—the barrier you grew up with."

Tune in to your tone   To convey gentleness and authority in an attractive, persuasive tone, we first have to hear ourselves. Voice specialist Arthur Joseph suggests you record and play back samples of your speech. What if you don't like what you hear? First, identify what you're conveying about yourself with your voice. Then, Joseph tells his students, "choose your vocal persona." He has them write down how they think they're perceived and how they'd like to be perceived. "What you write becomes a mission statement."

Say who you want to be   You can use your voice as a tool for change, says New York City psychotherapist David S. Wilson, Ph.D. He has discovered that if his patients speak about themselves positively and aloud, they become what they say. Do this positive "self-talk" as many times a day as possible, he says, and your own voice will begin to replace the formative voices of childhood that scolded you to "Be quiet!" or to "Speak up."

But first, according to Dr. Wilson, you need to hear your negative "self-talk," those self-defeating opinions about your self, whether it's "I'm fat" or "I'm no good at languages." You must hear yourself speak the accusation aloud because hearing it is how the thought originally got planted. Wilson points out that little children will say "I'm a

---

[4]Barbara Lazear Ascher, *Self,* August, 1995, p. 132.

bad girl or boy" because they hear their parents say it. "By the time you're in your teens *their opinion* has become *your belief,* a primal belief, so that even if you're a winner you think you're a loser," Wilson says. "People start saying, 'I'm no good at languages' or 'I'm no good at numbers,' and it becomes self-fulfilling."

Once you hear it, you can stop the negative self-talk and replace it with a positive statement that says what you want to be. Speak statements that contain no negatives. "I'm thin" rather than "I'm not fat," for example.

Repeat your positive statement aloud every chance you get, urges Wilson, and keep it simple. "I'm successful," for instance, or "I'm an adult in control." "If people stick with this," he says, "their self-image is changed—and the change begins with the first utterance."

Stand or sit tall   Physical tension and body position affect the sound of your voice, according to New York City veteran voice teacher Ralph Proodian. If your lower back is tight, then your chest tightens and that tension radiates into the larynx. Relax your shoulders and neck; when tense, they also raise the pitch. The free flow of breath that will bring the most beautiful resonance to your voice requires perfect posture.

Proodian recommends testing your posture by standing with your back to a wall with your heels almost against it, your shoulders touching it. Then, with your palm facing the wall, run your hands behind your lower back. If there is just enough space to slide your hand in and out, then your posture is speech perfect.

Take a deep breath   The vocal muscles are the only muscles that function through air pressure, according to Arthur Joseph. The velocity of air moving through the vocal folds creates vibration and pitch. "Inner conflict can stifle the airflow and prevent functioning," he says. When we're holding back feelings, we don't breathe properly, and our voice is thin, unpersuasive. We need to breathe freely in order to promote the richest cadence and melody in the sounds we make.

To breathe properly, Joseph reminds his students that breath is both emotional and physical. He instructs them to "allow a silent and loving breath" to move through the body before speaking. Then take another deep breath and send your voice out in an arc, as though it were a ski jumper.

Explore the emotional power of sound   Vocal *sounds,* even more than *words,* have tremendous power to release emotions and bodily tension. Don Campbell, founder and senior adviser of the Institute for Music, Health and Education in Boulder, Colorado, recommends making long vowel sounds like *aaaah, eee,* and *ooooh* to "learn the depths of your own personal voice." To do this, sit comfortably in a chair, close your eyes and begin with *aaah.* Make the sound as long and at as many different pitches as you like.

Experiment—let it sound like a yawn or a moan or a sigh. Go wherever your impulse leads you. Do this for three minutes and notice how you feel. Work your way through each vowel, noting how different sounds evoke different feelings, pitches, and rhythms. For most people, low slow sounds are soothing, while higher pitched sounds (like eee) are energizing and lift the spirits. Like deep breathing, vocalizing can calm you down, which is crucial to a melodic speaking voice.

Hear the music   "Listen to the French and Italians," suggests Dwight Owsley, a New York City cabaret singer with a voice you'd want to curl up with. "Notice how many different pitches their voices have. Americans tend to be very limited in their range, so that their voices, by comparison, seem flat."

It's true about the French. One of the many reasons that we find French women beautiful is the sound of their voices. Listen for a moment to the lilt, to the upward inflection and then the dip to a deeper range. They are able to convey tenderness and aloofness through the melody of their basic speaking voices.

The music of the voice is aesthetic, it's character forming and, according to Campbell, it can be good for your health. Campbell teaches that the sound of one's voice affects the body. Our voice, he says, is capable of harmonizing our inner and outer worlds—as the shamans and the singers of Gregorian chants know. Campbell tells the story of a French physician called in to treat a general malaise affecting monks in a Benedictine monastery. Following the reforms of Vatican II, the life of the monastery had changed radically. The physician determined that the problem was au-diological—not physiological—and prescribed a return to the pre-Vatican II "diet of Gregorian chant." The monks returned to their former practice of chanting eight or nine times a day for ten to twenty-five minutes, and the group was brought back into harmony with one another and their God. Their appetites returned and their fatigue vanished. "Within six months the monastery was intact," says Campbell.

The sound of their voices healed them.

Barbara Lazear Ascher is a noted essayist, novelist, poet, and lecturer. She's written and read essays for National Public Radio's *Morning Edition*. A lawyer-turned-journalist, she's most at home with essays because, she says, "I'm impatient," and short pieces enable you to "get to the point right away." Her article, "Voice Lessons," is an example of a short piece, loaded with useful information. *Courtesy of Barbara Lazear Ascher.*

Common Voice Problems

Nasality and Denasality

Nasality is caused by allowing air to exit through the nose, rather than the mouth, when sounding *M, N,* and *NG*. **Denasality** is caused by a blocked nasal passage, and often is present when one is suffering from a cold. Pinch your nostrils and speak a sentence or two; you'll find that by preventing air from passing through your nose, you're producing a certain vocal quality—this is denasality. Now, without holding your nose, try to speak with a nasal tone. You'll find that the sound can be generated only when you force air up through the nasal passage—this is nasality.

Proper use of the nasal passage involves selectively closing off sound with the lips or the front or rear of the tongue, to force sound through the nasal cavity. If you say, in turn, *sim, sin,* and *sing,* holding on to the last sound of each word, you'll find that for *sim* your lips close off the *M* sound, for *sin* the front of your tongue against the upper gum ridge (**alveolus**) creates the *N* sound, and for *sing* the rear of your tongue against the soft palate (or **velum**) produces the *NG* sound. These three nasal sounds are properly produced only by the correct placement of your articulators and an unblocked nasal passage.

If you have a nasal voice quality, your first problem is to determine whether it's caused by not properly sending the *M, N,* and *NG* sounds up through your nose, or whether it's the result of sending nonnasal sounds through the nasal passage. The following sentence should help you determine this. Read it very slowly, pausing to prolong every vowel sound that can be held without change. Record and play back the results.

Many men and women can do this in many differing manners.

All of the sustained *M, N,* and *NG* sounds should have resonance associated with them (as a matter of fact, unless these sounds are allowed to pass through the nose, they can barely be sustained). All nonnasal vowels should have no trace of nasality.

You can check for nasal resonance by placing the tips of your fingers lightly on either side of your nose. When holding a nasal consonant, you should feel a distinct vibration; when prolonging a nonnasal vowel, you should not. If you speak the word *women,* for example, the first prolonged vowel sound, WIII, should have only slight resonance. The WIIIII gives way to WIMMMMM, and this should produce nasal vibration. The next vowel sound is IHHHHHH, which should be free from vibration. The final sound, NNNNNNN, should bring back the vibration. If you find that your nose doesn't produce vibrations on the nasal consonants, your problem is typical of the most common type of nasality. If, on the other hand, you find that you're nasalizing vowels that should not be nasalized, you have a less common and more difficult problem to work on.

If you're not nasalizing the nasal consonants *M, N,* and *NG,* your problem may be a physiological blockage, or you may simply be experiencing nasal congestion. In either case, there's no point in working on nasality exercises as long as the blockage exists. Do whatever is appropriate to end the blockage, even if it means a trip to an allergist, or a nasopharyngologist. If you have no physiological problem or congestion and still lack resonance on the nasal consonants, the exercises on resonance at the end of this chapter should help. If your problem is nasalization of nonnasal vowels, those exercises should also help. Work to avoid any nasal resonance in nonnasal words, but don't try to eliminate it from words that legitimately call for nasality.

Huskiness

There *is* such a thing as a *pleasant* husky voice, one that suits a particular personality and is neither grating nor raspy, but an *excessively* husky or hoarse voice usually indicates a medical problem. Laryngitis, smoker's throat, infected tonsils, or infected sinuses can cause a husky voice. You should see an appropriate medical specialist for any of these conditions because they're a handicap for any type of voice work.

To some extent, huskiness can arise as the result of excessive nervous tension. If yours is an unpleasantly husky voice, and if there's no medical explanation for it, you might improve your performance by drinking warm liquids such as tea or water and by using exercises designed to relieve tension. A section of Chapter 5, under the heading "Lack of Preparation," presents one such relaxation exercise. Vocal exercises will help you overcome excessive huskiness or hoarseness only if your problem is the result of misusing your speech organs.

Excessive Sibilance

Because the sibilant *S* is a common source of trouble to announcers, a diagnostic exercise is included here. Read the following passage into an audio recorder, play it back, and determine whether you have the problem of excessive sibilance. Before working to soften this sound, however, you should experiment with microphone placement and even the use of a windscreen or pop filter, for you may find that the problem is with the equipment or the way you're using it, rather than in your speech.

Sideshows

How long has it been since you saw a first-rate sideshow? Some of us certainly should be sad over the disappearance of the classic circus sideshow, once a staple of civic celebrations—six or seven acts, set forth in circumstances that seemed awesome, or at least mysterious. Certainly, sideshows were sometimes scandalous, and sometimes in questionable taste, but they served to keep our curiosity in a steady state of astonishment.

PRACTICE

Achieving a Low Pitch

There's nothing intrinsically better about a low-pitched voice than a high-pitched one; either extreme can be unpleasant to the ears. A very high-pitched voice can remind listeners of fingernails being scratched across a chalk board; conversely, an excessively low-pitched voice can sound gutteral, one step removed from grunting. Many producers of commercials and documentaries are convinced that low-pitched *male* voices carry with them a certain "authority," despite the fact that many outstanding performances are regularly accomplished by both women and men with mid-pitch range voices. Extremely low voices continue to be heard on voice-over introductions to news programs and televised feature films, on car commercials, and for products of any kind that have "macho-type" men as their target.

Although you may not be set on driving your pitch down into the cellar, you may feel that your voice would benefit from a slightly lowered pitch. Many of us, male and female alike, speak at a higher than desirable pitch. You can evaluate the appropriateness of your pitch by recording some of the exercises found in Chapter 4, "Pronunciation and Articulation." If an analysis of your voice makes you decide to lower your pitch level, the following commercial may be used to see just how much lower you want to (or are able to) go. You should read and record this piece several times, listening between takes to judge each performance. If you already have a very low voice, make sure you don't creep along the bottom. Remember to work for variety in pitch (inflection). In addition to concentrating on pitch, try to read the commercial in exactly thirty seconds. If you read it in less time, you're probably not savoring the key selling words, and your speed may be interfering with the achievement of optimum pitch.

DAIRYLAND LONGHORN CHEESE

Mellow. Smooth and mellow. That's the way to describe Dairyland Longhorn Cheese. We use the finest Grade A milk from happy cows. Nothing but pure, natural ingredients. We take our time, letting the cheese age to the peak of perfect taste. We package Dairyland Longhorn in cheesecloth and wax, just like in the old days. And we speed it to your grocer, so that you get it at its flavorful best. Dairyland Longhorn Cheese. It's smooth and mellow.

 PRACTICE

Varying Your Pitch

Say these sentences, inflecting on the italicized word or words:

When did *you* get here?	When did you *get* here?
I *hope* you're right.	I hope you're *right.*
Which *one* is it?	Which one *is* it?
Which one is *it?*	*Which* one is it?
We *lost* the game!	*We* lost the game!
Don't say *that.*	Don't *say* that.
She found the key.	She *found* the key.
The *dog* ate the steak.	The dog ate the *steak.*

Inflect these words in isolation:

What?	Tremendous!
Certainly!	Ridiculous!
Maybe.	Surely.
Awful!	Life?
Sure!	How?
Try!	Stop.
Go!	Caught?

Note that the challenge is greatest with one-syllable words. The word *life*, for example, asked as a question, can accommodate both an upward and a downward inflection without becoming a two- or three-syllable word.

PRACTICE

Varying Your Tempo

The following commercial provides good opportunities for employing shifts in reading speed.

SFX: SOUND OF GRIZZLY MOTORCYCLE IN DISTANCE, GRADUALLY APPROACHING

ANNCR: I can hear it in the distance. (PAUSE) Can you? (PAUSE) The "grrr-ing" of the Grizzly motorbike. (PAUSE) No, not a "purring," a "grrr-ing." What's the difference? A "purr" comes from a contented cat—a "grrr" is made by a hefty Grizzly, looking for adventure. Cats are great, but they're usually gentle. The Grizzly is wild, but not unmanageable.

SFX: GRIZZLY VOLUME CONTINUES TO INCREASE.

ANNCR: The Grizzly doesn't "putt-putt," and it doesn't purr. It has a warm, furry sound, as befits a creature of the wild. (PAUSE) Here's the Grizzly, speaking for itself. (PAUSE)

SFX: SOUND UP FULL, THEN BEGIN FADE.

ANNCR: There it goes! (PAUSE) "Grrr-ing" its way to where it's going. Hear the "grrr"? You can own the "grrr"—if you don't want a pussycat and think you can tame a Grizzly. Check us out. (PAUSE) We're in the Yellow Pages. The Grizzly. (PAUSE) It's for people who want something on the wild side.

SFX: SOUND OF GRIZZLY TOO CLOSE

 PRACTICE

Working on Nasal Resonance

Speak each pair of nasal and nonnasal words, keeping the tips of your fingers lightly touching the sides of your nose. Work for vibration with the first word of each pair and for lack of it with the second.

(M)

aim—aid	beam—beet
arm—art	farmer—father
atom—attar	bump—butt
balm—back	summer—Sutter
calm—cot	ram—rat

(N)

earn—earth	bend—bet
barn—bard	bin—bit
bane—bathe	win—will
fawn—fall	own—oath
band—bat	friend—Fred

(NG)

link—lick	bunko—bucko
bank—back	tongue—tuck
blank—black	ming—mick
wink—wick	Manx—Max
singer—sitter	trunk—truck

CHAPTER 4

Pronunciation and Articulation

AFTER DRIVING HIS MOTOR HOME THROUGH NEARLY FORTY STATES OF the United States mainland, Nobel laureate John Steinbeck recorded these impressions in *Travels with Charley:*[1]

> One of my purposes [for making this trip] was to listen, to hear speech, accent, speech rhythms, overtones and emphasis. For speech is so much more than words and sentences. I did listen everywhere. It seemed to me that regional speech is in the process of disappearing, not gone but going. Forty years of radio and twenty years of television must have this impact. Communications must destroy localness, by a slow, inevitable process. . . . It is a rare house or building that is not rigged with spiky combers of the air. Radio and television speech becomes standardized, perhaps better English than we have ever used. Just as our bread, mixed and baked, packaged and sold without benefit of accident or human frailty, is uniformly good and uniformly tasteless, so will our speech become one speech.

These words, written in 1960, have not proved prophetic. People continue to speak with regional accents, despite the fact that, as John Steinbeck observed, an overwhelming percentage of broadcast

---

[1]Steinbeck, John. *Travels with Charley.* New York: Penguin Books, reprinted 1986, p. 106.

announcers at both the local and national levels speak the "homogenized" English of broadcasting. The *American Heritage Dictionary* defines **accent** as "a characteristic pronunciation," so, in truth, everyone speaks with an accent.

There are many different but acceptable ways of pronouncing American English. Think of differences in the speech of a native-born Georgian, a Texan, a New Englander, a New Yorker, a Hoosier (Indianan), an Oregonian, and a person from Ontario Province. The first section of this chapter investigates **pronunciation,** the way words are accented and inflected by a given speaker, and the second discusses a closely related topic—**articulation**—the breaking up of the sounds of speech into recognizable words. Pronunciation has to do with accent or dialect; articulation has to do with the precision or lack of it in sounding words and syllables.

Variations in United States and Canadian Speech

Despite the richness represented by regional differences in pronunciation, most broadcast executives long favored what came to be called broadcast speech, or, more precisely, **Standard American Speech** or **Standard American Dialect**. Although these terms are roughly defined as the native speech of well-educated Americans and Canadians of the Midwest and Far West, many acceptable variations of English are spoken

Figure 4.1

Sports producer and announcer Keith Jackson is one of many announcers with a pronounced southern U.S. accent. His Georgia manner of pronunciation gives his voice a mellowness and softness that have made him vocally identifiable for many years. *Copyright 2000 ABC, Inc.*

in this vast geographical area. These variations are reflected on radio, television, and cable by some news anchors and reporters, talk-show hosts, sports announcers, and stand-up comedians. Additionally, announcers doing cartoon voices and commercial voice-overs often employ accents or dialects. Announcers on stations that broadcast in every language from Korean to Spanish to Polish certainly do not employ Standard American Speech!

Standard American English is spoken by local announcers in every part of the United States, as well as by most television network announcers, and the prevalence of this mode of speech means that many broadcast executives still cling to belief in a "correct" way of speaking.

There are signs of change, most noticeable on cable and at the local station level. It's now possible to hear on stations in nearly every part of the United States and Canada voices that are identifiably African-American, Hispanic, southern, British, "country," New York–New Jersey, or New England. This trend will undoubtedly continue. At the same time, your chances of succeeding in many types of announcing work may be lessened unless you speak with a so-called broadcast standard accent.

As a student of announcing, you should consider the question of pronunciation: if you don't speak standard broadcast speech, you must decide whether or not you want to cultivate it. Because overall pronunciation is an important part of your speech personality, a decision to change it should not be made lightly. Keep this in mind as you consider modifying your mode of pronunciation: if you're truly an outstanding communicator with things of importance to say, the skill to say them clearly, and the ability to project an engaging personality, your regional, international, or ethnic dialect, whatever it may be, is of reduced importance.

Causes of Mispronunciation

Aside from regional deviations from Standard American English or broadcast speech, there are deviations that are not regional and are simply unprofessional. One or more of the following problems can cause mispronunciations.

Sloppy or Incorrect Articulation

If you say AIR for *error* or WIH-yum for *William,* you're mispronouncing because of laziness in the use of your articulators. Say the words *air* and *error* aloud. Note that *air* can be sounded by a simple closing of the mouth and a drawing back of the tongue; *error*, however, requires more effort—two distinct movements of the lips and two movements of the tongue. Other words often mispronounced because of sloppy articulation include *variable* pronounced VAR-uh-buhl instead of VAR-ee-uh-buhl, and *government* pronounced as GUV-munt instead of GUV-ern-munt. Articulation, which is related to pronunciation, is discussed later in this chapter. If you're guilty of sloppy articulation, you should work extensively with the practice exercises on voice quality and articulation.

Physical Impairment

Missing teeth, a fissure in the upper lip, a cleft palate, nasal blockage, or any degree of facial paralysis may make it impossible for a speaker to pronounce words clearly. If you have a correctable physical impairment that interferes with effective speech, such as missing teeth, you should consult an appropriate specialist.

Misreading

Mispronunciations may result from a simple mistake, such as reading *amendable* for *amenable, outrage* for *outage, meditation* for *mediation,* or *through* for *though.* If you consistently misread words, you may have a learning impairment (such as dyslexia and related challenges), or a problem with your vision; either condition calls for consultation with a specialist.

Affectation

Some Americans who employ Standard American English for nearly all their speech pick up a Briticism here and there, and this practice can be jarring to a listener. Saying *EYE-thuh* for *either* works well with New England or southern speech, but it usually sounds out of place when used by a westerner or a midwesterner. Affectation can be worked on and eliminated, but this task requires a keen ear and, in many instances, calls for the help of a qualified speech teacher.

Unfamiliarity with Correct Pronunciation

Most of us have a reading vocabulary that's far more extensive than our speaking vocabulary. From time to time, we err (correctly pronounced ER, not AIR) when we attempt to use a word known to us only through our eyes. The word *coup* (pronounced KOO), for example, might be pronounced KOOP by one who knew it only from the printed page. People who grew up in homes in which American English was poorly pronounced, or who learned English as a second language, sometimes must overcome a limited vocabulary and unfamiliarity with correct pronunciation by making an effort to become somewhat of a linguist.

To be truly professional, you must develop an extensive vocabulary and cultivate clarity and consistency in pronunciation. There are many books that can help you build your vocabulary, but be sure you're not simply adding to your *reading* vocabular.

 The web site for this text includes a list of three hundred words that are often mispronounced or that are uncommon but likely to turn up in broadcast copy. Examples are *bouclé* and *denier* from the world of fashion, and *sciatica* and *catarrh* from medicine. You can use this URL to access the text's web site:

www.hmco.com/college

In addition, Appendix C includes an extensive discussion of American English usage.

Pronuncia-tion

Speech Sounds of American English

In this discussion of the speech sounds of American and Canadian English, **wire-service phonetics** and diacritics are used to illustrate sounds. For the benefit of those who've learned—or are learning—the **International Phonetic Alphabet (IPA)**, those symbols are also given. Wire-service symbols are always enclosed in parentheses: (puh-REN-thuh-seez).[2] **Diacritical marks** appear between virgules: /vûr′gyōōlz/. IPA symbols are enclosed in brackets: [′brækəts].

---

[2]Wire-service phonetics were designed at a time when teletype machines were limited to capital letters only. An apostrophe was used to indicate the syllable to be stressed, as in (SILL-UH-BUHL). A better system of transcribing words uses both upper and lower case letters, as in (SILL-uh-buhl), and this practice is followed throughout this text. One-syllable words are capitalized when they're stressed, as in (TOY).

Figure 4.2

News anchor Rosie Allen prepares for her afternoon drive-time newscast. Born in Louisiana and reared in Denver, Colorado, Rosie speaks Standard American English. Her career has taken many turns, including vocalist for a band at age eighteen, three years in the U.S. Army, radio station news director, and head of public affairs. She's worked as a co-anchor with Ed Baxter since 1984. *Courtesy of Rosie Allen and KGO-AM, San Francisco, California.*

Speech sounds may be classified as vowels, diphthongs, and consonants. You may have been taught that the English language has these vowels—*a, e, i, o, u,* and, sometimes, *y.* While this is true of *written* English, the statement is misleading. Our language actually requires us to manufacture *twelve* vowel sounds.

A **vowel** is defined as a pure phonated (sounded) tone that doesn't use the articulators and can be held indefinitely without changing. If you say aloud the vowel (AH) /a/ [a] as in *father,* you'll note that you can hold it as long as your breath lasts without substantial change in its sound. If you say the diphthong (OY) /oi/ [ɔɪ] as in *toy,* you'll notice that it glides from (AW) /ô/ [ɔ] to (IH) /ĭ/ [ɪ] and that you can't hold its entire sound. You *can* hold the last part of this diphthong indefinitely, but only because it's actually the pure vowel (IH) /ĭ/ [ɪ] as in *it.*

Now say aloud the consonant *p.* You'll notice that you can't do so unless you add some vowel sound, such as *o.* The *p* sound is merely exploded air and can't be prolonged. Other consonants, such as *n,* can be prolonged; but as soon as you stop using your articulators (in the case of *n*, the tip of the tongue has been placed on the gum ridge behind the upper front teeth), the sound turns into a vowel sound such as (UH) /ə/ [ə]. Consonants, then, may or may not require phonation but always involve use of the articulators.

In come cases it becomes impossible to say whether an unacceptably uttered word has been mispronounced or sloppily articulated. Saying MIRR for *mirror,* for example, could be the result of either not knowing the correct pronunciation or simply not bothering to force the articulators to do their job. Many so-called pronunciation problems can be overcome by frequent use of the articulation exercises in this chapter.

Vowels

The English language contains twelve vowel sounds, if we ignore the three or four sounds that lie between some of these twelve and occur rarely—and only regionally—in American speech. Vowel sounds are usually classified according to the placement of the tongue in the mouth, the tongue being the only articulator that materially affects their production. The front vowels are produced through the vibration of the vocal folds in the throat and are articulated by the tongue and teeth near the front of the mouth. The back vowels are produced nearly the same way but they're articulated by the tongue and the opening in the rear of the mouth.

These are the front vowels:

(EE) /ē/ [i] as in *beet*

(IH) /ĭ/ [ɪ] as in *bit*

(AY) /ā/ [e] as in *bait*

(EH) /ĕ/ [ɛ] as in *bet*

(AAH) /ă/ [æ] as in *bat*

If you pronounce each of these sounds in turn, beginning at the top of the list and running to the bottom, you'll find your mouth opening wider as you move from one sound to the next. As your mouth opens, your tongue is lowered and becomes increasingly relaxed.

Here are the back vowels:

(AH) /ä/ [ɑ] as in *bomb*

(AW) /ô/ [ɔ] as in *bought*

(OH) /ō/ [o] as in *boat*

(OOH) /o͞o/ [ʊ] as in *book*

(OO) /o͞o/ [u] as in *boot*

If you pronounce each of these vowel sounds in turn, you'll find your mouth closing more and more, and the sound being controlled at a progressively forward position in your mouth.

There are two more vowel sounds that aren't classified as front or back: the (ER) sound, as in *her* (HER) and the (UH) sound, as in fun (FUHN). In the International Phonetic Alphabet, two symbols are used for the (ER) sound: one when the sound is stressed, as in *bird* [bɝd], and the other when the sound is unstressed, as in *bitter* [bɪtɚ].

The IPA also has two symbols for the (UH) sound: one when the sound is stressed, as in *sun* [sʌn], and the other when the sound is unstressed, as in *sofa* [sofə].

The twelve vowel sounds can be described according to the way each is manufactured. This is done in Table 4.1.

Vowel Deviations. In the section that follows, standard broadcast, or Standard American Speech, is the reference point for pronunciation. In other words, despite what was written earlier about the growing acceptance of regional and other variations in pronunciation, this section is written for those who want to practice standard broadcast speech.

Figure 4.3

Montreal Expos French-language announcing team Denis Casavant and Roger Brulotte must be fluent and articulate in two languages and pronounce words correctly in both. *Courtesy of Denis Casavant and Roger Brulotte.*

| TABLE 4.1 | HOW THE TWELVE VOWEL SOUNDS ARE PRODUCED |

Front Vowels

(EE), as in *beet*, is formed by holding the mouth slightly open, placing the tip of the tongue on the back surface of the lower front teeth, and arching the tongue toward the front of the mouth so that the sides of the tongue are in contact with the molars.

(IH), as in *bit*, is formed by placing the tip of the tongue on the back surface of the lower front teeth and lowering and relaxing the tongue slightly more than for (EE).

(AY), as in *bait*, is formed in much the same way as the (IH) sound, but the mouth is in a more open position and the tongue lies almost flat in the mouth.

(EH), as in *bet*, is formed with the mouth open still further than for the (AY) sound but with the tongue in just about the same relative position.

(AAH) as in *bat*, is formed with the mouth quite open and the tongue lying flat on the bottom of the mouth. A certain tenseness in the jaws is noticeable.

Back Vowels

(AH), as in *bomb*, is formed with the mouth quite open and the tongue lying flat and relaxed in the mouth.

(AW), as in *bought*, is formed by holding the lips open (but not rounded) and raising the tongue slightly in the rear. The tip of the tongue lies low on the gum ridge under the lower front teeth.

(OH), as in *boat*, is made by rounding the lips and raising the tongue slightly in the rear of the mouth.

(OOH), as in *book*, is formed in much the same way as (OO), except that the lips are more relaxed and slightly more open.

(OO), as in *boot*, is formed by holding the front of the tongue in approximately the same position as for the (EE) sound and the rear of the tongue in a raised position. The lips are rounded and extended.

ER and UH

(ER), as in *bird* and *bitter*, is formed by holding the tongue back in the mouth, with the tip poised somewhere about the midpoint between the hard palate and the floor of the mouth.

(UH), as in *sun* and *sofa*, is formed by holding the mouth slightly open with the tongue quite relaxed and flat on the bottom of the mouth.

Pronouncing vowel sounds in ways that deviate from standard broadcast speech shouldn't necessarily be regarded as "substandard."[3]

Some people have grown up in environments where scores of words were spoken with vowel sounds that deviate from broadcast speech. Those who say (MELK) for *milk* or be-KUZ for *because* are voicing vowel deviations. Vowel deviations can be changed, but first they must be identified.

It's not uncommon for speakers of American English to distort one or more vowel sounds. This doesn't refer to those who speak with regional accents other than Standard American. It's not incorrect for an easterner or a southerner to say (FAH-thuh) for *father,* but it *is* substandard for speakers of American English anywhere to say (fer-GIT) for *forget* or (JIST) for *just.* This type of vowel deviation is the focus of the following discussion.

Five vowel deviations occur with some regularity among Americans in any part of the United States and Canada, and several others occur less frequently. It's not surprising that these deviations take place between vowel sounds that are next to one another in the place of production in the mouth.

Five Major Vowel Deviations. The following five chief vowel deviations are accompanied by readings to help you discover whether you have problems and to provide you with exercises to overcome them.

1. **(EH) for (AY)**   /ĕ/ for /ā/   [ɛ] for [e]

Those who distort the (AY) /ā/ [e] sound, turning it into (EH) /ĕ/ [ɛ], usually do so only when it's followed by an (UL) sound. This is because it's quite easy to sound the (AY) in a word such as *pay* but more difficult to sound it in the word *pail.* Say, in turn, *pail* and *pell,* and you'll see why some speakers slip into the easier of the two, thereby distorting the vowel sound of this and similar words. Read, record, and play back this diagnostic exercise to see if you're distorting the (AY) vowel sound:

The pale graduate of Yale hailed the mail delivery daily.

She failed to go sailing, for fear of gales and whales, but

---

[3]Note that English-speaking Canadians manufacture the vowel sound in *out* in a way that differs from American broadcast speech; because this is consistent throughout Canada, it should be considered as standard for that nation.

she availed herself of the tall tales told her by the mail deliverer. "I shot a quail out of season and was sent to jail,"
he wailed, "but a female friend put up bail, so they failed
to nail me." The pale Yale graduate did not fail to hail the
mail deliverer's tale.

2. (AAH) for (EH)   /ā/ for /ĕ/   [æ] for [ɛ]

Unlike the problem just described, this deviation tends to be of regional or ethnic origin and isn't caused because one manner of pronunciation is easier than another. Those from cities or areas where there's a
sizable German-American or Scandinavian-American population are
most prone to make this vowel distortion. (FANCE) for *fence* and (TAL-
uh-fohn) for *telephone* are examples. Here's a diagnostic exercise for this
sound:

My friend, who is well but elderly, helped me mend my

fence. I telephoned him to let him know when to get

here, but he didn't answer the bell, so I guess he'd left.

He's a mellow friend who never bellows, but he some-

times questions everything a fellow does. He took some

lessons on television about fence mending, or else he

wouldn't be able to help me mend my fence.

3. (EH) for (AAH)   /ĕ/ for /ă/   [ɛ] for [æ]

Many Americans don't distinguish between the vowel sounds in the
words *Mary* and *merry*, giving both the (EH) /ĕ/ [ɛ] sound. Whereas
(AAH) /ă/ [æ] isn't often a source of trouble in the sounding of words
such as *bat, champion,* and *sedan,* it often slips into (EH) /ĕ/ [ɛ] in words
in which it's more difficult to sound the (AAH), such as *shall.* Here's a
diagnostic reading:

Mary left the Caribbean to visit Paris. She carried her

clothes in a caramel-colored carriage. Mary tarried at the

narrow entrance of the barracks. There was a caricature

of Mary that chilled her marrow. Mary said, "I shall never

tarry in Paris again."

Note the difficulty of hitting the (AAH) /ă/ [æ] sound when many words using this sound appear in rapid succession. Note, too, how the passage begins to sound "foreign" to our ears. The (AAH) sound will remain in American English speech, but there's no doubt that it's gradually disappearing from words in which its manufacture is difficult.

4. **(AH) for (AW)**   /ä/ for /Ô/   [ɑ] for [ɔ]

Some speakers don't distinguish between these sounds, giving the same vowel sound to the words *bought* and *bomb*. Of the following readings the first uses words for which the (AW) sound is appropriate, the second mixes words using both sounds.

We all talked about the day in the fall when Loretta

sawed off the longest stalk. Our jaws dropped in awe of

her raw courage. She caught the stalk in a bolt of gauze

and waited for the dawn to prevent the loss of all her aw-

ful haunted house of horror.

I saw them haul the bomb from the bottom of the

waterfall. All around, I saw the awesome possibility of

large-scale horror. Lost souls watched in a state of shock.

The bomb slowly fought its way clear of the pond. Water

dripped from the bottom of the bomb. I lost my fear, for I

saw that the bomb was not awfully large.

5. (IH) for (EE)   /ĭ/ for /ē/   [ɪ] for [i]

Sounding (EE) before an *l* calls for slightly more effort than sounding (IH) in the same construction. For this reason, some speakers habitually say (RIH-lee) for *really* and (FILL) for *feel*.

Sheila Fielding had a really strong feeling that something

really bad would come of her deal to have the keel of her

boat sealed. She wanted to shield the keel, so that peeling

paint wouldn't be a really big deal. Sheila really hit the

ceiling when she saw the bill. As Sheila reeled, she took

the wheel and dragged the keel with the peeling paint

across the pier and into the field, where her feelings were

really healed.

Several other vowel deviations are occasionally heard. Those whose speech includes these deviations (with some exceptions) tend to be quite consistent. Table 4.2 lists these deviations with examples of "standard" and "nonstandard" pronunciation.

Diphthongs

The **diphthong** or **glide** as it's sometimes called, is a combination of two vowel sounds, spoken in rapid order with a glide from one to the other. Note that this word is pronounced (DIF-thawngz). The diphthongs are represented as follows:

(Y) /ī/ [aɪ] as in *bite* (BYTE) /bīt/ [baɪt]
(AU) /ou/ [aʊ] as in *bout* (BAUT) /bout/ [baʊt]
(OY) /oi/ [ɔi] as in *boy* (BOY) /boi/ [bɔi]
(YU) /yōō/ [ju] as in *beauty* (BYU-tee) /byōō′tē/ [bjutˌi]

The vowel sound (AY) /ā/ [e], as you'll see by saying it aloud, is actually a glide; it definitely goes from (AY) to (IH). Because of this move from one sound to another, it's sometimes considered a diphthong and given the symbol [eɪ] in the IPA.

| TABLE 4.2 | SOME VOWEL DEVIATIONS |

Vowel Sound	Word	Standard Pronunciation	Deviation
(AW) for (OOH)	*poor*	(POOHR) /po͝or/ [pʊr]	(PAWR) /pôr/ [pɔr]
/ô/ for /o͝o/	*your*	(YOOHR) /yo͝or/ [jʊr]	(YAWHR) /yôr/ [jɔr]
[ɔ] for [ʊ] as in	*sure*	(SHOOHR) /sho͝or/ [ʃʊr]	(SHAWHR) /shôr/ [ʃɔr]
book	*tourist*	(TOOHR-ist) /to͝or′ĭst/ ['tʊr,ɪst]	(TAWR-ist) /tôr′ĭst/ ['tɔr,ɪst]
	jury	(JOOHR-ee) /jo͝or′ē/ ['dʒʊr,i]	(JAWHR-ee) /jôr′ē/ ['dʒɔr,i]
(ER) for (OOH)	*jury*	(JOOHR-ee) /jo͝or′ē/ ['dʒʊr,i]	(JER-ee) /jûr′ē/ ['dʒɝ·i]
/ûr/ for /o͝o/			
[ɝ·] for [ʊ] as in	*sure*	(SHOOHR) /sho͝or/ [ʃʊr]	(SHER) /shûr/ [ʃɝ·]
book	*insurance*	(in-SHOOHR-uns) /in-sho͝or′əns/ [in'ʃʊrəns]	(in-SHER-uns) /ĭn-shûr′əns/ [in'ʃɝ·əns]
	assure	(uh-SHOOHR) /ə-sho͝or′/ [ə'ʃʊr]	(uh-SHER) /ə-shûr/ [ə'ʃɝ·]
(IH) for (EH)	*tender*	(TEN-der) /tĕn′dər/ ['tɛndɚ]	(TIN-der) /tĭn′dər/ ['tɪndɚ]
/ĭ/ for /ĕ/			
[ɪ] for [ɛ]	*get*	(GEHT) /gĕt/ [gɛt]	(GIT) /gĭt/ [gɪt]
	send	(SEND) /sĕnd/ [sɛnd]	(SIHND) /sĭnd/ [sɪnd]
	engine	(EN-juhn) /ĕn′jən/ ['ɛndʒən]	(IN-juhn) /ĭn′jən/ ['ɪndʒən]
	friend	(FREHND) /frĕnd/ [frɛnd]	(FRIHND) /frĭnd/ [frɪnd]
(ER) for (UH), (AW), or (IH)	*familiar*	(fuh-MIL-yer) /fə-mĭl′-yər/ [fə'mɪljɚ]	(fer-MIL-yer) /fûr-mĭl′-yər/ [fɚ'mɪljɚ]
/ûr/ for /ə/, /ô/, or /ĭ/ [ɚ] for [ə], [ɔ], or [ɪ]	*forget*	(fawr-GET) /fôr-gĕt′/ [fɔr'gɛt]	(fer-GET) /fûr-gĕt′/ [fɚ'gɛt]
	congregate	(KAHNG-grih-gayt) /kăng′grĭ-gāt/ ['kaŋgrɪget]	(KAHNG-ger-gate) /kăng′gûr-gāt/ ['kaŋgɚget]
	garage	(guh-RAHZH) /gə-räzh′/ [gə'rɑʒ]	(ger-AHZH) /gûr-äzh′/ [gɚɑʒ]

Vowel Sound	Word	Standard Pronunciation	Deviation
	lubricate	(LOO-brih-kayt) /loō′brĭ-kāt/ [′lubrɪket]	(LOO-ber-kayt) /loo′bûr-kāt/ [′lubɚket]
(EH) for (IH)	*milk*	(MIHLK) /mĭlk/ [mɪlk]	(MEHLK) /mĕlk/ [mɛlk]
/ĕ/ for /ĭ/	*since*	(SINSS) /sĭns/ [sɪns]	(SENSE) /sĕns/ [sɛns]
[ɛ] for [ɪ]	*fill*	(FIHL) /fĭl/ [fɪl]	(FELL) /fĕl/ [fɛl]
	think	(THINGK) /thĭngk/ [θɪŋk]	(THENGK) /thĕngk/ [θɛnk]
	cent	(SENT) /sĕnt/ [sɛnt]	(SIHNT) /sĭnt/ [sɪnt]
(IH) for (EH)	*men*	(MEHN) /mĕn/ [mɛn]	(MIHN) /mĭn/ [mɪn]
/ĭ/ for /e/	*helicopter*	(HEL-ih-kop-ter) /hel′ĭ-kŏp′tər/ [′hɛlɪkɑptɚ]	(HIL-ih-kop-ter) /′hĭl′ĭ-kŏp′tər/ [′hɪlɪkɑptɚ]
[ɪ] for [ɛ]	*many*	(MEHN-ee) /mĕn′ē/ [′mɛn,i]	(MIHN-ee) /mĭn′ē/ [′min,i]
(UH) for (IH) /ə/ for /ĭ/ /ə/ for /ɪ/		it (as in *get it?*) becomes *uht* (as in *get uht?*)	
(UH) for (AW) /ə/ for /ô/ [ə] for [ɔ]		*because* becomes *be-KUZ*	

Diphthongs are a source of trouble to some speakers. Diphthong deviation tends to be regional and, though not necessarily substandard, is not compatible with Standard American Speech. If you have trouble with diphthongs, practice making each of the vowel sounds that form them and then speak the two sounds consecutively with increasing rapidity. These exercises will help only if you're producing the sounds of the diphthongs according to the standards of broadcast speech.

Read these sentences to practice the diphthong (EYE) /ī/ [aɪ].

1. I like my bike.

2. Lie in the silo on your side.

3. Fine nights for sighing breezes.

4. Why try to lie in the blinding light?

5. Cy tried to fly his kite.

6. My fine wife likes to fly in my glider.

7. Try my pie—I like it fine.

8. Shy guys find they like to cry.

9. My sly friend likes to be wined and dined.

10. Like all fine and right-minded guys, Mr. Wright liked best to try to find the slightest excuse to lie about his life.

These sentences allow you to focus on the (AU) /ou/ [aʊ] sound.

1. Flounce into my mouse's house.

2. Cows allow just about too much proudness about them.

3. Round and round went the loudly shouting lout.

4. A mouse is somewhat louder than a louse in a house.

5. A bounding hound went out on the bounding main.

6. Grouse are lousy bets when abounding results are found.

7. A cow and a mouse lived in a house.

8. The louder they proudly cried, the more the crowd delighted in seeing them trounced.

9. They plowed the drought-stricken cow pasture.

10. Allow the grouse to shout louder and louder, and
    you just about drown out the proud cows.

Use the following sentences to practice the diphthong (OY) /oi/ [ɔi].

1. A toy needs oiling.

2. The soybeans are joyously coiling.

3. Floyd oiled the squeaky toy.

4. Goya painted Troy in oils.

5. His annoying voice was boiling mad.

6. The oyster exploited the joyous foil.

7. Roy and Lloyd soiled the toys.

8. Joy, like a spoiled boy, exploited her friends.

9. What kind of noise annoys an oyster? A noisy noise
   annoys an oyster.

Read these sentences for practice with the (YU) /yōō/ [ju] sound.

1. I used to refuse to use abusive news.

2. The kitten mewed, but I refused to go.

3. The music was used to imbue us with enthusiasm.

4. The beautiful view used to confuse.

5. June was beautiful.

6. The newest pupil was wearing his suit.

7. The cute kitten mewed.

8. He eschewed responsibility for the news.

9. The few new musical numbers were confusing to the beautiful girl.

10. A few beautiful girls are using perfume.

Consonant Sounds

The English language contains twenty-five consonant sounds (*phonemes*), which are classified in a number of ways, the most basic of which is according to whether or not they're voiced. The letter *b*, spoken with a vibration of the vocal folds, is called a **voiced consonant**, whereas *p*, formed in exactly the same way but not phonated, is called **an unvoiced consonant**.

A more detailed and more useful system, based on how the sound is formed, classifies the consonants in this way:

- **Plosives** begin with the air from the throat blocked off, and the sound is formed with a release of the air. The plosive consonants are *p, b, t, d, k*, and *g*.
- **Fricatives** are created by the friction generated when air moves through a restricted air passage. The fricative consonants are *f, v, th* (as in *thin*), *th* (as in *the*), *z, s, sh* (as in *shoe*), *zh* (as in *vision*), *y* (as in *yellow*), and *h* and *hw* (as in *when*).
- **Nasals** are resonated in the nasal cavity. The nasal consonants are *m, n*, and *ng* (as in *sing*).
- **Semivowels** are similar to the true vowels in their resonance patterns. The consonants *w, r*, and *l* are the semivowels.
- **Affricates** combine a plosive with a fricative. The consonants *ch* (as in *choose*) and *j* (as in *jump*) are the affricates.

Still another system classifies consonants according to their place of articulation.

- **Labial,** or **bilabial, consonants** *Labia* is Latin for "lip." The lips are primarily responsible for the labial consonants *p, b, m, w*, and, in a less obvious way, *hw*.

- **Labiodental consonants** The lower lip is in proximity to the upper teeth. The labiodental consonants are *f* and *v*.
- **Interdental**, or **linguadental**, **consonants** For these sounds the tongue (*lingua*) is between the upper and lower teeth. The interdental consonants are *th* /*th*/ [θ] (as in *thin*) and *th* /*th*/ [ð] (as in *then*).
- **Lingua-alveolar consonants** For these sounds the tip of the tongue is placed against the upper gum ridge (*alveolus*). The lingua-alveolar consonants are *n, t, d, s, z,* and *l*.
- **Linguapalatal consonants** For these sounds the tip of the tongue touches (or nearly touches) the hard palate just behind the gum ridge. The linguapalatal consonants are *y* (as in *yellow*), *r* (as in *rain*), *sh* (as in *shoe*), *zh* (as in *vision*), *ch* (as in *chew*), and *j* (as in *jump*).
- **Linguavelar consonants** For these sounds the rear of the tongue is raised against the soft palate (*velum*), and the tip of the tongue is lowered to the bottom of the mouth. The linguavelar consonants are *k, g,* and *ng* (as in *sing*).
- **Glottal consonant** The glottal consonant, *h,* is formed by the passage of air between the vocal folds without vibration of those folds.

Phonetic Transcription

As an announcer, you face unique and challenging problems in pronunciation. In reading news, commercial, and classical music copy, you'll frequently encounter words of foreign origin, and you'll be expected to read them fluently and correctly. As a newscaster, you'll be expected not only to pronounce foreign words and names with accuracy and authority, but also to know when and how to Americanize many of them. Although British announcers are allowed to Anglicize categorically, you'd be seen as odd or incompetent if you said (don-KWIX-oat) for Don Quixote or (don-JEW-un) for Don Juan, as they do. Appendix B, "Phonetic Transcription," is devoted to helping you develop the ability to transcribe difficult words into phonetics. Wire-service phonetics, diacritics, and the International Phonetic Alphabet are discussed.

SPOTLIGHT

The Debate over Standard American Speech

From the very beginning of radio broadcasting in the United States, attempts were made to require announcers to use standardized pronunciation. In 1929, less than a decade after the first radio broadcast, the American Academy of Arts and Letters began the yearly award of a gold medal to the radio announcer who best exemplified the kind of speech of which the academy approved. In awarding the 1930 medal to Alwyn Bach of NBC, the Academy commented, "We believe the radio announcer can not only aid the European immigrant to acquire a knowledge of good English, but he can influence the speech of isolated communities whose young people have no other means of comparing their own accent with the cultivated speech of those who have had the advantage of travel and education"[4]

In taking the position that one style of American English speech was superior to others, the academy was following a European model. England and France each had a great variety of dialects within their borders. But not all those ways of speaking were considered "proper." Cockney, Midlands, and Cornish dialects in England and the speech of the people of Marseilles and Strasbourg in France were looked down upon by those who spoke with "correct" pronunciation. Also, during the eighteenth and nineteenth centuries, many small European kingdoms, duchies, provinces, church-owned lands, and independent cities were consolidated into the nations of Germany and Italy. The boundaries of these nations coincided roughly with language groupings. But the German spoken in Berlin was quite different from that spoken in Bavaria, and the Italian spoken in Genoa was not identical to that spoken in Sicily. Before long, "correct" or "official" ways of pronouncing the language were established in these newly formed nations. From this action it was but a short step to social discrimination based on regional accent or dialect.

Many feel that the United States, the land of equal opportunity and upward mobility regardless of origins, had no reason to follow Europe's lead. Until the advent

---

[4]"Broadcast Announcing Styles of the 1920s," by Michael Biel, a paper presented at the convention of the Broadcast Education Association, March 16, 1974.

of radio broadcasting, there were two standards for correct American pronunciation. The first was *platform speech,* an overarticulated, oratorical manner of speaking, with a strong Oxford-British flavor. The second was the speech used by "the enlightened members of the community." This phrase is significant, for it sanctions regional differences in pronunciation. Correct American speech could therefore vary—being that spoken by educated persons in New England, the South, the Midwest, or the West Coast, for example.

This acceptance of regional differences in pronunciation has been maintained by linguists and those who compile dictionaries, but was abandoned by broadcasters during the early years of radio broadcasting. Platform speech was precisely what the American Academy of Arts and Letters was promoting, as spelled out in its statement of criteria for good radio speech: "first, clear articulation; second, correct pronunciation; third, *freedom from disagreeable local accent;* fourth, pleasing tone color; fifth, evidence of cultivated taste."[5]

By the mid-1930s, objections to the stilted, quasi-English manner of speaking began to force change. However, despite the change to a more natural and conversational style of speech, the objective of standardized pronunciation remained. Standard American Speech became the standard for announcers all over the United States and English-speaking Canada. Standard American is thought to be pleasant, easily understood, and more common than any other regional accent. Even though it is not the only style of American speech that is pleasant and effective, for years those with southern, New England, eastern, or southwestern accents (as well as those with Asian, Latin American, or Middle Eastern accents) have been underrepresented on announcing staffs. A few exceptions may be noted: New England accents have long been accepted for the announcing of symphonic and operatic music; southern and eastern accents have been heard on many sportscasts; and nearly all regional accents have been accepted for news reporters, analysts, and commentators. All regional accents have been heard on commercials and talk shows. It may be that this trend will continue, and even accelerate. Regional pride may some day bring the full richness of our language in all its variations to the American radio and television public.

---

[5]Biel, "Broadcast Announcing Styles of the 1920's," *italics added.*

Figure 4.4

Amaury Pi-Gonzalez announces baseball games in Spanish for the San Francisco Giants. He represents thousands of announcers in the United States and Canada who perform in languages other than English. His delivery—as is true of all professional announcers—is marked by clear articulation, and his Spanish pronunciation is geared to that spoken by the majority of his Latino listeners. *Courtesy of Amaury Pi-Gonzalez and the San Francisco Giants.*

Articulation

Articulation problems arise from too fast a rate of delivery or from improper placement or faulty use of the articulators (the jaw, the tongue, and the lips). Read the brief selection that follows, and see if you have difficulty sounding all of the syllables of each word.

The Diagnostic Center

This is undeniably the most conscientiously designed diagnostic center imaginable. I recognize that, from an architectural standpoint, the building is magnificent. It also is strategically placed. At the same time, however, is it environmentally sound? Does it mirror our civilization's preoccupation with transcendental human competencies? Looking at the phenomenon from an unexpectedly malevolent point of view, we probably should ultimately

find an alternative.

Because many North American speakers suffer from poor articulation, many of the exercises in this chapter are intended to help improve articulation. Analysis of your performance with the diagnositc readings "William and His Friends," "The Battle of Atterbury," and "The Diagnostic Center" should tell you if you have difficulty with articulation, including slurring, mumbling, or omitting syllables and some speech sounds. If you find you have problems, perform the appropriate exercises daily for as long as necessary. The exercises will do you no good, however, unless you read the material *aloud,* while making a conscious effort to form successfully every syllable of every sentence. It's wise to exaggerate articulation at first, gradually moving toward normally articulated speech.

Articulation Problems

Several speech sounds are frequent causes of slurred, unpleasant, or "fuzzy" speech and should be corrected by anyone who intends to became a professional announcer. Of the twenty-five consonant sounds in the English language, the nine that cause most articulation problems are discussed here, along with exercises to help you overcome any problems you may have with them.

t   The consonant *t* is an unvoiced lingua-alveolar plosive. The *t* sound is formed by the release of unvoiced air that's been temporarily blocked off by the pressure of the tip of the tongue against the upper gum ridge. Note that *t,* like all other plosives, is best softened when speaking into a microphone.

The medial *t* is a problem for many American and Canadian speakers. In the West and Midwest, it's often turned into a *d,* as in saying (BAD-ul) for *battle* ['bædl for 'bætl]. In some parts of the East Coast, it's turned into a **glottal stop,** as in saying (BAH-ul) for *bottle* ['bɪʔ əl]. In some parts of Canada, Toronto becomes tuh-RAHN-o, To help you determine whether you have a medial *t* problem, record and listen to this reading:

The metal kettle was a little more than half full. I settled

for a little bit of the better stuff and waited while an Irish setter begged for a pitiful allotment of the fatter part of

the kettle's contents. The setter left, disgusted and a little

bitter over the matter of her lost battle for a better por-

tion of the beetle stew.

For extra work with the medial *t* try saying the following with increasing speed: *beetle, bittle, bayttle, bettle, battle, bottle, bootle, berttle, buttle.* Use the following sentences to practice the consonant *t:*

1. Tiny Tim tripped toward the towering Titan.

2. The tall Texan tried to teach the taxi driver twenty tall tales of Texas.

3. Attractive though Patty was, the battling fighters hesitated to attempt to please her.

4. The bottled beetles were getting fatter.

5. The fat cat sat in the fast-moving draft.

6. Herbert hit the fat brat with his short bat.

---

th   The consonant *th* (as in *thin*) is an unvoiced interdental fricative. (Diacritics use *th* for the sound in *then,* and *th* for the sound in *thin.*) This sound is frequently a source of trouble, because the microphone tends to amplify any slight whistle that may be present. In making this sound, place the tongue *up to,* but not *into,* the space between the upper and lower teeth, which are held about an eighth of an inch apart. Air passing over the top of the tongue and between its tip and the upper front teeth makes the (*th*) sound.

These sentences are for practicing the unvoiced (*th*) sound.

1. Think through thirty-three things.

2. Thoughts are thrifty when thinking through problems.

3. Cotton Mather lathed his bath house.

4. The pathway led to the wrathful heath.

5. The thought of the myth was cutting as a scythe.

6. Thirty-three thinking mythological monsters, wearing pith helmets, wrathfully thought that Theobald was through.

S   The consonant *s* is an unvoiced lingua-alveolar fricative. It's one of the more common sources of trouble for announcers. A slight misplacement of the articulators may cause a whistle, a thick fuzzy sound, or a lisp. There are two methods of producing *s*, neither of which seems clearly superior to the other. In the first, the sides of the tongue are in contact with the upper teeth as far forward as the incisors. The tip of the tongue is held rather high in the mouth, and a fine stream of air is directed at the tips of the upper front teeth. The teeth, meanwhile, are held slightly apart. In the second method of making *s*, the tongue is fairly low in the mouth at the rear and at the tip, and is raised just behind the tip to make near contact with the gum ridge. A fine stream of air is permitted to flow through this passage, down toward the front teeth, which are held slightly apart. Because most microphones tend to exaggerate any slight whistle or excessive sibilance, work for a softened *s*.

If you produce excessive sibilance, use these exercises:

1. Should Samson slink past the sly, singing Delilah?

2. Swimming seems to survive as a sport despite some strange circumstances.

3. Lessons on wrestling are absurd, asserted Tessie.

4. Assurances concerning some practices of misguided misogynists are extremely hysterical.

5. The glass case sits in the purse of the lass.

6. Past the last sign for Sixth Place, the bus lost its best chance to rest.

Figure 4.5

This AKG 414 condenser announce microphone has been fitted with a windscreen to reduce both sibilant and popping sounds. An alternate device, a screen of foam, is seen to the right of the mic. *Courtesy of AKG Acoustics, Inc.*

sh   The consonant *sh* (as in *shoe*) is an unvoiced linguapalatal fricative. It's made by allowing unvoiced air to escape with friction from between the tip of the tongue and the gum ridge behind the upper front teeth. Although this sound isn't a common source of difficulty, you should guard against its becoming a thick, unpleasant sound. To form (*sh*), make certain that air doesn't escape around the sides of the tongue; keep the central portion of the tongue fairly low in the mouth.

Exercises for sounding (*sh*):

1. Shortly after shearing a sheep, I shooed off a wolf.

2. The shapely Sharon shared her chateau with Charmaine.

3. Mashed potatoes and hashed cashews are flashy rations.

4. The lashing gale thrashed, lightning flashed, and the Hessian troops gnashed their teeth.

5. A flash flood mashed the cash into trash.

6. Fish wish that fishermen would wash their shoes.

n   The consonant n (as in *nothing*) is a voiced lingua-alveolar nasal. Unlike *m,* it can be sounded with the mouth open because the tongue, rather than the lips, blocks off the air and forces it through the nasal cavity. The sounding of n is responsible for much of the excessive nasality characteristic of many irritating voices. If you detect, or someone detects for you, a tendency to overnasalize such sounds, spend several sessions with an audio recorder learning how it feels to soften them.

You can use these sentences to practice the sounding of *n:*

1. Ned's nice neighbor knew nothing about Neil.

2. Now the new niece needed Nancy's needle.

3. Indigestion invariably incapacitated Manny after dinner.

4. Many wonderful and intricate incidentals indirectly antagonized Fanny.

5. Nine men were seen in the fine mountain cabin.

6. Susan won the clean garden award and soon ran to plan again.

---

ng   The consonant ng (as in *sing*) is a voiced linguavelar nasal. It's formed much as the consonant g, but it lacks the plosive quality of that sound. One of the most common problems with ng involves turning this sound into "in" in words that end with *ing,* saying *runnin* or *losin* for *running* and *losing.* Each announcer must, of course, determine whether it's appropriate to do this. A newscaster will undoubtedly decide not to. Drive time music and sports announcers, depending on their speech personality, may decide it's permissible. A less common pronunciation problem involving this sound is the practice in some parts of the East of adding g in the middle of a word such as *singing* (*SING*-ging) ['sɪŋgɪŋ].

Use these sentences to practice the ng sound.

1. The English singer was winning the long contest.

2. He mingled with winged, gaily singing songbirds.

3. The long, strong rope rang the gong.

4. Running and skipping, the ringleader led the gang.

5. Among his long songs, Engel mingled some lilting things.

6. Along the winding stream, the swimming and fishing were finding many fans.

❙ The consonant *l* (as in *willing*) is a voiced lingua-alveolar semi-vowel, formed by placing the tip of the tongue against the upper gum ridge and allowing phonated air to escape around the sides of the tongue. This sound causes little difficulty when it is in an initial or final position in a word, but it's frequently a source of trouble in a medial position. If you say aloud the word *William*, you'll notice that the tip of the tongue is placed low in the mouth for *Wi*, raised to the upper gum ridge for *ll*, and returned to the floor of the mouth for *iam*. Obviously, it's easier to speak this name without moving the tongue at all, but then it sounds like WIH-YUM (WIH-yum), and the *l* sound is completely lost. Unlike some English speech sounds that may be softened or dropped without loss of effectiveness, the lost medial *l* is definitely undesirable.

Here's a diagnostic reading for the medial *l*:

Millions of Italians filled the hilly section of Milan. The milling celebrants whirled all along the palisades, down by the roiling river. Lilting lullabies, trilled by Italian altos, thrilled millions as they willingly milled along the boulevard. "It's really thrilling," said William Miller, a celebrant from Schiller Valley. I'm compelled to call this the most illustrious fellowship in all of Italy.

If you have difficulty with the medial *l*, practice these exercises:

1. A million silly swallows filled their bills with squiggling worms.

2. Willy Wallace willingly wiggled William's million dollar bill.

3. Lilly and Milly met two willing fellows from the hills.

4. A little melon was willingly volunteered by Ellen and William.

5. Bill filled the lily pot with a million gallons of water.

6. The mill filled the foolish little children's order for willow leaves.

7. William wanted a million dollars, but he seldom was willing to stop his silly shilly-shallying and work.

8. Phillip really liked Italian children, although he seldom was willing to speak Italian.

9. Enrolling in college really was thrilling for William, even though a million pillow fights were in store for the silly fellow.

10. Billy Bellnap shilled for millions of collegians, even though his colleagues collected alibis galore in the Alleghenies at Miller's celebration.

---

hw   The consonant *hw* (as in *where*) is an unvoiced labial fricative. It's a combination of the two consonants *h* and *w* and is achieved by forming the lips for *w* but releasing the air that makes *h* first; then the *w* sound follows immediately, so the *h* sound is barely heard. Although the *hw* sound in words such as *when* is lost by most speakers, announcers should include it—at least until it drops out of our language altogether.

These sentences are useful for practicing the *hw* sound:

1. Mr. Wheeler waited at the wharf.

2. Wherever the whippoorwill whistled, Whitby waited.

3. Why whisper when we don't know whether or not Mr. White's whelp is a whiz?

4. "Why not whet your knife?" whispered the white-bearded Whig.

5. Whitney whittled the white-headed whistle.

6. On Whitsun, Whittier was whipping Whitman on a whim.

---

r   The consonant *r* (as in *runner*) is a voiced linguapalatal semi-vowel. In certain areas of the United States and Canada and in England, *r* is frequently softened or completely dropped. In Standard American, or broadcast, speech, however, all *r*'s are sounded, though they needn't and shouldn't be prolonged or formed too far back in the throat. A voice described as harsh is frequently one that overstresses *r* sounds. However, in attempting to soften your *r*'s, be careful to avoid affectation; a pseudo-British accent is unbecoming to Americans and Canadians.[6] Few speakers can successfully change only one speech sound. The slight softening of *r* should be only one part of a general softening of all harsh sounds in your speech.

Use these sentences to practice the consonant *r*:

1. Rather than run rapidly, Rupert relied on rhythm.

2. Robert rose to revive Reginald's rule of order.

3. Apparently a miracle occurred to Herman.

---

[6]This observation is true for those who want to sound "conversational" and unaffected. At the same time, one hears a great many commercial announcers—most often those for so-called prestige commodities—speaking with quasi-British accents.

4. Large and cumbersome, the barge was a dirty hull.

5. Afraid of fire and sure of war, the rear admiral was far away.

6. The bore on the lower floor left his chair and went out the door.

CHAPTER 5

Audio Performance

AUDIENCE RAPPORT

THE TERM **AUDIENCE RAPPORT** REFERS TO A BOND BETWEEN PERFORMERS and listeners. Most successful radio announcers have a special quality that's communicated through their voices, a quality that reveals the human being behind the voice. Without ever mentioning the word *rapport*, a popular Pennsylvania DJ wrote these words that reveal his thoughts on "being yourself."

GUEST EDITORIAL: BEING YOURSELF
Steve Walker, WMTZ, Johnstown, Pennsylvania

As I look at some of the stuff people have done on the air to be entertaining or a personality, most has nothing to do with *them as people*, and that's the weakness. You can make people laugh with a joke—anyone can tell a joke—but it's the *you*, the person who's on the radio, sharing the many facets of your life and comparing it constantly with the individual you talk to on the other end of the radio, who makes the distance between you and your listeners disappear.

You won't learn how to be a personality until you *have one*, and you won't be valuable to a radio station until you *are* a personality. Sharing your life with your listeners, little bits at a time, endearing yourself to them by dropping little embarrassments so they can learn to love you for being a human being.

123

Figure 5.1

DJ and operations manager Steve Walker is one-half of a morning drive-time team, Walker and Wild, on "The Mountain96.5," WMTZ, Johnstown, Pennsylvania. He's seen here on one of the station's many remote broadcasts. Steve's life follows that of all morning drive-time DJs, in that he's up by 3:45 A.M. in order to reach his station by 5:30 A.M. Unlike most DJs, Steve rides to work on his motorcycle! His station is active in such fund-raising events as the Relay for Life weekends and the St. Jude Radiothon. You can access The Mountain96.5, WMTZ, with this URL: *www.mountain 96-5.com/staff/onair/ Mornings/walker.htm.* If you'd like to read more of Steve's advice and opinions about music radio, go to the site for this textbook: *www.hmco.com/ college. Courtesy of Steve Walker and The Mountain96.5., WMTZ, Johnstown, Pennsylvania.*

If you are on the radio, and not just a voice doing liner cards selling the radio station and the music, but relating, (now there's an overused word, but necessary) and comparing your life to your listener's life, you'll find that you are someone at the station, not just another voice. Doing this in small quantities over a period of time lets listeners know *you,* and that makes *you* valuable."[1]

In this brief statement Steve does an excellent job of defining what rapport is about, as well as indicating how you might cultivate this quality. As you read the tips, suggestions, and guidelines throughout this text, never lose sight of the fact that to be successful you must project a personality that says to listeners "I am human, we share the same joys and sorrows, and I care enough about you to want to share my life with you."

All your preparation for radio announcing will culminate in performance, and it's your on-air qualities, including audience rapport, that determine success as a radio performer.[2] Before you can assume you're

---

[1]This guest editorial appeared in the web page "almostradio," a DJ prep service on the Internet created and maintained by Cosmo Rose. You can learn more about "almostradio," including how to access it, on the Houghton Mifflin Company web site: *www.hmco.com/college.*
[2]Of course, you must also acquire the ability to manipulate audio consoles, recorders, and playback units as you prepare for on-air performance. Course work in audio engineering and production are a must for anyone who intends to become a professional radio announcer.

ready to go before an audience, you must develop several qualities and abilities: a good and pleasing voice; interpretative skills; flawless pronunciation; competence in your area of specialization; and the ability to "sell," whether as a DJ, a commercial announcer, or a talk-show host.

This chapter addresses the topics of microphone fright and microphone consciousness and includes a number of tips for performers. Additional guidelines for performers are to be found in all chapters devoted to announcing specializations.

Microphone Fright

Many inexperienced performers have an almost uncontrollable fear of performing before a microphone. A few students will relish every opportunity to perform and will delight in performance playbacks. For most of us, though, it's normal to have butterflies before and during a performance and to feel disappointment on hearing the results during playbacks.

The good news is that some tension not only is to be expected but can actually help your performance. **Mic fright**, as this phenomenon is traditionally called, results in the release of adrenaline into the bloodstream,

Figure 5.2

Newscaster Ron Reynolds edits a radio commercial he has just recorded. A computer screen shows him a "picture" of his voice track, and a track ball helps him locate and delete unwanted sounds of breathing or to replace sentences in which he "stumbled." *Courtesy of Ron Reynolds and KCBS, San Francisco, California.*

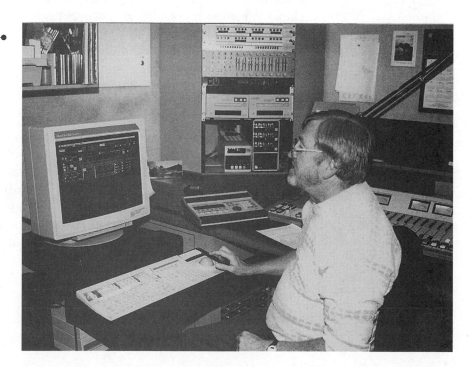

which causes one to become more alert and more energetic. A little mic fright can be an asset to a performer. A performer who's keyed up generates more positive energy than one who is routinely working through a piece of copy in an unfeeling manner.

The bad news is that *excessive nervousness* can seriously impair a performance. Extreme mic fright can lead to any combination of these symptoms: physical tension, shallow breathing, constricted throat, dry mouth, and (at an extreme) upset stomach, and shaking knees and hands. During performance, these conditions can cause your voice to go up in pitch or to break, or can make you run out of breath in the middle of a sentence, lose concentration, read or speak at an excessive rate of speed, or adopt a subdued attitude. Mic fright can also result in a completely dry mouth. At its greatest extreme, mic fright can make you entirely unable to communicate.

The **vocal folds** (often called **vocal cords**), which are central to good vocal tones, tighten up during times of moderate to extreme nervousness. The tighter the folds, the less they vibrate, which results in a lowered resonance and a strident sound to the voice. Hot liquids can help relax the vocal folds. Hot tea, bouillon, coffee, or even hot water can help you achieve a better speaking voice. (This advice remains true even after nervousness has been conquered.) Make certain that the beverage of your choice is not too hot, however, and avoid carbonated beverages and any beverage containing milk.

Generally speaking, mic fright is caused by one or more of the following conditions.

Lack of Experience

Nothing but time and regular performances will overcome inexperience. Performances need not occur on the air or in a class session. Perform a variety of written and ad-libbed or impromptu assignments and record them on an audio recorder. To speak *ad lib* is to perform without a script but with some preparation; *impromptu* means to speak without preparation or rehearsal. When talk-show hosts open on-air sessions with unscripted comments about a news development or a controversial film, these comments are *ad-lib* speech. When an on-the-scene television reporter, after delivering a report, speaks in answer to questions from an anchor, this is *impromptu* speaking. Both modes of unscripted performance require practice.

Lack of Preparation

It isn't possible to *prepare* for impromptu announcing such as a news report live from the field or the badinage expected of you as a talk-show host, but it *is* possible to *practice* impromptu performance. You can do this without equipment of any kind. To gain confidence and to develop a smooth delivery, practice by talking aloud. Walk through your living quarters and describe what you see; when driving, talk about what you see along the way. Sharpen your ability to hold your friends' attention as you relate anecdotes or discuss matters of mutual interest.

You can, of course, practice reading scripts. Though time pressures frequently make it impossible for professional announcers to rehearse, you're under no such restrictions. If you want to improve your performances, you must prepare thoroughly. Chapter 2, "The Announcer As Communicator," has exercises for evaluating, marking, and performing scripts.

 Appendix A has many scripts to use for practice, and our web site includes an additional supply of scripts for you to select, print, and use to polish your interpretative skills. The URL is:

www.hmco.com/college

Radio essay and commentary scripts from National Public Radio's *NewsHour with Jim Lehrer* may be found on the Internet. There you'll find several outstanding essayists from which to select. The URL is[3]:

www.pbs.org/newshour/essays–dialogues.html

---

[3]The Internet is changing constantly as new web sites are added and old web sites are abandoned. The URL listings in this textbook should be regarded as samples of the kinds of material available rather than as a stable index. If you seek a web site using one of these URLs and cannot connect, enter the key words for the topic into a search engine to find a site that may provide the information you want.

Fear of Failure

Most of us are more afraid of failing—of making fools of ourselves—than we are of physical dangers. You must conquer this fear and realize that you can progress only by daring to try a variety of approaches in your announcing work. To remain safely within a comfortable shell and perform in a laid-back, low-key manner is to sacrifice any chance of major improvement. If you're enrolled in a broadcast announcing class, keep in mind that you and your classmates are all in the pressure cooker together. Mature students will applaud and encourage one anothers' efforts to improve.

You can improve almost any performance by speaking with conviction. That is, if you believe in your message and if you sincerely want to communicate it to others, your fear of failure may be pushed aside by your conviction. Professional announcers don't always have the luxury of believing in what they're paid to say, but as a student you're usually free to choose messages that are of interest or importance to you. Take advantage of this opportunity and choose your topics wisely.

As you perform, try to concentrate on your message. Forget about self and forget about the audience. Assume that you're speaking to one or two people whom you respect and with whom you want to communicate. If you truly have a desire to get your message across, you can overcome your concern about failure.

Lack of Self-Esteem

Some of us simply feel that we're not important enough to take up the time and attention of others. This is an incredibly debilitating attitude that has nothing to recommend it. Modesty may be a virtue, but self-effacement is not.

Each of us is a unique creation. You are the only person just like you who has ever lived. Because you're unique, you have something special to offer. If you respect yourself, you'll perform at an acceptable level; if you respect your listeners, you'll find something worthwhile to say to them; if you respect your subject matter, you'll find ways to get it across. *Self*, *listeners*, and *topic* are interrelated variables that must mesh if you're to communicate successfully. Successful communication will inevitably increase your self-confidence and boost your self-esteem. Enhanced self-esteem will bring about further improvement in performances. Better performances will raise self-esteem—and so on. Believing that what you have to say is worthy of the interest and time of others is the start of a new and healthier attitude toward yourself.

But let's face it: if you're presenting dull material in a spiritless manner, you have no right to expect the rapt attention of your listeners. If you conduct a boring interview with a boring guest, there's no reason to try to tell yourself that what you're doing is important. This brings us back to conviction—the belief that what you have to offer is important and valid. To raise your self-esteem, be certain that what you offer your listeners is worthy of their attention.

Lack of Mental Preparation

During the minutes before a performance, remove yourself (physically if possible, but at least mentally) from the confusion of a typical production situation. Find a way to relax, to gather your thoughts, to concentrate on the upcoming performance. Think over what you're to say or read. Think about mood, about appropriate pace, about the importance of the message, about any potential problems of diction, pronunciation, and so on. Perform physical relaxation exercises. If possible, sit in a comfortable chair. Begin to relax physically—starting with your head, then your neck, your shoulders, and so on. After you've attempted to relax your entire body, imagine that the tension or stress is being discharged from the ends of your fingers. If you try, you can actually feel the tension leaving your body. At this point, think again about your assignment, and keep your message and your objectives clearly in mind as you prepare to perform.

Dislike of One's Voice

Students of announcing often dislike the way they sound on playbacks. This response isn't surprising, because we don't hear ourselves as others do. Most people don't believe that their voice sounds like what comes back to them from an audio recorder. The reason is simple: we hear ourselves speak through *both air and bone conduction.* The sound waves that emanate from our mouths are what others hear; only the person speaking hears the physical vibrations that go through the bones of the head to the tympanic apparatus of the ear. The combination of sounds conducted through air and bone is what we think we sound like to others. Only when we hear ourselves through air conduction alone, as from an audio player, do we truly hear ourselves as others hear us.

Figure 5.3

Radio news anchor Bob Price marks his script during his on-air shift. He uses the moments when recorded packages are being broadcast to check his script for pronunciation challenges and to underline words he wants to emphasize. *Courtesy of Bob Price and KCBS, San Francisco, California.*

If you truly understand that an audio playback of your speaking voice surprises only yourself and that others accept your recorded sound just as they accept you in person, you're well on your way toward overcoming mic fright.

Microphone Consciousness

Microphones are marvelous instruments, but they can do their job only when they're used properly. Improper use sometimes results from inexperience or ignorance, but is more often due to a lack of **microphone consciousness.** To be mic conscious is to be always aware that the misuse of a microphone will result in a flawed or failed performance. Typical examples of faulty microphone consciousness include these:

- Clapping with your hands near an open mic
- Making unwanted noises near an open mic, such as drumming fingers on a table near a desk mic

- Moving from side to side away from a mounted mic
- Moving in and out in relation to a mounted mic
- Failing to move a hand-held mic properly between you and a guest you're interviewing
- Positioning yourself and a guest improperly in relation to a desk mic
- Making sudden and extreme changes in the volume of your voice
- Failing to understand and properly relate to the pickup patterns of microphones
- Wearing jewelry, such as metal bracelets, that clanks when moved

One problem is so common that it deserves separate attention. The sound of paper being bent, turned over, or shuffled is the mark of an amateur. Learn to handle scripts in such a way as to avoid paper rattling. Never work from a script that's stapled or held together with a paper clip. Never turn script pages over as you move from one page to another; always slide the pages to one side when you're finished with them. Obviously, all scripts should be typed on only one side of the paper. When working with practice material from this or other texts, make copies on 8½-inch-by-11-inch paper, with double or even triple spacing.

Figure 5.4

Advertising agencies make frequent use of freelance performers. Here Peter Scott reads a script for a radio commercial. *Courtesy of Peter Scott.*

Ordinarily, the cheaper the paper, the softer it is and the less it will rattle. Work with the softest paper you can find.

During rehearsals and on the air, always assume that your microphone is open. Watch what you say. Always assume that profanity and backbiting comments about others will be heard by someone, possibly with devastating consequences!

Taking a Level

When working with an audio engineer, you'll be asked to **take a level** before each performance. This allows the engineer to adjust the volume control associated with your microphone. As a DJ or news anchor, you'll frequently do your own engineering, but as a talk-show host, or when performing voice-over commercials or narration, you'll usually work with an audio engineer who adjusts volume level as you speak into the mic. Because time can be wasted in taking voice levels and because getting faulty results will make the quality of the production suffer, it's necessary for you to understand this procedure.

Before taping or going on the air, the engineer sets the volume level of all audio inputs. In the simplest production, this means the volume level of the announcer; in elaborate productions, it might mean the levels of several voices, music, and sound effects. The engineer's job is to mix or blend audio inputs in the proper proportions. When taking a level, an engineer can tell you if you're off mic, if your volume is too loud or too soft, or if you're popping or creating excessive sibilance. **Popping** is an air blast when plosives are sounded; **plosives** are the consonants *p, b, t, d, k,* and *g.* **Sibilance** is the hissing sound made when the letter *s,* and sometimes *sh* or *z,* is sounded.[4]

You can't sound your best if you're misusing your mic. An audio engineer can help you make the most effective use of your voice, but you must cooperate. When you're asked to take a level, it's imperative that you *read from the actual script* to be used (or, if ad-libbing, that you speak at exactly the same volume you'll use during the performance), that you position yourself in relation to the mic exactly as you will during the show, and that you continue reading or ad-libbing until the engineer is satisfied with the result.

---

[4]Sibilance is a necessary part of spoken English, and to completely avoid sibilant sounds would be to speak with a lisp. The problem with many speakers who use a mic is not sibilance but *excessive* sibilance.

In taking a level, follow this procedure:

1. As you sit or stand before a mic, remain silent. Unnecessary chatter is distracting and potentially embarrassing if your mic is open.

2. Wait patiently and alertly for a signal to take a level; in a recording studio, the signal will probably be given orally by an engineer over an intercom. If you must depend on a visual signal, keep watching the engineer.

3. On receiving the signal, move into the exact position and posture you'll use during the performance, and read or speak exactly as you will later.

4. When working with a script, read from that script, using all of the vitality, emotion, and other qualities you intend to use in actual performance. Don't hold back, thinking that it's wise to save yourself for "the real thing."

5. As you read or speak, remain alert for any hand signals given by the floor director or engineer, which might indicate "louder," "softer," or "move closer to (or away from) the mic."

6. As you make the suggested adjustments (if any), continue to speak until the signal is given that everything is satisfactory.

Hand Signals

Hand signals were developed in the early days of radio because sound-proof glass partitions separated directors and engineers from performers. As radio turned more and more to recorded music, nearly all music announcers came to do their own engineering. Today, most radio stations don't even have a control room adjacent to the announce booth or studio, and hand signals aren't needed. However, hand signals are still used in a few radio applications. An announce booth director of live sports broadcasts—usually the audio engineer—uses a limited number of signals to cue sportscasters when coming back from commercial breaks. A few popular morning drive-time disc jockeys, especially those who work with sound effects and much "production," work in an on-air studio/control room complex and are provided with engineering help. Radio talk-show hosts generally work with a producer/phone screener, who may use some hand signals.

Most of the signals that follow are standard throughout the industry, but be prepared for variations.

- The *attention signal,* a simple waving of the hand, usually precedes the stand-by signal.

- The *stand-by signal* is made by holding the hand slightly above the head, palm toward the announcer. The stand-by signal is given at any time when the announcer can't judge the precise moment at which to pick up a cue.
- The *cue signal* is made by rapidly lowering the hand from the stand-by position, with the index finger extended and pointing directly at the person being cued. The cue signal nearly always follows the stand-by signal; neither signal is normally given alone.
- *Increase volume* (speak up!) is made by holding one hand, palm up, and raising it.
- *Decrease volume* is made by holding one hand, palm down, and lowering it.

Performance Skills

Preparing for a Performance

Preparation for a performance is necessary for all but the most seasoned veterans, and proper preparation involves several considerations. After you've worked in the field for even a few years, announcing will be as natural as breathing. Until then, follow the suggestions in this section to prepare for smooth and confident performances.

First, if you're working with a script, you should study and mark it.[5] Underline words to be stressed. Write, in phonetics, the correct pronunciation of difficult words or names. Note any words that might be mistaken for others. For example, the following words are sometimes confused because of similar spellings:

though—through
county—country
uniformed—uninformed
united—untied
mediation—meditation
complaint—compliant
impudent—imprudent
outage—outrage

---

[5]But, as noted elsewhere, be prepared to remark your script if your producer or director wants an interpretation that differs from the one on which you previously decided.

1. Study the script: mark it for correct pronunciation.
2. Use the final ten minutes before your performance to separate yourself from all distractions; concentrate on calming your nerves and "psyching up" your energy level.
3. Remind yourself to speak slowly, and if you should stumble, be prepared to continue in an unruffled manner with your broadcast.

To eliminate the possibility of reading such words incorrectly, mark your copy. You might write *tho* and *thru* for the first pair of words and use hyphens for the others: *coun-ty, count-ry; uni-formed, un-in-formed; u-nited, un-tied;* and so on.

The final ten minutes before a performance are critical. Try to separate yourself from any distracting activities and concentrate on your upcoming performance. If you're excessively nervous, try to relax; if you're apathetic, try to psych yourself up to an appropriate degree of energy.

If your performance is to be ad-lib, go over its objectives and make determinations about how you'll structure your ideas within the allotted time. How much time will you give to your opening? How much will you give to your conclusion? How much time remains for the body of your presentation?

Finally, remind yourself that you're going to control any tendency you may have to speak too rapidly; that if you make an error, you'll correct it as naturally and unobtrusively as possible and continue; and that if you stumble, you'll move on, putting the error behind you (dwelling on it will divide your attention and make further stumbles almost inevitable). Above all, do *not* stop to ask if you may begin again, unless such a possibility has been agreed to in advance. Even if your performance will never actually leave the classroom or studio, always adopt the attitude that it's going out live over the airwaves.

Achieving a Conversational Style

A conversational style is one that's natural to you, is appropriate to the intimacy of the electronic media, and sounds as though you're talking rather than reading from a script. Speaking naturally is one important element of building rapport. If you notice the speech of affected, stilted, and (perhaps) pretentious speakers who clearly enunciate every syllable of every word and who speak with repetitious changes in inflection,

Figure 5.5

For commercials, industrial videos, or feature productions, you may need to employ characterization to convey different sorts of personalities and voices. Here actress Katie Leigh records a child's voice for a television cartoon series. *Courtesy of Hanna-Barbera Productions.*

you'll recognize one extreme of spoken English. At the other extreme are those who mumble, who barely move their lips, and whose energy is marked by a scarcely audible volume level.

Good conversational delivery is somewhere in between. It avoids overarticulation and slurring. It's marked by variety in pitch (inflection) and volume level, and it uses changes in pitch and volume to stress words that help convey meaning. Much of our daily conversation with friends is natural and effective because it's designed to communicate ideas, points of view, or convictions. We automatically find the simplest and best words to make a point, and we naturally stress key words to get our points across. Because we use it every day, conversational speech should be easy to apply when speaking for the electronic media. It usually is not a problem when speaking impromptu or ad-lib, but can become a problem when working from a script. You can best achieve a conversational style by remembering a few simple principles.

First, don't hesitate to smile or laugh when it's appropriate. Don't be afraid to pause as you silently grope for an idea or a word, because pauses are perfectly natural. Fear of pausing can lead either to *ers* and *uhs* (**vocalized pauses**) or to spouting inanities as you try to fight your way back to where you left off.

Additionally, conversational quality is totally destroyed by reading AY instead of UH for the article *a*. Read this sentence, pronouncing the article as AY:

A good way for a person to make a fortune is to open a

savings account in a bank.

Now read the sentence again, substituting the sound UH for AY. Don't stress any of the UHs.

UH good way for UH person to make UH fortune is to

open UH savings account in UH bank.

Note how stilted the sentence sounded the first time you read it and how much more natural and conversational it was when you used UH for the article *a*.

The article *the* is sometimes pronounced *THEE* and sometimes *THUH*. The general rule is to say *THEE* before a word beginning with a vowel sound and *THUH* before a word beginning with a consonant.

SCRIPT: The appetite is the best gauge of the health of

the average person.

READ AS: *THEE* appetite is *THUH* best gauge of *THUH*

health of *THEE* average person.

Note, however, that when saying *THEE*, you should soften the *EE* sound. At times this general rule is broken for purposes of emphasis, as in "It's *THEE* best buy of *THUH* year!"

The conversational quality you already use when speaking with friends can be transferred to the reading of a script. Make recordings of impromptu discussions between you and one or more of your friends. Note on playbacks how you and other speakers use variations in pitch, volume, and tempo to stress important points. Note how speakers use pauses and how energy increases and decreases according to the significance of the point being made. Record yourself reading a script. Compare your deliveries in unscripted and scripted speech. It may take some time to transfer your conversational quality to the reading of scripts, but it's essential to achieving your optimal on-air conversational style.

Reading Telephone Numbers

When reading a telephone number that includes an area code, read it with a pause after each part, and always say "area code" before you give the code:

SCRIPT: Phone (332) 555–6666.

READ AS: Phone area code three-three-two / five-five-

five / six-six-six-six.

When reading a telephone number that includes zeros, you should, in most instances, use the word zero and never *oh* or *ought*.

SCRIPT: Phone 555–0087.

READ AS: Phone five-five-five / zero-zero-eight-seven.

However, when you repeat a number, you can vary the way you say it:

SCRIPT: Phone 555–8200; that's 555–8200.

READ AS: Phone five-five-five / eight-two-zero-zero;

that's five-five-five / eighty-two hundred.

Some sponsors have special numbers that must be read in a certain way. Part or all of the number may spell out a word, as in 555–SAVE. Often such numbers are given twice: once with the word(s), and then in the all-number version.

Toll-free telephone numbers should be read with the beginning given as "one-eight-hundred," "one-eight-seven-seven," or "one-eight-eight-eight." Increasingly, announcers are omitting both the phrase, "Call our toll-free number . . . ," as well as the first digit, "one."

Developing a Sense of Time

Announcers must develop a keen sense of time, for split-second timing is a part of most radio broadcasts. Most all-news stations follow a "clock," an hourly schedule of segments, such as local news, network news, commercial clusters, traffic reports, and so forth. Many music stations also have clocks that are to be adhered to by on-air DJs. Accurate timing also is essential when recording commercials, station promos, and public service announcements (PSAs). Disc jockeys at some popular music stations provide ad-libbed introductions that must end exactly when the commercial, promo, or announcement begins. Newscasters must work with precision so that there will be neither unwanted pauses nor overlaps when playing recorded actualities or musical IDs.

Other Tips for Improving Your Performance

First, there's no substitute for practice. Theoretical knowledge of broadcasting is important, and such knowledge will enhance your development, but without practice you'll never become truly professional. You don't need to confine your practice to class assignments. You can practice nearly anywhere, and you can practice without a single item of equipment. When reading newspapers, magazines, and books, isolate yourself from others and read at least some of the printed material aloud.

Second, if your budget permits, invest in a few basic items of equipment. Most practical is a good-quality, battery-operated audio recorder. With a recorder you can practice any type of announcing that appeals to you—news, interviewing, sports play-by-play, music announcing, or commercial delivery.

Most broadcast stations rely heavily on computerized operations. To prepare for work at a computerized station, buy a Macintosh or personal computer and use it for all your school reports, personal and business letters, and other writing. The computer need not be new or "state of the art." A factory-refurbished older model will allow you to become "computer literate"—assuming that you aren't already there!

Third, become honestly self-critical. As you listen to playbacks, imagine the voice you hear is that of another person. Listen for communicative values. Listen for voice quality, precise diction, and correct pronunciation. Experiment. Try various styles of delivery, levels of energy, and rates of delivery. You shouldn't try these things in imitation of another performer; rather you should experiment to find ways of bringing out the best that's in *you*.

When performing in a newscast, commercial, or interview, don't do takeoffs unless the assignment calls for you to do so. You may amuse yourself and others by doing a parody of your material, but it really affords you no useful practice unless, of course, you intend to make a career of doing spoofs and takeoffs. This warning doesn't rule out humorous commercials or humor-oriented interviews, as long as they're realistically related to your growth as an announcer.

Finally, save your recordings and review them from time to time to measure your progress. When you compare performances made four or five months apart, your improvement will be both impressive and encouraging—*if you've practiced!*

Evaluating Your Performance

Critical self-evaluation is the mark of the true professional in any of the performing arts. Here *critical* doesn't mean *disparaging*—it means careful, objective, and exact evaluation. Self-evaluation also requires the development of a mature attitude toward one's performance. A superior performance doesn't make you a superior person, any more than a wretched performance makes you a wretched person. Learn to distinguish between yourself as a *person* and your *performance* on any given assignment. Growth and improvement depend on your ability to learn from your mistakes, rather than being disheartened by them.

PRACTICE

Gauging Your Own Performance

Consult a daily news source (newspaper, radio, or television newscast) and write your own version of a local or national story. Prepare a script that will take two to two-and-one-half minutes to read. Read through your copy as you would if someone else had written it, marking for emphasis, pronunciation, and so on. Read it aloud several times. When you're ready, record your performance. Use the following audio checklist to evaluate all aspects of your performance.

CHECKLIST
EVALUATING AUDIO PERFORM- ANCES

1. **Pitch**
   Good_____ Too low_____ Too high_____

2. **Pitch variety**
   Good_____ Too little_____ Too much_____

3. **Volume**
   Good_____ Too weak_____ Too loud_____

4. **Tempo**
   Good_____ Too slow_____ Too fast_____

5. **Tempo variety**
   Good_____ Too little_____ Inappropriate variations_____

6. **Vitality**
   Good_____ Too little_____ Too much_____

7. **Articulation**
   Good_____ Underarticulated_____ Over-articulated_____

8. **Voice quality**
   Good_____ Nasal_____ Husky_____ Thin_____ Other_____

9. **Sibilance**
   Good_____ Excessive_____

10. **Plosives**
    Good_____ Popping_____

11. **Use of microphone**
    Good_____ Note any problems. _____
    _____
    _____

12. **Note any mispronounced words.**_____
    _____
    _____

13. **Give performance an overall evaluation.** _____
    _____
    _____

14. **Note specific things on which to work.**_____
    _____
    _____

 SPOTLIGHT

Breaking into the Announcing Field

Denny Delk has loved radio as long as he can remember. His mother, when reading bedtime stories, used her voice to add sound effects. As early as age four, he tried to emulate her. He started playing with a tape recorder when he was thirteen, varying sounds by speeding up and slowing down his recorded voice and trying out vocalized sound effects. Today, Delk does voice work for commercials, cartoons, and promos, and narration for industrials and documentaries.

Delk enjoys voice work more than any other mode of performance. "Radio, as has been said many times, is the theater of the mind," he says. "You can do anything you want to do. You can be anyone you want to be. You can make the imagination of the listener work by the way you treat the microphone, by the things the producer does with you, by the way you react with people—you can't raise an eyebrow; you can't give a sidelong glance—you have to do those things with your voice. And it's fun to be able to play that way."

Originally from Oklahoma, Delk got his start at a small-town radio station. There was a sign on the door that read "dollar a holler," meaning that each commercial message broadcast on the station cost only one dollar. It was a small beginning, but he loved radio. He later moved on to other jobs in broadcasting, all of them related to communication with an audience—camera operator, television director, studio engineer, sound technician for a television station, newspaper reporter, concert promoter, disc jockey, and radio talk-show host—all before becoming a voice-over announcer.

An English major who performed in many stage plays during his college days, Delk has worked in theater everywhere he's lived. He does improvisational comedy with the National Theater of the Deranged. He calls this "lazy man's theater—no need to memorize." Delk is convinced that doing theater helps a voice-over actor become a more complete performer. He urges students to become involved in college or community theater. Even behind-the-scenes work can teach you what communicating with an audience is all about.

Delk offers advice to aspiring announcers:

- How do you market yourself? Your first challenge is to get agents and producers to listen to your audition tape. Most likely, they're already working with a stable of regulars—outstanding voice-over people, with all types of personalities and ages—and you have to make them want to listen to your tape.

- The packaging of your tape can create a strong impression. Delk prefers to use standard audio cassette tapes. Sooner or later, individual auditions will be duplicated on CD ROMS—they already are by talent agencies—but, at present, cassettes are inexpensive and make your performance readily retrievable by agents. Delk includes visual material because when agents are listening to a tape there's absolutely nothing to do *but* listen. He encloses eight panels of humorous cartoons on a ten-inch-by-twenty-inch sheet. The cartoons relate to both announcing and his personality, and they catch the eyes of those who hire people to do voice work.

- *Never* include your photo for voice-over work. Your appearance has nothing to do with the job for which you're auditioning. Casting agents and producers will expect you—or want you—to sound like you look. Don't give them a chance to say "No, this person doesn't look right for the part." Force them to judge you *only* by the sound of your voice and your interpretive abilities, which are the only things that are relevant.

- Delk uses three separate "packages": one each for straight announcing, cartoon and character voice work, and industrial narration. Creating separate portfolio packages allows you to tailor each one to a distinct style and market.

- After sending an audition tape, follow with a card and a note that says "Hope you had a chance to listen." *Never* call the person. They don't have the time, and you really don't have anything to say. If you ask what was thought about the tape, you've put that person in a potentially awkward or difficult position.

- Put on your tape as many different things as you can do *well*. Don't include any voices or attitudes that are marginal or questionable. If you can't determine on

Denny Delk does more than send his résumé and audition tape; he gives potential clients something entertaining to look at while they review his tape. *Cartoon by Charles Oldham, Wonderworks, © 1981. Reprinted by permission.*

your own what things you do well, ask a qualified person, such as your instructor, for help.

- Your tape must never be longer than three minutes—two and one-half minutes is better. For industrial work or other tapes of voice-over narration, you may do a longer tape.

- You must have an attention-getter at the front. Use your best-sounding effort at the start. If you place it later, the agent may never hear it.

- Don't do complete spots—ten seconds is enough to establish any one thing.

- Show a variety of *attitudes* (better than *accents*): soft sell, snooty, seductive, down-trodden, and so on. Don't put them together in a haphazard or random order. Work for variety. Do a soft sell, followed by a hard sell. In other words, break up the pieces. This approach makes each segment more impressive than it would be if it stood alone or if it were surrounded by similar readings.

- Don't ask to have your tape returned. Audiotapes are inexpensive, and you want the tape to be sitting on producers' shelves. When the person they usually use is un-available, perhaps they'll remember your tape and listen to it again—and then they may call you.

- Even if a producer likes your tape, you'll still have to audition for a job. Sometimes tapes are better than people are, and they'll want to know if you're as good as your tape.
- Finally, remember that you won't succeed without the help of many others—agents, writers, producers, directors, sound engineers, advertising agency personnel, secretaries, union officials, and so forth. The profession is a highly rewarding one in which cooperation is eventually as important as talent, and people have feelings and very long memories.

CHAPTER 6

Video Performance

AUDIENCE RAPPORT

BECAUSE OF ITS OVERRIDING IMPORTANCE, THIS CHAPTER, LIKE THAT on Audio Performance, begins with a discussion of audience rapport, with a focus on television. Rick Houlberg, professor of broadcasting arts at San Francisco State University, made this pertinent comment after concluding a study of viewer preferences concerning television newscasters:

> After all the preparation, clothing, hard work, and luck, something more is needed for the on-air broadcaster to be successful. We know what that something is although we haven't been able to fully describe or study it. This something made us believe Walter Cronkite and send birthday presents to soap opera characters; this something makes us choose one television newscaster over another. . . . This something is a connection made between the on-air performer and the audience.[1]

---

[1]These comments were made by Professor Rick Houlberg after conducting a study of respondents in Ohio. The complete report is in the *Journal of Broadcasting*, Fall 1984. Houlberg cites later studies supporting his conclusions.

In his research Houlberg found that most respondents chose the television newscaster they watched because of these factors: "He or she made their problems seem easier"; "They would like to know more about the newscaster off the air"; "The newscaster is almost like their everyday friends"; and "He or she made them feel contented." Of course, audience rapport is not everything. News anchors and reporters, for example, must also have significant professional characteristics including objectivity, reliability, honesty, and appropriate preparation as journalists.

The messages here are clear: after achieving professional competency, and while maintaining the integrity that's expected of news personnel, broadcast performers must project an attractive and friendly personality to the audience. *Attractive* in this sense doesn't refer to physical appearance. Houlberg found that neither physical appearance nor gender was significantly important to his respondents. Synonyms for attractive are *appealing, engaging,* and *charming.* A sensitive performer can use these qualities to build audience rapport—a relationship of mutual trust or emotional affinity. It's not likely that every student can be taught these qualities because they come from within. Being aware of them can, however, help you channel your inner feelings of respect for your audience, concern for people, and dedication to your profession into more effective communication. Audience rapport is a state of mind. It relies heavily on your integrity. It's a reflection of who you are and what you care about.

Microphone Consciousness for Video Performers

To be mic conscious is to be always aware that the misuse of a microphone will result in a flawed or failed performance. Several examples of faulty microphone consciousness may be found in Chapter 5, "Audio Performance," most of which apply to television performance.

Television makes much use of lavaliere mics, and it's important to recognize the limitations of this convenient and unobtrusive instrument. Despite continual improvement, lavaliere condenser mics must be used carefully to prevent their picking up unwanted noise. A script being thumbed or rattled three inches away from the lavaliere will sound at least as loud as a voice coming from a foot or more away. Clothing brushing against the surface of the mic will sound like a forest fire. Nervous toying with the cable will transmit scratching and rumbling sounds directly into the microphone. If you tend to produce a popping sound as you pronounce *p, t,* or *k,* or excessive sibilance with *s* or *sh,* you may benefit from having a windscreen placed over the face of the microphone.[2] Several manufacturers supply open-cell polyurethane foam windscreens that only slightly affect the frequency response by eliminating some of the highs. Television performers should study the problems listed in Chapters 3 and 4, and consider also these that relate specifically to television performance:

- Failing to clip on a lavaliere mic before beginning a performance
- Attaching a lavaliere mic improperly—too far away from the mouth or under clothing that will muffle the sound
- Clapping with your hands near a lavaliere mic
- Failing to move a hand-held mic properly between you and a guest you are interviewing
- Walking away from the set after a performance without remembering to unclip a lavaliere mic

When rehearsing and performing for television, always assume that your microphone is open and that the camera is on. Watch what you say and do. Always assume that profanity and backbiting comments about others will be heard by someone, possibly with devastating consequences!

Figure 6.1

News anchor Cheryl Jennings checks the placement of her lavaliere mic, while co-anchor Dan Noyes waits for a cue to open the newscast.
Courtesy of Cheryl Jennings, Dan Noyes, and KGO-TV, San Francisco, California.

---

[2]See the discussions of popping and excessive sibilance in Chapter 3, "Voice Analysis and Improvement," and Chapter 4, "Pronunciation and Articulation."

Camera Consciousness

Just as a microphone initiates the process of sending your voice to listeners, a camera is the first element in the transmission of your physical image. **Camera consciousness** begins with understanding the needs and limitations of cameras and recognizing the problems faced by camera operators and those controlling robotic cameras. The discussion that follows covers only those technical aspects that are relevant to you as a performer.

A television camera picks up reflected light in much the same way the human eye does. Like the eye, a camera has a lens, an iris (or diaphragm), and a surface on which images are focused. The retina in the eye is like the photosensitive surface in the camera pickup tube. The lens focuses the picture, the iris opens or closes to control the amount of light entering the system, and the photosensitive surface converts the light patterns into electrical impulses.

Unlike the human eye, the television camera has a zoom feature that allows it to handle anything from a wide shot to an extreme close-up. To the human eye, a person standing ten feet away will always be on a medium shot, so to speak. Humans have the advantage of being able to rapidly move their heads approximately 180 degrees horizontally and can focus on one object at the start and on another at the end of the head movement without any sensation of blurring. A television camera can't do the same.

Keep these elementary facts about cameras in mind as you consider the aspects of television performance discussed under the following headings.

Hitting Marks

Hitting marks means moving to an exact spot in a studio or in the field marked by a piece of tape or chalk. During preparation for all but the most routine television productions, the director will "block" the movements of performers. **Blocking** is the term used in theater, film, and television for the planning of movements to be executed during the show by performers. When a specific movement is called for, it's important to move exactly as required and to stop in the predetermined position. There are at least three reasons why precision in hitting marks is critical:

1. The amount of light entering a lens determines the f-stop setting of the iris; the f-stop setting in turn determines the depth of field—the

extent of the area in front of the camera in which everything is in focus. (Objects closer or farther away will be blurred.) The greater the amount of light entering the lens, the smaller the iris opening and the greater the depth of field. Because zoom lenses have a great deal of glass through which the light must pass, because prompting devices cut down further on light entering the lens system, and because studio lighting is kept to the lowest possible level for the comfort of performers, the iris is generally quite open, and this setting reduces depth of field considerably. To put it plainly, if you don't hit your marks, you may be out of focus.

2. Another reason for hitting marks precisely is that the camera operator is responsible for the composition of the picture. Where you should stand for the best composition will have been determined earlier, and you must follow through in order to enable the camera operator to do a professional job.

3. A third reason for being meticulous about hitting marks is that studios often feature area lighting, which means that not all parts of the set are illuminated equally. If you miss your mark, you may be outside the area specifically prepared for your presentation.

Robotic cameras—cameras that move to predetermined positions, and are not controlled by human operators behind each camera—require announcers to be even more careful in hitting marks. Robotic cameras move to preprogrammed positions, and their lenses are prefocused. Although an operator sitting in a control booth can change the position and focus of each robotic camera, that operator is responsible for the control of three or more cameras, and the complexities of this task make precision in hitting marks extremely important to the technical quality of the show.

On-Camera Movement

Standing. When standing on camera, you must stand still and avoid rocking from side to side. Weaving or rocking from one foot to the other can be distracting on a long shot and disastrous on a close-up. In a television studio a monitor is placed where you can see it so you'll know whether the camera has you on a wide, medium, or close-up shot and you'll know if you're moving out of the picture. In the field you most likely won't have a monitor, so you'll have no way of knowing whether you're moving out of the frame.

Practice standing with a minimum of movement. To reduce a tendency to rock, stand with your feet slightly apart and with one foot turned out to form a 15-to-20-degree angle with the other foot; the turned foot should be four or five inches in front of the other. Standing in this manner should make it all but impossible to rock.

Sitting. You'll find it easier to avoid excessive random movement when seated, but remember that most movements appear exaggerated on television. If you find that you habitually move your upper torso and head in rapid or wide-ranging motions, you should work to reduce such movement—without at the same time seriously lowering your natural energy level. Sideways movement can be very annoying, especially on close-ups. Movement toward and away from the camera can take you in and out of focus.

Telegraphing Movement. When rising or sitting down and when moving from one part of the studio (or exterior location) to another, you must

Figure 6.2

Reporter–anchor Diane Dwyer demonstrates how rocking from side to side on camera appears on a medium shot, where it is not bothersome, and how it looks on a close-up, where the shot is badly framed. *Courtesy of Diane Dwyer and KTVU, Oakland, California.*

move somewhat more slowly than you ordinarily would, and you must telegraph your movement. To **telegraph a movement** is to begin it with a slow and slight motion followed by a pause before following through with the intended movement. Camera operators are trained to follow even fast-moving athletes, but you shouldn't test their skill unnecessarily. A little thoughtfulness on your part can guarantee that you'll not cross them up.

Don't sit down or stand up on camera unless the movement was planned in advance or is signaled by the floor director. When the camera is on a head shot of a standing performer and the performer suddenly sits, the head drops right out of the picture. When the camera is on a head shot of a seated performer who suddenly stands, the result is even worse; the viewer is treated to the infamous crotch shot. In Figure 6.3 Frank Somerville shows how this movement looks on television. If you find that you must stand up when no such movement was planned, telegraphing is imperative—it will give the director time to zoom out to a wider and safer shot.

Cheating to the Camera. To **cheat to the camera** is to position yourself so as to sustain the impression that you're talking to another person (as in an interview) while still presenting a favorable appearance on screen.

Figure 6.3

News anchor Frank Somervile shows what happens when he suddenly stands on camera without being cued to do so, or without telegraphing his move. *Courtesy of Frank Somerville and KTVU, Oakland, California.*

When a performer is speaking to a guest or a cohost, viewers want to see the faces of both persons and to believe that the two are speaking to one another rather than to the audience. So, to avoid presenting only their profiles as they speak, interviewer and guest position themselves at about a 25-degree angle from one another—thereby **opening up to the camera**—while continuing to speak as though they were facing one another directly.

When standing or sitting with another person—as when conducting an interview—position yourself nearer the other person than you ordinarily would. We are all surrounded by an invisible area we consider our own personal space. When talking with others, we usually sit or stand at a comfortable distance from them. Television, however, is no respecter of this psychological space. The intimacy of television is best exploited when both interviewer and guest can be seen in a medium shot. Sitting or standing too far from another performer forces the director to settle for close-ups of individuals, or wide-angle "two-shots" (two people in the picture). In unrehearsed programs, the director wants to have an acceptable cover shot, a shot that can be used regardless of which person is speaking. The farther apart the performers, the smaller they'll appear on the television screen. So, if the only two-shot available is a long shot, the director is forced to settle for a view that makes viewers feel they're watching from a distance, and intimacy is lost.

Addressing the Camera. When directly addressing the camera (the viewer, actually), look straight into the lens and focus your gaze about a foot behind the glass, for that's where your viewer is. When searching for a thought or a word, many of us tend to raise our eyes toward the ceiling as we pause for inspiration. This tendency is distracting and unflattering; if you have such a habit, work to overcome it.

Make certain you don't try to hold a smile on your face while waiting for the director to go to black, to another camera, to a recorded segment, or to a commercial. Try to make small and natural movements while you wait. Don't continue to stare at the camera unless you've been told to do so. If appropriate to the type of performance being given, look down at your script, pick up a pencil and make marks on your script, or when sitting beside another person—an interviewee or a co-anchor— start a conversation. Just remember that the mic may still be on. In Figure 6.4, Nerissa Azurin demonstrates the look that results when a director stays on a shot too long and the performer attempts to hold a smile. Television performers jokingly refer to this as the **egg-on-face look.**

Figure 6.4

Nerissa Azurin, a bit impatient to get out of the limelight, wears the egg-on-face look as she waits for the director to go to a commercial break. *Courtesy of Nerissa Azurin.*

In a studio production, you can expect to work with from two to four cameras: three are standard. From time to time you'll have to change your attention from one camera to another on cue. The cuing sequence begins when the floor director points both hands to the **taking camera** (the camera that's on, indicated by an illuminated red light called a **tally light**). On a signal from the director, the floor director rapidly moves one or both hands to point to the camera to which you're to turn. When you perform as a news anchor, you first notice the cue, glance down at your script, and then raise your head in the direction of the second camera. In Figure 6.5, Tori Campbell shows how to make a clean movement from one camera to another as she's cued by the floor director.

Don't stare at the camera. Just as staring at a person with whom you're speaking can make that person uncomfortable, staring at the camera lens can have the same effect on viewers. As you speak (read), let your head make small, subtle movements. These should be natural movements motivated by the words you're speaking. Be careful to avoid a machinelike pattern, one in which you automatically nod your head to emphasize every syllable. Make your movements small, motivated by the mood and meaning of what you're saying, and natural to you and your personality.

When addressing the camera, it's important to communicate through pitch patterns, rate of delivery, and nonverbal movements that are at a level of energy appropriate to the nature of the story. If you exaggerate any of these factors beyond what the story justifies, you'll come across as an actor who's *playing the role* of a news reporter. Believable

Figure 6.5

Floor director Charlene Johnson uses hand signals to alert anchor Tori Campbell to an upcoming switch from Camera 5 to Camera 6. This allows Tori to alter her eye contact by glancing down at her script and then up to Camera 6. *Courtesy of Tori Campbell, Charlene Johnson, and KTVU, Oakland, California.*

vocal variation and facial expressions and head, hand, and torso movements can add much to your communicative abilities.

Examine your appearance closely when viewing playbacks. In addition to watching for such obvious physical problems as poor posture, look at your mouth on a close-up. See if you've developed an unattractive and distracting habit of speaking out of the side of your mouth—speaking with one side of your mouth noticeably lower than the other. If so, practice straightening out your mouth while performing before a mirror; better still, practice while you videotape performances. A lifelong habit of speaking with a crooked mouth may be difficult to overcome, but correcting it will enhance your chances of having a successful career as a television announcer.

Holding Props

A **prop**, short for *property,* is an object that a performer holds or displays, or to which he or she points. Typical props are goods used in demonstration commercials, the food and utensils used in cooking shows, and books displayed by talk-show hosts.

Hold maps, sketches, books, products, or other props with a steady hand. Chances are the director will want an extreme close-up of the object, and even a slight movement can take it out of focus or off camera. Position the prop so that the taking camera has a good view of it. Glance at the floor monitor, and then position the prop correctly.

When pointing to an object or a portion of it, move your hand, with the index finger extended, slowly and evenly toward the spot to be highlighted. Hold that hand as steady as possible. Don't make quick motions here and there—the camera can't follow them. Always rely on a monitor to check both your positioning and your hand movements.

When holding any object that has a reflective surface, such as the dust cover of a book, check your monitor to make sure you're holding it at a correct angle. Studio lights reflected from any glossy object can totally wash out its details. If the object being held is reflecting light, tilt it forward or backward to correct the problem.

Additionally, few of us can easily speak fluently while using our hands to demonstrate. When demonstrating a product or a procedure on camera, don't feel compelled to keep up a nonstop narration. Constant chatter, especially when marred by hesitancy and repetitions, isn't good communication. Because television is a visual medium, action alone may sometimes work best. However, since commentary is sometimes helpful or even necessary, you should practice and perfect the skill of simultaneously speaking and demonstrating.

Holding Scripts

Scripts are used in live television primarily by news anchors. They're usually a backup to a prompting device. If the prompter fails or the person feeding it falls behind or rushes ahead of your delivery, you can refer to your script. At some stations, however, you won't have a prompter and must work entirely from hand-held scripts. (Working with a prompter is discussed in a later section.)

When working with a script, hold it with both hands, above the desk and tilted toward you at a comfortable angle for reading. You should hold the script above desk level for three important reasons: (1) to reduce the degree of up-and-down motion of your head as you look down to the script and then up to the camera; (2) to more easily keep the script in front of you as you look from camera to camera, thereby eliminating diagonal head movements; and (3) to avoid bending your head down to read a script that's flat on the surface of the desk, which restricts the airflow and thereby impairs voice quality.

Using Peripheral Vision

A periphery is a boundary. If you look straight ahead, you'll find that the left and right boundaries of your vision extend in an arc of about 150 degrees. This is the range of your **peripheral vision,** and you should be able to pick up movements, such as hand signals, given to you within this area. Actually, on-air you'll need to use only about a 45-degree arc of your peripheral vision, because floor directors will give you signals as near as possible to the camera you're addressing. When receiving signals, don't allow your head or even your eyes to turn toward the signaler. In Figure 6.6, Cheryl Fong shows how even a slight movement of the eyes to pick up a cue can look on camera.

Clothing and Makeup

When performing on television, plan your clothing carefully. If your station's system uses chroma-keying, you should avoid wearing any shade of the color used for the mattes (blue or green in most instances). **Chroma-keying** is a process that allows a picture from one camera to be keyed in to a portion of the picture from another camera. If blue is the color of the chroma-key backdrops (mattes) and you were to wear a blue shirt or blouse, the second picture would appear in the area of your blue clothing whenever a chroma-key matte was used.

Figure 6.6

It is important to use peripheral vision. Reporter Cheryl Fong shows what happens when a performer on a close-up glances away for a cue. *Courtesy of Cheryl Fong.*

Avoid, too, any article of clothing that has small checks or narrow stripes. The television cameras can't handle fine, high-contrast patterns, and a wavy, shimmering look, called the moiré effect (pronounced mwah-RAY), results. Also avoid black-and-white clothing. Pastel colors are best for nearly all broadcast purposes and are complimentary to people of all skin shades. Performers with extremely dark faces should wear clothing somewhat darker than that worn by people with light skin tones. The principle to follow is to avoid excessive contrast between your face and your clothing and to avoid clothing of the same shade and color as your skin.

Jewelry can cause video problems, as can sequins. Studio lights reflected directly into the camera lens cause **flaring**—light reflected from a highly polished object causing signal overload, which results in a flash on the television screen. This effect may be used to assert the glamour of a particular guest, but it's very distracting if created regularly by a program host.

If your vision needs correction, contact lenses will usually give you your best on-camera appearance. If you prefer to wear glasses, have their lenses treated with an antiglare coating. The frames you choose are an important aspect of your appearance, so look for frames that are flattering and suit your on-air personality. Generally speaking, frames should not be so unusual as to call attention to themselves. Eyeglass frames made of metal may cause flaring, so choose plastic frames.

Makeup for television performers is usually quite simple and quickly applied. Makeup can help reduce skin shine, eliminate "five o'clock shadow," improve skin color, and hide minor blemishes. It's seldom intended to drastically change the appearance of a television performer. Close-ups too readily reveal attempts to change basic facial features. If your complexion is sallow, be careful to cover your entire face, neck, and ears with makeup, because the contrast between the near-white of uncovered skin and almost any color of makeup is noticeable. If your complexion is quite dark, you won't have the same problem of contrast, but you should experiment with a variety of shades of makeup, including eyeliner and, for women, rouge and lipstick. Dark skin should be toned down to avoid unflattering highlights; find a pancake hue that works well with the bright lights and the technical requirements of television. Some men, even when freshly shaven, show a dark cast in the beard and mustache area. Although pancake makeup helps cover five-o'clock shadow, a special beard stick eliminates the problem in nearly all cases.

Always have powder or pancake makeup near you. Some sets are brightly lit, and the heat from lighting instruments may cause you to perspire. Check frequently to make sure you're not perspiring; if you are, apply powder when you're off camera.[3]

Working with Cue Cards

Cue cards are used at most television stations for short announcements to be made by an on-air performer; to list items to be mentioned, such as the names and professions of program guests; or to supply some bit of information to the performer, such as a telephone number or a reminder to mention an upcoming segment of the show. For lengthy messages that on-air announcers are to read, nearly all television stations use electronic prompters.

Some college departments of broadcasting don't own prompting devices, and students who must deliver lengthy messages word for word must rely on memorization or cue cards. Memorization involves a greater risk of failure. The pressure of performing before one's peers along with the normal distractions of the television studio—bright lights in one's face, time cues, signals from a floor director to change cameras—makes concentration on a memorized script quite difficult. For most learners, cue cards are the best option.

---

[3]An informative and more extensive discussion of makeup and clothing for television may be found in Herbert Zettl's *Television Production Handbook,* 7th ed. (Belmont, CA: Wadsworth, 1999).

Cue cards are generally made in one of two configurations. If the message is brief enough, the cue card will be a single sheet of poster board measuring twenty-eight by forty-four inches. The script is written on the card with a black felt-tip marker. During rehearsals and performance, a floor director holds the card to the right of the camera lens and moves the card slowly upward as the performer reads it so that the line being spoken is always alongside the lens. Although standard poster board is twenty-eight inches wide, a wide right margin is generally left so that the reader/performer can minimize left-to-right head movement.

Smaller cue cards are used for longer messages. These are generally wider than twenty-four inches and no more than twelve to fifteen inches high. Although less information fits on each of these smaller cards—a thirty-second commercial will require several of them—they help the performer maintain better eye contact with the viewer than is possible with the larger cards.

Cards should be held as close to the lens as possible; the best placement is just below the lens, because this allows the performer to look directly at the viewer. If the script calls for a switch from one camera to another, either the cards must be duplicated, with one set held at each camera, or they must be divided according to the lines that are to be addressed to each camera.

When working with cue cards—especially with multiple ones—it's imperative that you practice with the person or persons who'll be holding them during your performance. Even a slight hesitation in changing the cards can cause you to stop in midsentence. As you read from cue cards, practice looking as directly as possible into the lens, using your peripheral vision to its greatest degree. It isn't easy, but with regular practice you can develop this skill.

Working with Prompters

Television stations use prompting devices to enable performers to maintain eye contact with viewers. Most **prompters** are entirely electronic; scripts are typed on a word processor, stored, and transmitted to a display terminal. Older prompters combine mechanical and electronic components. With both systems the image appears on a monitor attached to each television camera; a mirror reflects this image onto a sheet of glass mounted at a 45-degree angle in front of the camera lens. The performer sees the script while looking directly at the lens. The speed of the moving script is regulated to match the reading speed of the performer. Both systems require **hard copy**—a script printed on sheets of 8½-inch-by-11-inch paper—for use by producers, directors, news anchors, and others. The script may be written on an electronic keyboard and then duplicated in the number of copies required for production, or the script may be entered directly onto **copy sets**, multipart forms that yield several copies. (A camera-mounted prompter is shown in Figure 6.7).

Prompters are used extensively on television newscasts. On talk, interview, game, variety, and other programs that are predominantly ad-libbed, prompters are used only for short messages that must be delivered verbatim (word for word) and, in some operations, to pass on information such as the nature of an upcoming program segment.

When delivering a television commercial or commentary, you'll seldom have a script in your hands or on a desk in front of you. Nearly all such performances are recorded, and can be redone if the prompter malfunctions. During a live newscast, on the other hand, you must have a complete script to turn to in case the prompter ceases to work or gets out of phase with your reading.[4]

Figure 6.7

Sports reporter Fred Inglis reads from a prompter as he delivers a breaking sports story from the newsroom. *Courtesy of Fred Inglis and KTVU, Oakland, California.*

[4]See also the discussion of prompters in Chapter 10, "Television News."

Instructions and Cues

Nearly all television performers work as members of teams and must therefore develop harmonious relationships and efficient means of communicating. Because cooperation is necessary, you must learn to coordinate your efforts with those of others.

Television performers receive instructions and cues from floor directors and producers during real-time broadcasts.[5] Floor directors use either oral or visual means of communicating. Oral instructions are preferred whenever possible, as during a commercial break. Producers of television newscasts, infomercial programs, play-by-play sports broadcasts, and some talk shows communicate by way of an **interruptible foldback (IFB)**, a small speaker that fits in a performer's ear. In general, instructions from floor directors are confined to details such as cuing, indicating an upcoming program break, and signaling the improper use of equipment or of lights.

Producers of television commercials usually concern themselves with matters of interpretation and timing, whereas news producers are alert to changes of plan, such as dropping a news story. Regardless of who issues the instructions, it's your responsibility to carry them out promptly and effectively.

Achieving Good Working Relationships

Several considerations are involved in developing good working relationships. For example, you may find yourself disagreeing with a director on interpretation of lines and want to express your point of view. Sounds reasonable, but there are acceptable and unacceptable ways of doing this. To openly and directly challenge a director's instructions is to defy established authority and bring into question the director's competence. Needless to say, unless you're in such demand that you can get away with any degree of rudeness, you may soon be without a job! At the same time, as an announcer you're not expected to act like a mindless automaton. Ample opportunity exists to discuss your ideas and concepts with producers or directors, but you must choose the right time, and adopt an appropriate and nonthreatening manner.

---

[5] In this context, *real-time* refers to programs that are produced without stopping and without postproduction editing. A real-time program may be shown as it happens—as with "live" newscasts—or may be recorded and shown at a later time, as with some sports events.

Scripts of complete television dramas, both serious and comic, may be found on the Internet. One source, Drew's Script-o-Rama, may be accessed with this URL[6]:

www.script-o-rama.com/tv/tvscript.shtml

The Television Transcript Project includes commercial scripts, arranged by category—headache remedies, restaurants, and so forth. Open, print, and you'll have copy to use for practice. Note: most of these spots have the product name changed, so you may want to enter a real product name before printing. *Most important, you must not use these spots for any on-air performance, because they are copyright protected.* The URL is:

www.tvtp.simplenet.com/

The Chicago Tribune maintains a web site that will lead you to scripts of many kinds. The URL is:

www.chicagotribune.com/news/columnists/zorn/feature/0,1438,9554-9554,00.html

For a complete, updated list of URLs for this textbook, please see the text home site available at *www.hmco/com/college.*

When rehearsing or when making a number of takes of a performance under the coaching of a producer or a director (for example, when recording the narrative for a television documentary or doing voice-over commercials), do your best to implement instructions. If your director welcomes it, you may discuss alternative ways to deliver lines, but always remember that the producer's word is final. One effective way to express your opinion is to say, "what if I tried it this way?"

---

[6]The Internet is changing constantly as new web sites are added and old web sites are abandoned. The URL listings in this textbook should be regarded as samples of the kinds of material available rather than as a stable index. If you seek a web site using one of these URLs and cannot connect, enter the key words for the topic into a search engine to find a site that may provide the information you want.

This approach is tactful and nonthreatening and will most likely be productive.

During rehearsals, avoid continually explaining why you did something this or that way or why you made a mistake. No one is really interested, and alibis and explanations only delay the project.

Always remain alert for cues and instructions. Sometimes you'll wait an eternity for a problem, usually a technical one, to be ironed out. This is no time for daydreaming and certainly no time to leave your position. When the problem is corrected, you'll be needed—at once.

Always treat every member of the production team with respect. No one is unimportant, and your success—and that of the production—depends on the degree of commitment and the quality of performance of every member.

Hand Signals

In television, **hand signals** are used for communication between members of a working team. Most of the signals that follow are standard throughout the industry, but be prepared for variations.

- The *attention signal,* a simple waving of the hand, usually precedes the stand-by signal. It's given by the television floor director, sometimes called the stage manager.
- The *stand-by signal* is made by holding the hand slightly above the head, palm toward the announcer. The stand-by signal is given at any time when the announcer can't judge the precise moment at which to pick up a cue.
- The *cue signal* is made by rapidly lowering the hand from the stand-by position, with the index finger extended and pointing directly at the person being cued. The cue signal nearly always follows the stand-by signal; neither signal is normally given alone. At some television stations the cue signal is thrown toward the camera that is going on the air.

The attention, stand-by, and cue signals are mainly used in television newscasts and talk shows. When given at the start of the show, or when returning from a commercial break or recorded package, the attention signal is given near the lens of the camera to be called up, and after the stand-by signal is given, the cue is thrown and the announcer begins addressing the indicated camera.

- The *switch-camera signal* tells you to look from the taking camera to the camera to which you've been waved. The floor director will progress from the stand-by signal to the switch-camera signal by moving one or both hands from the first to the second camera. Figure 6.5 shows how this transition is best made when working with a script and a prompter.
- The *break signal*, used chiefly on interview and talk programs, tells you that you need to wrap up the present segment for a commercial break. The signal is made by holding the hands as though they were grasping a brick or a stick of wood and then making a breaking motion.
- The *introduce-report* signal consists of a thumbs-up sign given to a news anchor to indicate that a planned report from the field is ready to go on the air. The *drop-report signal* is a thumbs-down sign meaning that the report is not to be introduced. Reports may be dropped because of technical difficulties or because of time pressures.

It's natural to want to acknowledge that you've received and understand a hand signal. Experienced performers working with professional crews don't send back a signal indicating "message received, will comply." At some television stations, however, and especially when new, unrehearsed, or unusually complex programs are being produced, performers are asked to acknowledge hand signals. In some instances this acknowledgment is conveyed by an unobtrusive hand or finger movement, in others it may involve a larger gesture. Follow the practice preferred by the director or producer of the show.

- The *cut signal* is made by drawing the index finger across the throat. This signals an emergency; on receiving it, stop speaking at once. After stopping your performance, wait for oral or visual signals before beginning again.
- The *slowdown or stretch signal* is given by a television floor director. It's made by pulling the hands apart, as though pulling taffy. Because slow down and stretch mean somewhat different things, you must rely on the context in which the signal is given to know how to interpret it. When you are reading from a script, the signal means to slow the pace of your delivery; when you are ad-libbing, it means to stretch (in other words, to keep talking until a further signal is given).

- The *speed-up signal* is given by holding the hand before the body, index finger extended, and then rotating the hand. On receiving this signal, you should increase the pace of your delivery. The signal is imprecise; it doesn't tell you how rapidly you should speak, or for how long. Later directions or signals will give you this information. Be careful not to confuse this signal with a wrap-up sign.

- The *wrap-up signal* is made by holding both hands in front of the torso and then rotating them about eight inches apart so that first one hand and then the other is on top. On receiving this signal, you should bring the program or the segment to a close as soon as possible in a smooth and natural way.

As a program nears its conclusion or as a segment of a program nears a station break, it's important for you to know the exact number of minutes or seconds remaining. Time signals are no longer used in radio or recording studios, but are very important in television. They are as follows:

- *three-minute signal*—three fingers held up and waved slowly
- *two-minute signal*—two fingers held up and waved slowly

Figure 6.8

Floor director Anthony Brock gives the stand-by-to-switch-camera signal. *Courtesy of Anthony Brock and KTVU, Oakland, California.*

- *one-minute signal*—the index finger held up and waved slowly
- *thirty-second signal*—the right and left arms crossed, or the index finger of one hand crossed with the index finger of the other
- *fifteen-second signal*—a clenched fist held upright and near the head
- *ten-to-zero signal*—all fingers on both hands held up and then lowered one at a time as the seconds are counted down

Be prepared for local variations of these signals.

Performance Skills

Preparing for a Performance

On entering the television studio for a rehearsal or performance, make note of the placement of microphones and cameras. Note where you'll sit or stand and decide where you'll hold or place your script (if any). Check out the lighting and determine exactly where you'll stand or sit and how far you may be able to move in each direction without moving into shadows. If appropriate, consult the floor director to make sure you know which camera will be called up to open the scene, and ask about any critical or unusual camera shots.

If you're to hold or demonstrate an object, decide exactly where and how you'll hold it and to which camera you'll present it.

Finally, to repeat a caution from the chapter on audio performance, remind yourself to avoid speaking too rapidly and, if you make an error, to correct it as naturally and unobtrusively as possible and then continue. If you stumble, move on and put the error behind you—dwelling on it will divide your attention and make further stumbles almost inevitable. Above all, don't stop your performance and ask if you may begin again unless such a possibility has been agreed to in advance. Even if your performance will never actually leave the classroom or studio, always adopt the attitude that it's going out live over the airwaves.

In television you'll be given time signals by a floor manager or floor director. In a newscast or an interview-talk show, you'll often be given a countdown as you introduce recorded stories. The floor director will first hold up the correct number of fingers and then, on instructions from the director, lower the fingers one at a time. When the countdown is completed, the director has gone to the recorded insert.

At other times during a program, you may be given a hand signal meaning that you have ten seconds in which to wrap up, or that there are three minutes, then two minutes, then one minute left in the program or in a segment of it. It's important that you develop a sense of how long these periods of time are. Smooth transitions and unhurried endings require accurate timing. To develop this sense, you must practice extensively using a stopwatch. Without looking at the watch, start it and then stop it when you think that a given number of seconds has passed. At first, you'll typically think that a minute has passed when the actual elapsed time is closer to thirty or forty seconds. With practice, you should become quite accurate at estimating elapsed times. Then you should practice speaking and reading lead-ins and program closings, pacing your words to match a predetermined number of seconds.

Other Tips for Improving Your Performance

You can practice television delivery with or without equipment. Of course, using a camcorder is the most desirable way of practicing on-camera delivery, and several cameras of adequate quality are priced under four hundred dollars. A camera plus a tripod, will, in most cases, give you the basics for television practice. An external mic is desirable because the built-in mic will be several feet away from you as you speak.

If video equipment isn't available to you, you can place some object on a wall (a drawing of a television lens will help) and use it to practice eye contact. There's no perfect substitute for performing before a camera with later playbacks for critical evaluations, so perhaps you can volunteer as talent on the projects of others. You may also obtain on-camera experience at a local cable station.

Evaluating Your Video Performances

As with audio performances, you should critically review your television performances to identify areas to work on and to assess improvements. The checklist presented on the following page covers the physical aspects of television performance. You should also use the checklist for audio performance found at the end of Chapter 5.

Television reporters engage in a great range of specalizations; one of these is feature reporting. **Feature reporters** write, edit, and announce soft news stories that engage audiences with stories that move, entertain, amuse, and/or illuminate. One outstanding feature reporter is Wayne Freedman. This chapter's Spotlight focuses on him; reveals how he regards himself and his work; follows him through a day in his life as a writer, producer, and performer; and includes his advice to those who want to excel in this demanding specialization.

CHECKLIST

EVALUATING TELEVISION PERFORM-ANCES

1. **Eye contact**
   Good_____   Needs work_____

2. **Use of peripheral vision**
   Good_____   Needs work_____

3. **Posture**
   Good_____   Needs work_____

4. **Standing on camera**
   Steady_____   Rocking_____

5. **Moving on camera**
   Telegraphed movement?_____

   Moved smoothly?_____

   Sat correctly?_____

6. Were transitions smooth when switching cameras?_____

7. Were props held correctly for cameras?_____

8. Was pointing clear and even?_____

9. Was eye contact with camera maintained while using cue cards?_____

10. Were cues correctly responded to?_____

11. Was dress appropriate?_____

12. Facial animation
    Appropriate?_____   Too much?_____   Too little?_____

    _____

    _____

13. Note specific areas on which to work._____

    _____

    _____

14. Note areas that showed improvement._____

    _____

    _____

SPOTLIGHT

Feature Reporting As Storytelling

"Most good stories boil down to five key elements . . . beginnings, middles, endings, main characters and simple truths." With this sparse description, KGO-TV feature reporter Wayne Freedman summarizes his approach to the creation of stories that have earned him thirty-eight Emmys, nine awards from the Associated Press, six from the United Press, and nine from the Radio and Television News Directors Association.

Freedman considers himself, first, a writer and storyteller. He began his career as a photographer in Louisville, Kentucky, but switched to reporting because "it's the best way to tell stories." As to his record number of awards, he comments "I guess it says I'm consistent. Above all, I think a newscast needs someone to remind viewers that, even with all the lunacy in this world, normal people still exist. I look for the untold story, and the person—a main character—and that person's simple truth." As a feature reporter, Wayne ignores the sensational story because his vision of reporting doesn't lend itself to hard, breaking news. Hard news is impersonal; a feature report should be the opposite.

A few of the hundreds of stories told by Wayne indicate what he looks for as a storyteller: a focus on an entertainer facing the closure of his nightclub, a child entrepreneur running a lemonade stand, a man who specializes in photographing cemetery art, and two women who worked for years, five feet apart, one inside and one outside separated by a window, who were strangers to one another. Simple stories. Simple truths.

Skill in revealing the inner person sets Freedman apart from most television reporters. He offers this advice: "You want to get ahead in television news? Then remember that, day to day, this is a business of little stories. Learn to do those well, and the big ones will fall into place because you've learned how to tap into concerns and values, not only of the people whose stories you tell, but also of those who are moved by them. Why do so many reporters make pieces so complicated? This should be an emotional medium. The path to the head runs through the gut." He adds, "You'll serve a piece better by staying out of the story's way."

Wayne believes that you shouldn't invent the story, but instead try to discover it from the inside. You'll inevitably be *in* the story, but it's your responsibility to *tell* the story without *becoming* the story. "I want to be thought of as a good writer and storyteller. I know I'm different. I try to respect the viewers and let the person in the story be the star of that story. Many feature reporters spend too much time trying to feature themselves, writing the proverbial elephant. I think the most important difference would be that beneath the surface, even the most simple story contains layers and subtleties. A good feature story is often about something other than the main subject. If I do my job exceptionally well, viewers may not remember me, but they'll remember the story—not for minutes or days, but for years."

To illustrate this point, one of Wayne's stories on the 11:00 P.M. news was about a three-legged dog. The next day, a great number of calls came to the station from people offering help. For Wayne, the dog was the surface story; the more important story lay beneath this. "People pass others daily who need help, and turn away, yet they'll rush to the aid of an animal in distress." Wayne then raised the question, "Why do we animalize humans and humanize animals?" Again, a simple story, a simple truth. Something for viewers to remember the following day and, perhaps, ponder. Maybe even act on.

Asked if his intimate stories are tough sells to news directors, Freedman replies: "Generally, they trust that if I see a story, I'll deliver a story. Call it the 'inside strike' syndrome. I've hit enough round-trippers by now that they figure I know the zone. By my standard, a story that humanizes a person is often a good, solid triple; maybe even an inside-the-park job. Very good for a five-hour turn. And off-beat stories are a lot like baseball. Don't think. Trust your instincts, your reactions, and swing."

A Day in the Life . . .

Two factors are key to understanding the unique success of Wayne Freedman. The first is his thorough preparation for, and meticulous execution of, each story. It isn't unusual for him to spend nine hours on a report that runs under five minutes.

The second is his instinct for selecting people who lend themselves to being humanized through their stories. His objective is to give viewers a reason to care. He says, "I try to do that with everything."

The following sketch provides a glimpse of the effort that goes into his making of a feature report.

The Scene: The Newsroom of KGO-TV, an ABC Affiliate

2:00 P.M. Wayne and James Sudweeks, Wayne's long-time video editor, spend an hour and a half editing material shot a week earlier. A once-popular nightclub is closing after sixty-three years. The recordings were made in advance to be run on the night of the closing. The digital tape had been logged by Wayne, and the report is now edited into a package for the 6:00 P.M. news.

3:30 P.M. Sitting at his desk, Wayne prepares a brief script. It's to be his live introduction to the report, delivered by him from the sidewalk before the club, and run on the 6:00 P.M. newscast.

4:00 P.M. Wayne goes to the nightclub where camera operator John Griffen has parked the remote truck. John has set up lights and a tripod, and has spent time looking for interesting backgrounds. After arriving, Wayne decides on the shot sequence and his on-camera movements, and then rehearses his introduction. A field monitor is placed atop the remote truck, so later Wayne will be able to watch the 6:00 P.M. news. Audio levels are set.

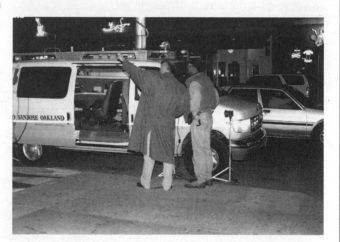

5:00 P.M. With an hour available before he's cut into the early news, Wayne and John go backstage to shoot scenes of the nightclub performers arriving, getting into their costumes, and applying their makeup. Brief comments from the performers on closing night are recorded.

6:00 P.M. All is set for the live introduction. One more rehearsal, and it's time for the stand-up.[7]

[7]A *stand-up* is a statement by a reporter directly into the camera lens. A stand-up may come at any point in a recorded story, but it nearly always closes the story.

6:15 P.M. The introduction is delivered, and the report is on the air. At the close of the package, Wayne tosses back to the station with "This is Wayne Freedman, reporting live." Wayne returns to the station and logs the recordings just made at the club for later editing.

7:30 P.M. Back at the club, hundreds of people are lined up at the ticket booth. Wayne interviews a few of them, and then conducts a lengthy conversation with one of the nightclub performers he's chosen to carry the essence of the story. The conversation isn't recorded; its purpose is to cement a relationship with the performer, to develop two-way empathy before the on-camera interview. Wayne doesn't reveal the questions he'll ask later during the interview. He wants spontaneity. When he's satisfied that he's found the right person to carry the story, he interviews the person on camera.

8:30 P.M. Back at the station, Wayne writes a script that now ties together all of the recorded elements of the piece. He enters a small

announce booth and records voice-over narration.

Wayne then moves to an editing booth and works with video editor James Sudweeks to edit the entire piece into its final form. It's then duplicated and fed into a computer.

11:15 P.M. Back in front of the nightclub, Wayne introduces the recorded report and, when it ends, he makes closing comments live. He then tosses back to the news anchors. He and John Griffen strike and stow equipment, and both enter the van for the return to the station. Wayne's workday is over.

Freedman joined KGO in 1991 after moving from CBS News, where he traveled throughout America as a feature correspondent for CBS. In his twenty years of reporting he's done general assignments, politics, and investigative reports. He began his television career in Louisville, Kentucky, took a reporting job in Dallas, Texas, and then moved to San Francisco, California's, KRON in 1981. Wayne's syndicated program *California Offbeat* is heard on Britain's Channel Four. Respected for his lectures on the craft of television news writing and reporting, Wayne's taught at stations in most of the United States, in parts of Canada, and in Europe.

Becoming a television writer and performer came naturally to Wayne. He grew up in and around television. His father, Mike, pioneered the first live hand-held camera for ABC in the late 1950s and 1960s—". . . the first guy to walk a football sideline, to go underwater, to walk a convention floor, live." Wayne's mother was a ballerina who, among other performances, danced the part of Laurie in the original cast of *Oklahoma!*

Wayne earned his bachelor's degree in political science from the University of California—Los Angeles, and graduated from the University of Missouri with a master's degree in journalism.

Photos courtesy of Wayne Freedman, John L. Griffen, James Sudweeks, and KGO-TV, San Francisco, California.

CHAPTER 7

Commercials and Public-Service Announcements

CHAPTER OUTLINE

- In-House Production of Radio Spots
- The Announcer's Role
- Analyzing and Marking Commercial Copy
  - Analyzing Structure
  - Analyzing Mood
  - Marking Commercial Copy
- Recording a Commercial in a Studio

Working with Commercials During an On-Air Shift
Character Voices
- SPOTLIGHT: Tips from a Voice-Over Pro
- Radio Public-Service Announcements
- Television Commercials

ADVERTISING IS THE LIFEBLOOD OF AMERICAN COMMERCIAL BROAD-casting. Advertising supports nearly ten thousand American radio and more than a thousand television stations; it's also the major financial support for most cable channels other than so-called premium channels.[1]

Commercial stations offer the public hundreds of hours of information and entertainment daily. Although commercials are often maligned, they sometimes are amusing; frequently provide useful information; help fuel our economy; and offer work for writers, producers, directors, audio engineers, sales personnel—and announcers. Often, commercials surprise us with their creative use of new technologies. Some commercials are so creative and engaging that reels of both radio and television commercials are bought and enjoyed by thousands. The annual CLIO Awards broadcasts, on which awards are presented to creators of outstanding television commercials, are eagerly anticipated by sizable television audiences.

Public-service announcements (PSAs) resemble commercials in some respects. Both are informational in nature and considered non-entertainment. Radio commercials generally are longer than PSAs; commercials may be fifteen to sixty seconds in length, while most PSAs are brief mentions of a nonprofit cause on a "community billboard" segment

---

[1]Approximately 2,000 noncommercial radio and nearly 500 television stations operate in the United States. Up-to-the-minute figures may be obtained from the FCC at *www.fcc.gov/mmb/asd/totals/index.html*.

of a day's programming. Radio commercials and PSAs differ considerably from those on television, so the challenges presented by the two media will be discussed separately. Note, however, that the suggestions for analyzing and marking copy apply to both.

Announcers at most commercial radio stations—whatever their announcing specialization—often combine on-air announcing duties with production of radio commercials (also referred to as **spots**).[2] The first section of this chapter explores the announcer's work with respect to radio commercials; the second discusses **PSA**s; and the last provides information on delivering television commercials.

In-House Production of Radio Spots

In major markets, most commercials run by radio stations are supplied by advertising agencies. By contrast, in smaller markets, advertising agencies may supply only 10 percent of the commercials broadcast; the other 90 percent are written and produced by station staff for local merchants. Here are common practices in smaller markets:

- A station sales representative (or an announcer in some cases) sells time to a client and obtains essential information about the nature of the business and specific objectives of the spot. The station representative enters the details on a standard information form and later transfers these data to a **fact sheet** to be turned over to a sales manager. Few small radio stations employ full-time continuity writers, so they usually assign script development to management personnel, time sellers, announcers, or production specialists. When the spot has been written, it is given to a producer, often an announcer, who works from the script to produce a commercial. The producer adds such embellishments as a **music bed** (recorded instrumental music), sound effects, voices, and other available elements that seem appropriate. On-air announcers almost always provide the voiced portion of such spots. At larger stations, full-time account executives sell time and write and produce commercials, often using station announcers as talent.

---

[2]Major market television announcers may also be involved in the production of commercials, especially in voice-over work.

- A merchant comes to the station to deliver a commercial, and the commercial is recorded for later editing, which may include special audio effects and music. The final version is stored on a storage device such as a hard disk.
- A merchant is recorded on location at the merchant's place of business, such as an auto dealership or a furniture store. Post-production includes the same possibilities as those listed for in-studio recordings.

The Announcer's Role

Most radio announcers deliver commercials as part of a job that includes other duties, such as music announcing (DJ work), traffic reporting, sportscasting, or performing as talk-show hosts. Some staff announcers, particularly DJs on highly rated stations, receive extra payment beyond their salaries—performance fees—if they can perform well as commercial announcers. Many staff announcers earn additional money by doing freelance work at professional recording studios. These announcers are represented by talent agencies and are hired through them by advertising agencies.[3]

More than 90 percent of commercials broadcast by radio stations are recorded before they're broadcast. However, as an announcer, you may have to read some commercials live, with very little time to study the copy. As a professional, you'll be expected to sight-read without stumbling or misreading. Sight-reading in an authoritative and convincing manner is difficult. Take advantage of any spare moments to look over the copy you're given to read—even if this means arriving for work earlier than scheduled. Remember to read the copy aloud when practicing.

Many commercials written and produced for local clients are straightforward catalogings of items, prices, phone numbers, and other basic information, and such commercials give you little opportunity to "showboat." Your challenge is to read unfamiliar copy in such a way as to capture and hold the attention of listeners, while delivering a message that "sells" a product or service. In many respects, reading straight informational copy effectively is the greatest announcing challenge of all.

A key to success in delivering commercials is taking time to **wood-shed** your copy—*woodshedding* is a long-standing radio term that

---

[3]National radio and television networks prohibit news anchors and reporters from performing in commercials.

means *reading, rehearsing aloud,* and *marking copy.* You'll record most of your commercials before they're broadcast, and this will grant you several moments to analyze and mark your copy before recording it. However, the sheer volume of commercials for a wide range of products and services will present you with multiple challenges to sound fresh, interested, and convincing as you interpret your scripts. Working for variety in delivery to give each commercial a unique sound without abandoning your distinctive style and individuality is a formidable challenge. Your best option is to adopt a mental attitude that allows you to concentrate completely on the spot before you at any specific moment. Imagine that the spot you're working on is the only spot that exists. Don't think about commercials you've already done or those ahead of you, or you'll be overwhelmed. Take it one step at a time.

If you're fortunate enough to work for a classical music station, a low-key FM station, or any station that limits the number of commercials, your opportunities to be effective are greatly improved. Take advantage of such ideal working conditions to spend more time woodshedding. The results will benefit you, your station, your client, and your listeners.

Analyzing and Marking Commercial Copy[4]

Chapter 2 presents analyses of several types of broadcast copy, including commercials. Because both structure and mood must be communicated effectively in sixty seconds or less, commercials present a unique challenge. You'll be better able to meet this challenge if you've analyzed and marked your copy.

Analyzing Structure

An important consideration is the *structure* of a commercial. Most outstanding commercials are both subtle and complex. Chapter 2 provides many points in the analysis of structure; the discussion here adds one more consideration—the **rule of three**. This long-recognized principle says that the sharpness and punch of one's comments are diluted by going beyond three words or phrases in a given sequence. To demonstrate the rule of three, the following three commercials are analyzed.

---

[4]This section on marking copy assumes that you're working alone, without benefit of a producer or director. When working under a supervisor, you'll be expected to analyze and mark copy according to a mutually agreed on vision.

AGENCY: Ketchum Advertising, San Francisco
CLIENT: The Potato Board
PRODUCT: Potatoes
TITLE: "Versatile"
LENGTH: 60 seconds

ANNCR: Here's another message from the Potato Board. Don't we American's love food? Fast food . . . slow food . . . all kinds? But, above all, don't we love that good food—the potato? Today, the potato stands alone as the number one vegetable of versatility. And our friends at the Potato Board remind us that Americans crave potatoes in any and every form, for every meal. Why, Americans love potatoes as appetizers, in soups and salads, as entrees and side dishes, and . . . yes . . . even as desserts. The Potato Board says any way you serve the all-American potato, you'll be getting an economical vegetable that has lots of nutrition, but not—I repeat not—lots of calories. So, whether you serve potatoes scalloped, hashed, or mashed . . . sliced or diced . . . French fried, boiled, or baked, in all their delicious versatility, the Potato Board says potatoes are America's favorite vegetable. Well, aren't they in your house?

Note that in this commercial the first grouping of three comes early: "Fast food . . . slow food . . . all kinds?" Also note that the first three sentences (beginning with "Here's another" and ending with "the potato?") form a complete expository unit and should be read so as to give a sense of a beginning, a middle, and an ending—though not so obvious an ending as to make what follows seem tacked on.

The next set of three is less obvious. Here are the three parts of this segment of the Potato Board commercial.

1. "Why, Americans love potatoes as appetizers"
2. "in soups and salads"
3. "as entrees and side dishes"

Then comes what seems to be a fourth element, "and . . . yes . . . even as desserts," but the ellipses indicate that this is to be set apart from the preceding sequence of three by a pause. These words become a group of three in themselves if you pause slightly between each word—"even . . . as . . . desserts." In analyzing and marking this copy, you should not see "appetizers," "soups," "salads," "entrees," "side dishes," and "desserts" as six points receiving equal stress.

The final set of three consists of the phrases "scalloped, hashed, or mashed," "sliced or diced," and "French fried, boiled, or baked." Two of the three phrases in this sequence are made up of three units each.

Now consider another outstanding commercial, which requires a British accent. This Schweppes commercial has a Monty Python quality, and you should enjoy it as an exercise in mock disdain. Be sure to avoid a Cockney dialect—it calls for your best Oxonian accent.

AGENCY: Ammirati & Puris, Inc.
CLIENT: Schweppes
LENGTH: 60 seconds

ANNCR: (BRITISH ACCENT) I have before me a bottle of Schweppes Bitter Lemon. The soft drink loved by half of England. We British love the way it looks: a fine, sophisticated mist, with morsels of crushed whole lemon. We love the way it sounds: (BOTTLE OPENS) a particularly masterful rendering of Schweppes cheeky little bubbles. And we especially love the way it tastes: (POURS) refreshingly brisk, cultivatedly crisp and thoroughly Schweppervescent. It's no wonder that Bitter Lemon is adored by half of England. Now, what about the other half, you might ask? The half that doesn't adore Bitter Lemon? Well, let me assure you, they're all whining children, grubby little urchins whose opinion is completely and totally insignificant. They

are youthful upstarts and, as such, absolutely incapable of appreci-

ating anything as forthrightly crisp as Bitter Lemon. The frightfully

grown-up soft drink from Schweppes. The Great British Bubbly.

The first 60 percent of this commercial is to be read in a precise, dignified, and restrained manner. Then, beginning with "Now, what about the other half," you must begin to build in emotion, intensity, volume, and rate of delivery. As you reach the end of the third-to-last sentence, begin decelerating on "as forthrightly crisp as Bitter Lemon." The last two sentences should see you returning to the dignified mood with which you began.

Note how this copy applies the rule of three. The first group is

1. "We British love the way it looks"
2. "We love the way it sounds"
3. "We especially love the way it tastes"

Near the middle is this sequence of three:

1. "refreshingly brisk"
2. "cultivatedly crisp"
3. "thoroughly Schweppervescent"

Then, finally, the children are

1. "whining children"
2. "grubby little urchins"
3. "youthful upstarts"

Dialogue on television commercials often follows the rule of three, but because the visual element usually overshadows the words to be spoken, the principle isn't as obvious as it is in radio scripts. The following television commercial for Du Pont—one of the most moving commercials ever produced—does show use of the rule of three.[5] (Note: VO is the abbreviation for *voice-over.*)

---

[5]Bernice Kanner, in her book *The 100 Best TV Commercials . . . And Why They Worked,* selected this spot as one of her favorites, and added this comment: "Demby, intended as a short-term corporate ID, became a corporate image spot and ran for two years. It attracted the attention and interest of key business prospects while changing people's perceptions about Du Pont."

AGENCY: BBDO
SPONSOR: Du Pont
TITLE: Seattle Foot

VIDEO	AUDIO
A YOUNG MAN LIMPS TO AN URBAN SCHOOLYARD WHERE A BASKETBALL GAME IS IN PROGRESS	**ANNCR:** (VO) When Bill Demby was in Vietnam he used to dream of coming home and playing a little basketball with the guys. That dream all but died when he lost two legs to a Vietcong rocket.
DEMBY ARRIVES AT THE SCHOOLYARD WHERE FRIENDS GREET HIM. AS HE SITS ON A BENCH TO REMOVE HIS SWEAT-PANTS, THE CAMERA PANS TO A TEAMMATE GLANCING SIDE-WAYS AT HIS LEGS: PROSTHETIC LIMBS.	**ANNCR:** (VO) But then a group of researchers discovered that a remarkable plastic from Du Pont could help make artificial

limbs that were more resilient, more flexible, more like life itself.

DEMBY GOES FOR A SHOT, FALLS, AND SOFTLY GROANS. BUT HE REFUSES HELP AND PULLS HIM- SELF UP AS IF HE HAD LEGS OF FLESH AND BONE.

ANNCR: (VO) Thanks to these efforts, Bill Demby is back. And some say he hasn't lost his step. At Du Pont, we make the things that make a difference.

FRIEND: Hey Bill, you've been practicing.

SUPER: DU PONT, BETTER THINGS FOR BETTER LIVING.

ANNCR: (VO) Better things for better living.

The first group of three is "more resilient, more flexible, more like life itself." The second group follows:

"Thanks to these efforts Bill Demby is back."
"And some say he hasn't lost his step."
"At Du Pont, we make the things that make a difference."

And, had Du Pont retained the slogan it used for many years, the tag line would also have reflected the rule of three: "Better things, for better living, through chemistry. When analyzing copy, always look for *structure* as revealed by the *parts*.

Advertising Age magazine hosts a web site that includes insightful and often devastating reviews of current commercials. It may be accessed at this URL[6]:

www.adage.com/news_and_features/ad_review/index.html

For a complete, updated list of URLs for this textbook, please see the text home site available at *www.hmco.com/college.*

Analyzing Mood

Read the following two commercials and the brief analyses that follow them; then practice them aloud, attempting to project clearly differentiated moods. (Note: UP means the volume is raised; UNDER means the volume is lowered or fades.)

AGENCY: Yamashiro Associates
CLIENT: Webster's Department Stores
LENGTH: 60 seconds

ANNCR: Webster's has you in mind!

MUSIC: UP-TEMPO INSTRUMENTAL, UP AND UNDER

ANNCR: Webster's announces the sale of the year! Up to one-half off on thousands of items! Arrow and Van Heusen mens' shirts. 50 percent off. All shoes in stock, one-third off. One dollar above our cost for men's three-piece, all-wool suits. Save dollars on neckties, belts,

---

[6]The Internet is changing constantly as new web sites are added and old web sites are abandoned. The URL listings in this textbook should be regarded as samples of the kinds of material available rather than as a stable index. If you seek a web site using one of these URLs and cannot connect, enter the key words for the topic into a search engine to find a site that may provide the information you want.

socks, and sport shirts. In the women's department, one-third to one-half off on designer pants, blouses, and blazers. Entire dress inventory reduced by 50 percent. Even homewares are going at all-time low prices. Rag rugs from India—were $69, now only $39. Bath and beach towels, all prices cut in half. Fifty-piece stainless tableware, down by one-third. All radios, portable TVs, and home recorders, just dollars above our cost. Now's the time to take advantage of low, low prices, while enjoying the traditional high value of Webster's! Three stores to serve you. Sorry, at these prices, no free delivery and no layaways. Come see us today. Webster's has you in mind! Webster's, where you'll save dollars, with no sacrifice of quality!

AGENCY: Ketchum Advertising
CLIENT: Lindsay Olives
LENGTH: 60 seconds

MUSIC: FRIENDLY MUSIC IN BACKGROUND

ANNCR: (FRIENDLY OLIVE) Hi! Hi! How are ya? Good. I'm Ted. I'm a friendly olive. In fact, most of my true-blue friends are olives, too. Yeah, yeah, sure they are. Now, my friends are all mature—strictly high-quality guys. That's why they're Lindsay Olives. We were all very close friends on our branch. We did everything together: soaked up the sun, talked to the girl olives, read the classics. Yeah. Honest. We read the classics. I told you we were high-quality olives. Well, one day the Lindsay picker came for the final inspection. He took all my friends, but rejected me. He said I had a bruise. Yeah, a bruise. I don't know how I got it—but I got it. We all argued, but the inspector wouldn't take a flawed olive for Lindsay. Well, I was quite upset. Upset! 'Cause I knew some day I'd end up like this in some obscure can of olives, and all my pals would be Lindsays.

ANNCR: (FEMALE VOICE) An olive is just an olive, unless it's a Lindsay.

ANNCR: (FRIENDLY OLIVE) Hey, you look friendly. Let's have lunch sometime.

Note the striking difference of mood in these two examples. The first, for Webster's, is designed to hold attention through vitality and the illusion of importance. Every effort is made to encourage direct and rapid action from the listener. The second commercial, for Lindsay Olives, is light, humorous, and wistful. Both pieces contain the same number of words (182) and therefore must be read rather rapidly. Be careful not to turn the Lindsay Olive spot into a hard-sell commercial.

 Television commercial copy may be obtained on the Internet at this URL:

www.tvtp.simplenet.com/

See the note about this web site in Chapter 6, p. 162.

For a complete, updated list of URLs for this textbook, please see the text home site available at *www.hmco.com/college.*

Marking Commercial Copy

Once you analyze the structure and mood, you mark the commercial copy. As a DJ or news anchor recording commercials prior to your air shift, you'll have little time for **marking copy**, but you should do so whenever possible. As a freelance announcer working in a recording studio, you'll be expected to mark your copy both before and during each recording session.

This copy for Middlesex Bank was marked by a freelance voice-over announcer after he arrived at the recording studio. Read it aloud according to the marks made for pauses and stresses. One virgule (/) means a brief pause; two virgules(//) mean a longer pause. One line under a word means stress; two lines indicate fairly heavy stress. Note that since this is a **soft-sell commercial**, even your heaviest stress should be consistent with the mood and style of the piece. (SFX is the abbreviation for *sound effects*; SEGUE means to transition directly from one section or theme to another.)

AGENCY: Ingalls Associates, Inc.
CLIENT: Middlesex Bank
SUBJECT: Home Improvement Loans
LENGTH: 60 seconds

SFX: CHILLING WIND SOUNDS UP AND UNDER

VO: This harsh and untimely interruption of summer/is brought to you by/Middlesex Bank. As a reminder that this summer is no time to forget about/next winter.

SFX: STORM SOUNDS UP AND UNDER

VO: The heating. Those storm windows. That leaking ventilation system. If your house could use a little winterizing, summer is the time to do it. Because right now, the prices are right. And/right now, Middlesex Bank is standing by, ready with a home improvement loan.//We interrupt this interruption of winter/with summer.

SFX: SEGUE FROM STORM TO SPLASHES OF SWIMMING POOL

VO: As a reminder, that with <u>gas</u> prices the way they are, you might

even consider turning your house into a <u>summer</u> place . . ./*/*/

by putting in a <u>swimming pool</u>. No matter what part of your home

you'd like to improve, we've got a <u>Home Improvement Loan</u> to help

you do it. We're <u>Middlesex</u>. The Little <u>Big</u> Bank.

Now read the following commercial and note how it was marked
during a recording session. Also observe how it follows the rule of three.

AGENCY: Allen and Dorward
CLIENT: New Century Beverage Company
LENGTH: 60 seconds

ANNCR: Wherever you go in San Francisco (SFX: FOG HORNS), the executive

bistros (MUSIC: CONTEMPORARY)/ in the bustling <u>financial district</u>,

the elegant homes of <u>Pacific Heights and Sea Cliff</u>, or the lavish

rooms of the major hotels, you'll hear the inviting sound of

<u>Schweppervescence</u>.///(SFX: HISS AND POUR) That curiously refresh-

ing sound when the mixer meets the ice, is an <u>irresistible</u> call to

<u>pleasure</u>./And whether you're pouring Schweppes Tonic Water, Club

Soda, or Ginger Ale, the sound is the same.///(SFX: HISS AND POUR)

But <u>each</u> has a <u>taste</u> all its own. You'll find the unchanging quality

of Schweppervescence <u>immediately</u> apparent in the company of

kindred spirits or/straightaway. That <u>curiously</u> refreshing sensation

found only in Schweppes that makes your drink <u>so</u> extraordinary.

San Franciscans are not alone in their refreshing appreciation of

Schweppes, for Schweppes Mixers are accepted around the world by those with a taste for quality. The great taste of Schweppes Mixers cannot be silenced. (SFX: HISS AND POUR) Tonic Water, Club Soda, Ginger Ale. Listen to the sound of Schweppervescence. Call for Schweppes. Curiously refreshing since 1783. (SFX: FADE OUT HISS)

Recording a Commercial in a Studio

As a voice-over commercial announcer, you'll be hired through your agent by an advertising agency. Normally a commercial recording studio will be rented, along with the services of an audio engineer. Usually your script will be faxed to you, so you'll have time to study it. At the studio, a producer or sometimes the writer will discuss the spot in general terms—the overall mood, the characterization expected of you, and so forth. You'll have a few minutes to further study, analyze, and mark your copy. Be sure to bring pencils and erasers.

Despite the analyzing and marking you've done just before the recording session, be prepared to make changes during the ten, twenty, or more takes that are necessary before the person producing the commercial is satisfied. A typical recording setup for a radio commercial requires from three to five persons: one or two announcers, an agency producer, an audio engineer, and, sometimes, the writer of the commercial. Music is recorded in advance and added by the engineer.

As each take is recorded, the producer or writer gives instructions to the announcer regarding changes to be made to eliminate awkward phrases, to delete or alter sentences with too many sibilant sounds (i.e., "that's because Bonnie's citrus scouts search the finest orange groves"), to change the emphasis of words or phrases, and, most often, to delete words or short phrases to conform to time limits. The producer or writer may also offer suggestions for interpreting the copy. The producer will inform an announcer who's going too fast or too slow, is mispronouncing a word, or is slurring or having some other articulation problem. The writer (if the writer isn't also the producer) will decide what words to change or cut. As the announcer, you're expected to follow all instructions without comment or argument.

Not all agency representatives are competent in coaching performers. Some will give you vague instructions such as "give me more,"

"bright and perky," or "try it another way." As a freelance voice-over performer, you'll work with many different producers. Some will be able to give you clear and helpful directions, others will be vague or confusing. There may be times when you'd like to offer suggestions, and to do so is appropriate if you're confident that the producer feels secure and is open to your ideas. Be very careful when attempting to offer suggestions for changes in commercial copy. Remember that even constructive suggestions from you may be considered unwelcome by some agency writers and producers.

Not all aspects of commercial recording are standardized, but you'll soon learn what's expected of you. In some instances, for example, if you stumble or slur a word, you're expected to pause, say "pickup," pause again, and begin reading from the beginning of the sentence in which you stumbled.[7] This practice makes it easy for the audio engineer

---

[7]The term **pickup** is used in at least two other ways in voice-over work. A **pickup session** is a recording session in which specific lines, recorded during an earlier session, have been judged unusable and must be recorded again. *Pickup* also refers to picking up one's cue—in other words, speaking more closely on the heels of a line delivered by another performer.

to edit the recording. In other operations you'll begin again at the very opening of the spot.

Working with Commercials During an On-Air Shift

As an announcer on a music, news, or talk-radio station, you'll likely record some commercials *before* your regular on-air shift, working in a small production studio to engineer, deliver the lines of the commercials, mix your voice track over a music bed, and record the mixed spot on a hard disk or on digital audiotape (DAT). Later, during your shift, you'll play these along with spots recorded by other staff members as well as commercials sent by advertising agencies. You'll play the commercials in the order given by your station's **traffic** or **continuity department**, which is responsible for scheduling commercials. A large station will maintain a log, most likely stored on a hard disk, that shows on a display screen the commercials, jingles, station IDs, and promos to be played during your shift, and the times at which each is to be broadcast. The commercials themselves are stored on another hard disk and can be summoned by using the computerized workstation next to your audio console.

In a technologically less up-to-date station, you might have a printed log and a **copy book**, sometimes called a **continuity book**. The traffic department will prepare seven such books weekly, one for each day of the week. Each book will contain, in order of presentation, commercial copy for spots that are taped or are on mass-storage hard disks. You merely keep track of the sequential placement of the commercials by entering a mark on the program log as you punch up each commercial and send each out over the air at times stipulated in the log. A turn of the page brings you to the next commercial.

If you work at a station that still works with both carted and live commercials, the on-air procedures are more complex. The commercial copy of your entire shift will have been logged by the traffic department, and you'll have a copy of that log. The log indicates the order of the commercials, whether a given commercial is recorded or is to be read live, the cart number for carted commercials, and the time each commercial is to be broadcast. If your station has a tight format, the times will be precise; if the format is casual and relaxed, the times will be approximate.

At stations where limited budgets dictate fewer staff members, there often is only one copy book. Commercials are inserted alphabetically by sponsor name. The program log contains an entry such as "live #4,

Malagani Tires" or "cart #23, Red Boy Pizza." The first of these examples indicates that you should look up the Malagani copy, commercial number 4, in the alphabetically arranged copy book and read it at the appropriate time. The second indicates that, because you're working combo, you should locate cart number 23 and play it at the correct time.

Commercials with a script and a recorded portion are often **cart with live tag**. This phrase means that the commercial begins with the playing of the cart, which may be only a jingle or music with recorded speech, and the station announcer comes in at the end to provide a tag that gives local or extra information, such as the current price or a local phone number. In other practices, the recorded portion of such commercials may begin with a brief jingle and then fade under while the announcer reads the entire sales pitch. **Donut commercials** are similar. A jingle opens the spot, the music fades down for a pitch by the announcer, and then the music is faded up just as the announcer completes the message. The term *donut* arose because music begins and ends such a commercial, with the announcer filling in the middle. Both cart with live tag and donut commercials usually are recorded by staff announcers and are dubbed to a hard disk or other storage equipment.

Figure 7.2

Popular music announcer Carter B. Smith stands as he reads a commercial. He knows that both his posture and his performance are improved by standing. *Courtesy of Carter B. Smith and KABL, San Francisco–Oakland, California.*

In working with commercials that are part live and part recorded, it's necessary to develop split-second timing. A script for a cart with live tag follows:

CLIENT: Bellach's Furniture
LENGTH: 60 seconds
TYPE: Cart with live tag

CART #: L-66

BEGIN: 8/12

JINGLE: (5)

VOICE: "Chicago's newest shopping mall"

CART CLOSE
AND TAG CUE

VOICE: "Open Tuesdays 'til nine."

SFX: (1)

TAG IN AT: (45)

LIVE TAG: Visit the home furnishings display at Bellach's. Fine leather sofas and lounge chairs are on sale at 25% off! Bedroom sets by Heritage now marked down a full 30%! Lamps, end tables, occasional chairs, and desks—all on sale at prices you have to see to believe! Bellach's, at the Stonestown Mall!

How do you work from this script? First, you must understand the symbols used. The numbers following CART # identify the particular cart to be played. BEGIN: 8/12 gives the starting date for air play. JINGLE: (5) identifies the specific music identification cart to be played. CART CLOSE means that at this point, the recorded portion of the spot concludes. TAG CUE and VOICE indicate that the last line of the recorded portion is "Open Tuesdays 'til nine." SFX: (1) identifies the sound effects cut to be played. TAG IN AT: (45) tells you to begin the closing live tag 45 seconds into the commercial, which gives you 15 seconds to read the tag. In practicing this commercial, use a stopwatch and work until you're able to read the tag in exactly 15 seconds.

Most radio production and announce booths are equipped with a mounted stopwatch or an electronic digital clock that can be programmed to show elapsed time or remaining time. When performing commercials, whether delivered live or recorded, time is important. Use a stopwatch or clock each time you practice. Time is what radio stations sell, and clients expect precisely what they pay for.

Character Voices

Despite the exceptions noted in the Spotlight discussion in Chapter 4, Standard American English has been the accepted manner of speaking by both men and women announcers since the beginning of radio broadcasting in the United States. However, broadcasters have also used foreign accents, regional dialects, and character voices in some dramas and in a great many commercials. If you have a good ear for speech sounds and find that you're able to perform competently while using a character voice, you may want to develop a number of dialect specializations, especially if you intend to become a freelance performer of commercials.

Saturday morning children's television shows make use of character voices in animated program material and commercials. The types of voices used in both include pretend animal voices (such as that of Barney), monsters, aliens from other planets, and superheroes and heroines, to name a few.

 More information on character voices, as well as practice copy, may be found on the text web site:

www.hmco.com/college/communication/index.htm

Tips from a Voice-Over Pro

When it comes to voice-over, Voicetrax founder Samantha Paris has done it all. Her credits include more than a thousand national and regional commercials, major roles in nearly two hundred animated television cartoon shows, three CLIO Awards for outstanding commercial performance, and the National Gabriel Award for public-service announcements. Samantha Paris also narrates corporate-industrial and documentary films, provides character voices for CD-ROM and interactive games, teaches voice-over performance to students, and, on occasion, loops a voice for a theatrical feature film. All of this is in addition to founding and supervising Voicetrax, a training academy and placement service for those preparing for careers as voice-over performers.

From her home in Northern California, minutes away from San Francisco, Samantha spends her days doing the things she loves within this industry: teaching, directing, casting, and running her two businesses—Voicetrax, Inc., and Voicetrax Casting. Both are housed in the same location in Sausalito and have grown rapidly since 1991, when they opened. Voicetrax is the most comprehensive voice-over training facility in the country, offering nearly eighty introductory lectures, workshops, and seminars throughout the year, seven days a week, with cutting-edge instruction from top San Francisco and Los Angeles producers, agents, and directors.

Now entering her twenty-fifth year in the industry, Samantha attributes her success to years of hard work. Knowing from a young age that this was the profession she wanted to pursue, she began taking voice-over lessons at age fifteen for four evenings a week. While the rest of her high school peers were socializing after school, Samantha was immersed in her lessons, spending extra hours each week practicing. This early training has been invaluable and has carried her through many high-pressure situations: how to size up a piece of copy in seconds; how to make instant decisions about character and moods; and how to adapt her voice quality and personality for any situation. At age seventeen—two years after she began her training—she started auditioning for voice-over work as well as throwing her hat in the on-camera arena, auditioning for television commercials, episodic television, and feature films.

Although she was quite successful in these mediums, there was one major obstacle overshadowing her—the pain of rejection. "For every job I landed, there were twenty that I didn't get. I was constantly focusing on those and feeling like I wasn't enough." So at age twenty-three she decided to take a break and became a voice-over agent. After six months of directing other actors and promoting their voices, she quickly realized that not only were there many enormously talented actors out there but that she was one of them! Not landing a role didn't have anything to do with a *lack* of talent, it was just a matter of who they (the producer or client) would *select.* It was with that revelation that Paris returned to her acting career focusing solely on voice-over and became one of the nation's top voice-over artists. "There were lots and lots of tears back then" she says, "but you can't give up. If you want it badly enough, you've just got to believe that you're good, and you can't give up . . . Sometimes it's painful, but you've just got to stay with it and keep the faith. When you're first study-ing, you can't be looking down the road, wondering, 'Well, how long is it going to take?' You have to love what you're doing, and just enjoy the journey."

This is the philosophy Samantha instills in the students and professionals who come through the doors at Voicetrax. The following are some suggestions she offers to help performers achieve their highest potential:

- Read, read, read aloud. Use anything from actual scripts to newspaper articles, or if you're interested in character work for cartoons and CD-ROMs, start by putting voices to the comics in newspapers. Do not record and play back your performances on your own. Concentrate on your work, and rely on qualified teachers and coaches to judge your taped performances. We all sound pretty bad to our own ears.

- Always have a clear picture of who you are, to whom you're talking, and where you are. Make sure that each listener feels that you're talking only to her or him.

- Choose an *attitude* before you choose a *character.* Characterization comes only af-ter all other decisions as to purpose, place, mood, nature of listener, and so forth have been made. The decision about attitude must be precise: *motherly* is not the same as *caring; caring* is not the same as *neighborly; neighborly* is not the same as *friendly.*

- It isn't nearly enough to decide that in your performance you will be, for example, a middle-aged mother. You have to go deeper than that. As a mother, how do you feel about the child you are addressing? Are you talking to one child or two? How old are the children? How old are you? What is the setting in which you speak to the children?

- When you're given a technical direction such as "I want you to really punch that word," make sure that your attempt to carry out the instruction fits your attitude and character. Make it believable.

- Techniques eventually come into play. For example, emphasis can be accomplished by intonation, by pauses before and after the words of importance, by a break in delivery, or by a change in rhythm or volume. However, before you even think about such techniques, make sure to establish your attitude, your objectives, and your character.

Voice-over actress and teacher Samantha Paris demonstrates how to convey specific moods when interpreting commercial copy. Note that she uses nonverbal communication, even though her audience cannot see her. *Courtesy of Samantha Paris.*

Radio Public-Service Announcements

Nearly all commercial broadcast stations provide free time for **public-service announcements (PSAs)**. A public-service announcement is a message promoting a nonprofit agency such as the Red Cross, Mothers Against Drunk Driving (MADD), or the United Negro College Fund, or local, state, or federal government programs, such as the National Crime Prevention Council, the Federal Highway Administration, or the National Safety Council. These may be read live by a local announcer, may be recorded in-house by staff announcers for later playing, or may come on CDs prepared by an institution such as the Advertising Council.

Most broadcast stations limit PSAs to organizations that are tax exempt, as defined by the Internal Revenue Service. Despite deregulation, nearly all radio stations continue to carry PSAs. Along with the tradition of community service on the part of broadcasters, station managers know that the goodwill of community members is important to the success of the station.

Some announcements of community interest are paid for by local merchants who realize that their interests are served by supporting important local causes. These are not truly PSAs, because PSAs are broadcast without charge, but except for the mention of the sponsor, these read like PSAs. Such a sponsored announcement will be broadcast during any daypart the sponsor pays for, because it's treated like a commercial. Here's an announcement paid for by a brake and tire service:

ANNCR:

Brandon's Brake and Tire reminds you that, with the opening of the school year, it's extra important to keep alert on the road. A child often forgets all the safety rules that are taught by parents and teachers. Drive carefully and cautiously, and be prepared to stop in a hurry if you see a ball bounce into the street—a child may be right behind it. As adults, we need to do some thinking for children. This message is brought to you by Brandon's Brake and Tire, Clement and 14th Streets, in Madison.

Although PSAs and commercials have much in common, PSAs tend to be shorter, some constituting only a brief mention on a community billboard feature. PSAs seldom are augmented by elaborate production, such as music and sound effects. In addition, PSAs are more likely to be broadcast during off hours—those times of the day that are least attractive to advertisers.

Other important differences lie in the objectives and in the motivational devices used. Many commercials present rational arguments to sell a product or a service, such as a spot for a supermarket that lists the weekend specials. Other commercials are designed to arouse the emotions of fear, greed, or insecurity. Public-service announcements should avoid such tactics. Fear, greed, and insecurity are basic human emotions, and it's rather easy to exploit them. A campaign for famine relief or one to save the whales should indeed appeal to basic human emotions, but the producers of PSAs for such causes traditionally avoid emotional overkill. Because of these considerations, you should give PSAs an unadorned, straightforward delivery in nearly all instances.

At a prosperous large-market station, the PSAs you're to read will be neatly typed, duplicated, and placed in your copy book. You may read some PSAs during a broadcast, but more often, you'll record them, along with commercials, as part of your production duties. In smaller markets, PSAs will come to you in a variety of ways. Where there's a staff member assigned to public affairs, PSAs may be typed on 3-inch-by-5-inch index cards. At regular intervals you'll read two or three of the brief messages as a **community calendar.** The following is typical:

MISSION HOSPITAL
OUT[8]: APR. 5

The Sunrise Unit of Mission Hospital will present the film *Chalk Talk*

and a discussion on alcoholism on April 5th, 6:30 P.M., at the hospi-

tal. Info: 555-9333.

Figure 7.3

Jerry Dean ad-libs public-service announcements from notes. He is an authority on all types of jazz, and uses soft jazz background music as a "bed" behind his voice. *Courtesy of Jerry Dean.*

---

[8]OUT means that the spot should be played as scheduled, but "pulled" or "killed" on the day of the event.

At times, you may have to ad-lib an announcement based on a fact sheet such as this:

Dixie School
1818 Morgan Drive
Outland, MI

Dear Friends:

I'd appreciate having this announcement read on your Community

Billboard:

Parental Stress Workshop

Wednesday, February 24

Dixie School, Room 23

- Child Care   • Refreshments

Thank you!
Janice Decker

Here are some suggestions for practicing the delivery of radio commercials and PSAs:

- Practice reading aloud and recording ten-, twenty-, thirty-, and sixty-second commercials as well as ten-, twenty-, and thirty-second PSAs, always working with a stopwatch. Listen carefully to playbacks. Ask yourself: Does this voice please me? Does the delivery hold my attention? Does the meaning come through? Is the rate of delivery too fast or too slow? Is there variety in pitch, rate, and emphasis? And, most importantly, am I sold on the product or the cause?
- As you practice ad-libbing PSAs from brief fact sheets, try to convey the essential information in ten seconds.
- Produce and record a commercial that requires sound effects, music, and dramatization.

- Ask a radio station or advertising agency for copies of recorded donut commercials, complete with copies of the scripts, and practice with the commercials until your timing becomes razor sharp.

Appendix A includes several public-service announcements to provide you with opportunities for practice. Additional PSAs may be found on our web site.

Television Commercials

Most television commercials differ from radio commercials in several ways. They're usually briefer than most radio commercials; running from fifteen to thirty seconds, they use music and sound effects more often; and they are almost never performed live. Because television is a visual medium, most advertisers want to show their products or services, and as a result, the majority of television commercials feature voice-over narration. The face of a television commercial announcer seldom appears on the screen, unless that person is a famous actor, singer, or dancer. Even in commercials that show an announcer, the appearance is usually confined to a few moments of introduction at the beginning.

These comments don't apply to two types of television commercials: those on "shopping channels," such as QVC, and program-length commercials, known as *infomercials*. Hosts on **shopping channels** make lengthy pitches for products shown to viewers, and they mix their sales presentations with interviews and information on the quantity of pictured items that remain. Hosts also engage in chatty conversations with viewers who call in to say hello or to praise some product they purchased previously. Shopping hosts also interview jewelry or clothing designers who appear as guests.

Infomercials typically are half-hour sales pitches, with two or more announcers demonstrating such products as exercise machines, hair restorers, cooking equipment, fishing equipment, and beauty aids. Studio audiences sometimes are included in these programs. Both shopping channel and infomercial announcers speak ad-lib and are expected to know a great deal about the products they promote.

Aside from these lengthy television commercial presentations, most commercials are brief, and almost without exception, they are recorded. As a television commercial announcer for pitches of thirty seconds or

Figure 7.4

Program hosts on shopping channels must ad-lib for extended periods of time about the products offered. From left to right, Colleen Lopez and Suzanne Somers appear on air at HSN to sell Suzanne's jewelry line. *Courtesy of the Home Shopping Network, and Suzanne Somers.*

fewer, you'll have time to prepare and discuss interpretation with a copywriter or agency producer. Recording and re-recording—seemingly without end—will give you a margin of safety.

Television commercials reach the air by processes similar to those for radio commercials. Advertising agencies provide some commercials, almost always on tape. Some are produced by nearby production companies and sent to stations by courier. Others are produced by a station's retail services unit and are played on that station and then dubbed and sent to other stations. If you're an announcer specializing in television commercials, you'll most likely receive your assignments through a talent agency. You'll perform in one of these settings: a sound recording studio (for voice-over commercials), a television station studio, a video or film studio, or the field, with a remote crew.

Many television commercials that appear to be locally produced actually originate in major production centers and are offered to local merchants as cooperative commercials. A **cooperative commercial** is one for which a national advertiser pays the cost of production and then shares the expense of broadcast with a local merchant. The bulk of such a commercial arrives on tape at the local station or local production house, where a closing tag on behalf of the local merchant is added. The following is a script for a cooperative commercial produced by Serta. (Note: SUPER is short for *superimposition*, a picture or slide shown over another picture on a television screen.)

AGENCY: Allen and Dorward
CLIENT: Breuner's
PRODUCT: Serta Mattresses
LENGTH: 60 seconds

VIDEO	AUDIO
	MUSIC UNDER
WOMAN TOSSING AND TURNING IN A TRAIN SLEEPING COMPARTMENT	SHE: I want my Serta!
	ANNCR: (VO) Here's why people want their Serta—why they're spoiled for any other mattress— Only Serta goes beyond just
ANNOUNCER STANDING NEXT TO SERTA MATTRESS	being firm, beyond what others do.
SUPER: SERTA PERFECT SLEEPER	We top our support with the extra comfortable Serta surface—
SHOTS OF COILS AND TOP SURFACE	a unique difference you can feel in a Serta Perfect Sleeper.

ART CARD: SERTA LOGO	**BREUNER'S ANNCR:** (VO) Save
"I WANT MY SERTA"	50% off original prices on the
	clearance of all Serta Perfect
PERFECT SLEEPER HOTEL 50%	Sleeper Hotel sleep sets, with no
OFF (DISSOLVE) NO PAYMENTS	payments 'til November!
UNTIL NOVEMBER (DISSOLVE)	
BREUNER'S FINE HOME	
FURNISHINGS SINCE 1856	

If you work as a radio or television announcer, you may pick up extra money by freelancing as a television commercial announcer. Network news anchors and reporters are barred by contract from advertising products, but most other television performers, including announcers on local stations, are free to **moonlight** (to work at a second job during one's spare time, often at night). Television commercial announcing at the national level pays well, but it's a difficult field to enter. Most performers for national spots live in New York, Chicago, San Francisco, or the Hollywood area, and a small number of them dominate the field.

Locally produced television commercials offer employment to many performers, mostly in voice-over roles. Portable electronic production equipment, along with character generators, graphics generators, digital video effects (DVE) equipment, and chroma-keying, makes it possible for even small local stations to create elaborate and effective commercials. Videotapes can be made on location—at a carpet store, an auto parts dealer, or a grocery store—and then, during **postproduction,** station personnel add written information, draw images onto the screen, create and manipulate multi-images—such as changing a picture into a mosaic or swinging a picture through space—or key two or more pictures onto the same screen. A typical locally produced television commercial may show an announcer at or near the beginning of the spot and then show images of products or services while the announcer continues with voice-over narration.

Voice-over narration for television commercials differs from radio delivery only in that the words must be timed to match the pictures being seen by the viewers. This coordination is achieved through one of three production routines:

1. The announcer reads the script, and in postproduction the pictures are timed to match the words.
2. The visual portion of the commercial is shown on a monitor, and the announcer's voice-over performance is recorded as the words and pictures are synchronized.
3. During postproduction, the recorded performance is edited to match the pictures.

In most instances the announcer is long gone before the commercial is completed, and perhaps may never see the finished product.

Some television commercials are produced in the field, with the announcer playing a visible role. Because you won't have a teleprompter in the field, you'll have to ad-lib from cue cards and make a direct address to the camera. Although on-camera commercial delivery is rare, it's worth practicing. Elsewhere in this book—particularly in the chapters on performance (Chapters 5 and 6), interviewing (Chapter 8), and television news (Chapter 10)—many suggestions are offered for improving your on-camera performance. Nearly all of these suggestions apply to on-camera commercial announcing.

In addition, the checklist presented in this section includes tips that apply to performing commercials in the classroom or studio.

Try to reflect your own personality when you deliver radio and television commercials. Some commercials call for a slow, relaxed delivery, and others for a hard-sell approach. Often sponsors will ask for a particular style of delivery. But appropriately changing pace, volume, and level of energy doesn't mean you must transform yourself totally each time the style or mood of a commercial changes. If you don't maintain and project your own personality, you run the risk of sounding like an impersonator rather than a communicator.

CHECKLIST

MAKING
EFFECTIVE
TELEVISION
COMMER-
CIALS

1. When practicing on-camera performance, dress as you would if you'd been hired to deliver the commercial.
2. Understand and convey the impression the sponsor wants to create.
3. When handling props or pointing to signs or products, make your movements slow, deliberate, and economical.
4. If television equipment is available, try to simulate actual broadcast conditions.
5. Adhere scrupulously to the time limits of the commercial.
6. When appropriate, look into the camera lens, but don't stare.
7. In on-camera performance, practice switching smoothly from one camera to another on cue.
8. Don't do a parody or a travesty of a commercial unless the assignment calls for it. Your ability to sell a product or a service cannot be judged if you turn your performance into a lampoon.
9. Communicate!

PRACTICE

Delivering Radio Commercials and PSAs

Appendix A offers several commercial and PSA scripts. These materials provide practice with most types of commercials and PSAs heard on radio today. Find additional practice material and write some of your own.

PRACTICE

Producing Your Own Commercial

Ask a local merchant—the owner of an independently owned small grocery store, restaurant, or gift shop, for example—to help you fulfill a class assignment. Make sure the merchant understands that you have nothing to sell—be clear about who you are and what you're asking the merchant to do. Use a note pad to record basic information about items the merchant wants to promote. Write scripts, record them on audio and videotape, and then return to obtain the merchant's feedback.

PRACTICE

Delivering Television Commercials

Because television commercials usually involve elaborate visual effects, students of announcing have difficulty finding opportunities for realistic practice. Appendix A includes many radio scripts and a few television scripts. Some of the practice commercials call for animation, film inserts, or properties that may not be available. There's no ideal way of working with such commercials, but they're included here because they represent a large number of current commercials, and it would be unrealistic to exclude them. You can adapt some of the radio scripts for television performance, but you'll generally be limited to a straight, on-camera presentation.

The following exercises should help you achieve satisfactory results with a minimum of production support:

1. Practice on-camera delivery with some of the simple presentational commercials included in Appendix A. Use demonstration commercials and those incorporating studio cards or one or two slides instead of those that involve elaborate production. Work for exact timing as well as camera presence. Practice with an electronic prompter, if available, or with cue cards.

2. Prepare slides and adapt a thirty-second or sixty-second radio commercial for voice-over presentation. Practice synchronizing your off-camera delivery with the visual images as they appear on the screen.

3. Record television commercials currently being broadcast. Write out a script of the spoken portions of each commercial. Then, with the sound turned off, run the recording and practice voice-over delivery.

4. Produce a commercial with one person on camera demonstrating a product or a process while you're off camera delivering the voice-over narration.

CHAPTER 8

Interview and Talk Programs

THE WORD *INTERVIEW* COMES FROM THE FRENCH AND MEANS, ROUGHLY, "to see one another." Interviews fill a great many hours of every broadcast day. Some are brief, such as a ten-second **actuality** or **sound bite** on a news broadcast.[1] Others are longer and make up the substance of hour-long talk programs. Interviewing eyewitnesses at the scene of a fire, an airplane crash, or similar event for a news broadcast is only one aspect of news-gathering by reporters. However, conducting interviews and discussions with guests is the chief activity of hosts of talk and interview shows. Interviewing for news broadcasts is discussed in Chapters 9 and 10. This chapter is devoted to practices and techniques appropriate to television talk and radio call-in shows.

---

[1]**Actuality** is the radio term for a brief statement by someone other than station personnel. **Sound bite** is the television term for the same feature.

209

Talk and Interview Shows Today

When considering changes in talk and interview programs in recent years, an old song, "What a Difference a Day Makes," comes to mind. The subtitle of this chapter could well be "What a Difference a *Decade* Makes!" In 1987, there were 238 talk shows on American radio; by 1995, the number had increased to more than one thousand.[2] Listeners in most markets today receive several stations that feature all-talk formats or a combination of news and talk. Much of this programming is of local origin, but several syndicated talk shows are delivered by satellite to stations in all parts of the country.

As the number of radio talk shows increased throughout the 1990s, so, too, did the excesses of their hosts. Deregulation of radio and the ending of the Fairness Doctrine and Equal Time Provisions coincided with the so-called sexual revolution to make radio a medium on which, to cite another old tune, "Anything Goes."

Two outcomes of the spread of radio talk shows are undeniable: Much of the talk generated by the new breed of talk-show host has been angry and often tasteless, but talk shows have revitalized AM radio. Having lost much of its audience for music programming to FM, with its vastly improved sound quality, AM radio needed a new challenge, and it found it in talk radio.

While AM radio was undergoing its transformation, daytime television also underwent significant change. Interview talk shows proliferated, and previously unheard of hosts, some with no apparent qualifications, were given hours of airtime. By the mid-1990s, most television stations had dropped local shows that combined news, traffic, weather reports, and interviews and turned to syndicated programming. A number of talk-show hosts became noted for their handling of controversial and sometimes shocking topics.

Bill Carter of the *New York Times* described a type of talk show that consumed many hours of daytime television by the late 1990s:

Lowdown TV Talk Shows Flying High
Bill Carter

A new breed of television talk show, specializing in salacious subjects and emotional confrontations, has become so successful in drawing audiences that few producers of the programs, executives

---

[2]These figures are from *Broadcasting & Cable Yearbook,* 1996, p. B-590.

of the companies that own them, or advertisers who support them raise any questions about their content.

For a successful show, like the ones presided over by Jenny Jones and Ricki Lake, profits can reach $50 million to $60 million a year, comparable to what Jay Leno brings NBC with his *Tonight Show.*

So, despite a killing in Michigan last week that the authorities have linked to an encounter on *The Jenny Jones Show,* few industry executives expect any serious attempt to change the broadcasts.[3]

The contempt reflected in this report shouldn't obscure the fact that the programs it refers to attract large audiences and are valued by many viewers. In the television documentary, "Signal to Noise Ratio," a husband and wife describe their feelings about television. And, while no claim is made that they represent all television viewers, it's clear from other evidence—including audience ratings—that they're far from alone:

> **Man:** Oh, God, I just *love* talk shows! Y'know, when you're having a rough time in your life, and you watch a talk show, and they're on, discussing something that you relate to— like low self-esteem, or marriage problems, or children— and *you're* dealing with that; you hear what these people are talking about on TV, and . . . uh . . . you feel like you're *them!* . . . TV—it's like it has *arms,* 'cause it just *holds* me; it holds me, and I cannot get up. I won't be able to get up.
>
> **Woman:** Television is, for me . . . um . . . an escape from everyday chores, everyday duties, work. It's just a time for me to come and say "hello" to my couch, and just become one with my couch, and just relax.

Aside from sensational shows, talk and interview programs of substance and integrity continue to draw audiences. There are two types of talk shows. The first is a direct, one-way presentation from program to audience, as in interview, dialogue, and panel discussion shows. Both radio and television share in the production of such programs. The

---

[3]"Lowdown TV Talk Shows Flying High," by Bill Carter, *New York Times,* published in the *San Francisco Chronicle,* March 14, 1995.

second involves two-way communication, in which people call in to ask questions or offer opinions; programs of this type are almost exclusively found on radio. Many programs, such as single-subject call-in programs about financial advice, home improvement, health concerns, travel, sports, and recreation are available in almost every market. Such shows may serve as models of good communication.

Whether talk-show producers and hosts aim high or low, successful interviewers observe several time-tested principles. The suggestions for effective interview and talk performance described in this chapter are not advice on how to go for the jugular or how to humiliate guests, but rather how to support compelling discussions suitable for the public airwaves.

Some interviews are essentially question-and-answer sessions, often with controversial guests. Many are single-subject interviews on topics such as gun control, health care, or illegal immigration. Other interviews are essentially conversations that may bring out interesting or amusing anecdotes from famous guests. Each type of interview demands a special technique, and technique is determined by purpose.

Every interview should have at least one clearly defined objective, and it's important to determine that purpose before beginning an interview. Some interviews—especially those with outstanding storytellers—are meant to entertain and require a lighthearted approach. When you interview a gifted teller of anecdotes, be prepared to let the guest narrate humorous or otherwise entertaining stories with little interruption. In the Spotlight within this chapter, Professor Arthur S. Hough, Jr. describes his first on-air interview with a famous movie star. He says that he soon realized that he had one job to do, to listen and respond, and adds: "Of course there is a lot more to interviewing than effective listening, but it still is at the top of the list of things to do well."[4]

Establishing the purpose of an interview before starting it is one of the most important decisions you can make as a talk-show host.[5] When interviewing a writer who has a book to promote, your aim should be to explore in an engaging way the most interesting, amusing, controversial, or noteworthy parts of the book. Your audience may also receive enough information about the book to motivate its purchase; at the

---

[4]From an unpublished manuscript, "The Perfect Listener," by Arthur S. Hough, Jr. Reproduced with his permission.
[5]The term *host* is used to identify both female and male interviewers on talk shows. *Hostess* is neither necessary nor appropriate when referring to a female host.

Figure 8.1

The late Harry Caray is seen interviewing a Chicago Cubs player prior to game time. Caray called more than 8,000 games for the St. Louis Cardinals, the Oakland A's, the Chicago White Sox, and the Chicago Cubs. On learning of Caray's death in 1998, Hall of Fame sports announcer Jack Buck said: "There's going to be a loud silence." Stan Musial added: "We're going to miss old Harry. He was always the life of the party, the life of baseball." *Stephen Green Photography/Courtesy of the Chicago Cubs.*

same time it's important to keep the interview from becoming merely a puff piece for the author. Interviews on serious social problems should be designed to provide useful information on critical issues and should be approached with a serious, but not somber, attitude.

Television makes almost exclusive use of studio guests for interview programs, while radio utilizes both guests and telephone callers. However, the two media are alike in that in each the key to success is the program host's interviewing ability. The intimacy of talk shows makes them naturals for radio and television. Also, they present contemporary issues, are entertaining and informative, offer variety, and often directly involve listeners or viewers. Talk shows also are relatively inexpensive to produce; many guests receive no compensation for their appearances. Others receive transportation, lodging, and per diem pay for meals. Some are required by their performer's union to receive at least minimum scale.

Jobs as talk-show hosts aren't *numerous,* but they *are* rewarding and challenging. You may or may not succeed in having your own talk show, but the skills you develop as you work toward that goal will be useful in a range of announcing specializations. Some of those skills can be practiced; others come with experience. You can practice interviewing, discussing music, sports reporting, commercial delivery, and news reporting—all of which will help you become competent as a talk-show host—but the true measure of your effectiveness will be how well you put it all together on a live broadcast. Talk-show hosts are among the few announcers whose auditions usually coincide with their first air experience in that capacity. You may not be able to practice in an integrated way all the skills you need for the job, but you can study the practices and procedures you would encounter if you were to work as a radio or television talk-show host.

Principles of Effective Interviewing

Avoiding Abstraction

One of the fundamental aspects of interviewing that affects every interviewer's approach is what semanticist S. I. Hayakawa calls the **abstraction ladder**. This phrase refers to the fact that several terms are usually available for the same phenomenon, some precise and some general. Take, for example, *food, fruit, apple,* and *Granny Smith.* An apple is a type of fruit, and it's also a food, so all terms are accurate. The term *food* is a high-level abstraction; *fruit* is below it on the ladder; *apple* is quite specific; *Granny Smith* (a tart, green apple) is at the lowest rung on the ladder. Some interview guests consistently speak at a level that's high on the ladder of abstraction; that is, they consistently use vague and general terms rather than precise ones. It's up to you as the interviewer to "pull" such guests down the ladder of abstraction when appropriate. For example, consider this exchange:

ANNCR:

And just what does the administration intend to do about the problems of the inner cities?

GUEST:

We're extremely aware of the seriousness of the situation. We feel that the development of human resources in our cities must come before we can expect to overcome the problems of the physical environment.

What this guest is saying in an abstract way is quite simple: we need to find jobs for people before we can hope to clean up and rebuild. The interviewer's challenge is to find a way to get the guest to express this thought in clear, specific language. One approach is to ask directly for clarification of terms:

ANNCR:

And just what do you mean by "the development of human resources"?

A later question would steer the guest toward an explanation of the phrase "the problems of the physical environment."

Avoiding Bias

A second basic consideration for any interviewer is *bias*. When interviewing a person on a controversial or extremely important subject, one has a natural tendency to accept without question comments that one agrees with. This isn't a problem when the statement is a matter of common knowledge or of record, as in this example:

ANNCR:

How do today's students compare with students of twenty years ago?

GUEST:

Well, standardized test scores of college-bound seniors have fallen pretty regularly over the past two decades.

On the other hand, a guest may state opinions or theories:

ANNCR:

And how do you explain the drop?

GUEST:

Television viewing is the primary culprit.

As a *person* with many opinions of your own, you're free to agree or disagree with this statement. As a *responsible interviewer,* however, you have an obligation to ask further questions to bring out any facts that led your guest to the conclusion reached. Probing may reveal that the statement is based on hard fact—or that it's simply an unsubstantiated hunch. In either case, you've provided a service to your audience by nailing down the statement's truth or lack of it. Whatever the outcome, you owe it to your listeners to question undocumented assertions. To put it simply: Never allow your personal beliefs to keep you from questioning unsubstantiated statements.

Tips for Conducting Successful Interviews

Ernie Kreilling, a syndicated television columnist, has compiled a list of do's and dont's that are especially helpful to radio or television talk-show interviewers. These suggestions provide an excellent framework for discussing interviewing and are therefore used as subheads in this section. Think about them and work them into your practice where appropriate. It is also helpful to refer to them after each interview.

Note that the tips cover three general areas: preparation for the interview, treatment of guests, and the interviewer's strategy and contributions.

Preparing for the Interview

Carefully Research the Guest's Background, Accomplishments, Attitudes, Beliefs, and Positions. You'll generally know from one to several days in advance who your guest will be, so you'll have enough time to do some research. If your guest has written a book, and if the interview is to focus on it, you should read the book, make notes, and read some reviews.[6]

---

[6]There are exceptions to nearly every broad statement: Larry King claims he *never* reads the books of authors on his highly successful program!

Figure 8.2

Intern Julie Dickson is interviewed on her arrival at the University of Houston where she will enter its graduate program. Her interview will later be played on the university's radio station, KUHF-FM, Public Radio licensed to the University of Houston. *Courtesy of KUHF-FM and the University of Houston, Houston, Texas.*

 Biographical sketches of thousands of people may be found on *Web Sites for Students* under such categories as: African Americans, Artists, Astronauts, Authors, General Biographies, Government and History, Mathematicians, Miscellaneous, Musicians, Scientists, and Women. To access this information, enter this URL on a New Web Browser[7]:

www.ad12.k12.co.us/northglennhigh/nghs/bio.html

For a complete, updated list of URLs for this textbook, please see the text home site available at *www.hmco.com/college.*

---

[7]The Internet is changing constantly as new web sites are added and old web sites are abandoned. The URL listings in this textbook should be regarded as samples of the kinds of material available rather than as a stable index. If you seek a web site using one of these URLs and cannot connect, enter the key words for the topic into a search engine to find a site that may provide the information you want.

Aside from the Internet, you'll find biographical information in such standard reference works as *Who's Who* (in politics, in education, in medicine, and so on), the *Europa Year Book,* the *Book of the States,* and the *Municipal Year Book.* Most radio and television stations, as well as public libraries, have access to computerized data banks that provide information on nearly anyone of importance. If your guest isn't a person of national prominence, you may find background information through local newspapers, libraries, or chambers of commerce. If your guest has been scheduled by a booking agent, you most likely will be provided with a **press kit** containing useful information.

When time and circumstances permit, researching your guest's background is as important as all other factors combined. No amount of style, personality, smooth performance, or perfect timing can compensate for a lack of such knowledge.

Be Sure the Topic to Be Discussed Is of Interest or Importance. Although a dull guest can make even the most exciting subject boring, an interview always benefits if the topic itself is truly interesting or important.

When practicing interviewing as a student, don't settle for the most readily obtainable guest. Interviews with parents, siblings, classmates, and others you know well are seldom of interest to anyone, the participants included. A special energy is generated when you interview people who are strangers to you, and an even greater intensity develops when you interview people of real accomplishment.

Where Appropriate, Limit the Number of Topics to be Explored So That They Can Be Discussed in Depth. Depending on the intended length of the interview, it's best to explore only as many topics as can be dealt with in some depth. The least interesting interviews are those that randomly skim the surface of one topic after another.

Don't Submit Questions in Advance, Unless You'd Lose an Important Interview by Refusing to Do So. Hostile guests and some politicians may ask you to submit your questions in advance. This practice is a bad one, because spontaneity demands that guests not rehearse their answers. On the other hand, it *is* good practice to let an interviewee know the general areas to be covered. To help relax an inexperienced guest, you might even reveal your first question slightly in advance.

There's one exception to this rule: if you're going to ask a guest for his or her most interesting, funniest, or most unusual experience, advance notice will provide time for reflection. Most interviewees draw a blank when asked such a question abruptly, but a little advance notice may make the answer the highlight of the interview.

Write out, or at Least Make Notes on, the Introduction and Conclusion. Writing out or outlining the beginning and ending of an interview will free you during airtime to focus on its body. Note, however, that unless you're able to deliver your opening and closing in a totally conversational manner, the shift from reading to ad-lib speaking will be quite noticeable. In most instances the conclusion should include a summary of important or interesting information revealed during the interview. This cannot, of course, be written in advance, but your prepared conclusion can indicate the point at which you'll ad-lib this summary.

Plan at Least a Few Questions to Get the Interview Started and to Fill Awkward Gaps. Few sights are more painful than those of interviewers struggling to come up with a question. Plan ahead, but be ready to drop questions if they prove unnecessary.

The Guest

Make Your Guest Feel at Home. Introduce your guests to studio and control room personnel when it's convenient. Show your guests the area where the interview will take place and give them an idea of what's going to happen. Such hospitality should help relax your guests and make them more cooperative. With seasoned guests (people used to being interviewed) you can plunge right into the interview. With inexperienced guests it helps to spend a few minutes explaining how you'll conduct the interview and what you expect of them.

Establish the Guest's Credentials at the Start of the Interview. Station personnel usually select guests they believe are knowledgeable and responsible. The audience also needs to know how and why they're qualified to speak on a particular subject. The significance of a partisan statement about heart transplants differs depending on whether it's made by a heart surgeon, a heart recipient, a representative of a health plan, or a politician. One opinion is not necessarily better or more newsworthy than another, but your audience must be aware of the specific credentials of the speaker in order to assess statements in a meaningful way.

At the same time, confine your introductory comments to the bare essentials and give your guest an opportunity to be heard early in the interview. You can add additional biographical details later.

Occasionally and Indirectly Reestablish the Guest's Name and Credentials. On television, guests are identified periodically with **supers** at the bottom of the screen.[8] It's also customary to mention a guest's name when breaking for a commercial—"We'll be back with author Annie LaMott right after these messages." On radio, of course, reminders must be done orally, and, because listeners can't see the guest, frequent reintroductions are essential. Always end your interview by once again identifying your guest. Many people are likely to have tuned in during the interview, and they could anxiously be waiting to hear the name of the person who has so charmed or outraged them.

Remember That the Guest Is the Star. Rarely is the interviewer of more interest to the audience than the guest. Oscar Levant, a famous pianist, wit, and raconteur, consistently upstaged his guests, and the audience loved it. In general, however, dominating an interview is not only contrary to its purpose of drawing the guest out but is simply rude.

Remember That the Guest Is the Expert. At times, you'll be an authority on the subject under discussion and will be able to debate it with your guest, but in most cases your guest will be the expert.

Do Not "Preinterview" a Guest. Your conversation will lose spontaneity if you and your guest discuss the upcoming interview in detail before going on the air. Confine your contact with your guest to a general "ice-breaking" conversation unless your judgment tells you that you must mention a critical or sensitive topic.

Avoid Entrapment. Some "trash" radio and television interviewers deliberately mislead guests by hiding from them a sensitive or sensational item that the guest would prefer to leave undiscussed, then springing the question during the on-air interview. As mentioned at the opening of this chapter, several such hosts have appeared in the last few years.

---

[8]**Super** is short for *superimposition*, a picture or slide shown over another picture on the television screen.

The term *trash television* (or *trash radio*) has arisen to describe their efforts. Such interviewers put two important concepts in conflict: the belief in freedom of expression versus the concept of a person's right to privacy. The First Amendment guarantees the right of freedom of expression. No such constitutional guarantee of right to privacy exists for a person who agrees to appear on a talk show, so the integrity of the talk-show host is the only guarantee that a guest's privacy will be protected.

Conducting the Interview

Discuss the Subject with the Guest. On typical talk-shows, hosts aim for a conversation with their guests. They seek to avoid a mere **question-and-answer session (Q & A)**. Successful talk-show hosts participate in the discussion, adding information, anecdotes, and insightful comments. Unlike reporters, they don't rapidly fire questions, hoping to obtain sound bites from newsmakers. Questions are essential to an interview, but if you simply move from one question to another without revealing your feelings about the answers, you run the risk of seeming indifferent or unimpressed by what your guest is saying. Feel free to express honest reactions, including laughter when appropriate.

Try to Establish a Nonthreatening Atmosphere. Don't cross-examine or otherwise bully guests. Because they may be nervous, it's your responsibility to put them at ease, no matter how much you may dislike or disagree with them. If you show hostility, unfairness, or lack of common hospitality, both your guests and your audience will resent it.

There are a few talk-show hosts who make it a practice to bully their guests or insult call-in listeners. They thrive on dissension. These hosts are willing to ask any question, however tasteless, and to make any statement, however outrageous. Remember that viewers or listeners don't see a talk-show host as an actor playing a role; to them your role is the *real you.* If you value your reputation, you'll treat guests with fairness and respect.

Establish the Importance of the Topic. Topics that are obviously noteworthy need no special buildup, but others may require a brief explanation. People are interested in almost anything that directly affects them, so your interview will increase in significance if you can establish its relevance to your listeners or viewers. One simple way of doing this is to ask your guest early in the session why the issue is important.

During the Interview, Listen Attentively to the Guest's Replies and React with Appropriate Interest. Next to preparation, listening is the most important aspect of interviewing discussed in this section. Listen carefully and follow up important statements with appropriate questions. Also, don't feign interest. If your interest isn't genuine, you're either conducting a bad interview or not listening to your guest's responses.

Another reason for careful listening is to avoid the embarrassment of asking a question that has already been answered. The ultimate penalty for inattention to guests' remarks is to have them say on the air, "Why, I already answered that!"

In General, Base Questions on the Guest's Previous Statements. Don't hesitate to dispense with preplanned questions if more interesting ones arise naturally from the discussion. The following dialogue is an exaggerated example of failure to switch to a new topic:

ANNCR:

Now, Mayor Lutz, your opponent has charged you with a willful and illegal conflict of interest in the city's purchase of the new park. What's your answer?

MAYOR:

Well, it hasn't been revealed yet, but I have evidence that my opponent is a parole violator from out of state who served five years as a common purse snatcher!

ANNCR:

The *News-Democrat* claims to have copies of the deeds of sale and is ready to ask for your resignation. Will you tell us your side of the story on the park purchase?

Clinging to a planned question when a more important topic clamors for recognition may be caused by rigidity. In reviewing your recorded interviews, be alert for moments when you've sacrificed effectiveness because of a previously determined plan. Have a plan, but don't be a slave to it. A related mistake is caused by inattention to a guest's answers. If you "tune-out" your guest's comments as you frame your next question, you may miss an opportunity to follow up on an unexpected but intriguing statement.

In Particular, Follow Up on Important Contradictions. Public figures, especially politicians, often make contradictory statements that can be developed into good dialogue. But if you perceive that your guest is going to be evasive, adopt another line of questioning.

Try to Build an Interview Toward a High Point or Climax. Hold back an especially interesting or provocative question until near the end of the interview. Try to lead up to that question. However, don't spring an important question too late; it's unacceptable to abruptly cut off the answer to a significant question because you've run out of time.

Avoid Referring to Conversations Held Before Airtime. Ideally, you'll have an opportunity to chat with your guest before airtime. This conversation will help you determine areas of questioning, the general mood you want to establish, and other matters of importance. At the same time, an audience will feel excluded by a question such as "Well, Pat. I'm sure the folks would find interesting that new hobby you were telling me about just before we went on the air. Will you tell them about it?" Listeners or viewers want to feel that they are taking part in the interview, not as if most of it has already taken place.

Seek out a Guest's Deep Convictions. Don't settle for mentally rehearsed platitudes and clichés. Probing usually means that you must reveal something of yourself. Your guest isn't likely to open up unless you do.

Be Tenacious. Don't be put off with evasive answers. Keep probing until you see that you can't get any further; then drop the line of questioning and turn to something else.

Don't Interrupt with Meaningless Comments. "I see," "Uh huh," "Oh, yes," and "That's very interesting" add nothing to an interview and actually detract from what your guest is saying. Another reason for not peppering an interview with these meaningless interjections is that they quickly become predictable and annoying. Some interviews are intended for editing (usually for newscasts or documentaries), and your words will be edited out and replaced with narration. If your voice can be heard uttering meaningless "I sees," it may be impossible to eliminate them in the editing. All announcers should cure themselves of the habit of using such vocal reinforcement when they interview. Practice giving *nonverbal* reinforcement and work to eliminate voiced encouragement. At the same time, because a good interview frequently is a conversation, don't be afraid to make meaningful responses that are appropriate to the interchange, such as "I can't believe you didn't know about your nomination." When giving nonverbal responses on television, be careful when shaking or nodding your head—these motions could be interpreted by your viewers as agreement or disagreement with your guests' statements.

You'll usually know in advance whether or not an interview will be edited, so you'll be able to differentiate between times when interjections are acceptable and times when they're not. The nature of the interview will determine the extent to which you should speak up.

Point Out and Emphasize Important Answers. But don't parrot responses. Here's a good example of how a significant answer is given emphasis:

ANNCR:

Senator, if you were offered your party's nomination, would you accept it?

SENATOR:

I've given much thought to that possibility, and my present inclination is to accept such a call, provided that it's a mandate from the rank and file as well as the party leaders.

ANNCR:

Senator, you've just said—for the first time, I believe—that you're willing to run for the presidency. That sounds firm and unconditional. Am I right in drawing that conclusion?

Paraphrasing the senator's answer emphasizes its importance; giving the senator a chance to confirm or deny it will nail it down. On the other hand, avoid the meaningless repetition of answers, as in the following:

ANNCR:

You've been married five times. If you had your life to live over, would you try to stick with one of your wives?

MILLAR:

No, I wouldn't do anything differently.

ANNCR:

You wouldn't do anything differently. Well, which of your five partners did you love the most?

MILLAR:

I loved every one of them.

ANNCR:

You loved every one of them. Does that include spouse number three, with whom you lived for only two days?

Don't Patronize Your Guest, and Don't Be Obsequious. Avoid phrases such as "I'm sure our viewers would like to know" and "Do you mind if I ask?" A few guests may be reluctant or hostile, but most have come to be interviewed and need no coddling.

Keep Cool. Interviewing is your specialization, and you should feel at ease. Your guest may be a stranger to the interviewing situation and may be awed by the equipment, a bit afraid of you, and worried about saying something wrong. If you fail to remain calm or are distracted, you'll only rattle your guest further.

Keep Control of the Interview. Experienced guests, particularly politicians, can take over and use an interview for their own purposes. Keep the questions coming so that guests don't have time to digress from the subject or the opportunity to indulge in speechmaking.

Make Logical, Smooth Transitions to New Topics. Here's a bad example of making a transition—one actually made by a novice talk-show host:

ANNCR:

You said a few moments ago that your most memorable experience was the time you nearly drowned. Tell us, are you into any other sports besides swimming?

Always Be Ready with Your Next Question, but Don't Allow It to Distract You from the Comments Your Guest Is Making. Be prepared to alter your plan on the basis of an unexpected answer, but don't be caught with no question at all in mind. The problem of thinking ahead to the next question without tuning out the present is solved only with practice and experience.

Don't Ask More Than One Question at a Time. It's poor practice to combine questions into a multipart form, as in this example:

ANNCR:

Where did you get your inspiration for "Moonlight on the Ohio," and is it true that "Love Song" was inspired by your first wife?

There's a good chance that you'll end up with muddled answers to multiple questions.

Make Questions Brief and to the Point, but Don't Be Rude or Brusque. Don't be afraid to ask more detailed questions when the circumstances warrant, but avoid rambling questions such as this:

ANNCR:

Pat, I remember when you won the Academy Award for *Broken Hearts*—that was '93, I believe—and at that time you said you wanted to give up motion picture directing and do something on the Broadway stage. That's when you got involved in directing a modern-dress version of *Uncle Tom's Cabin,* and I guess they'll never let you forget that disaster. Well, looking back, is there any one moment you consider to be the turning point in your career? Any moment when you should have done something other than what you did?

PAT:

Z–z–z–z–z–z–z . . .

Don't Ask Questions That Invite Yes or No Answers. Try instead to draw your guest into an amplified response. The key point is that your interview will flow better and elicit interesting answers if you concentrate on asking "why," "what," and "how" questions *rather than* "are you," "did you," or "can you" questions.

Here are a few examples, both good and bad:

ANNCR:

Are you working on a book now?

AUTHOR:

Yes.

ANNCR:

What are you working on now?

AUTHOR:

I'm still looking at possibilities. I'm curious about. . . .

ANNCR:

How did you decide on a topic for a book?

AUTHOR:

I don't think "decide" is the right word—it's more like, "what topic has discovered *me?*"

Even if the author weren't writing at the time, it would be impossible to respond to the second question with a simple yes or no. If your guest does answer yes or no, and the point is of significance, ask for an explanation of the response.

Ask Questions a Layperson Would Ask. Don't be afraid to ask some questions that are fundamental. Most of your listeners will need basic information on the topic.

Go a Step Further, and Ask Interesting Questions Most Laypersons Wouldn't Think of. Outstanding interviewers bring out information that the audience wants but doesn't know it wants.

Avoid Obvious Questions. For example, don't ask a famous baseball player, "You were a baseball player, weren't you?"

Avoid Predictable Questions. Word some of your questions from a point of view that's opposite to that of your guest. Fresh and unexpected questions are necessary in two common circumstances: when the guest is someone who regularly appears on interview shows and whose opinions are, therefore, widely known, and when the topic has been so thoroughly chewed over by experts and amateurs alike that the audience can anticipate the questions that are likely to be asked. Because your primary task is to give your audience interesting and useful information, try to break away from the known, the obvious, and the redundant.

Don't Answer the Question As You Ask It. For example, what could the senator say in response to the following question except "That's right"?

ANNCR:

Senator, you voted against the treaty. Just what were your feelings about it? Your statement to the news media

indicated that you felt we were giving up more than we
were gaining.

*Don't Feel Compelled to Jump in with a Question the Second a Guest
Stops Talking.* Some interviewers feel that any dead air is unacceptable.
One popular talk-show host was notorious for interrupting guests in
the middle of amusing anecdotes out of a fear of a moment of silence.
Because good interviews are usually *conversations,* pauses are appropriate. Silence, together with an expectant expression, will often encourage a guest to continue in more detail.

A memorable example of a pause more eloquent and moving than
spoken words came in the televised court hearing of a boxing champion
accused of "throwing" a fight. After the momentous question was asked,
at least eight seconds elapsed as the boxer gulped, drew a deep breath,
began to answer, paused, blinked several times, and then—in a voice
choked with emotion—quietly answered, "Yes sir, I did." It's unlikely
that such a dramatic exchange will occur on a television interview program, but the principle remains valid: always be aware of when you, as
the interviewer, should just remain silent!

The panic that can set in when you can't come up with a question
can make a bad situation even worse; fright can cause you to think
about the *problem,* rather than allowing your mind to search for a logical question or comment to continue the interview. When appropriate,
ask your guest to elaborate on the statement just made. Ask if there's
anything she or he wants to comment on that hasn't been covered in the
interview. However, the best protection for avoiding such a tense moment is to be a *very careful listener. Going blank usually is the result of
inattention to what your guest is saying.*

*Don't Hesitate to Interrupt if Your Guest Uses Jargon not in Common Us-
age.* The term *jargon* has several negative connotations, but it also has
a neutral meaning: "the specialized or technical language of a trade,
profession, or fellowship." When guests use jargon, you may need to
ask for clarification so the audience won't be confused.

ANNCR:

And what did you find?

GUEST:

There wasn't a single PFD in the boat.

ANNCR:

PFD? I'm not sure what that is.

GUEST:

A personal flotation device.

ANNCR:

What I'd call a life jacket?

GUEST:

Yes.

Another example:

GUEST:

He showed negative life signs.

ANNCR:

You mean he was dead?

GUEST:

Correct.

During an interview, you'll often find it necessary to make quick decisions about asking for clarification of jargon or in-group terminology. When interviewing a nurse, you may hear "ICU," and you may decide almost at once that most of your listeners will know that, especially in a hospital context, this means "intensive care unit." On the other hand, if the nurse speaks of "NIC units," you most likely will decide to ask at once what this term means ("newborn intensive care").

Interviewers and reporters on the *NewsHour with Jim Lehrer* are excellent judges of the occasional need to stop a guest for clarification of an obscure term or phrase.

On Television, Check Your Notes Openly, Not Furtively. There's no reason to try to hide your notes. Their use doesn't in any way detract from a good discussion. Notes can be on a clipboard or small file cards.

On Television, Be Aware of Your Posture and Your Facial Expressions. Don't slump, and always be aware that your facial expressions are visible to your viewers. Grimaces, frowns, nervous mannerisms, and the like are seldom appropriate for interview hosts.

Before Ending an Interview—Especially if You've Run out of Questions—Ask the Guest Whether He or She Has Anything to Add. Aside from its obvious value when you're unable to come up with another question, this practice gives your guest one last chance to express something interesting or important that didn't come out earlier in the interview.

Avoid Ending an Interview with "Well, I See Our Time Is up." Of course your audience knows you're ending the interview because time is up! However, there are less hackneyed ways of indicating this: "I've been speaking with . . ." or, "I've enjoyed our conversation . . ." The problem with "I see our time is up" is that it's a cliché that merely states the obvious.

At the Conclusion of the Interview, Thank the Guest Warmly but Briefly. Don't be effusive. Move on quickly to your concluding comments.

CHECKLIST

BECOMING A
SKILLED
INTER-
VIEWER

Preparing for the Interview

1. Carefully research your guest's background, accomplishments, attitudes, beliefs, and positions.
2. Be sure the topic to be discussed is of interest or importance.
3. Where appropriate, limit the number of topics to be explored so that they can be discussed in depth.
4. Don't submit questions in advance, unless you'd lose an important interview by refusing to do so.
5. Write out, or at least make notes on, the introduction and conclusion.
6. Plan at least a few questions to get the interview started and to fill awkward gaps.

The Guest

7. Make your guest feel at home.
8. Establish your guest's credentials at the start of the interview.
9. Occasionally and indirectly reestablish your guest's name and credentials.
10. Remember that your guest is the star.
11. Remember that your guest is the expert.
12. Don't "pre-interview" your guest. Spontaneity is lost if you conduct an in-depth prebroadcast interview.
13. Avoid entrapment.

Conducting the Interview

14. Discuss the subject with your guest. Don't make your interview a mere Q & A session.
15. Try to establish a nonthreatening atmosphere.
16. Early in the interview, establish the importance of the topic.
17. During the interview, listen attentively to your guest's replies and react with appropriate interest.
18. In general, base questions on your guest's previous statements.
19. In particular, follow up on important contradictions.
20. Try to build an interview toward a high point or climax.

21. Avoid referring to conversations held before airtime.
22. Seek out your guest's deep convictions.
23. Be tenacious.
24. Don't interrupt with meaningless comments.
25. Point out and emphasize important answers.
26. Don't patronize your guest, and don't be obsequious.
27. Keep cool.
28. Keep control of the interview.
29. Make logical, smooth transitions to new subjects.
30. Always be ready with your next question, but don't allow it to distract you from the comments your guest is making.
31. Don't ask more than one question at a time.
32. Make questions brief and to the point, but don't be rude or brusque.
33. Avoid questions that invite yes or no answers.
34. Ask questions that a layperson would ask.
35. Go a step further and ask interesting questions most laypersons wouldn't think of.
36. Avoid obvious questions.
37. Don't ask predictable questions.
38. Don't answer the question as you ask it.
39. Don't feel compelled to jump in with a question the moment your guest stops talking.
40. Question jargon unless its use is so widespread that you're sure the audience will understand it.
41. On television, check your notes openly, not furtively.
42. On television, be aware of your posture and your facial expressions.
43. Before ending an interview—especially if you've run out of questions—ask your guest whether he or she has anything to add.
44. Don't end an interview with "Well, I see our time is up." If you need to let both guest and listeners know that the program is ending, find a less hackneyed way of saying so.
45. At the conclusion of the interview thank your guest warmly but briefly.

SPOTLIGHT

The Art of Interviewing

By Arthur S. Hough, Jr.

I was a young, "floating intern" at San Francisco's educational television station, KQED, when out of the blue one day, a producer came to me and said, "Robert Taylor, the actor, is showing up unexpectedly today. Could you be ready to interview him by two o'clock?"

"Of course," I said, although I'd never conducted an on-air interview in my life. I raced to the library to study up on Robert Taylor, and to my horror found that most of his off-screen life was either completely dull or hotly controversial.

Taylor appeared at two o'clock, huge, handsome, and completely poised. I still had not found a way to conduct the interview, so, as our mics were being clipped on, I said in complete frustration, "Mr. Taylor, I've never done this before, and I'm at a loss as to how to approach you." He gave me the most welcome smile I've ever known and said in his deep voice, "Arthur, don't worry about a thing. I'll carry it."

I can't remember how I got him started, probably with some dumb question like, "What has it been like all these years, to be a Hollywood star and celebrity?" And off he went, like a finely tuned machine. I realized that I really had one job to do, to *listen* and *respond*. We had a great interview. We talked and laughed and I made it through to the end just by being there, listening, following, listening, following.

Of course there is a lot more to interviewing than effective listening, but it still is at the top of the list of things to do well. Personal, in-depth interviewing is an art, badly done by most interviewers, mainly because they cannot let go enough to truly listen to their guests. The ace television interviewer, Ted Koppel, has said about himself, "I listen. Most people don't. Something comes along—and whoosh!—it goes right past them."

The considerations that I believe make a brilliant on-the-air interview are steeped in listening:

How do you prepare to listen?

How do you open up your guest to get something worth listening to?

How do you participate and still listen; how do you follow and lead?

How do you make listening an obvious part of your physical style?

How do you get out of it when the time is up?

Interviewing on the air takes everything you've already learned about listening, and puts it on a professional, expert level. Like skiing, it is fast, exhilarating, full of unexpected soft spots and high lumps, and a constant test of your most delicate balance and skill.

You can learn the principles in minutes, but it may take years to incorporate them into your own personal style. Here are some quick starting rules:

Preparation

Conduct whatever research you can on your guest, but don't conspire with him or her in a preinterview discussion. Preinterviewing kills spontaneity.

Accumulate questions ahead of time to give yourself some feeling for the structure you want to follow; write down key phrases on cards, but know that in a really sparkling interview, your prepared questions will fade in importance. Don't be rigid. Follow the flow; be flexible.

Introduction

Introduce quickly and let the guest speak up early. More introductory material can be woven in later. This is especially true on radio where the audience has no contact at all with your guest until they hear his or her voice.

Ask your guest to explain whatever you think the audience might not understand, special vocabulary, abbreviations, and "in-talk" as in "When you speak of Otto, do you mean Otto Preminger?"

Avoid trivia, or hackneyed questions, such as "How did you feel when you knew you'd lost the game!"

Participation

Be entirely quiet when the guest is speaking. Do not accompany him or her with little grunts like "Uh-huh," "I see," "Okay." Talk-along interruptions intrude on the audio of the interview and kill crispness.

Keep control, but do not dominate. This is a delicate skill. Learn to interrupt, but not to intrude. When you must, be sure you break into the guest's stream at phrase endings and breath points. Slip in between thoughts and snip him or her off without intruding. Don't wiggle into the conversation—break in with a strong (but not harsh) voice.

To stop a long monologue, listen closely, pick up the guest's point and grab it. That is, feed back his or her point, and then, without pause, move the guest on, as in "You had a narrow escape there, but how did you finally find the treasure?"

Break the guest's "tape." Many guests are obviously well prepared on some topics; they've been interviewed before and have developed an inner tape that they play for you. You must get the guest to *think* rather than *recite;* break in with the pertinent but unexpected question, such as "It must have taken some courage to do that; were you frightened?"

Do not kill a good guest run just because you have an agenda. If what you're getting is interesting, let it roll. The audience will hate you for spoiling an interesting chain of thought.

Show evident interest, not perfunctory, distracted, or obsequious attention. Keep eye contact with your guest, but don't just stare.

Participate in the interview, the content, and the feelings. Don't stand off with the objectivity of a scientist with a microscope. Every comment you make should not simply be another question. Feedback that leads to a further or deeper thought is good. Injecting your own opinion or experience is fine so long as it adds to the guest's contribution, and does not compete with it. Don't hog the time.

Get rapport—an easy, even, equal relationship with the guest. Make your contribution friendly, not an interrogation, but don't fall into a style of exaggerated awe. Psychologically join your guest, unless your special purpose is to keep perspective.

Avoid these clichés:

So . . . (in introducing your next remark or question)

Right! . . . (to indicate you understand)

That's very interesting.

Thanks for joining us.

Nice to have you with us.

We'd like to thank you . . .

. . . needs no introduction

Listening

Feelings follow facts. Feed back content, and then go for the *feelings beneath* that *content.* State, as feedback, what feelings you think you are hearing, as in "It irritates you that people don't understand your position on this."

Follow subtle clues. Listen for the throwaway phrase, the thing NOT said, or said hurriedly, the inconsistencies, the unusual or out-of-place adjective, as in "You said 'unfortunate' accident. Do you think it could have been avoided?"

Ending

When your time is up just say so and stop. The time limit is a real and acceptable factor, nothing to be embarrassed about.

End clean: no fuss, no cliché, no speech.

Dr. Arthur S. Hough, Jr. is an author and professor emeritus of broadcast communication arts at San Francisco State University. He has years of on-air interviewing experience and has taught interviewing technique in a variety of performance courses.
Courtesy of Arthur S. Hough, Jr.

Radio Talk-Show Hosts

More than five hundred radio stations in the United States describe themselves as talk stations.[9] More than one thousand stations are classified as news/talk stations that schedule at least some talk shows during their broadcast week. At some stations, talk and call-in programs are broadcast twenty-four hours a day with program hosts generally performing in four-hour shifts. In contrast, some stations have only one talk or call-in show a day, and this may be devoted to sports talk, pet care, or computer troubleshooting. Regardless of the number of hours devoted to talk programming, the procedures used to produce them are fairly standardized.

As an announcer for a talk program, you need to develop two major related skills: conducting interesting and informative interviews (or

---

[9]Radio and television station formats are listed annually in *Broadcasting & Cable Yearbook*. The publisher is R. R. Bowker, New Providence, New Jersey.

conversations) with studio guests, and conversing engagingly with the full spectrum of strangers who call in on the telephone.

Preparing for the Shift

At a typical talk-radio station, you may expect to work a two- to four-hour air shift, five or six days a week. If you work on weekends or the **graveyard shift** (from midnight on), longer hours may be assigned. Most stations, however, choose to limit talk-show announcers to a maximum of four hours, which is about as long as anyone can be expected to remain sharp, energetic, articulate, and patient. These may seem short working hours, but talk-show announcers work many additional hours a day preparing for their airtime.

As a talk-show announcer, you may work with a producer, a **phone screener,** and (at most stations) an engineer. The program director or other designated administrator will suggest guests, will in some cases instruct you to schedule a certain guest, and will evaluate your work frequently. The producer will assist you in scheduling guests, will handle correspondence, and will act as traffic director for arriving and departing guests. The phone screener will handle all incoming calls during your air shift, will cut off obvious cranks or other undesirables, and will line up calls in order of their calling or according to station policy. The engineer will play recorded commercials and station logos, will cut in the network for news summaries or breaking news events, and will operate the **time-delay system.**[10] At smaller-market stations, one person may perform the tasks of producing, screening, and audio board operation.

Your first task in preparing for a shift is to develop at least three or four timely, universally interesting, or controversial topics for discussion. Whether or not you have guests, you must open your program with talk that will stimulate listeners' interest and motivate them to phone in to offer their opinions. Naturally, you won't speak about all of your prepared topics at the outset of your program. You'll begin with the most logical one and save the others to be used if the first topic bombs. In nearly every instance, your first topic will be of current importance.

In order to be timely and interesting on the air, you must be widely read and conversant with an extremely broad range of topics. There's an

---

[10]A **time-delay system** records the voices of both host and caller, and delays their comments for several seconds before being broadcast. This is done to avoid accidentally broadcasting libelous or indecent statements.

absolute limit to the number of times you'll be able to get away with saying, "Never heard of it." Unless you're hired specifically to do a sports or other specialized talk show, you must be a generalist. You can expect to find yourself discussing such diverse topics as local politics, conservation, and the details of a new and important book at any given moment. This means that you must read several newspapers and magazines regularly and keep abreast of television, movies, books (both fiction and nonfiction), and other important media.

A typical talk-show host daily will read two local newspapers, as well as the *New York Times,* the *Wall Street Journal, USA Today,* and the *Christian Science Monitor.* Weekend reading might include the *New York Times* and the *Los Angeles Times,* as well as two local newspapers, and weekly reading will include *Newsweek, Time, Brill's Content,* and other magazines to keep current on developments in technology, space exploration, medicine, economics, politics, or other areas of knowledge. The host may also read (mostly by skimming) three to five books a week.

Although having studio guests isn't required, radio talk-show announcers frequently use guests to add variety to programs. Even the most famous and sought-after guests seldom are paid for appearances on talk shows, so they represent a cost-effective source of program material. Most guests agree to appear on a program because they see it as an opportunity to promote a book, a film, or a cause. There's nothing inherently wrong in such a tradeoff, as long as both parties understand the conditions and as long as the announcer stays in control of the show. Well-known guests are usually on a circuit of appearances on both radio and television talk programs in a number of markets. Such guests know or soon learn that they'll be welcome only as long as they help their hosts deliver an engaging program. If you take time to explain to your guests the nature of your show, the kinds of listeners you're attempting to reach (your **audience demographics**), and any station policies that may be relevant, you should have little trouble in gaining their full cooperation.

When you schedule guests, you'll be expected to inform your station several days in advance. This will give the promotion department time to publicize appearances, generally by sending notice of scheduled guests to local newspapers and by writing promotion copy to be read by other talk-show announcers at your station during their shifts.

Some stations maintain a log to keep control over the appearance of guests. They want to avoid overexposing guests as well as repetitiveness in the type of guest or subject covered. A **debriefing log** contains post-broadcast comments, an evaluation of a guest's performance that usually consists of answers to the following questions.

What topics did the guest actually cover?

Did the material covered match the preshow expectations?

How well did the guest perform?

How much interest did the guest generate as measured by phone calls?

Performing As a Radio Talk-Show Announcer

As a talk-show announcer, you'll sit in a small studio immediately adjacent to a control room that houses the engineer and phone screener. You won't use a telephone for your conversations with callers; their voices will be amplified so you can hear them over a special speaker. You'll speak directly into an ordinary mic. A soundproof separation of studio and control room is absolutely necessary, because a time delay is used as a precaution against the broadcasting of profanity and slander. It's imperative not to be distracted by the sound of your own voice and your guest's voices as they go out over the air approximately seven seconds after the words have been spoken. Do not allow the conversation between the screener and the callers to distract you.

In most cases the studio will have a special telephone console that handles several incoming lines from which you can select callers by punching the appropriate button on the phone base. Calls are fed to the phone base by the screener after the calls have been sifted to eliminate cranks; a light that illuminates a push button tells you that you have a caller on a particular line. The lines are usually identified by geographical location: for example, line 1 may be the South Side; line 2, Oak Manor; and line 3, Outer Vista. At most stations, a video display terminal shows the name and hometown of the next person on the line.

Most radio talk-show hosts give out a fax (**facsimile transmission**) number so that listeners can send hard copies of newspaper stories, letters, or other material. Hosts also mention their e-mail address from time to time but especially at or near the beginning of their show.

At the start of your shift you'll ad-lib your introduction along predetermined lines. You'll state the opening topic for discussion and include an identification of yourself, the station, the length of your program segment, and the guests who'll appear later. You'll repeat the call-in telephone numbers on a regular and frequent basis, and you'll occasionally mention your fax number and your e-mail address.

Stations have many policies for performance; these are not standardized, but they do tend to be similar. Most stations ask talk-show

Figure 8.3

Sports director Gary Radnich hosts a daily call-in show. Gary lists these qualities as requisite for success as a sports talk-show host: a passion for sports; a broad, up-to-date knowledge of the field; high energy (but not forced); respect for callers' opinions; ability to listen; and a sense of humor. *Courtesy of Gary Radnich and KNBR, San Francisco, California.*

hosts not to talk at the start of the program for more than a certain number of minutes before taking a phone call. A related policy insists that you never talk for more than a certain number of minutes during your segment without taking a call, even when you have a fascinating in-studio guest. Your station may ask for more and shorter calls, and if you ask, "More and shorter than what?" the answer may be, "More than you're taking and shorter than you're allowing." The aim of talk radio is maximum listener involvement.

Talk stations **cluster** their commercial announcements. Unlike a popular-music station, where program segments (songs) last three minutes or less, talk shows can't tolerate constant interruptions. A **commercial cluster** may consist of three or more commercials. It's mandatory that you, as the organizer and director of your own show, not get so carried away by the ongoing dialogue that you forget to deliver the commercial clusters at the times designated. Since sponsors pay for the programming, all commercials must be read or played, and they should be spaced properly to avoid piling up toward the end of your shift. All radio announcers work with a log—called the **program log** by people in programming but referred to as the **billing log** by the sales department. It's your responsibility to initial all commercial and public-service announcements as they're broadcast. The Federal Communications Commission (FCC) no longer requires program logs, but most stations continue to maintain them.

Legal and Ethical Concerns

Despite deregulation of radio by the FCC, broadcasters continue to be legally responsible for what is sent over the airwaves by their stations. Many stations give talk-show hosts detailed instructions on their legal and ethical responsibilities.

Payola and plugola are illegal practices. *Payola* refers to the undisclosed payment of something of value to a station employee for the on-air promotion of goods, services, or events. *Plugola* is the promotion by a station of an item or event in which the station or one of its employees has an undisclosed financial interest. Plugola is not illegal *if* the management of the station is aware of the arrangement and *if* appropriate sponsorship information is announced. When FCC rules on payola or plugola are violated, fines or even the loss of a station's license could be the outcome.

Challenges and Responsibilities

One of your challenges as a radio talk-show announcer will be to motivate many new or infrequent callers. To guarantee fresh call-in talent, you must repeat the phone numbers often on the air and tell your listeners from time to time which lines are open. Even if few listeners respond to your invitations, don't beg people to phone in. If the telephone lines are dead and cannot be resuscitated by your best efforts, you may conclude that one of the following problems exists: (1) your comments are so fascinating that your listeners don't want to interrupt; (2) you're so dull and uninspiring that no one is motivated to call; (3) the transmitter has shorted out.

Occasionally callers may use profane language, mention the names of people other than public figures in a derogatory way, or make defamatory statements. Because your station's license may be at stake in such cases, you must develop quick reflexes with the **panic button**, which takes the offending comment off the air and replaces it with a beeping sound or a prerecorded warning about such utterances. It's far better to overreact in questionable situations than to let a caller's comments go beyond the point of safety. You can always apologize if your finger was too quick on the button, but there's little you can do constructively once things have gone past the point of no return. You will, of course, be extensively briefed on do's and don'ts.

One of your responsibilities may be to call your audience's attention to other segments of your station's broadcast day. In some cases you'll promote the news, music, contests, sports, or special features such as farm information. In other instances you'll have to speak favorably of people who have comparable shows on your station—that is, people who might in some ways be considered your competition. Unless there's some station-endorsed mock feud between talk-show announcers, you'll be expected to do a conscientious job of fairly promoting your co-workers.

Hosting Television Talk Programs

Television talk shows can be seen at nearly every hour of the broadcast day. At both the network and the local level, talk shows are usually broadcast live, even though some segments may have been taped in advance. Local stations also rely on taped talk programs that have been syndicated for distribution. Network programs are early-morning (*Good Morning America*) and late-night offerings (*Letterman*); most local talk shows are broadcast in the midmorning or in the afternoon.

As a television talk-show announcer, you'll face constant demands on your abilities to ad-lib, to cover quickly for slip-ups, to concentrate in the face of multiple distractions, and to help produce a smooth show without scripts or rehearsals.

 You can find transcripts of interview shows on the Internet. One rich source is found on the CNN web site. Use this URL:

www.cnn.com/TRANSCRIPTS/

You'll find transcripts of interviews by Larry King and Jesse Jackson, and the programs *TalkBack Live, Crossfire, Burden of Proof, Reliable Sources,* and *The Capitol Gang.*

For a complete, updated list of URLs for this textbook, please see the text home site available at *www.hmco.com/college.*

Types of Talk Shows

Network and nationally syndicated talk shows are produced by large staffs. Guests are booked well in advance, and transportation and lodging are arranged for them. Staff members thoroughly research each guest's background and provide the program host with copious notes. Other staff members obtain photos or recorded material that will add to the show's effectiveness. The result is a fast-paced, smoothly produced program with enough variety to retain and please the viewers.

Most locally produced television talk shows are put together by small staffs with limited budgets. Small-market stations provide little support for the host. You likely will spend the first several years of your career as a talk-show host at a station with limited resources. Some small stations lack even a floor crew and instead may have two cameras locked in fixed positions and a director sitting at the **switcher**, cutting from one camera to another as appropriate. Working at such a station will allow you to learn every aspect of talk-show performance and production and prepare you for a move to a station in a larger market. Medium-market stations offer more support, but still work with somewhat limited resources. Program quality need not suffer because of modest support, but interview programs require great effort and adaptability from all members of the team.

PRACTICE

Interviewing

Interviews serve several different ends. The exercises that follow relate to interviews on talk-show programs and person-in-the-street features, sometimes called **vox pops.**[11] A practice section at the end of this chapter suggests interviews for news packages and documentaries.

Before beginning any interview, decide on the interview's *purpose;* this will help you focus on the best approach (guarded or open, light or somber), the approximate length of the interview, and whether you should stay with one topic or go into two or more areas of discussion. Generally speaking, multiple-topic interviews are appropriate when your guest is a celebrity who can talk on several subjects; single-topic interviews are proper when your guest is a specialist in some area such as pediatrics,

---

[11]**Vox pop** is an abbreviation of the Latin *vox populi,* literally translated as "voice of the people." The term is interchangeable with **MOS,** or "man-on-the-street," which has fallen into disfavor because of its gender bias. Both refer to brief sound bites of randomly selected people expressing opinions on a topic or event in the news.

investments, or gardening. Vox pop interviews are by necessity single-topic interviews, as are interviews designed for later use in a documentary.

Like most other exercises in this book, those that follow are designed for the simplest possible production, using only a portable audio or video recorder. Any of these exercises can be adapted to full-studio television production.

1. For a multiple-topic interview, select a person you consider unusually interesting. Make sure you do some research about your guest so that you have at least a general idea of what can be discovered and discussed. Notes on areas to be explored are almost a necessity for this type of interview. Plan to interview without stopping your recorder for at least ten or, preferably, twenty minutes.

2. For a single-topic interview, choose a specialist whose field is of great interest to you and interview this person at length without significantly changing the subject. A list of possible questions should help you "stay the course."

3. Choose a topic and conduct vox pop interviews. Here are a few suggested questions:

   - What's the most useless gadget on the market?
   - What job would you most like to have?
   - What's the worst advice you've ever received?
   - What would you do if you won the lottery?

You can also obtain samples of public opinion by asking more serious questions, such as probing people's feelings about an item in the news. Editing the responses and organizing them into packages—with appropriate opening and closing remarks—will complete this exercise.[12]

4. Occasionally it's effective to conduct an interview for which all or most of the questions have been written out in advance. For example, you may want to pin down a guest by asking a string of precisely worded questions, such as these:

   - Why did you vote against the treaty?
   - Last May, in your Tulsa speech, didn't you say that you favored the treaty?

---

[12]Don't include non-newsworthy and pointless comments you've recorded at the scene of a story as part of your on-air report. Broadcast journalism is plagued by reporters' misconception of what constitutes a response worth sharing with an audience. "I dunna know . . . I guess, like, maybe he shoulda been more careful," "I guess it's all right, but who knows?" Statements such as these should die a merciful death during editing for a package. Inarticulate and uninformed bites add nothing of value to a story.

- On May twentieth, the *Tulsa Record* printed this quote: "I fully support the administration, and therefore I support the proposed treaty." Do you still maintain that you never expressed support for the treaty?
- Here's a quote from the *Dallas Advance,* dated May thirtieth: "Senator James stated that, while he had some minor reservations about the treaty, he would support it when it came to a vote." Did the *Advance* also misqoute you?

Select an interviewee and a topic that lend themselves to a scripted approach and practice this unusual, but sometimes highly effective, interview technique.

PRACTICE

Interviewing for Radio News

These suggestions are offered to help you practice some of the varied assignments given to radio journalists.

1. Cover news conferences with a portable cassette tape recorder. Record the entire conference and then record interviews with appropriate persons—including the spokesperson, if possible—as well as those who favor and those who oppose the speaker's position. Edit the statements to create actualities and wraps with the recorded material. Follow the procedures described in Chapter 9, "Radio News," for writing and recording lead-ins, lead-outs, and connecting commentary.

2. Practice interviewing. Conduct a range of interviews that demonstrate different types appropriate for radio newscasts: actualities about a specific hardnews incident, position statements of politicians, vox pop interviews, and features interviews, with, for example, a zoo keeper about the birth of a rare animal, or with a city bus driver about the advantages and disadvantages of that vocation.

CHAPTER 9

Radio News

NEWS ON RADIO RANGES FROM IN-DEPTH COVERAGE AROUND THE clock, to brief hourly summaries, to no news coverage at all on some stations. Many popular music stations have no news director or reporters, and broadcast news reports only in emergencies. At some talk and music stations, news reports are provided by a national news service such as Associated Press Radio, CNN Audio, National Public Radio, or the United Press International (UPI) Audio Network. At other stations, reports from a wire service are taken directly from a computer terminal, printed, and read without being edited. Announcing at such **rip-and-read** operations requires considerable skill in sight-reading, but no journalism skills. This chapter discusses news operations at radio stations where news is taken seriously and where specialized news personnel are employed full time.

Nearly every broadcast market now has or can receive signals from one or more radio stations that feature news. Some stations have an all-news format, some provide news during morning and evening drive times, and some give hourly reports researched and written by a news staff. News operations rely on news from station field and beat reporters, wire services, audio feeds from news services, off-site employees, a parent network, and **stringers.**[1] Any station that takes news seriously relies heavily on the efforts of its field reporters, newswriters, and anchors.

---

[1]A **stringer** is a part-time reporter who is paid only for stories that are chosen and used by a station's news department.

Most all-news stations offer more than news. Typical features are stock market and business reports, sports, traffic and weather, and a community billboard. Some stations also feature special interest programs such as cooking programs featuring local chefs or food and wine specialists or a call-for-action consumer complaint program. Some special-interest programs are performed by station news personnel; others rely on outside specialists, with a station announcer serving as host.

As you read this discussion of the performance and production aspects of radio news at the local-station level, keep in mind that only larger stations have the resources to provide the support described.

Anchoring Radio News

As a radio news anchor, you'll prepare much of the copy you read. There are advantages to this. First, as you write copy, you can contact sources to gather more details or to learn the correct pronunciation of any names or words that might otherwise cause trouble during delivery. Second, investigating stories and writing your own copy will help you develop into a journalist rather than a mere reader of news scripts.

Figure 9.1

News anchor and reporter Ed Baxter records promos or "teases" prior to his daily afternoon newscast. Ed received his bachelor's degree from California State University—Northridge, in radio-television journalism. He has received awards from the Associated Press, the United Press International, and the San Francisco Bar Association for his work as a reporter. *Courtesy of Ed Baxter and KGO-AM, San Francisco, California.*

In preparing a news script, you'll work with an editor who decides what stories will be broadcast and the order of their delivery. You'll work from a log listing the sequence of the components of the newscast. Most news-oriented stations follow a cyclical format—called a **clock** or **newswheel**—that is repeated on an hourly basis. Some news clocks divide a drive-time hour into forty or more segments. A typical clock, or newswheel, is shown in Figure 9.2. A typical format begins or ends each hour with five minutes of network news, it provides national and world news headlines at or near the half-hour, and it has features such as sports, weather, traffic, stock market reports, and local headlines at regularly established intervals. Commercials are also scheduled at stipulated times.

News Sources

When preparing copy for a news shift, you may expect to work with news from several sources. Some stories will be generated by station

Figure 9.2

The program clock (hot clock) is a radio station's strategic tool for gaining and keeping audiences; the schedule for each hour is carefully divided into segments of news, sports, weather, headlines, and features. This one-hour clock, from an all-news commercial AM station, shows the broadcast schedule during morning drive time.

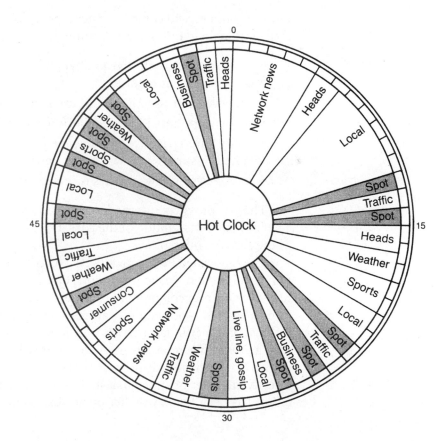

TABLE 9.1	TERMS USED ON A NEWSWHEEL

Term	Meaning
Net news	Network news
Heads	News headlines
Local	Local news stories
Spot	Commercial
Traffic	Traffic reports
Sports	Sports briefs from station's sports reporter
Weather	Weather report from station's meteorologist
Business	Business report from station's business reporter
Live line, gossip, etc.	Special features done by news anchors, just for fun
National	National news reported by local anchors
Consumer/medical	A consumer report from station's consumer reporter or a medical report by a doctor or other medical specialist

reporters; others will come from news providers. Here are resources typically available to radio news personnel:

- Audio reports, both live and taped, from station, field, and special assignment reporters
- Associated Press (AP) and Reuters news wires
- Associated Press Radio Network news feeds
- A city wire service, which may be independently owned and operated or supervised by a major news service
- Interviews or news reports received by telephone

The AP provides international, national, and local news services. The following description of the AP services will give you a general idea of the services offered.

The Associated Press provides AP NewsPower, subscribed to by many radio stations and smaller television stations. The Associated Press sends news stories from computer to computer to member stations. From "custom categories"—a **menu** of features such as state news, national news, international news, farm news, business stories, sports scores and stories, and weather reports—news directors select and receive only those stories that interest them. News stories in selected categories are printed directly on paper or stored in a station's computer and printed after a decision has been made whether or not to use the stories. In this way, an all-news station, a rock station, and a Classical-music station can choose assortments of news stories appropriate to the stations' differing formats.

Another feature of AP NewsPower allows station newswriters to call up a story paragraph by paragraph on their computers. At the push of a button, the paragraph from the news service moves to one side of the video display terminal, permitting the operator to paraphrase or to add a local angle by typing the story on the unoccupied portion of the screen. The push of another button directs the computer to print the rewritten story. At some radio stations, on-air newscasters read their scripts directly from a video display terminal. For editing at a radio station, AP NewsPower includes an integrated pronunciation look-up and insertion, as well as a thesaurus look-up and replacement.

AP NewsPower sends timely features throughout the year, including special reports on income tax tips and a year-end review. It also sends complete newscasts, developing news stories, and bulletins.

The Associated Press also maintains the APTV wire, a service mainly used by television stations but also subscribed to by the largest radio stations. This service carries some of the same written material as AP NewsPower, as well as in-depth newspaper-style stories. Stations using APTV receive more copy on each story than is provided by AP NewsPower, giving them a wealth of source material to augment their local coverage. Among APTV's offerings are in-depth newspaper-style state and regional news; national and international news; weather bulletins, warnings, and reports; detailed sports stories, including the scores of ongoing games; detailed business news; entertainment news; and many seasonal features.

The AP Radio Network delivers five-minute audio newscasts at the top and bottom of each hour, twenty-four hours a day, as well as brief sports, business, weather, features, and headlines several times each hour. For music stations, AP Drive Time provides a special service for stations that broadcast news only during morning drive time. AP Headlines, which is also tailored to music stations, provides a service for stations with a "limited appetite for news and information." All AP reports can be inserted into locally produced newscasts and thereby provide expanded coverage to stations that can't afford teams of national and international correspondents.

When using stories from the wire services, you have four options:

1. Read the story as you find it.
2. Leave the story unaltered but add a lead-in of your own.

3. Edit the story to shorten it, sharpen it, or give it a local angle.

4. Completely rewrite the story.

Whatever you decide, the story must be entered in the running sequence of the newscast. At some stations you'll make a copy for the files and insert the original in a loose-leaf book from which you'll work during your shift.

Most radio stations that feature news ask reporters to work the **beat check** (also called the **phone beat**, or the **phone check**). This consists of making phone calls to agencies and persons who are most likely to provide news items regularly. A typical beat list includes phone numbers and names of contacts for all nearby police, sheriff, disaster, fire, and weather departments; federal agencies such as the Federal Bureau of Investigation, the Secret Service, the Alcohol, Tobacco, and Firearms Bureau, the civil defense headquarters, and the National Guard; local and nearby jails and prisons; all local hospitals; all nearby airport control towers; and specialized agencies important to listeners in your community (for example, the farm bureau and earthquake stations).

When you work the beat check, plan to call each listed agency at the same time each day. Try to establish a personal relationship with the contact there. Discover how each contact prefers to work with you—whether you're allowed to tape the conversation or are permitted only to paraphrase statements. If it fits the news report, give credit to the people who supply your station with news items; most people are pleased to hear their names on the air. At the same time, you must respect requests for anonymity.

A related assignment is searching for and selecting news releases on the Internet. Using your station's computer, you can access government agencies and other organizations that may have news of interest to listeners. Copy to a storage disk or printer newsworthy stories or policy statements. When using any of these feeds, it is important to check controversial information against other sources and clearly mention the source.

Preparing for a Shift

When preparing for a news shift that will keep you on the air for two to four hours, you'll typically write, rewrite, and assemble about two hours' worth of material, including live copy, recorded reports, features, and commercials. While you're performing, a newswriter will be writing and assembling material for the remaining hours of your shift.

The checklist that the news editor prepares for you will include the stories to be featured, the order in which you should give them, and the **sounds** with which you'll work. **Sounds** are different from **sounders**, which are short musical **IDs** or **logos** that identify a particular feature such as a traffic or sports report. Sounds come in several forms:

- An **actuality** is a brief statement made by someone other than station personnel, such as a newsmaker or eyewitness. It's recorded in the field on a battery-operated recorder or at the station by way of a cellular telephone.
- In a **wrap**, or wraparound, a reporter records an opening that leads into an actuality, which is followed by the reporter's closing comments. The conclusion may be a brief summary, followed by a tag line such as, "Bill Hillman, KZZZ News."
- A **voicer** is a report from a field reporter, usually sent to the station by a cellular phone, short-wave radio, or a conventional phone.
- A **scener** is a report on a breaking event. It's usually broadcast live, but may also be taped for incorporation into a later broadcast.
- **Raw sound** refers to what may be called "news noise"—protesters chanting or funeral music with no reporter commentary.

Actualities and wraps need **lead-ins** and **lead-outs,** sometimes called **intros** and **outros.** As you prepare for your shift, you listen to the sounds with which you'll work and write introductions and ending statements. In preparing lead-ins and lead-outs, follow established practice at your station. Practices vary from station to station, but most follow a general pattern.

First, you'll make decisions about editing the actualities, voicers, and wraps with which you'll work, as well as any taped sceners to be repeated after their earlier live presentation. As you listen to each tape, you'll make decisions about the various segments you'd like to use on the newscast. Some of these will have been edited by a field reporter, a newswriter, or another newscaster, so you may add them to your on-air material without alteration.

Since there are fewer station personnel to help you prepare or update material during off-peak hours, such as in the middle of the night or on the weekend, you'll most likely rely on recorded stories prepared by others. Most recordings used in newscasts are edited electronically. The excerpts you intend to use must be dubbed to a storage medium.

Figure 9.3

An actuality log prepared
by a reporter.

RADIO NEWS ACTUALITY LOG			EDITOR: HEWITT

STORY AND REPORTER: Forest Fire, Hewitt

CART #	SUBJECT	TIME	END CUE
N-35	Mt. Sakea forest ranger James Cleary—fire has burned more than 3,000 acres	:16	"as of now."
N-99	No evidence as to cause. Arson not ruled out. Man seen leaving area at high speed in green sports car.	:11	"in a green sports car."
N-83	Should have it surrounded by tonight, and contained by midday tomorrow— depending on the weather.	:15	"a lot of tired firefighters will be able to go home."

One actuality or recorded telephone interview often provides several sounds for a newscast. On your script you'll indicate the words that close each segment of the report so that the announcer who uses them will know the **out cues.**

You'll also write a log that lists the general nature of each actuality, the running time of each, and their out cues, or end cues. Figure 9.3 shows one example of current practice in logging actualities. The log shows that the editor (who was also the reporter) was able to obtain three brief actualities from one recorded telephone conversation with a forest ranger. The general nature of each actuality is listed under SUBJECT, and the end cues allow the anchor to pick up immediately when the cut ends. When the precise end cue is also spoken earlier in the actuality, the person preparing the log writes **double out** in the END CUE column to indicate that fact. For example, if the phrase "as of now" had been used by the ranger twice in the first actuality, *double out* would have warned the newscaster against picking up the cue prematurely.

In preparing for a newscast, you must have a fairly accurate idea of the number of lines or pages you'll read in the allotted time.

To project the amount of time it will take to read copy, count the number of lines on a typical page of copy and time yourself as you read aloud at your most comfortable and effective speed. If you read at about 180 words a minute, you'll read the following numbers of lines in the given time:

15 seconds = 4 lines

30 seconds = 8 lines

45 seconds = 12 lines

60 seconds = 16 lines

If a page of copy has thirty-two lines, for example, you'll read a page in about two minutes. With such information you can easily project the number of lines of copy needed for a newscast of a specific length.

Of course, a time chart is useful only for developing a sense of the relation between space (the physical copy) and time (the newscast). Experienced reporters have so developed this sense that they can prepare newscasts without conscious thought of lines per minute or of their reading speed. As you work with a time chart, remember that actualities, commercials, and sounds—as well as your desire to vary your pace of reading to match the moods of the stories—will complicate your timing.

Writing News

As a radio journalist, you'll be expected to write well and rapidly. To help you develop your writing skills, Chet Casselman, a highly experienced news director and former national president of the Radio-Television News Directors Association, offers the following guidelines.[2] They are, for the most part, equally applicable to writing news for television.

Write for the Ear Rather Than the Eye. Your audience doesn't see the script; it only hears it. Sentences should be relatively short, the vocabulary should be geared to a heterogeneous audience, and potentially confusing statistics should be simplified. Some specific rules:

- Say it the simple way. Eliminate unnecessary ages, middle initials, addresses, occupations, unfamiliar or obscure names, precise or involved numbers, incidental information, and anything else that slows down or clutters up the story.

---

[2]Chet Casselman, *KSFO Stylebook* (San Francisco: Golden West Broadcasters), pp. 4–7.

- Convert precise or involved numbers to a simplified form. For example, change 1,572 to "almost sixteen hundred," 2.6 million to "slightly more than two and a half million," and 35.7 percent to "nearly 36 percent." Unless a number is an essential part of the story, it should be dropped.
- Express names of famous people and their relatives carefully to avoid confusion. For instance, "The wife of famous architect Sydney Nolan is dead; Mary Nolan died today in Chicago of heart failure" is much clearer than "Mary Nolan, 67, wife of famous architect Sydney Nolan, died today in Chicago."
- Avoid indiscriminate use of personal pronouns. Repeat the names of the persons in the story rather than using *he, she,* or *they* whenever there's the slightest chance that the reference may be misunderstood.
- Report that a person pleads "innocent" rather than "not guilty." The latter may be too easily misunderstood as its opposite.
- Avoid the words *latter, former,* and *respectively,* which are acceptable in print but shouldn't be used on the air because listeners have no way of referring to the original comment.
- Avoid hackneyed expressions common to newscasts but seldom heard in everyday conversation. Say *run* instead of *flee, looking for* instead of *seeking,* and *killed* or *murdered* instead of *slain.*
- Change direct quotations from first person to third person whenever the change will help listeners understand. It's clearer to say "The mayor says she's going to get to the bottom of the matter" than to say "The mayor says, and these are her words, 'I'm going to get to the bottom of the matter,' end of quote."
- Always use contractions, unless the two words are needed for emphasis.

Avoid Confusing Words and Statements. The following lead-in to a news story is seriously misleading: "We have good news tonight for some veterans and their families. A House committee has approved a 6 percent cost-of-living increase." People unfamiliar with the legislative process might assume the money was as good as in the bank.[3] Confusion can

---

[3]Money bills are originated by a committee of the House of Representatives. Measures that are passed by that committee face possible alteration or defeat at several other levels: from the full House membership, from the Senate, and from a possible Presidential veto.

CHECKLIST

WRITING
EFFECTIVE
NEWS COPY

1. Write for the ear rather than the eye.
2. Avoid confusing words and statements.
3. Avoid excessive redundancy.
4. Use the present tense and the active voice.
5. Avoid initials.
6. Don't give addresses.
7. Use official job titles.
8. Proofread for badly cast sentences.
9. Avoid using *we* to refer to yourself.
10. Don't refer to a suspect's past criminal record.

also arise from using *homonyms,* words pronounced the same as others with different meanings. For example, in 1999, when there was an outbreak of the deadly Ebola virus in Africa, radio listeners must have been puzzled when they heard. ". . . ninety people were killed by *Ebola virus*" and thought they heard ". . . ninety people were killed by *a bowl of iris.*"[4]

Avoid Redundancy. Repeating important facts is advisable, but too frequent repetition is dull. For example, a newscaster might say, "Senator Muncey has called the recent hike in the prime lending rate outrageous," and then go to an actuality in which we hear the senator say, "The latest hike in the prime lending rate is, in my opinion, outrageous." Work always for lead-ins that promote interest but don't duplicate the story that follows.

Use the Present Tense and the Active Voice. Because the electronic media can report events as they happen, the present tense is appropriate. It automatically gives news an air of immediacy. The active voice uses verbs that give sentences power. Instead of writing "The passenger ship was rammed by a submarine in Hampton Roads," write "A submarine rammed a passenger ship in Hampton Roads."

---

[4]Another example: the word, *expatriate* may easily be confused with *ex-patriot*. The word *expatriate* can mean one who's renounced his or her native land. Its more common meaning, though, refers to one who lives abroad. As an announcer, be alert for homonyms that may confuse, and find ways to paraphrase when there is any doubt as to their meaning.

Avoid Initials. Use initials only when they're so well known that no misunderstanding is possible. A few standard abbreviations are readily identifiable; examples are FBI, U.S., YMCA, and CIA. Most abbreviations, not as well known, should be replaced with the correct title, for example, "The Michigan Teacher's Association," followed later in the story by an appropriate phrase such as "the teachers' association."

Don't Give Addresses in News Copy. You may give addresses if they're famous or essential to the story. *Ten Downing Street,* the home of the British prime minister, is a safe address to broadcast. The address of a murder suspect or an assault victim is not.

Be Careful to Use Official Job Titles. Use *firefighters, police officers,* and *mail carriers,* rather than *firemen, policemen,* and *mailmen.*[5]

Be Wary of Badly Cast Sentences. This example from a wire-service bulletin shows the peril of careless writing:

> Detectives found two and a half pounds of Asian and Mexican heroin in a large woman's handbag when the car was stopped in South Central Los Angeles.

Listeners probably missed the next two news items while trying to decide whether the heroin was found in the handbag of a large woman or in a woman's large handbag.

When Referring to Yourself, Use I *Not* We. Such use of *we* is inaccurate and pretentious. No one person can be "we," although monarchs and high church officials have traditionally used *we* this way.

Don't Refer to a Suspect's Past Criminal Record. Unless it's known to be true and is an important aspect of a present case, a suspect's past criminal record should not be mentioned. In most instances, a suspect's crim-

---

[5]Words help determine and define reality, so the terms used for numerous occupations were changed officially by the U.S. Department of Labor to eliminate gender and age bias in our everyday language. These changes were made in the U.S. Department of Labor's *Dictionary of Occupational Titles,* 4th ed. (2 volumes, revised 1991), in which the official terminology for nearly 3,500 occupations was changed to eliminate discriminatory referents.

inal record should be reported only after the suspect has been formally charged. Also, don't refer to any history of mental illness or treatment unless the information is essential to the story and has been checked for accuracy. Not only may reporting such information be defamatory, it may also prejudice the public against the person accused of a crime but not charged, tried, and convicted.

Avoid the Misuse of Allegedly. Perhaps the most overused word in broadcast news reports is *allegedly*. It's impossible for a person to steal, kill, or lie in an alleged way. "Twenty people were allegedly killed or injured by the crazed gunman" makes no grammatical sense. The use of *allegedly* does not always protect the station from charges of libel. You aren't protected when using the term unless the story includes the name or title of the person doing the "alleging." It's safe to say "Police Captain Caprio alleged that the man threatened to kill his hostage," without any added form of "allege." When you state the name or title of a person who is qualified to make an allegation (such as a police captain), you can omit the qualifying term "alleged" altogether.

The only sound reason for using any of the derivatives of *allegation* is to help preserve the notion that all people are innocent until proven guilty. There are, however, correct and incorrect ways of using these words. Here are three misuses noticed recently:

1. "The bullet allegedly fired at the president. . . ." This is ludicrous. The reporter can't possibly question the fact that a gun was fired and a bullet whizzed past the president, when viewers can see the incident on their television screen.
2. "Jones will stand trial for alleged auto theft." The notion of a trial carries with it the allegation, by a district attorney, of guilt. Therefore, *alleged* is unnecessary in this sentence.
3. "The experts have examined the alleged bullets used in the assassination." There are many kinds of bullets, but no one has ever examined an alleged one.

When considering the use of any term of *allegation*, ask yourself these questions: (1) Is the word necessary to qualify the statement? (2) Am I using it correctly? Clearly, *allegedly* and *alleged* are unnecessary in the three examples given. Is it possible or useful to say who is doing the alleging? "Meyer is alleged by his estranged wife to have set fire to the store" is longer and more cumbersome than "Meyer, the alleged arsonist," but it contains more useful information and is fairer to Meyer than the shorter version. The indication that Meyer's wife did the alleging also removes the possibility of your being sued for libel! However, is the term, *is alleged,* the best way of saying this? Instead, say "Meyer's wife claims that . . ." The following are some correct and incorrect uses of these terms:

Correct	Incorrect
"The principal alleged that the striking teachers destroyed their attendance records."	"The striking teachers allegedly destroyed their attendance records."
"Benson is alleged by the State Department to be an undercover agent."	"Benson is allegedly an undercover agent for a foreign power."
"Chang is reported to be set to buy the hockey team at the end of the season."	"Chang allegedly is set to buy the hockey team at the end of the season."*

*Note that this example is wrong in two ways. First, it isn't possible to buy anything in an alleged manner. Second, terms of *allegation* should be reserved for instances in which there's possible wrongdoing.

Allegedly is a poor reporter's cop-out. This word fails to tell us who is doing the alleging. You may not know who's doing the alleging, but it's part of your job to find out and to include that information in your report.

Checking Your Newswriting Style

A simple way to check the clarity of your broadcast newswriting was developed by Irving Fang, who calls his system the easy listening formula (ELF).[6] It's applied by counting, in each sentence, every syllable above one per word. For example, the sentence "The quick brown fox jumped over the lazy dog" has an ELF score of 2: 1 for the second syllable in *over* and 1 for the second syllable in *lazy.* To find the total ELF score for a script, compute the ELF scores of all the sentences and average them.

---

[6]Irving E. Fang, *Television News, Radio News,* 4th rev. ed. (St. Paul: Rada Press, 1985), pp. 42–43.

Fang's investigation of a wide variety of broadcast news scripts showed that the ELF scores of the most highly rated newswriters average below 12. If your sentences score consistently above that figure, you may not be writing well for aural comprehension. Fang points out, however, that no mechanical system of measuring language is infallible. Common sense must be applied at all times in using his formula, because "it is easy to devise a confusing sentence with a low ELF score, just as it is easy to devise a simple sentence with a high ELF score. . . . What the easy listening formula shows is tendency and trend."

Delivering the News

When you've written and rewritten the copy you'll use during your air shift and when the sounds have been assembled and logged, you're ready to go on the air. As you sit in the on-air studio, you'll have before you the following items:

- The **running log**, sometimes called a **run sheet**, follows the established format of your station and indicates the times at which you'll give headlines, features, time checks, commercials, and other newscast elements or the times at which they'll be played. The log may be on sheets of paper, on a computer screen, or on both.

- The **continuity book**, which contains notations of recorded commercials you'll play.

- Your **news script**, which will be loose sheets or which may appear on a video display screen.

- An **elapsed-time clock**, which you can start and stop to help you time the commercials you'll read.

- **Switches**, or **buttons**, that allow you to open and close your announce mic, to open and close the intercom or talk-back mic, and to open a mic in the newsroom for feeding out a news bulletin.

- Equipment for playing actualities, commercials, station IDs, jingles, and such. Depending on the sophistication of your station's announce studio, you may use **tape carts**, **DAT** (**digital audiotape**) cassettes, **CDs**, or a computerized storage system.

- One or more lights to send information to you while you're on the air. (For example, a red light might indicate that the newsroom has a bulletin to be read; a yellow light might tell you that the station's traffic reporter has a traffic alert.)

The on-air studio may be equipped with a comfortable chair without armrests (they'd restrict movement) and castered legs that enable you to scoot in and out, or from side to side. The chair may be designed to promote good posture, but no chair alone can make anyone sit up straight. The quality of your voice is directly affected by your posture; remember to sit comfortably, but try to keep your spine as straight as possible. A slumping person can't breathe correctly, and weakened abdominal muscles and diaphragm can't push air from your lungs through your phonators and articulators with sufficient strength.

Position yourself so you can easily reach the script, the continuity book, and the controls of both the elapsed-time clock and your mic. You'll be checking off commercials, PSAs (public-service announcements), and other program elements as they occur, so make sure that you're in a position to reach the running log with your pencil. Unless you have an unusual voice or speech personality, you should position yourself six to ten inches from the mic. If you experience problems with excessive sibilance or popping, or if your voice sounds thin or strident, work with a station engineer to find a better way of using your mic.

When you're on the air with the news, you're the **anchor**. At times you may be joined in the booth by a feature reporter, a field reporter who's returned from the scene of a news event, or a **co-anchor** (a second newscaster who'll alternate with you in the reading of news stories).

Most news announcers read copy at 175 to 200 words a minute. This speed is considered fast enough to give the appropriate degree of importance to the material yet slow enough to be understood easily. At a station that carries only infrequent and very brief reports, you may be asked to read at a much faster rate. The overall sound of the station will determine reading speed. To prepare for all eventualities, you should practice reading news in at least four different ways:

1. Practice reading the news slowly and casually, as preferred by many low-key stations.
2. Read the news at the rate you feel brings out the best in your voice, interpretive abilities, and personality.
3. Practice at a rate of approximately two hundred words a minute. This is the rate that may be expected of you.
4. Practice reading at your absolute maximum rate, with the realization that you're reading too fast if you stumble, slur words, have trouble maintaining controlled breathing, force your voice into stridency, or lose significant comprehensibility.

As you read, be prepared for mistakes you may make from misreading or stumbling over words, introducing the wrong recorded message, or cuing prematurely. Some argue that mistakes should be covered up rather than acknowledged, but the best practice is to acknowledge mistakes as frankly but as unobtrusively as possible. Here's an example of a weak cover-up:

ANNCR:

. . . and they'll have your car ready in a half-hour, or an hour and a half, whichever comes sooner.

The script said "in an hour and a half." The cover-up is improper because it gives false information. Here's another example:

ANNCR:

The press secretary delayed and relayed the president's statement on the meeting.

Here the cover-up is so obvious that it would have been far better to have said, "The press secretary delayed—sorry, relayed—the president's . . ."

When giving cues to a co-anchor, stop talking after throwing the cue. If you ramble on, you'll talk over your partner's opening words. No well-run station will tolerate such sloppiness. In throwing cues, don't think it amateurish to make your gestures big, clean, and precise. The best professionals never lapse into practices that can damage the program or their own performance.

You may be handling a great deal of paper during your air shift, so develop skill in shifting papers without allowing the sound of rattling paper to be picked up by your mic. You'll need to lift script pages from the pile in front of you, move them to one side, and turn script pages in the continuity book. No materials should be stapled together, so there should be no need to turn over pages while on the air.

There will be many times during a normal shift when you'll have an opportunity to talk directly with your producer, co-anchor, or sports, traffic, or weather reporter. Use these opportunities for consultation wisely, but not too often. It's important that you not lose track of what your audience is hearing at such times. Check details that might prevent errors. Tell the producer that you're going to shorten or dump a story because you're running late. If in doubt, ask what the next sound is to be. But be aware at all times of what's going out over the air. More than one anchor has followed a tragic actuality with an inappropriate wisecrack. Also, there's the possibility that the wrong package has been played. If you are not listening, you can't possibly correct the mistake.

Be prepared to make constructive use of the minutes you have during your shift when you're not actually on the air. During breaks of thirty to sixty seconds, bring your logging up to date; check out the next few sounds you'll introduce or cue; and see whether you're running ahead of, behind, or right on schedule. During longer breaks, you may have to write intros to actualities or voicers that were received and edited while you were on the air.

Three- or four-hour shifts aren't uncommon at stations that feature news. It takes a healthy speech mechanism to continue to perform well day after day. You'll very quickly become aware of any misuse of your vocal apparatus because you'll suffer from hoarseness, sore throat, or similar disorders. Always have such symptoms checked by a doctor.

Long before you apply for a position as a news anchor, you should practice performing as you'll be expected to perform on the job. Practicing means not only learning to work with all the elements of a con-

Figure 9.4

During morning commutes, 5:30 to 7:00 A.M. each weekday, Stan Burford reports from a helicopter to inform television viewers of traffic conditions. During afternoon drive time, he works in a radio newsroom with a bank of audio monitors to keep drivers informed of traffic problems and alternate routes they may take. *Courtesy of Stan Burford and KGO-TV and KGO NewsTalk Radio, San Francisco, California.*

temporary newscast but also reading the news for extended periods. Such practice can't ordinarily be accomplished in a classroom, so you're encouraged to look for opportunities to perform wherever they present themselves. College radio stations offer realistic challenges to students preparing for careers as radio news personnel.

The Radio Field Reporter

Field reporters are responsible for (1) live coverage of events as they occur; (2) recorded actualities, voicers, and wraps; and (3) occasional research for, and production of, **minidocs**, brief documentaries presented as a series, usually over several days. Radio field reporters are sometimes called *general-assignment reporters, correspondents,* or *special-assignment reporters.* Their work is similar to that of their television counterparts, with obvious variations because of differences in electronic technology.

Live Reporting

When reporting live, it's your responsibility to create a word picture of a scene, including sights, sounds, smells, tension in the air, and factual details—for example, the extent of a blaze, the names of the victims, or the value of stolen goods. When reporting live, you may be equipped with a cell phone. You'll use it to indicate when you're ready to give your report, and you'll hear your cue to start as the program line is fed to you. Even when you're describing events as they occur (a *live scener*), as opposed to reporting at the conclusion of an event, you may work from notes that you scribbled as you gathered information.

As you give a live report, keep these suggestions in mind:

- Don't report rumors, unless they're essential to the story—and then report them only as rumors.
- Don't make unsubstantiated guesses as to facts, such as numbers of people injured or the value of a gutted building.
- Control your emotions, but remember that a bit of genuine excitement in your voice will convey the significance of your report.
- Don't identify yourself at the start of the report, because the anchor will already have given your name. Identify yourself at the close of the story, following the policy set by your station.
- In the event of physical danger—a police siege or a confrontation between rival groups or street gangs—don't become so

absorbed in your story that you endanger yourself or your station's equipment.

- Be prepared to discuss the event with the anchor after you've given your report. This means doing sufficient investigation prior to going on the air so that you can answer questions.

Voicers, Actualities, Sceners, and Wraps

Most of your work as a field reporter won't be broadcast live but will be in the form of **packages**, which consist of wraps, voicers, and edited sceners. When recording in the field, you'll likely use a cassette tape recorder. When making packages at the station, you'll usually dub from cassettes to a mass storage disk or to DAT cassettes. These will be the sounds introduced by news anchors during their shifts.

Field voicers usually are transmitted to the station by cell phone. After making notes, you call the newsroom of your station and notify a reporter or producer that you're ready to file a report. The person taking your call will prepare to activate a storage medium—hard disk, tape

Figure 9.5

Dr. Dean Edell is one of the first "media doctors" in the nation. He appears on both the five and six o'clock evening newscasts on KGO-TV. His syndicated talk radio show is heard in more than 400 markets. In addition to discussing medical problems and breakthroughs, he also takes phone-in questions in a segment he calls "Housecalls." Dr. Edell earned his M.D. at Cornell University Medical School. *Courtesy of Dr. Dean Edell and KGO-TV, San Francisco, California.*

cart, or DAT cassette—and will place an index finger on the start button. You give a brief countdown—"three, two, one"—and start your report. The person taking the call will press the start button just after you say "one." If all goes well, the recording and your report begin at the same time. Voicers made at the station are produced in essentially the same way, although you'll typically perform all of the work without assistance.

Some field reporters must use a conventional telephone to send in voicers. If you're reporting live, your voice is put directly on the air. The process becomes less desirable when you're sending a report with one or more actualities that you've recorded previously. You'll have to speak into the mouthpiece of a conventional or cellular phone, roll your tape, quickly move the telephone's mouthpiece down to the speaker of your recorder to send the bulk of your report, and then move the handset up to your mouth to make your closing comments and tag.

If you're reporting from one of your station's "bureaus," such as city hall, the court house, or a police station, you'll most likely use a telephone that's been rewired by a station engineer. The handset will have been outfitted with a miniplug that allows the cable from your recorder to bypass the telephone's built-in microphone and pass directly over the line to your station. The signal quality is excellent.

A **wrap** is phoned in essentially the same way as a voicer except for this difference: When all elements are connected, your tape is cued, your mic switch is on, and the record key is depressed, you give the countdown and begin your introduction to the actuality live. When you finish, you depress the play key and the tape rolls. When the actuality is completed, you hit the record key. This cancels the play key, so the tape stops rolling while you give your closing tag live.

In making voicers at the station, you'll write a script. In this case the log will simply indicate "script attached," the duration of the voicer in seconds, and the end cue, which is nearly always your name followed by the call letters of your station.

In making wraps at the station, you begin by making and recording telephone calls. If there's a news story of an impending strike, for example, your phone calls may be to the union leader, the speaker for the company or agency being threatened, and a labor negotiator. From the telephone interviews you should be able to make several usable wraps—carted, timed, and ready to be logged.

Philosophies of Radio and Television Journalism

As a journalist working for a television, radio, or cable news station (such as CNN), you'll make important decisions daily. The way you report stories will influence attitudes and actions of your listeners and viewers. Because of this, it's essential that you develop a working philosophy of broadcast journalism. When an important story breaks, it's far too late for you to start making decisions about your responsibilities, values, and philosophy of broadcast journalism.

In a democracy there are only two theories of the press worthy of consideration. The first, the **libertarian theory,** is based on the belief that, except for defamation, obscenity, or wartime sedition, there should be no censorship or suppression of news whatsoever. The second theory, which Wilbur Schramm named the **social responsibility theory,** maintains that journalists must exercise judgment as to whether a particular story should be covered or ignored and, if covered, how it should be covered.[7]

The libertarian theory of the press grew out of democratic movements in England near the end of the seventeenth century and received renewed momentum a hundred years later through the writings and speeches of Thomas Paine, Thomas Jefferson, and other American revolutionaries. Essentially, the libertarian theory was a response to centuries of suppression and censorship by church and state. Jefferson believed that the only security a democratic people have is grounded in a fully informed electorate. "If a nation expects to be ignorant and free, in a state of civilization, it expects what never was and never will be," wrote Jefferson in 1816. The implementation of this statement is clear: allow full and free publication of all shades of opinion and all items of information. The basic assumption of the libertarians was (and is) that a free people in full possession of the facts will act responsibly.

The social responsibility theory was a response to what many saw as shortcomings in the idealistic libertarian theory. In practice, the public simply wasn't receiving all of the facts necessary to make responsible decisions. In the wake of the civil disorders of the late 1960s, a presidential commission called attention to what was seen as the failure of the press to adequately inform the public. "Disorders are only one aspect of the dilemmas and difficulties of race relations in America. In defining, explaining, and reporting this broader, more complex, and ultimately far more fundamental subject, the communications media, ironically, have failed to communicate."[8]

---

[7]Wilbur Schramm, *Responsibility in Mass Communication* (New York: Harper & Row, 1957).
[8]*Report of the National Advisory Commission on Civil Disorders* (New York: Bantam, 1968), pp. 382–383.

A libertarian approach to riot coverage was unacceptable to the commission for several reasons: reported facts may have been exceptional rather than typical; disclosing some facts may have caused even more serious incidents; and, although the reported fact indeed may have happened, it may have occurred only because the news media were encouraging certain actions by their very presence. The social responsibility theory of the press asks that journalists report not only the facts but also *the truth behind the facts.*

The concerns expressed regarding a libertarian approach to journalism are understandable when one thinks of serious news events such as riots, wars, or insurrections. The social responsibility theory demands that journalists apply their best judgment and weigh their conduct on a daily basis without regard to the nature or scope of the story being covered. Both the libertarian and the social responsibility theories of news coverage ask that reporters be responsible journalists; all reporters should start with good intentions, but a well-meant beginning is not enough. Only a solid education in broadcast and journalistic law, ethics, and investigative reporting can lead to success as a responsible broadcast journalist.

Preparing Feature Reports: Minidocs

Radio stations that emphasize news sometimes vary their programming by broadcasting feature reports or short documentaries. These may be a series of three- or four-minute programs, made up of as few as three or as many as seven individual segments, each focusing on a different aspect of a topic. Feature reports deal with people, problems, events, or anything else that's of general interest but lacks the "hard news" character that demands coverage on a regular newscast. Breaking news stories, in fact, frequently inspire feature reports, but features differ from news stories in that they provide much more detail, offer greater perspective, and often express a point of view.

Preparing a series of feature reports begins with the selection of a topic. An editor may assign a topic to you, but as feature reporter you're expected to come up with promising ideas of your own. It's obvious that your overriding responsibility is to report on issues of general interest. That's the easy part. The more difficult task is finding ways to make your reports appealing. As a reporter on *radio,* one of your first considerations should be *sounds.* Ask yourself what kinds of sounds, both spoken and natural environmental sounds, can be used to take advantage of your medium. No report can be considered a success unless it captures

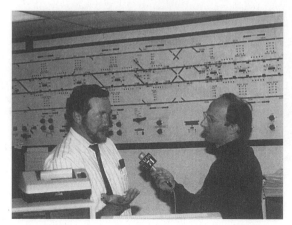 

Figure 9.6

Left: Special assignment reporter Mike Sugerman interviews municipal railway official Len Olson as Sugermen gathers information for a five-part minidoc on public transportation. Each segment runs from 2 minutes, 17 seconds, to 2 minutes, 37 seconds. *Right:* Back at the station, Sugerman listens to the material he recorded in the field, edited, and assembled in the order in which it will be broadcast. He then records his connecting narration. *Courtesy of Mike Sugerman and KCBS, San Francisco, California.*

and holds the attention of your listeners. A succession of statements by public officials isn't likely to be dramatic or even interesting, but official position statements interspersed with more dramatic actualities, sound effects, and narration can deliver a series that first grabs audience attention and then satisfies audience curiosity through a fast-paced, varied, and aurally stimulating presentation.

Once you've chosen or been assigned a topic, your job will include researching the subject, identifying and interviewing people you hope will contribute the information you need, editing and organizing the taped materials, writing the connective and interpretive narration, voicing the narration, and producing the final mixed versions of the program segments. The steps in creating a series are illustrated in the following example on the topic of homelessness.

Researching the Topic

Your research plan is essential to the success of the series. Developing a personal system for doing research can save hours, reduce the possibility of mistakes, and result in a superior product. You most likely will want to begin your research with an on-line **search engine**, such as Yahoo!, Hotbot, Alta Vista, or Fast Search. These engines operate on the basis of author, title, or key words. In searching for information on *homelessness,* type "homelessness" on the keyboard, and the display will show the number of articles available and give the title and the gist of each entry.

If you ask a search engine for articles on *homelessness,* the number you'll find will be staggering, so you'll want to narrow it down by city or state, age, socioeconomic group, or some other criterion. As an example of the wealth of information available, entering the key word "homelessness" on Fast Search produced references to 66,466 articles and reports in 0.0220 seconds search time! To illustrate further, entering the names of specific cities, chosen at random, plus entering "homelessness," produced 3,514 documents for Seattle; 1,962 for Kansas City; 2,178 for Houston; 1,854 for Miami; and 4,353 for Toronto. Combining the key words "homelessness," "mental illness," and "Texas" produced 1,113 documents. In all examples, the search engine found and listed documents that included only one key word, as well as documents that included all key words. As a result, most of the "hits" found weren't useful to the researcher. However, by reading the titles and a few descriptive words about each entry, complete articles that seem relevant to your project can be brought up on your computer screen, examined, and printed for further appraisal and possible use. Eventually, you'll be able to select a number of articles and activate a printer to produce hard copy.

Other sources you can use to find information on your topic include the *Reader's Guide to Periodical Literature, Facts on File,* the *New York Times Index,* the U.S. Government's *Statistical Abstract,* and a number of encyclopedias and almanacs. With a few hours of searching, you'll gather many basic facts and representative opinions about homelessness.

Outlining the Series

Having read several articles and learned some basic statistics about the homeless and homelessness, you're ready to make some tentative decisions about the series. If you and the news director agree that the topic is important and complex, perhaps five or six segments will be allotted to it. You may decide that your final segment will provide explicit recommendations. You'll also decide on the people to be interviewed and the contributions you hope will be made by each. The following lists the subjects you will likely cover in each segment of your report on homelessness.

- Segment 1—Basic facts about homelessness and statistics. To make listeners aware that the problem of homelessness is large and growing, you include many sound bites of homeless people, citizens who are angry about people sleeping in parks or doorways, and some who are genuinely concerned about the safety and welfare of homeless people. You also "tease" a number of questions that you'll address in later broadcasts.

- Segment 2—What a homeless person goes through. This segment is made up of edited comments by several homeless people, recorded in a park, under a viaduct, or at any other site where you've found the homeless congregate.

- Segment 3—A police view of the homeless. This segment features the edited comments of police officers as well as one or more police officials. It discusses the problems of sanitation and aggressive panhandling that are caused by some who are homeless.

- Segment 4—Attitudes of neighbors, tourists, and businesspersons. This segment shows a range of attitudes held by people who are not themselves homeless but who nonetheless are affected by homelessness.

- Segment 5—Causes of homelessness. This segment includes comments from social workers, psychiatrists, or other authorities on the subject.

- Segment 6—What society should do to help the homeless. This last segment consists of suggestions offered by several of the people interviewed for the series.

Recording Interviews

Because all of your interviews will be in the field, you'll need a high-quality, lightweight, battery-operated tape recorder. You'll also need a professional external microphone.

Before making dates for interviews, speak with the people you've selected tentatively for the program. Tell them that you want ideas and information, but don't invite them to be interviewed until you're satisfied that they're articulate, knowledgeable, and cooperative. You may find you must look further for your talent. However, you won't be able to phone homeless people to screen them or set up appointments, so there's no reason to delay taping them. Obtain their permission to tape. Then roll your cassette and start asking questions. Then, after you've completed your interviews, have them sign permission forms. Be prepared to play back the interview you've just conducted if requested. Interviewees may want to hear the tape before they sign a permission form!

Before each recording session, prepare a list of questions. Be as thorough as possible in your preparation; the audio quality of your program will suffer if you have to record the same person on two or more occasions or in different locations. Ambient noise and acoustics should be as consistent as possible within each program segment.

Tips on interviewing are given in Chapter 8. The following checklist and comments add some suggestions that are applicable to recording material for feature reports.

CHECKLIST

RECORDING INTERVIEWS SUCCESSFULLY

1. Test your equipment before beginning an interview.
2. Explain your taping and editing procedures to the interviewee.
3. When you're ready to begin, ask the guest to remain silent and then start recording.
4. Avoid giving vocal reinforcements such as "uh-huhs" during the guest's remarks.
5. Keep the recorder running.
6. Limit your recording sessions to a reasonable length.
7. Keep your station's format restrictions in mind.
8. If there is ambient noise, keep the mic close to the interviewee's mouth.

Test your equipment before beginning the interview, no matter how experienced you are. Even professionals sometimes complete interviews only to discover that their batteries were weak, the machine was not recording, the volume level was too high or too low, or the absence of a windscreen on the mic resulted in excessive wind blast. Try to test your equipment under the exact conditions and in the precise location of the interview. After completing your taping, spot check your tape to make sure your equipment worked properly.

Take time to explain taping and editing procedures to the interviewee. It's important for your guest to know that all of your comments and questions will be removed from the tape and replaced by narration recorded in the studio. This means that the interviewee should make direct, complete statements that are not preceded by references to the questions. Here are two responses to the same question, one useful and another that will cause a problem in editing:

ANNCR:

What do you feel should be done to combat homelessness in America?

ANSWER 1:

To make a dent in homelessness, we need to find out just who the homeless are and how they became homeless.

ANSWER 2:

I don't really have the answers. Maybe we need to know more about them and why they're without homes.

Both statements say approximately the same thing, but it's obvious that the first answer will be easier to edit, will provide more precise information than the second answer, and will allow a smoother flow from narration to statement. You can't expect every person you interview to overcome a lifetime of conversational habit, but you can expect reasonable cooperation.

When you're ready to begin the interview, ask the interviewee to remain silent and then start recording. Record about thirty seconds of dead air. This precaution provides you with **ambient sound** for insertion at any point at which you want an undetectable pause. All rooms other than those designed for scientific tests have ambient noise, and no two rooms are acoustically alike. Splicing in the ambient sound from another interview, or blank tape, would be noticeable to any attentive listener. Ambient sound is rarely needed, but when you do need it you'll be grateful for having developed the habit of recording it before every interview.

It's also good practice to allow the recorder to run for a few seconds after your guest has stopped speaking. Later, when you're editing and writing your script, you may want to do a fade-out at the end of one or another of your guest's comments. If you've abruptly stopped the recorder immediately at the conclusion of your guest's remarks, there's no way to do a fade.

When recording in the field—as for the homelessness series— record every sound you might conceivably want to use later as you edit your tapes and write narration. If you realize you need a particular sound after you've returned to the station, it's probably too late to return to the field to record what you missed because timelines are so tight. Therefore, when interviewing a person living in an automobile, for example, record the sound of a car door slamming. Record the sound of a dog barking, if that's an appropriate (and genuine) sound relating to a pet-owning homeless person. Record traffic sounds and the sounds of buses, streetcars, and trains if they'll add a touch of honest reality. Record the songs of birds and of wind whistling through trees if those sounds are actually present in the environment about which you're reporting. Radio, being an aural medium, benefits greatly from the ambiance of an environment established through its sounds. At the same time, never resort to the use of faked sound effects in a piece that's offered as reality.

As you interview, avoid giving your guest vocal reinforcement, such as "uh-huh" or "I see." These will be impossible to edit out when you assemble the program. Nonverbal support—for example, a nod of the head or a smile—is sufficient to encourage a guest to continue.

During the interview, try to keep the recorder running. Don't hesitate to stop it, however, if the session's going badly. The reason for an uninterrupted take is that most people are more alert and energized when they feel that what they're saying will be heard later on the air. Constant stopping and starting saps energy and reduces concentration.

Keep your taping sessions to a reasonable length. A ninety-minute interview to be edited as part of a three-minute program segment could cost you hours of production time. Therefore, work for interviews that are long enough to supply you with the material you need, but not so long as to saddle you with hours of editing.

As you interview, keep the format of your station's feature reports in mind. If, for example, your station prefers to use both your questions and your guest's answers as recorded in the field, your interviewing technique should reflect that fact. You won't have to ask guests to answer your questions in the form of self-contained statements.

Train yourself to detect slurred speech patterns. Some people run words together so habitually and consistently that it's impossible to edit their comments effectively. If you aren't alert to this potential problem, it'll be too late to do much about it when sitting at a tape-editing station. When your ears tell you that you're working with someone who slurs, do your best to slow the person down. If this attempt fails, ask the guest to repeat single phrases and sentences that seem to be the most important contributions you'll use later in your report.

When recording at any location that has a high level of ambient sound (machinery, traffic, crowds), hold your mic close to your guest's mouth. As mentioned earlier, authentic background sounds can enhance the realism of your report, but they mustn't be so loud as to drown out your guest's remarks. If you'll later edit out your questions, you needn't move the mic back and forth between you and your guest. If, on the other hand, you're to retain even some of your questions or comments, then you must develop skill in moving the mic. To avoid mic-handling noise, wrap the cord around your wrist. Mic-handling noises are especially troublesome because they can be heard only on playback or by monitoring during the interview, a practice seldom engaged in by people working solo.

It's essential that you follow station policy in having those interviewed sign release or permission forms. This requirement may not be a problem when interviewing a public official or other person who can be contacted later for the signing, but anyone who doesn't have a permanent address—such as a homeless person—must sign a form before you leave the site of the interview.

After completing each interview, make notes that later will help you in editing—for example, name of guest, topics covered, comments of special importance, and so on. And, of course, label each tape!

Your next step will be to do a rough edit of your tapes. You'll audition each tape, and dub statements that seem likely for inclusion in your final version to another cassette recorder—most likely DAT—or to a storage disk. If you have access to state-of-the-art equipment, your work can be done entirely on an editing system, such as Digi-cart, a digital hard disk recorder.

If time permits, make a typescript of each roughly edited interview on a word processor for easy cutting and pasting. The written word is far easier to identify, retrieve, manipulate, and edit than are words on an audiotape. When writing the narrative script, you'll find it easier to develop a smooth flow with precise lead-ins when working in print. Making a typescript may actually save time.

Having completed the script, do the fine editing of the rough dub. Editing allows you to remove unwanted pauses, *ers* and *uhs,* or even single words. It also allows you to take a portion of an answer from one part of the interview and join it to an answer from another part of the interview. A word of caution: It's critical that such editing preserve the sense of your guest's comments and never be used for any purpose other than clarifying your guest's position and making your report as factually honest as it can be.

When editing your tapes, you may find that some statements that looked good in the written script don't come out well in sound. Be prepared to go back to the roughly edited version to look for substitute statements or to rewrite your script to make the narrative sound better or more clear.

Finally, record your narration. Often, you'll have to sit in an announce booth or a small production room and do a real-time recording, alternatively feeding your voice and the edited and carted actualities to a tape recorder. It's also possible to record your narration without the edited inserts and to mix the entire report later.

PRACTICE

Reading News Copy Cold

As indicated in Chapter 2, you or your instructor can obtain printouts of up-to-the-minute news copy through the Internet using this URL[9]:

fullcoverage.yahoo.com/

Among many others, Reuters, Pan Africa News Agency (PANA), Agence France Presse, and Voice of America offer current headlines, complete news scripts, and features. These can be selected and printed for practice in news reading. Note: some news providers restrict their service to those that subscribe to the service on a contractual basis.

---

[9]The Internet is changing constantly as new web sites are added and old web sites are abandoned. The URL listings in this textbook should be regarded as samples of the kinds of material available rather than as a stable index. If you seek a web site using one of these URLs and cannot connect, enter the key words for the topic into a search engine to find a site that may provide the information you want.

PRACTICE

Rewriting News Copy

Because most news copy on the Internet is written in newspaper style, you can use it to practice rewriting for a better news sound. Convert newspaper copy to shorter, crisper sentences; round out numbers (change "3.89 million shares" to "nearly 4 million"); and look for homonyms that may cause misunderstanding. Follow the suggestions noted earlier in this chapter for writing news for aural comprehension.

PRACTICE

Performing Commercials on the Side

Some stations have policies that prohibit news reporters or newscasters from reading commercials; most do not. To practice delivery of commercial copy, choose three scripts from Appendix A and read them aloud until you feel confident enough to record your performance. Listen to your performance closely, noting pacing, tone, and pronunciation. Decide what types of commercials are best suited to your personality and your voice.

CHAPTER 10

Television News

TELEVISION NEWS VARIES FROM BRIEF VOICE-OVER SLIDE BULLETINS TO the twenty-four-hour coverage of Cable News Network (CNN). Most large television stations produce two or three news program daily; some are thirty minutes in length, while others last an hour. These are typically broadcast at noon, at the dinner hour, and at ten or eleven o'clock at night. A few stations have an early morning newscast. Except for those in small markets, most news departments are large relative to a station's total employment. Departments range from about a dozen to nearly one hundred employees. Television news programs are put together by reporters, anchors, newswriters, remote crews, mobile van operators, operators of special-effects generators and computer graphics systems, video editors, and a production crew working in the studio, the control room, and master control.

Television Reporters

Journalists who work away from the station are called **field reporters**, **general-assignment reporters**, or just plain **reporters**. Reporters stationed some distance away are called **correspondents**. As a **special-assignment reporter**, you might cover a regular beat such as crime, politics, or a particular section of an extended metropolitan area. Stations that can't afford such specialists on a regular basis often place field reporters on special assignment.

As a field or general-assignment reporter, you'll receive your daily schedule from an **assignment editor (The Desk)**. Some assignments will be to cover **hard news**—serious accidents or crimes, fires, explosions, chemical spills, tornadoes, and other unanticipated events. Other assignments will be concerned with **soft news**—meetings, briefings, hearings, news conferences, and so on. News departments maintain a **future file**, consisting of thirty-one folders (for the days of the month), into which is placed information about scheduled soft news events. As notices of planned events reach the station, they're placed in the folder bearing the appropriate date. Each day the assignment editor searches the file for the most promising news stories and schedules reporters and camera operators to cover the stories. Scheduled coverage of soft news is often dropped at the last minute in favor of late-breaking hard news.

As a field reporter, you'll work live and record on tape or on a digital hard drive.[1] When recording a story, you'll have an opportunity to plan your coverage, engage in on-site investigation, think through and write your opening and closing stand-ups, and record a second or third take if the first effort falls apart. A **stand-up** is a statement by a reporter directly into the camera lens (in other words, addressed to the viewers). It may come at any point in a recorded story, but it nearly always closes the story.

When reporting live by way of microwave or satellite transmission, you'll report events as they happen, and this precludes scriptwriting and reshooting. Your ability to ad-lib an unfolding news event in an accurate, effective manner is an essential key to success in live reporting.

Recorded and live field reports on television newscasts are often longer than stories prepared for radio. Television coverage is much more expensive and time consuming, and involves greater technical complexities. Therefore, you'll be expected to cover only one or two

---

[1]Field cameras may use videotape as the recording medium or a digital hard drive. Throughout this chapter both terms are used.

Figure 10.1

A control center, known as "The Desk," is a prominently placed, high-energy site found in television newsrooms the world over. An assignment editor is stationed there to assign reporters, camera operators, and newswriters to every detail of the day's effort. A record is maintained that follows the progress of each story from the time it's chosen, to when and whom it's assigned, and when it's delivered. The Desk is essential for the coordination of television news personnel and resources. *Courtesy KTVU, Oakland, California.*

stories in a day. You must not assume that your field reports will dominate a newscast; most packages run only between thirty seconds and three minutes. Creating a usable sixty-second report may take several hours, both in the field and at your station. You'll use part of the time investigating the story, lining up witnesses or others you want to interview, conducting interviews, making notes for stand-ups, and recording the stand-ups. More time is consumed after you return to the station because, at nearly every station, reporters edit their recorded material, write voice-over narration, record the narration, and assemble a complete **package** (a report that will need only a lead-in by a news anchor).[2]

Preparing a Package

As a reporter, you'll follow certain steps in making a news package. The assignment editor will give you your assignment on a daily basis. Depending on the kind of news that is breaking, you'll be given either a

---

[2]Many stations use digital video cameras in which a high-capacity hard drive replaces videotape. The recorded material can be edited in postproduction without having to transfer it to another hard drive.

Figure 10.2

Figure 10.2

Feature reporter Bob MacKenzie reviews tapes sent from various organizations and sorts out those that may be of use. In creating a package of his interview with an opera star, for example, he may intercut taped scenes of the singer in performance from a tape supplied by the opera company. Selected scenes are dubbed up to a digital Beta recorder and mixed with the interview. *Courtesy of Bob MacKenzie and KTVU, Oakland, California.*

hard news or a soft news story to cover and, perhaps, be asked for ideas. After receiving the assignment, you leave the station with an **electronic news-gathering (ENG)** operator.

You may travel in a station wagon with little equipment, in a van with equipment for viewing and editing on your way back to the station, a truck equipped to send recorded reports to the station via microwave transmission, or a truck with uplink equipment that bounces program material off a satellite to a receiver at the station.

When you arrive at the scene of the story, you undertake appropriate research to learn what's happened, who's involved, what's going on at the moment, and why the event is happening. In other words, you pursue answers to the traditional *who, what, when, where, why,* and *how* of journalism. As you investigate, the ENG operator records whatever is essential or potentially useful in telling the story, including general scenes of action: for example, the overall wreckage of a multiple-car accident, waters spilling through gaps in a levee, or picketers marching and chanting.

As you gather information, you take notes. At this stage you haven't decided how you'll structure the report, so you commit to your notes almost anything that seems likely to become a part of your story. As the story begins to take shape in your mind, you ask the ENG operator to record this or that person or object, most particularly interviews with eyewitnesses or spokespersons whose edited comments may become **sound bites**, the television equivalent of radio **actualities**. After all notes have been taken and all visual material has been recorded, you perform your stand-ups. You may begin your report by addressing the camera with an introduction, and you may record one or more on-camera comments to be edited into the completed package. You then do an on-camera summary, closing with the phrase that "tosses" your report to the anchor.

Before leaving the scene of your report, you may ask the ENG operator to record material to be used as **cutaway shots**, or **cutaways**. Cutaways are a form of insurance used to avoid **jump cuts**. When editing an interview, you may want to delete some comments the speaker made while in front of the camera. The insertion of a brief shot of you apparently listening to the speaker will camouflage this kind of cut and keep viewers from noticing any change in positions—a jump—of the speaker between comments. To prepare for the possible need of cutaways, you'll

Figure 10.3

KTVU reporter Thuy Vu interviews a protester representing restaurant employees who lost their jobs when ownership of the restaurant changed. Thuy was born in Saigon, and left Vietnam with her family when it fell to the Vietcong. She says: "I think my experience as an immigrant actually gives me more insight as a reporter. When I cover stories about immigrants or disenfranchised communities, I have a fuller understanding of the issues because I have been in their shoes." Thuy received her bachelor's degree, with honors, in rhetoric from the University of California, Berkeley. *Courtesy of Thuy Vu and KTVU, Oakland, California.*

ask the ENG operator to record you after the interview as you look past the camera lens. If possible, do your cutaways while the person you've interviewed is still present. Also, remember that because a cutaway is not an actual, real-time shot of you listening to the speaker, it's *imperative* that your reactions be as true to the spirit of the interview as possible. A popular motion picture of 1988, *Broadcast News,* made contrived cutaway shots the focus of its condemnation of unethical journalistic practices.

Back at the station—if you've not already done so on the drive back—you sit at an editing console in or near the newsroom to view the recorded material, make editing decisions, and write a script that you'll record in an announce booth equipped with a microphone and an **equalizer.** You'll have worked with a station engineer to learn how to adjust the equalizer so your voice will sound as close as possible to the way it sounded when recorded in the field. In writing a script, you'll use a conventional format and certain abbreviations. Many of the abbreviations (and their meaning) used in television scripts are listed in Table 10.1.

Your final step is to mix recorded shots that tell the story, general shots of the scene, sound bites, stand-ups, and your voice-over audio narration into the package.

The script you'll prepare for each package will list all cuts (scenes) to be used, identified by time code address. The **time code** is an elec-

Figure 10.4

News anchor Tori Campbell seated at a video editing station reviews a taped story and writes lead-ins for it. She'll see her lead-ins later on an electronic prompter as she co-anchors the News at Noon. Tori majored in French literature at Hamilton College. *Courtesy Tori Campbell and KTVU, Oakland, California.*

TABLE 10.1	ABBREVIATIONS USED IN TELEVISION SCRIPTS

Abbreviation	Meaning
TS	Tight shot
CU	Close-up
MCU	Medium close-up
ECU or XCU	Extreme close-up
MS	Medium shot
WS or LS	Wide shot or long shot
ELS or XLS	Extreme long shot
OS	Over-the-shoulder shot (usually over the reporter's shoulder and showing the person being interviewed face-on)
RS	Reverse shot (reporter listening to person being interviewed)
TWO-SHOT	A shot with two people in the frame
PAN	Camera moves right to left, or left to right
TILT	Camera moves up or down
SOT	Sound on tape
SLO-MO	Slow motion
VO	Voice-over
CUT	A brief recorded scene, an actuality, a voicer, or a wrap
IN	Indicates the words that open a sound bite
OUT	Indicates the words that end a sound bite
SLUG	The slug line, a brief title given to a news story for identification purposes
TRT	Total running time

tronic readout that gives an address (number) for each frame. Figure 10.5 shows the opening portion of a typical format for editing and assembling a package. *TAL* means talent, and the initials below it (LC) identify the reporter. *SLUG* is the slug line, a brief title given to identify the story. *TIME* gives the running time. The left side of the script is the video information column, with the time code information, descriptions of what is being seen, and *CG* instruction. The abbreviation CG stands for **character generator,** a computer that creates letters and numbers. In Figure 10.5, CG indicates that the words following the abbreviation are to be created by the character generator operator and superimposed on the video screen. The audio column is on the right. The words to be spoken by the reporter are in UPPERCASE, and the words spoken by the witness are in lowercase. *SOT* means **sound on tape,** a term used even in instances in which digital cameras have

Figure 10.5

A script for a video package identifies the cuts used by tape number and time code address.

Thurs, Aug 19 11:18		Page 1		
TAL	STORY SLUG	GRAPHIC	VIS	TIME
LC	BAD TEMPER?		SOT	2:58

CG Ripton
me with Simpsen

28-YEAR OLD EDWIN SIMPSEN CLAIMS THAT RIPTON MOTORIST FRANK LEWIS SEVERELY BEAT HIS PASSENGER AFTER A MINOR FENDER BENDER ON AUGUST FIRST.

various shots,
tape 1, 5:57 on
or :40 on.
street signs,
10:39

THE INCIDENT BEGAN AT LINDARO AND LINCOLN IN RIPTON WHEN SIMPSEN AND HIS COMPANION SIDESWIPED A SPORTS UTILITY VEHICLE.

intersections,
10:55
rolling shots
through streets,
11:50 on

THE TWO MEN STARTED TO PULL OVER, WHEN THEY SAY THEY THOUGHT THEY SAW LEWIS PULL A GUN FROM HIS GLOVE COMPARTMENT. THEY TOOK OFF AT HIGH SPEED THROUGH SEVERAL NEIGHBORHOODS TO AVOID A CONFRONTATION.

shot of railroad crossing
tape 2, 3:31–3:50
CG 2 line
Edwin Simpsen,
witness
tape 1, 1:56–2:03

THEY WERE FORCED TO STOP AT A RAILROAD CROSSING, AND LEWIS CAUGHT UP TO THEM.

Lewis approached the driver's side, pulled open the door, and dragged Larry out and started beating him.

SIMPSEN SAYS THAT LEWIS USED A TIRE IRON IN THE ATTACK. HE ADDS THAT HIS COMPANION DID NOT FIGHT BACK.

CG 2 line
Officer Jackson
Ripton Police
me with officer
tape 2, 16:11–16:21

ARRESTING OFFICER JERRY JACKSON CONFIRMED THAT THERE WAS A VIOLENT ATTACK.

All of us in our business see . . . preserve and protect at all costs.

SOT more Simpsen
tape 3, :54–1:13

I saw Lewis grab . . .
no, it was only him.

replaced cameras that use tape. In the final sound bites, the script indicates only the in cue and the out cue.

In some cases, you'll create a package by returning to your station after covering the assignment and writing a script to accompany your visual images. You alternate your voice-over narration with excerpts that include sound, and mark your script for use by an editor. Some portions of your script may require you to enter a small announce booth to record your comments for inclusion in the completed package. About a half-hour before the ten o'clock news goes on the air, you return to the scene of the news event with a camera operator. Holding your script—usually below camera range—you perform a live ad-libbed introduction to your story on cue. After the director cuts to your package, you can bring your script up to a comfortable reading distance and read at least some of your voice-over narration live. You lower the script out of camera range before you're once again seen live on the television screen to make your closing tag. At that time you may engage in a brief on-air discussion with the news anchors.

At a small television station, you may do your own camera work. You go to the scene of a story, conduct your investigation, and record sound bites, including interviews. Before leaving the scene, you place the camera on a tripod, start the recorder, walk to a position in front of the camera lens, and perform your stand-up. When you return to the station, you write the script and edit and assemble your package.

Reporting Live from the Field

Most television news operations make use of one or more remote vans equipped with ENG equipment: **minicams (miniaturized cameras)**, microwave transmitters, and, in some cases, an uplink to a satellite. Vans are used for conventional coverage of news stories (recording reports in the field), but they also enable reporters to cover events and to transmit their stories directly to the station, often live during a newscast.

Only reporters who are excellent journalists, have widespread knowledge of many subjects, and can ad-lib fluently and informatively are outstanding at live reporting. Excellence as a reporter begins with a solid education. Studying journalism in college will prepare you to size up a story quickly, make judgments about its potential news value, identify the most noteworthy points about the event, and organize that information so that it's readily understandable to viewers. When covering slow-breaking stories (in fact, whenever time permits), your background in journalism will enable you to engage in investigative, or depth, reporting.

Knowing how and where to look for hidden information is essential for depth reporting. Finally, journalism courses will familiarize you with laws regarding libel, contempt, constitutional guarantees, access to public records, the invasion of privacy, and copyrights. Of course, all reporters should be competent journalists, but those who report the news live must be especially well prepared. If you make a defamatory statement on a live broadcast, there's simply no way to undo it.

Reporters also need extensive knowledge of many subjects, especially those who report live. You need a broad education in the arts and sciences, and you should consider yourself a lifelong student. The reading of selected new books, several newsmagazines, and two or more daily papers should be routine for you as you prepare to work as a reporter.

It's common practice for anchors to follow a live report with a **Q & A** (question-and-answer) **session** with the reporter. The stories you report may vary from a demonstration at a nuclear power plant to the birth of a rare animal at the zoo. A good Q & A session requires you to speak knowledgeably about the general subject area of the story you're reporting. Blank looks, incorrect information, and the response "I don't know" are unacceptable.

Along with the confidence that comes of a solid educational background, reporters who work live during a newscast must be able to concentrate under pressure and sometimes in the midst of confusion, to speak smoothly, coherently, and in an organized fashion. Sometimes you'll address the camera amid high levels of ambient noise; you may be distracted by onlookers; you may even be in a position of danger. You'll work with notes, rather than a script. You won't have a monitor to show what's being seen by the television audience, though you will hear the words of the director and anchor on an earpiece, an **interruptible foldback (IFB)**.[3]

When you communicate with the anchor by way of satellite, you need to anticipate a delay of about one and one-half seconds between the time the anchor speaks and the time you hear the anchor's voice. It's necessary to pick up cues as rapidly as possible to make this delay less noticeable. You can also expect to hear your own voice coming back to your ear one and one-half seconds after you've spoken. Engineers can **minus out** your voice so that the anchor and the viewers hear it but you don't, but when this technical adjustment isn't made, you must give your report smoothly despite the distraction of hearing your words on delay.

---

[3]*Foldback* is the term for an earphone system; *interruptible* indicates that with this system a director or producer can interrupt an announcer with questions or instructions.

The News Anchor

Performance abilities are as important for a news anchor as journalistic knowledge. News directors look for anchors who are physically appealing (which doesn't necessarily mean young or good looking in the conventional sense), have pleasing voices, are skilled in interpreting copy, can work well with a prompting device, and can ad-lib smoothly and intelligently. In addition to on-camera performance ability, most successful news anchors have a background in field reporting.

The chapters that discuss interviewing, voice and diction, and principles of communication, provide suggestions and exercises that will help you perform well as an anchor. Some of the discussion in Chapter 9 of radio news, especially the section on newswriting, applies to the work of the television anchor. Chapter 6 provides details of working with scripts and prompters, addressing cameras, and moving, standing, sitting, and holding props on camera. The following section concentrates on aspects of preparation and performance that are unique to television news anchors.

Working Conditions and Responsibilities

Working conditions vary from station to station, but at a typical medium-market or large-market television station your news anchors' job may involve

- Writing twenty-five to fifty percent of the copy you read on the air
- Covering some stories in the field
- Preparing occasional feature reports
- Working with a co-anchor as well as sports and weather reporters
- Preparing and delivering one or two newscasts daily, five days a week
- Meeting daily with newsroom management to discuss and help decide on the stories to be covered and the order in which they'll be presented to viewers

At some stations you might work three weekdays as a field reporter, and Saturday and Sunday as evening news anchor.

As an anchor, you'll work with materials from a variety of sources: field reports, stories written by newswriters, wire-service agency copy, recorded reports from a parent network or a cooperating station in a nearby market, and reports from CNN's NEWSOURCE or Reuters. Final decisions on the content of newscasts rest with the news director (or the news producer), but you'll be involved in nearly every step in preparing for a broadcast. You were hired partly because of your journalistic judgment, so you keep abreast of developing stories. You'll check with reporters as they leave on assignment and as they return; you'll scan wire reports and newspapers; you'll confer at regular intervals with your producer; and you'll view recorded reports, both to determine their usability and to write lead-ins for those chosen.

Preparation and performance demand that you know the technological possibilities and demands of your medium and that you write well and rapidly, can cope with confusion and last-minute changes, work well with all members of the production staff, and possess your own performance style. Although it's true that a few stations permit anchors to merely show up in time to look over the news script, apply pancake makeup and contact lenses, and spend the next thirty to sixty minutes playing the part of a broadcast journalist, you shouldn't settle for such make-believe: there is little satisfaction or professional pride in doing so.

In general, your preparation is similar to that of a radio news anchor. You'll write lead-ins for packages, voice-over narration, and straight news stories that have no accompanying video, and you'll make notes for teases. A **tease** comes just before a commercial break and is designed to hold viewer interest by headlining a news item to be delivered after the break. Teases must be planned but are seldom written out. Be sure to review any news item or feature you tease; viewers are resentful of teases that keep them watching yet don't live up to advance billing. Viewers also resent teases if they believe that the information itself should have been given instead. Who wouldn't object to hearing "And you'd better be on the lookout for an escaped lion—details when we come back"?

A **toss** is a brief introduction to the weather or sports reporter, consumer affairs consultant, or other member of the news team. Tosses are indicated on the script but are delivered ad lib. You toss the program to someone else by turning to that person and making a smooth and quick transition to the next segment.

In writing your share of the news script, you'll begin with the standard opening used by your station on all newscasts: for example, "These are the top stories this hour." The opening is followed by headlines of the major stories of the day. As you write your copy, you may decide that you need graphics. Anchors sometimes are responsible for suggesting when a graphic aid is appropriate.

Most likely you'll work on a word processor with a video display terminal. Such computers are flexible and make adding or dropping stories easy. They also allow you to move a wire-service story to the side or to the top of the screen, leaving room for you to paraphrase the story in your own style. **Hard copy** (a printed script) is generated on a word processor. As noted in Chapter 6, the script is printed on copy sets— prepared forms with five or more sheets, sometimes color-coded. In some operations, only the edges of tractor-feed copy sets are color coded. Many news scripts are typed in capital letters only.[4] Scripts that go to production personnel use the left side of the script for video information and the right side for audio information. The video column is seldom marked by anyone other than the director, who indicates the shots to be taken. However, scripts on studio prompters—those read on-air by anchors—don't use the two-column format.

Using a Prompter

When you go on the air for a thirty- or sixty-minute newscast, you'll have a complete script, but expect it to be revised during the broadcast. Runners will bring new copy to you, the camera director, the news producer, and the prompter operator. Instructions to toss to a reporter in the field or in the newsroom will be given to you by a director or producer over an **IFB**, also called an **earprompter.** You'll also receive instructions passed to you by the *floor manager* (sometimes called the *floor director* or *stage manager*) during commercial breaks, reports from the field, or recorded stories.

Skill in sight-reading is extremely important. You won't be able to study stories written and delivered after the start of the newscast. You may have a chance to skim the new copy for names of people, places, or things that you may have trouble pronouncing, but there's no guarantee that anyone in the studio or control room will be able to help you with the pronunciation. For this reason, you should establish an understanding with newswriters, assignment editors, and associate producers that unusual words or names will be phoneticized on the copy that goes to you and the prompter. An example of how your script may read follows:

---

[4]The practice of writing news copy in ALL CAPITAL letters originated at a time when teletype machines that carried news stories from the Associated Press, United Press International, and other news organizations were limited to upper-case letters only. Most broadcast journalists today prefer copy that features both upper- and lower-case letters.

> The East African nation of Djibouti (jee-BOOT-ee) has been
> hit by a severe plague of locusts.

In this instance, the newswriter took the phoneticized spelling from the
pronouncer included in the wire-service copy. **Pronouncer** is the term
used by news services for the phonetic transcriptions of words and
names that accompany wire-service stories. Another example required
the newswriter to research the pronunciation of medical terms:

> **(Washington)** A dietary supplement that may cause a fatal
> blood disorder has been removed from sale by its manufac-
> turer. L-Tryptophan (el-TRIP-toe-fan) has been linked to the
> potentially fatal blood disease eosinophilia (EE-uh-sin-uh-
> FEEL-ee-yuh). A national consumer organization praised the
> manufacturer's decision, and called the halt in sales, quote:
> "a prudent and cautious course of action."

If you type your own script, make certain that each sentence is indented four or five spaces. In the event the prompter fails, this will help you quickly spot the part of the story you're reading. As you read from the prompter, slowly move a thumb down the side of your hand-held script. With practice, you'll eventually become quite precise in keeping your thumb positioned at the point of the story as you read it from the prompter.

Never hyphenate a word at the end of a typewritten line in a script. You must be able to see entire words without having to shift your eyes back to the beginning of a new line for the conclusion of a word. If, for example, a line ended with *con-,* you'd have no way of knowing whether the rest of the word was *-tingent, -tinuous,* or *-vict.*

When working with a prompter, the camera usually will be ten to fifteen feet in front of you. Eye movement as you scan the projected script will be less noticeable at that distance. Glance down at your script frequently. This habit not only eliminates the staring look but keeps you in touch with the ongoing script—a necessity in case the prompter fails.

SPOTLIGHT

A Representative Television News Operation

There's a discernible pattern to a daily television news operation. In the newsroom, hours of anticipation are followed by sudden quiet as the action moves to the news set and control room. The show goes on the air in an atmosphere of concentrated effort and often some anxiety. As closing credits roll, there is satisfaction, relaxation, and even exhilaration.

The following sketch describes one day in the life of a news department.[5]

The Scene: A Television Newsroom

1:00 A.M.: First to arrive are an editor and a newswriter. They watch television news on CNN, check wire-service stories fed to a computer, and generally get things rolling.

---

[5]The practices described in this section are those of KTVU, Oakland, California, a consistent Emmy Award–winning television news operation.

4:00 A.M.: The executive producer arrives and, after sizing up ongoing news events, makes phone calls to ENG operators to assign stories. ENG camera operators often work alone to cover news conferences, fires, accidents, and similar events. Their raw footage is screened, edited, and completed by a reporter or a newswriter.

4:30 A.M.: The assignment editor and a field reporter arrive. Field reporters are assigned to overlapping shifts so that some will be available every hour of the day.

5:00 A.M.: Other members of the large team trickle in—news director, producer, co-anchors, editor in chief, newswriters, desk assistants, field reporters, on-air director, editors, interns, and others. At first, everything seems uncoordinated. Gradually, as each team member completes preliminary preparations, small groups begin to form. The pace accelerates but without confusion. All know their duties and prepare without receiving instructions.

Some reporters at KTVU, Oakland, California, work from early morning until early afternoon. During their shift, they report some stories live during the noon news. They also work with ENG operators to record material for complete reports or packages. They perform stand-ups and return to the station to edit their recordings, write and record narration, and add the narration to the edited packages. Reporters cover one story a day, though they sometimes are asked to record a sound bite for another reporter.

7:00 A.M.: The two-hour morning show begins. It features news and in-station interviews presented by the co-anchors, and it features on-location interviews conducted by feature reporters. The morning show includes time checks, traffic and weather reports, and more interviews than do the other news shows.

9:00 A.M.: After the morning program, a conference is held to discuss and select news stories for the noon news. Key members of the news staff, including the assistant news director and the editor in chief, are present.

A **format,** a rundown of the stories to be included in the newscast, is generated on a computer. Stories are discussed by all, but are selected by the news director on the basis of the stories' significance, viewer interest, and timeliness. The format will undergo several changes before airtime, as breaking stories replace others that are less urgent.

News scripts are written on desktop computers by newswriters and anchors. Eventually, the stories are printed on five-page copy sets. Script copies go to the news producer and anchors for editing. The director marks a copy for camera directions. Other copies go to the prompter operator and the character generator operator.

10:00 A.M.: One anchor delivers a live tease before a fixed camera in the newsroom. Also, by 10:00 A.M., ENG operators arrive with recorded material to be viewed, edited, and supplied with voice-over narration and appropriate lead-ins.

10:05–11:50 A.M.: Anchors and writers continue writing scripts; changes are made as updated information and new stories are received.

12:00 P.M.: The half-hour newscast begins. At its conclusion, most of the early-arriving personnel, including anchors, leave for the day. The newsroom grows quiet except for those reporters preparing packages for the nightly ten o'clock news.

3:00 P.M.: The nightly news team arrives to prepare for the ten o'clock news.

3:20 P.M.: Anchors meet with the news director, producer, reporters, and other key members of the team. A list of available stories, called a **situationer,** is distributed. Stories are discussed, one by one. The group can view sound bites and packages from the station's reporters, from CNN's NEWSOURCE, Reuters, and other news providers. Preliminary story selections are made. Near the end of the discussion, the evening news reporters receive their assignments, and the news producer assigns writing responsibilities to anchors and newswriters.

4:30 P.M.: Anchors and newswriters write scripts while other members of the operation keep up with developing stories. Anchors write intros; newswriters write voice-over narration. The bulk of each newscast comes from news packages and live reports.

Through the afternoon and evening the work continues. Eventually, scripts, recorded packages, and inserts are assembled.

9:50 P.M.: The newsroom falls quiet. Only a few people remain: the assignment editor, two assistants, a newswriter, and two news interns. The interns act as runners, replacing script pages as the show is rewritten because of new or updated stories. The action has moved to the control room and the news set. On the set, the anchors take their places to tease the upcoming broadcast.

9:55 P.M.: Both co-anchors give a live tease from the news set.

10:00 P.M.: The recorded program introduction is rolled, followed by a cue from the director.

For the next hour the program unfolds. Revised scripts (hard copy) are brought to the control room and are noted by the producer and assistant director and given to news anchors. Revisions are fed electronically to the prompter. Noise in the control room is considerable. The audio feed of the newscast is played at a high volume to be heard above ringing telephones, phone conversations between producer and newsroom personnel, the director's orders, and occasional comments from the producer.

11:00 P.M.: Recorded closing credits roll. Earpieces and headset microphones are removed. On-the-set lights are dimmed. In the control room there is little sound.

The show has kept team members in a state of tension for several hours. One by one, team members drift back to the newsroom—some to relax, others to pick up personal items as they leave for home. If significant problems arose during the newscast (a rare occurrence), the news producer, assignment editor, anchors, and other key personnel meet with the program producer for a brief **postmortem** (a discussion of what worked, what didn't work, and why). The newsroom will not be completely quiet until nearly midnight. The effort starts all over again at 1:00 A.M.

Weather Reporting

Weather reporting on regularly scheduled newscasts may be as simple as having weather news delivered by an anchor. At other stations, particularly major-market stations and stations in any location where weather information is of exceptional importance, professional meteorologists report the weather. Some weather reporters go beyond the bare facts of weather predicting to explain the causes of meteorological phenomena, subtly and gradually educating their audiences. Many meteorologists engage in television reporting as only part of their professional careers. At some stations a professional announcer who isn't a trained meteorologist may become a specialist in weather reporting.

Nearly all television stations use chroma-keyed maps and satellite photos for weather information. The weather reporter stands before a large blank screen, usually a medium shade of blue, and points out noteworthy features of the day's weather while looking at a monitor that carries a picture of the reporter and the weather map.

Weather maps are stored in the station's computer. After determining weather patterns from the complex information sent by the U.S. National Weather Service, the meteorologist creates graphics showing weather fronts, storms, high and low temperatures, and similar information. Satellite photos are received directly from the National Weather Service's satellites and are stored in the station's computer until used.

As a weather reporter, you may do special features occasionally. If the area experiences a snowstorm of unusual proportions or at a time of year when it's not expected, or if there's prolonged rain or a drought, you may be asked to conduct street interviews to assess public opinion.

In doing so, you will follow essentially the same techniques as for any other interview of randomly chosen passersby, but unless the weather news is serious or tragic, you may want to look for humorous or offbeat comments.

When reporting the national weather, remember that most people don't really care what the weather is like anywhere other than where they are, where they may be traveling to, or where they've come from. Unless a weather report from 2,000 miles away is unusual, as with tornadoes, floods, or hurricanes, it's seen by most viewers as not being news at all. Although people in Georgia may care nothing about the weather in Kansas, they *are* interested in the price of wheat and pork, and while New Englanders may feel that the weather in Florida doesn't affect them, they'll care about Florida's weather when they learn that a winter freeze there will send the price of citrus and other produce soaring. Therefore, whenever possible, tie weather reports to something about which people care. In other words, when reporting the weather from distant places, try to arouse interest by interpreting the weather's significance.

It's obvious that weather is newsworthy when it's violent. However, slow-developing conditions brought on by weather, such as two-year drought, also must be reported, and such nearly imperceptible events can't be adequately covered by a mere recitation of statistics. To best serve your public, you must go beyond the kind of weather news traditionally offered by wire services. In a drought, for example, you could periodically record telephone interviews with experts on several drought-related problems. Ask the Farm Bureau about the drought's effects on farming. Ask a representative of the Audubon Society about the effects of the drought on birds in your area. Ask a fish and wildlife expert about the prospects for survival of fish and wild mammals. Get drought information from professional gardeners, and share plant-saving tips with your listeners.

In short, as a weather reporter, you should use your imagination and constantly ask yourself these questions: Why should viewers be interested in today's weather report? What am I telling them that will be of use? Too often weather reports become routine recitations of fronts, temperatures, inches of precipitation, and predictions for tomorrow. Most viewers and listeners find this information somewhat interesting, but aside from frost, flood, or storm warnings, it's of little use. Always work creatively to make your weather reports useful to your audience.

PRACTICE

Comparing Local and National Newscasts

Record both a local and a national newscast—that of an independent station and that of a major network or CNN. Study the performances and list the ways local television news differs from national coverage. Omit obvious differences such as "national newscasts feature reports from all over the world." Look instead for differences in length of stories, use of visuals and computer-generated graphics, and inclusion of specialized reporters who focus on the environment, business, weather, sports, and entertainment.

CHAPTER 11

Music Announcing

MUSIC ANNOUNCING IS OLDER THAN RADIO ITSELF. IN VAUDEVILLE AND burlesque houses, it was customary for a master of ceremonies to introduce singers and instrumentalists, often with brief biographical commentary, together with the names of the selections to be played or sung.

Thereafter, announcers became associated with publicly performed music. When radio, the "blind" medium came along, it was a natural step to have announcers perform the same kinds of introductions. Throughout most of radio's history, announcers—soon to be dubbed *disc jockeys*—have filled this role.

This chapter features the operations of popular-music radio stations, with a focus on radio disc jockeys, but both *streaming audio* and *club* or *mobile DJs* may find much in this chapter that's applicable to their work.[1]

Recorded music predominates on radio in the United States and Canada. There are more than twelve thousand AM and FM radio stations in the United States, and approximately eleven thousand are all-music or nearly all-music stations.[2] About five hundred stations play Classical music, and most are noncommercial. Most of the popular music stations are FM. Many AM stations have turned away from all-music formats because the AM sound simply can't compete with FM.[3] As a result,

---

[1]Later in this chapter a few additional comments are made about streaming audio DJs and club or mobile DJs.
[2]Statistics from *Broadcasting and Cable Yearbook,* 1999 edition.
[3]Some AM music stations broadcast in stereo, and the sound quality comes close to that of FM stereo.

numerous AM stations have moved to all-talk, all-news, news/talk, agriculture, and sports, as well as religious and non-English-language broadcasting. However, music on AM does remain well represented by stations playing Country, Middle-of-the-Road, Gospel, and "Oldies."

About six hundred U.S. radio stations are ethnically oriented or broadcast in a language other than English.[4] Many are all or mainly music. If you're qualified (or qualifiable) to announce on these stations, you may want to include them in your career plans.

Popular-Music Announcing (DJ)[5]

The DJ

The term **disc jockey** was coined years ago to identify radio announcers on popular music stations. The term had logic behind it, because those who announced on music stations worked with "discs" and "jockeyed" them, in the sense that DJs manually cued, introduced, and then "spun" their records.[6] Today, music announcers work with compact discs (CDs) or hard drives, and many no longer want to be called *disc jockeys*. Most who perform this function prefer to be called **personalities** or **on-air talent**, even though these terms refer to *qualities* and not to *people*. An informal survey of several music announcers failed to find a term preferred by all; however, most accepted the term *DJ* but did not care for the terms *disc jockey* or *jock*. Since DJ is well established, people no longer think of its literal meaning, and the term *DJ* is a convenient parallel to music video's *VJ*. Throughout this chapter, the term *DJ* is used.

Whatever the degree or nature of equipment manipulation, the most important work of DJs—introducing or **back announcing** musical selections, engaging in pleasant chatter, delivering or playing commercials,

---

[4]The category "Spanish" includes all Spanish language stations. Some five hundred radio stations in the United States are listed as "Spanish," and those that feature music are included with other formats. They're listed within such categories as SS-RA (Ranchero), SS-EZ (EZ Listening), or SS-TJ (Tejano).

[5]Ron Rodrigues, editor in chief of *Radio & Records,* and veteran DJ Carter B. Smith, contributed much of the information relating to recent changes and practices in the field of music radio.

[6]Music discs used on radio stations began with ten-inch records that revolved at 78 RPM (revolutions per minute). Then came vinyl discs called "LPs" (long playing) that turned at $33\frac{1}{3}$ RPMs. A later competitor, 45 RPM discs, were significantly smaller than LPs. In the 1990s, records of all speeds and sizes gave way to tape cartridges (carts); these, in turn, were superseded by digital audiotape (DAT), then by compact discs (CDs), and, more recently, by mass storage hard drives.

and promoting contests—continues to be the common denominator for success. DJs offer a great range of announcing styles, from rapid delivery to casual, or laid-back delivery but they're associated only with popular music. Announcers on Classical-music stations aren't included in this term, even though their work has much in common with that of DJs. This chapter discusses the work of both the DJ and the Classical-music announcer.

Working Conditions

As a DJ, you can expect working conditions to vary widely from station to station. If you're talented and lucky enough to become a popular drive-time DJ on a prosperous major-market station, your salary could be in six figures—or even above.[7] High salaries generally are paid only to morning drive-time music announcers in major markets. Even announcers in major markets whose shifts are afternoon (both midday and afternoon drive times), evening, or overnight no longer draw the huge salaries they once commanded.

If you begin your announcing career at a small-market station or at a financially marginal station in a market of any size, you can expect to work a four- to six-hour air shift and to perform other duties for additional hours each day. At a thriving major-market station, your board shift will seldom exceed four hours.

Whether working for a major- or a smaller-market station, your job will be demanding, because many hours a week of off-duty preparation are required for continued success. Successful DJs at both large and small stations spend considerable time each week preparing for their shifts (*showprep*), checking prep sites on the Internet, reading music trade magazines, and preparing informative or humorous pieces for their shows. Although most popular music radio stations, large and small, require DJs to do their own engineering, an exception is sometimes made during morning drive time. At a "personality intensive" station—a station that features a very popular DJ or a team of announcers noted for their repartee—an engineer may operate the board, and cue and play music and sound effects.

---

[7]Although definitions of market size aren't standardized, generally speaking a major market has a potential audience of more than one million listeners; a secondary market is one having between two hundred thousand and one million potential listeners; a smaller market has a potential audience of fewer than two hundred thousand.

At a small station, in addition to your on-air work, you'll likely spend additional hours performing other assigned chores: selling commercial time, writing and recording commercials, producing spots for local retailers, performing routine equipment maintenance, and/or reporting news and weather.

During your air shifts, you'll work in a combined announce booth and control room, called an **on-air studio**, and you'll perform the combined functions of announcer and engineer. This is called **working combo.** You may be responsible for assembling and delivering brief hourly news headlines, although few music stations still produce newscasts, preferring instead to take a feed from a news service or to drop news coverage altogether.

Additional duties may be reading or ad-libbing brief public-service announcements—often on a **community bulletin board** or **community calendar** feature—playing commercials and station IDs (on tape carts at some stations, and on hard disks, DAT, or programmable CDs at others), making entries in the program log, and, in some operations, especially on weekends and holidays, answering the telephone.[8] Many music stations run contests and promotions, and as the on-duty DJ, you'll tease and then conduct the contests with phone-in callers. While doing all this, you're expected to be alert, witty, and personable.

Working at a Tapeless Radio Station

A considerable number of radio stations are tapeless operations at which music, jingles, commercials, and similar material are recorded and stored on digital hard drives. The scenario that follows will give you an idea of how this may affect you if you work at a tapeless station.

When you report for work at your Adult/Contemporary station, for instance, you're given scripts for the commercials you're to produce prior to your on-air shift. You enter a small production studio, where a digital workstation—complete with audio console and computer system—is available. You manipulate a track ball (which functions as a mouse) to select a music bed. You activate the recorder, which mixes your voice and the music background onto a hard disk, and begin to record a commercial. As you speak, a "picture" of your reading appears

---

[8]Although the Federal Communications Commission (FCC) no longer requires radio stations to maintain program logs, you may be required to work with one because some stations continue to maintain them for billing purposes.

on the video display monitor. It progresses across the screen from the start to the finish of your reading.

With the aid of the track ball, you later edit any portion of the recording to eliminate or replace unwanted sounds, such as a sneeze or the wheeze of overaspirated intake breaths. Most audio workstations' equipment is set to apply **automatic gain control** (AGC) when a reduced or barely audible sound is detected, so the sounds of your intake breaths are increased in volume as the AGC "searches" for sound. To eliminate unwanted sounds, you locate on the computer screen the point at which the sound begins, press a key to mark it, then find the ending point, and make a second mark. These marks "surround" the segment you're editing. A keystroke deletes the sound between the two marks.

Another option allows you, not to delete, but to exchange sounds. It permits you to re-record one or more sentences, to place marks at the start and end of the unwanted sentence, or sentences, and to simultaneously erase them and insert the preferred version. Other features allow you to change the volume or the equalization of any portion of your recording, or to remix the volume balance between the voice and the music bed. When you're satisfied with your edited commercial, you give

Figure 11.1

DJ Tom Plant works with a keyboard, a track ball, and a video data monitor to select and "stack" commercials stored on a hard disk. He follows a log, prepared by the traffic department, which lists in order the commercials to be played during his four-hour shift. *Courtesy of Tom Plant and KZST, Santa Rosa, California.*

it an identification name and number, and store it on a mass storage hard disk. You may produce between two and twelve commercials in a single day. On other days when there are few commercials to produce, you may record promos for your station.

Later you will enter the on-air studio, ready to start your shift as a DJ. Before you take over from the DJ whose shift precedes yours, you begin your preparations. Working from a log prepared by the music director, you access the hard disk that stores the music library, and select and stack in order the music cuts you'll play during your time on the air. You then go to a computer terminal, complete with keyboard, a track ball, and a video data monitor. A log, prepared by the traffic department, lists the commercials to be played during your shift, as well as the order and the precise times at which they'll be broadcast. Many of the commercials were sent from advertising agencies to your station over high-quality telephone lines and then digitally reconstructed on a hard disk. Some commercials and nearly all of your public-service announcements (PSAs), jingles, and station promos were created in your production studio by you and your co-workers and were then transferred from an audio console/video terminal system to the same mass storage disk that holds the agency-produced commercials. With the aid of the track ball, you select all stored commercials to be played and assemble them in the order in which they'll be broadcast. Recorded station IDs, jingles, promos, and PSAs also are stored on a hard disk, and these have been scheduled by the traffic department.

None of the recorded material is in your announce booth: it exists only on the computer hard disk in an adjacent room, or even on another floor of the radio station building. As the time comes to play each program element—music, commercial, jingle—you use the track ball to *find,* the video screen to *see,* and the computer keyboard to *select* each segment. When the time comes to play each program element, you press the "play" command, and the cut you've previously selected is sent to the audio console and then out over the air.

While music is played, you may receive telephone calls from listeners. As you answer the phone, you inform callers that their call will be recorded. If there's no objection, you then activate a recorder to make an audio record of the conversation. There are two reasons for recording these calls: the first is to preserve actual conversations to avoid problems later regarding prizes, prize winners, or other issues that could arise from misunderstandings; the second reason is to collect comments that later may be edited into sound bites to be used in station promotions.

Preparing for Work at a Tapeless Radio Station

The scenario just presented for working at a tapeless radio station examines just one particular operating system. At some stations, DJs have before them a computer screen that lists, in order, every program element for the entire day as developed by the station's program or music director. As each program unit is activated, it's sent out over the air, and at its conclusion its listing on the computer screen moves up to be replaced with the next element. Music and all other recorded materials are broadcast without assistance of the DJ. Interspersed are breaks that require the DJ to back announce the songs played in a **sweep** (several songs played without interruption), give weather updates, comment on some item of interest or amusement, and, occasionally, read a commercial. When comments by the DJ are recorded in advance, the computerized system can enter the recordings as program elements. Hence, announcers can be away from the station (for example, on a holiday) and their voices can be heard by their audience.

Figure 11.2

Veteran DJ Carter B. Smith analyzes and comments on the day's stock market developments during his afternoon drive-time shift on KABL. This station features Swing, Big Band, and Standard Oldies, and its relaxed format permits DJs to engage in nonmusic topics of interest to listeners. Such discussions are, of course, subject to overall station policies, but the station's format, which appeals to mature listeners, works well with business news after the daily closing of the stock market. The ability to make interesting and informative comments about topics aside from music is an asset to any popular-music announcer. *Courtesy of Carter B. Smith and KABL, San Francisco, California.*

If you remain in radio for even a few years, you'll need to operate hi-tech equipment immediately, and eventually use equipment that hasn't been developed yet! Even if you begin your career at a small-market station, you may be asked to work with highly sophisticated computerized operations. In the past, in terms of technology, equipment at smaller stations lagged decades behind that found at large and prosperous stations, but today sophisticated apparatus may be found at stations of every size. The twin factors of reduced equipment costs and the ability to operate stations with fewer employees combine to make technological upgrading economically attractive to station owners.

If the equipment found at a tapeless station is not available to you currently, how can you prepare to use it in the future? Your educational goals should be twofold: (1) develop your performance abilities and (2) learn operational skills, including audio engineering and computer operations. Most of the chapters of this text are devoted to assisting you in becoming an engaging performer; the following are suggestions to assist you in developing technical skills.

- First, take at least one, and preferably two or more courses, in audio engineering. To be of practical use, the courses should include in-studio recording on multichannel recording consoles, mixing of multiple inputs, editing, use of board equalization, reverberation systems, graphic equalizers, limiters, overdubbing, and sound reinforcement. Although later you may operate a board during an air shift that requires you to do little but occasionally press busses (or buttons) to open and close your announce mic, a comprehensive knowledge of board operation is necessary to perform the production tasks described in the section in this chapter titled "Working at a Tapeless Radio Station."

- Second, enroll in a number of both Macintosh and personal computer courses to gain hands-on experience using major computing programs such as Microsoft Word, MacWrite II, Claris Works, WriteNow, Microsoft Excel, and so forth.

You must realize, however, that taking a few courses in computing will not prepare you adequately to work in a tapeless, computerized station. Although undoubtedly your school has computer labs, you should own your own computer; used and refurbished Macs and PCs are available at very low cost.

As you choose your courses, remember that education for any sort of technical operation isn't limited by the sophistication of the tools you use for practice. Learn what a board does and how it operates. While you practice with a specific console, your understanding of audio recording, collecting, mixing, equalizing, editing, and so forth can be transferred quickly to a board you've never seen or touched.

The development of your talent to make you an effective and compelling communicator should receive your highest priority. A sound working knowledge of audio engineering and computer operations should be your second goal.

The Realities of Music Radio Today

Music radio broadcasting is constantly changing. At the turn of the millennium, music radio is dominated by station managers who are convinced that people tune into a particular station for the music, not to hear the voice of a DJ. In apparent contradiction to this notion, the same executives demand that morning drive-time DJs entertain their listeners with witty or wise chatter, whereas DJs in other time periods are often given strict time limits for any impromptu remarks. This is discouraging to prospective DJs who know that their initial employment will be in non-prime-time hours, where they'll be unlikely to impress management or listeners with their repartee.

Advancements in technology and changes in broadcast practices reduced the number and the importance of music announcers. The rapid spread of syndicated programming has led to fewer jobs for DJs. Program syndicators tailor programming for specific markets and audience demographics and sell these services at a cost that's less than that of full local production. In some instances, the programming is sent to stations as part of an automated operation. Increasingly, satellites are used to deliver programming to stations. Syndicators can provide stations with anything from brief features to complete program services, including music, jingles, promos, and the services of DJs. This leaves station management free to concentrate on sales. This trend, of course, means fewer opportunities for music announcers at the local station level.

Local marketing agreements (LMAs) have expanded in the field of radio broadcasting. In this practice, two or more stations enter into an arrangement in which facilities, staff, equipment, and, in some instances, even a frequency are shared. LMAs are able to operate with one announcing staff for several stations, rather than separate staffs for each.

Also, increased use of computers has resulted in changes in production practices. These changes have reduced music stations' dependence on announcers as operators of broadcast equipment, so the role of DJs as manipulators of recorded music on discs, carts, and CDs has lost its former importance. Some stations are run on "unattended operations," in which no announcer of any kind need be present.

If these words sound discouraging, take heart. Good communicators, those announcers who care about people and who have ideas, values, and insights—and some good laughs!—to share will always be in demand. And, there are opportunities for DJs outside of radio. As a person seeking a career in music announcing, you shouldn't ignore other, related, job opportunities. **Streaming audio** (sometimes called **streaming radio**) refers to the playing and announcing of music over the Internet. **Club** or **mobile DJs**, who perform live in dance halls, as well as at birthdays, company parties, weddings, reunions, and similar festive events, represent a large and growing number of music announcers whose work isn't broadcast.[9]

To learn more about club or mobile DJs, check out these web sites through their URLs[10]:

search.yahoo.com/bin/search?p=mobile+disc+jockeys

www.altavista.com/cgi-bin/query?pg=q&what=web&q= Disc+Jockeys&user=yahoo

www.realnames.com/Resolver.dll?provider=1&realName= disc+jockeys+

For a complete, updated list of URLs for this textbook, please see the text home site available at *www.hmco.com/ college.*

---

[9]**Streaming audio** is the term applied to music sent over the Internet that can be downloaded and burned onto a recordable CD. It later can be listened to on any CD player. **Club DJ** or **mobile DJ** are broad terms for those who perform as DJs, almost always with a public address system, and whose audience is physically present.
[10]The Internet is changing constantly as new web sites are added and old web sites are abandoned. The URL listings in this textbook should be regarded as samples of the kinds of material available rather than as a stable index. If you seek a web site using one of these URLs and cannot connect, enter the key words for the topic into a search engine to find a site that may provide the information you want.

Steve Walker, a popular DJ at WMTZ, Johnstown, Pennsylvania, whose comments on rapport are outlined in Chapter 5, views present practices as only a blip in a continuing series of changes in music radio. He recognizes that automation has reduced the prominence of DJs, but he feels that this is a temporary state. He has this to say about availability and job security questions facing DJs:

> Here are some thoughts on the fear of losing your job to a satellite or the dreaded hard drive. The bean counters that make these kinds of decisions will find it works some places but not others. I've been doing this for twenty-five years and have seen cycles where DJs went from talking and saying as much as they wanted as long as they didn't tick anyone off, to the "shut up and read the card" days when you were just a warm body.[11]

Steve is convinced that, because most trends are cyclical, DJs will one day reclaim their prominent role in delivering not only music but commentaries about life, events, people, and other topics.

Cosmo Rose, a DJ whose show preparation advice constitutes the Spotlight for this chapter, adds the following thoughts that underscore the value of DJs who "connect" with their listeners:

> I am amazed at what about my show gets reflected back to me when I meet listeners out in public. It's never the goofy contest or the funny joke that I hear about. Instead, it's that little story I told about my daughter . . . or the funny thing my wife said. And as the listeners reflect this back to me, I realize they've probably told a few friends about it as well. There's the chatter component.
>
> Now, sharing these types of stories may not make me that crazy, irreverent morning man in the eyes of my listeners, but it does make me human. Perhaps connecting with the audience on a human level can be equally as important . . . if not more.[12]

This is uplifting advice from those who've seen trends shift as capriciously, though not as frequently, as the daily weather.

The chapters on audio and video performance begin with discussions of *audience rapport,* and the comments quoted here from two of the most successful and respected DJs in the business complete a three-way focus on that priceless commodity. The moral of these messages

---

[11]Excerpt from editorial "Be Yourself," by Steve Walker. Almostradio web site, Volume 2, 39, October 27, 1997.
[12]Excerpt from editorial "Showprep Is Everything and Everything Is Showprep," by Cosmo Rose. Almostradio web site, Volume 2, 51, January 19, 1999.

from Steve Walker and Cosmo Rose is to work to become a compelling communicator, prepare yourself for success and expect to achieve it, and realize that you'll only "make it" if you truly want to build a relationship and make a positive difference in the lives of your listeners. You have to earn your success; you can become important only if you deserve to be important.

Music Station Practices

At most popular music stations, the program director develops a **clock** or **wheel** (often called a **hot clock**) that divides each hour of a particular time period into sixteen or more segments. Each segment specifies a certain activity for the DJ. In one segment, a sweep of music selected by the music director is played. In another, called a **stop set** or **spot set**, a commercial cluster is run. In yet another, a contest is announced, and in several segments, weather updates are given. Music is categorized, according to the program director's concept of competitive programming, as Instrumental, Vocal, Up-Tempo, Top 10, Top 5, Nostalgia, Easy Listening, and so on. The days of DJs choosing the music they play are over. Station managers set radio station music policy, and at major stations, a program director develops the playlist. At medium- and smaller-market stations, the selections and placement of songs may be made by a program director who probably has a regular air shift.[13] For one example of a "hot clock," see Figure 11.3.

As a DJ on a larger station, you'll have some of the same problems and challenges as your counterpart on a small station. However, generally speaking, you'll have more help. A traffic department will have arranged your running log in the most readily usable manner, and the log will appear on a computer screen atop the audio console. The days of six-hour air shifts will be behind you. However, show preparation and public appearances at fairs, parades, and similar events will extend your work time.

Regardless of variations, the technical and manipulative skills involved in DJ work can be acquired in a few weeks, *assuming that you're computer literate*. The challenge isn't merely to be able to perform all of the routine duties well but to project an attractive and unique personal-

---

[13]College radio stations, both on air and carrier current, often permit student DJs to select music within categories established by a music or program director.

Figure 11.3

Popular-music stations often use a clock as a programming tool to ensure a balance of music, news, commercials, and features. This clock, which was created for the afternoon drive time, reflects the importance of frequent traffic updates. But clocks do more than manage what gets broadcast and at what times. When entered into a computer, a clock can be altered daily to keep listeners alert and competing stations confused.

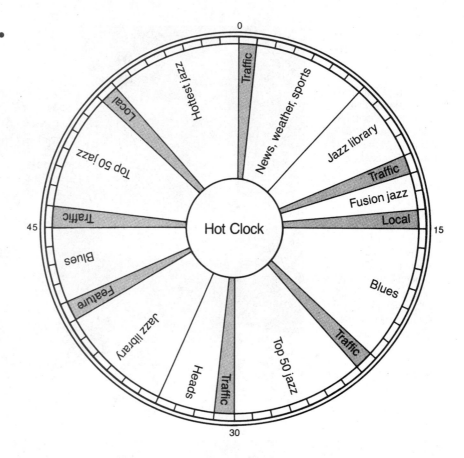

ity and to be energized and articulate during the few minutes each hour when you're in direct communication with your listeners.

Showprep for Music Announcers

Showprep is an abbreviation of *show preparation,* and to DJs it has several meanings. Many of the most successful morning drive-time DJs believe that conscientious and regular showprep is what keeps audiences tuned in and makes the DJ stand out. In the Spotlight that follows, Cosmo Rose defines *showprep* and explains how he prepares for his morning drive-time show on WXKC-FM, Erie, Pennsylvania. The advice given is particularly applicable to a morning drive-time DJ or a DJ in any time slot on a personality-intensive station.

Figure 11.4

Afternoon drive-time DJ Ray White teases upcoming songs on KKSF, San Francisco, California, an FM station with a Smooth Jazz format. Ray became committed to music radio at the age of fifteen. "After my first visit to a local station, I was hooked on radio. And, I realized that the magicians on the air, much like the Wizard of Oz, were just regular people who had a knack for talking into a microphone—and a love for music." Ray majored in history and minored in communications at the University of Connecticut, Storrs. You can visit KKSF through this URL: *www.kksf.com/. Courtesy of Ray White and KKSF, San Francisco, California.*

SPOTLIGHT

Showprep Is Everything and Everything Is Showprep

By Cosmo Rose

The title of this week's editorial is a phrase that I coined (I think I coined it, anyway) for a presentation my producer and I will make at a local university. The course is about *showprep* . . . the kind of course I wish had been offered at the school I attended and at the many schools where I was an instructor.

In today's radio climate, showprep is more important than ever. The competition for the best radio jobs is getting fierce as opportunities shrink. Only the best people will get on the air . . . and that's not only for high-profile shows like A.M. or P.M. drive. Marginal talent doesn't really have a place in today's radio, except maybe as board ops. That's why it's a great idea to get our future broadcasters acquainted with good showprep habits.

Of course, as a great believer in showprep, it follows that I'm also a believer in "presentation" prep. I've spent the past few weeks outlining the types of showprep I do and how I do it. Rather than use this stuff on one class (which, of course, is honor enough), I figured I'd share it with you as well.

My first golden rule is spelled out in the title of this editorial: "Showprep Is Everything and Everything Is Showprep." The first part was explained when I told you that good showprep is necessary to separate the good broadcasters from the mediocre. The second part refers to my belief that as entertainers (like stand-up comics) we are always preparing our shows. Many things that happen to us during the course of a day could potentially be used on the air as bits . . . or may give you an idea for a bit.

My second golden rule is that everyone who is successful is organized. Now, let me explain that I don't necessarily mean organized in the strictest sense, having a calendar, elaborate file system, and everything neatly in its place. But if you're successful, you most likely are at least an organized thinker when it comes to your chosen career.

Third golden rule . . . attitude makes a difference. As the job field narrows and the supply of radio applicants continues to grow, arrogance will be tolerated less and less . . . particularly at the hiring stage. After you start earning monster ratings, you may get away with a little more. However, that's a gamble too because ratings don't always stay high forever.

Those are the three rules that guide me through each workday and drive the level of showprep that I do. I've learned those rules mostly through either making mistakes or watching others making mistakes. It is via this same school of hard knocks that I also arrived at all the different types of showprep that exist . . . and there are probably many more than I use.

The first type of prep is vertical prep. In effect, this refers to looking at an individual day's show and planning it out break by break until every slot is filled. It is important to master this type of prep first because it will have the most immediate impact on the structure and presentation of your show.

The second type of prep is horizontal prep. At this level, you plan show ideas day by day . . . week by week. Here is where a calendar becomes most useful. If you get an idea for Easter, write it down on your calendar for one day during the week before Easter. At that point, you may not know what time you'll do the bit . . . you'll save that for vertical prep closer to the show date.

The last aspect of showprep I'll discuss is the sources of prep. My favorite source for prep is life experience or life stories. In my career I have found that I receive the greatest amount of feedback on those little life stories I tell about growing up, about my wife or daughter, or even about my cat. Those are the bits that listeners reflect back to me when they meet me at a live broadcast. And, the best part is, they can't effectively be stolen by anyone else.

A second major source of showprep is observation. Perhaps you've noticed a trend in TV commercials or a plethora of potholes in your town . . . whatever. Chances are your listeners have noticed it too . . . or at least will come around to your way of thinking.

The third source of prep is the most readily available: prepackaged prep. This is in the form of prerecorded comedy bits and song parodies, magazines, weekly radio newspapers, and e-mailed publications. There are also many sharing networks and computer bulletin board services that provide prep ideas for broadcasters.

A fourth source for showprep is your local newspaper. By being up on what's going on, you'll avoid becoming a generic morning show that could be playing anywhere in the country.

The final source of prep is: the moment. Many times we'll be planning one thing for our show when we get a call from a listener who introduces a topic so compelling, we're forced to shift gears. Or perhaps a side comment by a co-host will send you in an interesting direction. Being attuned to those opportunities when they present themselves can often yield some of the best shows of one's career.[14]

[14]Cosmo Rose invites you to visit his web site at *www.almostradio.com*. Send an e-mail to cosmo@almostradio.com explaining that you are a college student, and he'll give you special free access to the "Members Only" section.
"Showprep Is Everything and Everything Is Showprep." Almostradio web site, Volume 2, 51, January 19, 1999.

Cosmo Rose is the host of The Breakfast Club on WXKC-FM, Erie, Pennsylvania. Cosmo began his professional career at the age of 19 as a news anchor-reporter. After two years, he pursued his true interest, becoming a morning drive-time DJ on WJRZ-FM in Toms River, New Jersey. In 1996, he began the Almost Radio Network, one of the first showprep sites on the Internet. Cosmo received his bachelor's degree in communications from Glassboro State College in Glassboro, New Jersey. In addition to his on-air hosting and showprep site management, he's taught broadcasting courses at Cabrini College, Ocean County College, and Monmouth College, all in New Jersey. *Courtesy of Cosmo Rose,* and WXKC-FM, Erie, Pennsylvania.

You can access showprep sites through these URLs:

dir.yahoo.com/News_and_Media/Radio/Show_Preparation/

www.almostradio.com/

For a complete, updated list of URLs for this textbook, please see the text home site available at *www.hmco.com/college.*

Popular-Music Station Formats

Music stations range from those that play one narrowly defined type of music to those playing a broader spectrum. The style of music featured by a station is called its *format.*[15] Music stations describe their formats in a number of ways. A Country-music station may call itself "Modern Country," and a particular type of Rock station may advertise itself as "Lite Rock."

During the 1970s and 1980s, most popular-music station formats fit into one of a limited number of clearly defined categories. In the 1990s, two developments made it more difficult to categorize music stations. Some stations became quite diversified in the music they played, while other stations became more narrowly focused. To illustrate: many Country stations no longer confine themselves to songs that are clearly of the Country genre, enlarging their scope (and, they hope, their audiences) by playing Pop songs with a broader appeal, as well as Pop Classics recorded by Country artists. At the same time, the once clearly defined category of Adult/Contemporary (AC) has splintered into more focused formats by stations that call themselves Hot AC, Soft AC, or Urban AC. Each has a distinct sound. Some stations play music that doesn't fit any standard format, including Contemporary Religious, Gospel-Inspirational, and Country-Spanish, which is sometimes designated Ranchero.

---

[15]*Format* is used in several ways in broadcasting. A television talk-show outline is called a *format.* In radio, *format* refers to the kind of programming provided by a station (*all-talk format* or *Country-music format*). Stations may also be described as having a *tight* or *loose* format.

M Street, an influential trade publication, currently uses twenty-four categories of music formats.[16] They range from Country, represented by nearly 2,600 stations, to Easy Listening, a format used by only 70 stations. The formats described in the following paragraphs are neither rigid nor unchanging. Nearly any type may be automated and may be found in a market of any size. Format codes, such as AC for Adult/Contemporary, are those used by *M Street.* The format categories are listed alphabetically with brief descriptions of the type of music featured.

AC Adult/Contemporary. An adult-oriented Pop/Rock station, with no Hard Rock, possibly some non-Rock music, and often a greater emphasis on noncurrent music. AC-OL (Adult/Contemporary–Oldies) would be a gold-based AC, "gold" being the term for hit songs, mainly from the 1950s and 1960s. Typically, AC stations provide hourly news reports, traffic information during peak drive times, sports reports, business reports, and sometimes live play-by-play coverage of professional baseball and football games. Adult/Contemporary stations are tightly formatted, but morning drive-time DJs are allowed to chatter with few restrictions on time or topics. Success at an AC station is tied to a DJ's ability to develop a personal following.

AH Hot AC or Adult/Contemporary Hit Radio. A more up-tempo Contemporary Hits format, with no Hard Rock and no Rap.

AP Adult Alternative. Eclectic Rock, often with wide variations in musical style. It is sometimes called *AAA.* Alternative Rock stations play some Rock music from the latest charts, but rely heavily on Classic Rock hits of the 1970s and 1980s, targeted to older listeners. Adult Alternative stations are tightly formatted, with all music chosen by a music director.

AR Album Rock. Mainstream Rock 'n Roll. It can include more guitar-oriented Heavy Metal.

---

[16]*M Street Publications,* with headquarters in Nashville, Tennessee, offers a comprehensive service for radio stations and associated businesses, including record companies. One of its major offerings supplies to subscribers up-to-the-minute data about music radio trends. *M Street* granted permission to include its radio format information in this text.

AS Adult Standards. Standards and older non-Rock popular music. It often includes softer current popular music. Music on these stations is targeted to an older adult audience. The music covers a wide range of styles and is taken from playlists from four decades: 1940–1980. Rock music of any genre is seldom heard on Adult Standards stations, but softer versions of currently popular music may be included in AS formats.

BG Black Gospel. Religious music in the Gospel tradition.

CHR Contemporary Hit Radio (Top 40).[17] Current popular music, often encompassing a variety of Rock styles. CHR-RB (R & B/Urban) would be Dance/CHR, CHR-AR would be Rock-based CHR; CHR-NR (New Rock) would be New Rock or Modern Rock–based CHR. Some Rock stations call themselves Classic Rock, while others are known as New or Modern Rock and feature mostly new bands along with Rock hits of the last ten years. A typical Top 40 or CHR station rotates the top thirty to forty hits of the day with some older titles interspersed according to a formula. Station policies vary, but most stations repeat all of the current hits within two to three hours of broadcast time. They feature songs that are (or are predicted to be) highest in CD sales. Disc jockeys on CHR stations generally are upbeat. Their delivery is rapid but does not include the piercing high-volume frenzy of earlier days. Most CHR stations limit DJ talk and feature a seamless sound—one with no gaps or pauses between program elements.

CR Classic Rock. Rock-oriented Oldies, often mixed with hit Oldies of the 1960s, 1970s, and 1980s, sometimes called Classic Hits. The Oldies format is also known as Classic Hits, Rock 'n Roll Classics, Nostalgia, Golden Oldies, Old Gold, Solid Gold, or Classic Gold. Disc jockeys at these stations are expected to build a personal following and demonstrate in-depth knowledge of the music they play. Many Oldies stations carry newscasts, weather reports, and traffic reports, and feature contests and call-in listener conversations. A variation on the Oldies format is one that aims for the over-thirty age group by playing Rock 'n Roll hits from the 1970s and early 1980s.

---

[17]*M Street* uses the designation CH for Contemporary Hit Radio, but most others in music radio use CHR as the abbreviation for this music station format.

CW   Country. Country music, including contemporary and traditional styles, CW-OL (Oldies) would be Country Oldies. Sometimes known as Contemporary Country or Modern Country, Country-music stations tend to be moderately paced, even though they're as tightly formatted as Adult/Contemporary stations. Country music is incompatible with a frenetic pace.

CZ   Classic Hits. Classic Rock and Pop hits from the late 1960s through the early 1980s. These stations play Rock 'n Roll hits of the past, and on occasion, they'll add non-Rock hits of the past to their playlist.

EZ   Easy Listening. Primarily instrumental cover versions of popular songs. More up-tempo varieties of this format include Soft Rock originals, which may also be mixed with Smooth Jazz or Adult Standards.

FA   Fine Arts–Classical. Fine Arts (Classical) music. It often includes opera, theatre, and culture-oriented news and talk.

JZ   Jazz. Mostly instrumental, often mixed with Soft AC. This format classification includes both traditional Jazz and what is called Smooth Jazz or New AC.

MA   Modern Adult/Contemporary. A softer spectrum of Modern Rock.

NR   New Rock. Modern Rock.

OL   Oldies. Popular music, usually Rock, with 80 percent or greater non-current music. The abbreviation CW-OL indicates Country Oldies; RB-OL indicates R & B Oldies; and OL-70 indicates Pop-based 1970s Oldies.

PT   Preteen. Music, drama, or readings intended primarily for a pre-teen audience.

RB   R & B/Urban. Can cover a wide range of musical styles, often called Urban Contemporary.

RC   Religious/Contemporary. Modern and Rock-based Religious music.

SA   Soft Adult/Contemporary. Primarily noncurrent Soft-Rock originals. A cross between Adult/Contemporary and Easy Listening, these stations present older non- or Soft-Rock originals. This format may include Smooth Jazz or music usually heard on Adult Standards stations. Disc jockeys at these stations are chosen for their easy-going, friendly manner and are allowed to "chat" with their listeners.

SB   Soft Urban Contemporary. Soft R & B sometimes mixed with Smooth Jazz, and often heavy in Oldies. Some stations additionally play Soul, Jazz, and Soft Black Rock music.

SS   Spanish. Many stations listed as Spanish are full-time music stations, featuring music from Latin America. The actual number of Spanish-language music stations is unknown, but they're of great and growing importance to their audiences. In the early 1990s, a Spanish-language music station, KLAX, featuring Ranchero music, became the number one station in the huge Los Angeles market.

Spanish-language music stations play songs appropriate to the origin of their listeners. Stations in Florida favor Cuban music; stations in the Southwest generally feature music from Mexico; Puerto Rican and other Caribbean music is popular in the American Northeast; and

Figure 11.5

DJ Chuy Gomez back announces a music sweep on KMEL, San Francisco, California, an Urban Contemporary station featuring Hip-Hop and Rhythm and Blues. Chuy was born in Tepatitlan, Mexico. He received a 1995 Billboard award for Local Video Show of the Year. In addition to his afternoon drive-time shift on KMEL, Chuy hosts a weekly show that is broadcast in Japan, "All Japan Dance Top Ten." He studied broadcasting at the College of San Mateo, a community college in California. You can visit the KMEL web site at *www.106kmel.com/ MEETAIR.html. Courtesy of Chuy Gomez and KMEL, San Francisco, California.*

stations serving a sizable population of Central Americans—Guatemalans, Costa Ricans, Salvadorans, Hondurans, Nicaraguans, or Panamanians— feature music of those countries. Spanish stations generally provide more nonmusic programming than do English-language music stations. They may carry baseball games from Latin America, U.S. games broadcast in Spanish, and interview and religious programs.

The popularity of some music formats varies from region to region. Country-music stations are far more prevalent in the South than in the East. On the other hand, some formats, including Gold/Classic Rock, show nearly the same degree of popularity in all regions of the nation, ranging from eight to ten percent.

Announcing Styles

Many music stations—including those formatted as Easy Listening, Adult/Contemporary, Country, or Oldies—feature DJs with a conversational style of delivery, with a minimum of "chatter." On the other hand, Top 40, or CHR, stations ask DJs to project more energy, but the vitality is expressed in a moderate volume, medium-paced delivery. Urban Contemporary stations, featuring music by African-American and Latino artists, often ask for a low-pitched, conversational, noticeably masculine style of delivery.

Because of the range of announcing styles on the air, you'd do well to practice a number of stylistic approaches to popular-music announcing. At the same time, it's important to be yourself. You must be able to project your individuality while speaking at different rates and levels of intensity.

Preparing for a Career As a DJ

In preparing for a career as a DJ, your highest priority must be to develop a compelling air personality. Beyond this, you must be able to use microphones correctly and to operate audio consoles and computerized work stations. Solid preparation also includes skill in the use of tape cartridge machines, compact disc players, digital audiotape players, and even reel-to-reel tape recorders. It is also important to become an authority on the type of music you intend to announce.[18]

---

[18]Although most music radio stations no longer play selections recorded on tape carts, DAT, or reel-to-reel tape recorders, station executives agree that students of announcing should still learn to operate such equipment. An announcer who's unable to operate these systems would not be able to function if the computers went down.

Concentrate on the sections in this book that discuss performance, interpreting copy, ad-lib announcing, commercial interpretation and delivery, news writing, news delivery, and interviewing.

CHECKLIST

IMPROVING YOUR POPULAR-MUSIC ANNOUNCING STYLE

1. Become an authority on the type of music you intend to announce.
2. Work to develop an engaging and unique on-air personality.
3. Cultivate your sense of humor.
4. Learn to operate audio equipment efficiently.
5. Practice announcing for several types of formats.
6. Practice delivering commercials, PSAs, and station promos.
7. Perfect your ad-libbing skills.
8. Learn to match music and chatter to a specific station sound.

Although your success as a DJ will depend on your ability to develop a *unique* and attractive air personality, it's helpful to listen to a wide range of successful announcers. The best approach is to listen to all of the popular-music stations in your reception area, rather than concentrating on the one or two stations whose music you prefer.

Successful DJs have a well-developed sense of humor, usually of the "off-the-wall" variety. It's unlikely that anyone without a sense of humor can develop one after reaching adulthood, but it's possible to improve one's skills in almost anything, including comedy. An analysis of puns, jokes, and one-liners that you find funny will tell you much about your sense of humor. It may be helpful to invent gags and test them on your friends. Most DJs demonstrate their sense of humor by making ironic or satirical ad-lib comments about current events and noteworthy people. Although a sense of humor is invaluable, it is equally important that you be willing to share yourself with your listeners, even when this means revealing painful or embarrassing experiences or minor problems in your life.

Disc jockeys also need considerable knowledge of music and musicians, including historical facts, trivia, and current developments. This is best gained by reading on a regular basis several trade magazines and newspapers. Among the most useful are *Billboard, R & R (Radio & Records), Gavin,* and a variety of tip sheets.

If you don't have an opportunity to do on-air work as a DJ, you can still practice introductions to recorded music and the kind of humorous chatter required of some DJs. Use the practice suggestions that end this discussion of DJs.

Practice announcing for both fast-paced and more relaxed station formats. Research the music you're playing: find out when a recording was made, who some of the key artists are, and anything of significance about the recording techniques used or the time and place at which a live recording was made. Refer to a news service for information about important anniversary dates (for example, Woodstock 1, the breakup of Led Zeppelin, and the death of Jerry Garcia) and the music happenings of one, five, and ten years ago. Publications such as *R & R* include this information; the publications are expensive, but you may be able to examine a back issue at a local radio station. Once you're on a station's payroll, you'll have regular access to a number of trade publications.

Here are a few more suggestions for practicing DJ work:

- In choosing music to introduce and play, choose performances you know and like. Look especially for music about which you can talk. You won't select your own music when working for a station, but it's good practice to begin with the easiest possible challenge.

- When you practice, actually play your songs, and play them all the way through. Pacing and mood demand that you and your music work together for a total impression.

- Practice headlining songs you'll play later. This is a realistic technique used to hold listeners who might otherwise switch to another station.

- Practice giving the name of the songs and their performers at the end of a sweep. All stations have policies on music identification, and you'll have to conform to them, but as you practice, aim for the communication of a maximum amount of information.

- Practice delivering commercials, ad-libbed public-service announcements, and station promos.

- Practice working with an audio console. You'll almost certainly be expected to operate your own console as a professional DJ.

- Practice performing intros. First, time the music between the start of the song and the start of the vocal. Then, work to introduce the number so that your voice stops just as the vocal begins or where there's a natural change in the music, as when the horn section begins. Although you may not appreciate DJs who talk over music, some stations require it.

- Practice ad-libbing about the music, the day's events, or ideas that intrigue you. You'll have little chance to ad-lib on a station with a tight format, but many stations will consider you for a job only if you're able to entertain in a spontaneous, ad-lib manner.

- Introduce songs ad-lib. Scripts (other than for commercials, some PSAs, and news briefs) are not used by DJs.

- Avoid corny clichés. Try to develop your own announcing style. The creative expressions of popular DJs become the clichés of unimaginative and unoriginal announcers.

- Before engaging in practice sessions, remember that all music stations work to achieve a particular **sound**. A station's sound is the result of a number of factors: the type of music played, the voices and personalities of the announcers, their energy level, the kinds of things they say, whether they speak over instrumental introductions or endings of songs, and the general pace of music and speech. Useful practice includes determining the specific sound you're attempting to achieve and the selection of music appropriate to that sound.

For information on job seeking, see Chapter 13, Above all, remember that there are jobs available if you're well trained, have native talent, and are willing to begin at a modest salary, work hard, and move to any geographic location.

 PRACTICE

Tracking Rate of Delivery of DJs

Make audio recordings of several popular-music announcers, each chosen to represent a different sound: the first from a low-key noncommercial station; the second from a fast-paced CHR station; the third from a Country station; and the fourth from an AC station. Play each tape, and make a typescript of any sixty-second portion of the performance. Count the number of words delivered during the sixty seconds. Compare rates of delivery according to types of stations.

The Classical-Music Announcer

There are Classical-music stations in all parts of the United States and Canada, and they add up to about six percent of radio stations that feature music.[19] With just slightly more than five hundred Classical-music stations on the air, it should be apparent that job opportunities in this demanding specialization are limited. You shouldn't single-mindedly prepare for a career strictly as an announcer on a Classical-music station unless your love of both Classical music and radio is so strong that you're willing to put practical considerations aside. On the other hand, preparing for Classical-music announcing as part of your study of the entire field of broadcast announcing can be of great value. Exploring the great treasure of music, learning musical terms, and practicing the foreign pronunciation that's required of all Classical-music announcers will enrich your life and make you more competent in any announcing specialization.

As an announcer on a Classical-music station, you'll have some duties in common with a DJ. You'll operate an audio console, ad-lib introductions to musical selections (usually from information contained on three-by-five cards), and read public-service announcements.[20] Because noncommercial Classical-music stations outnumber commercial Classical-music stations about six to one, it's unlikely that you'll work with commercials. You will, however, have a number of other collateral duties such as dubbing music to DAT, CDs, or mass storage hard drives; preparing newscasts and summaries; and maintaining an operating log.

Unlike a DJ, you won't be concerned with hit records. You will, however, be expected to keep abreast of new recordings of standards, releases of music not previously recorded, and a small output of new works. You'll be required to have an extensive knowledge of Classical music and be accurate in pronouncing French, Italian, German, Spanish, and Russian. Acceptable pronunciation of Czech, Slovak, Swedish,

---

[19]*Classical* is not really the best label for stations featuring concert and operatic music. An important period in music history, roughly the last half of the eighteenth century, is known as the Classical Period. The music of that time—represented by Haydn and Mozart, among others—is, strictly speaking, Classical music. *Classic,* which means "of the highest or best order," is a better choice to name stations of this type. One station calls itself "your classic music station," but most stations that feature operatic and concert music refer to themselves as Classical-music stations. Because the usage is widespread, it's followed here.

[20]Occasionally on certain stations, scripts are prepared for specialized programs, such as complete operas. Before each act or scene, a synopsis of the story is read by the on-air announcer.

Figure 11.6

Classical-music announcer Al Covaia reads information about musical events of the week in all areas reached by his station's signal. He prepares his copy from newspaper ads, concert listings, telephone calls, and brochures. *Courtesy of Al Covaia and KKHI, Corte Madera, California.*

Polish, Romanian, and other languages of composers who've contributed to Western Classical music would be desirable.

As an announcer on a Classical-music station, your name may or may not be known to your listeners. Stations on which announcers perform live usually ask you to give your name at the start and end of a shift, with occasional mentions in between, but automated stations almost never reveal the names of those making the announcements. In either case, it's unlikely that you'll be expected to build a personal following.

If, on the other hand, you're assigned to, or develop, a specialty program (a music quiz, a telephone talk show centering on Classical music, a program of operatic arias, or a program featuring the best of the new releases), you might become well known to your listeners, but such prominence is rare. Station and program managers believe that most Classical-music fans turn to stations because of the music, not because of the announcers.

No ladder extends from the small Classical-music station to the big time. Most Classical-music stations are noncommercial FM stations, and working conditions and salaries tend to be uniform. There are profitable FM Classical-music stations in major metropolitan areas, and salaries there are quite good, but those stations employ only a small percentage of professional radio announcers.[21]

Your announcing work at a Classical-music station will be more relaxed than that of a DJ on a popular-music station. Musical selections are longer, many running thirty minutes or more. You'll spend most of your time announcing general music programs consisting, for example, of a Bach fugue, followed by a Strauss tone poem, a Vivaldi concerto, and a Mozart symphony, rounded off by ballet music by Tchaikovsky.

The selection and placement of music recordings are made by the music director, who's responsible for the total sound of the station. There usually is a coherent plan to a broadcast day: brisk and lively short works are played during morning drive time (especially by commercial Classical-music stations), concert programs during midday, shorter works again during evening drive time, and longer works—including complete operas, symphonic programs recorded during performances, masses, and oratorios—throughout the evening. Music directors keep a list of all musical selections played, complete with date and time of each playing. Most Classical-music stations have a policy requiring the lapse of a certain number of weeks or months between playings.

Several scripts for practicing Classical-music announcing, featuring names and words in various European languages, may be found on the web site for this book. URL:

www.hmco.com/college

CHECKLIST

POLISHING YOUR CLASSICAL- MUSIC ANNOUNCING

1. Perfect your foreign language pronunciation.
2. Perfect your use of phonetic transcription. Although wire-service phonetics may be adequate for most announcers, as a Classical-music announcer, you should master the International Phonetic Alphabet.
3. Practice reading and ad-libbing PSAs.
4. Practice cuing and playing the music you introduce.

---

[21]Ninety-seven percent of Classical-music stations are FM; only three percent broadcast on the AM band.

5. Create music programs. Invent titles, write openings and closings, select theme music, and make sample program offerings.
6. Practice ad-libbing with only the name of the composer, the title of the composition, and the names of performing artists before you.
7. Practice reading news headlines and five-minute news summaries, because this is a typical part of a Classical-music announcer's broadcast day.

As you practice Classical-music announcing, keep the suggestions in the checklist in mind.

Concert music usually is introduced by giving the name of the composer, the selection, the orchestra (or other musical group), the conductor, and, when appropriate, the soloist (as in a concerto or an aria). At some stations you'll be asked to add the name of the recording company. When introducing opera, you'll most likely give a résumé of each act or scene and identify the leading singers. *Schwann Opus*, issued quarterly, includes extensive information on Classical recordings and furnishes birth and death dates of composers and, when known, the date of composition of each work.

The most important requirements for employment as a Classical-music announcer are impeccable foreign language pronunciation and a thorough knowledge and appreciation of Classical music. If you choose to specialize in this type of announcing, you should enroll in as many general courses in music as are offered to nonmajors. Of course, if you're a musician, more specialized courses will be available. Listen to Classical-music broadcasts; collect records, tapes, and CDs; practice aloud the introductions to musical selections; and learn to use some of the source books mentioned in Appendix D under Chapter 11.

CHAPTER 12

Sports Announcing

CHAPTER OUTLINE

- Working Conditions of Sports Announcers
- Interviewing Athletes
  - Editing Considerations
- Sports Reporting
  - The Television Sports Reporter
  - The Radio Sports Director
- The Play-by-Play Announcer
  - Working Conditions

- Practicing Play-by-Play Announcing
- Preparing for Play-by-Play Announcing
- Calling the Game
- Additional Tips on Sportscasting
- SPOTLIGHT: Plea to Radio Sportscasters: Give Us the Details
- The Play Analyst

MOST ANNOUNCERS WHO REACH THE TOP OF THEIR SPECIALIZATION spend years of preparation before achieving success; nowhere is the struggle and its potential reward seen more clearly than in sports broadcasting. Sports announcing is extremely competitive and demands years of dedicated effort before there's any likelihood of significant return. Despite this, the dream of spending a career in sports broadcasting is so appealing that scores of young people eagerly make the effort and assume the risks associated with the gamble. If you're determined to become a sports broadcaster, you should weigh carefully the advice of Russ Hodges. First, to succeed you must love both *sports* and *broadcasting* and fully commit yourself to both. Second, you must truly believe that you'll succeed. Third, you must prepare yourself educationally for a different career just in case you're one of the ninety-five out of one hundred who don't succeed in sports broadcasting.[1]

To become a successful sports announcer, you must have a *passion* for your work. You'll need it because sports announcing can be a stressful and exhausting way of life. You may find yourself traveling with a team, living out of a suitcase, putting in long hours, eating in restaurants and fast-food shops, and leaving your family for extended periods. Only a passion for your work can sustain you in such a job. Sports

---

[1]Russ Hodges was sports announcer for seven major-league baseball teams, including the Yankees and Giants. He also announced football, televised boxing matches, horse racing, hockey, polo, golf, and nearly every other major and minor sport. His broadcasting career spanned forty-one years, from 1929 to 1970.

reporters who don't travel outside their immediate geographical area still work long hours and seldom have a day off.

Sports announcing includes *sports reporting, play-by-play coverage,* and *play analysis.* Most sports announcers become expert in one of these specialties. Nearly all beginning sports announcers must become competent at all three specialties. Interviewing sports figures and delivering commercials are additional challenges that you must manage well in order to succeed in sports announcing.

The Entertainment and Sports Programming Network (ESPN and ESPN2) considerably expanded the range of sports events shown on television. ESPN covers traditional mainline sports such as football, basketball, baseball, golf, hockey, boxing, and tennis, but in addition, to fill its many hours of daily cablecasting, it televises such events as bicycle racing (the Tour de France, for example), rodeos, billiards, volleyball, horse show-jumping, bodybuilding championships, roller hockey, surfing, waterskiing, gymnastics, hydroplane racing, and even tractor-pulling contests.

In addition to ESPN, many regional radio and television sports networks offer employment to sports announcers. The Fox Sports Network has stations in Chicago, New York, Ohio, Pittsburgh, and the San Francisco Bay Area. Other cable sports networks are the New England Sports Network (NESN), Classic Sports Network, Empire Sports Network, and the Midwest Sports Channel.

Figure 12.1

Before, during, and after the game, sports announcers spend hours researching team and player histories, statistics, and interesting sidelights. Play-by-play announcer Bill King goes over his detailed stat book just before the start of a baseball game. *Courtesy of Bill King and the Oakland A's, Oakland, California.*

Working Conditions of Sports Announcers

As a sports announcer, you'll work for a radio or television station (perhaps both), for a broadcast or cable network, for an athletic team, or as a freelance announcer. Your working conditions, responsibilities, and income will be determined by your affiliation.

Network sports announcers, whether play-by-play, analysts, or reporters, are generally at the top of the salary range and have the least strenuous schedules. Network sportscasters seldom broadcast more than one game a week, and even those who add reporting duties to their schedules are responsible for only a few minutes of sports news a day. Sports announcers for national or regional cable systems are well rewarded, but their work schedule is heavy: they may find themselves calling several games each week during basketball, hockey, and baseball seasons.

Radio station sports reporters are usually responsible for delivering one or two hourly reports during their shifts, as well as taping additional reports to be broadcast after they've left the station. Television sports reporters produce several minutes of visually informative sports news each day and also record sports features to be run on the weekends.

Sports announcers who work for athletic teams have the most strenuous but perhaps the most exciting and rewarding jobs. As an employee of a professional baseball, basketball, football, or hockey team, you'll travel with the club. You owe loyalty to your employer, even though you may occasionally find it difficult to reconcile your judgment with that of your boss. Most team owners require their sportscasters to advertise special-promotion days and push ticket sales. Some demand that their play-by-play sportscasters openly root for their team. Some ask their announcers to favor their team but to do so with discretion. Other owners make no demands on their play-by-play staff but expect announcers as well as all other members of the organization to maintain loyalty to the team, especially when the team is on a losing streak. Even when working for the most genial or detached owner, you won't have as much freedom as does a reporter who works for a newspaper or a radio, television, or cable operation.

Most sports announcers fill a variety of professional roles. The most simple combination is doing play-by-play baseball during its long season and basketball, football, or hockey during the fall or winter. Other sports announcers combine five days a week of sports reporting for a station with weekend play-by-play reporting of college sports. If you become a sports announcer, you'll probably begin at a small-market radio station doing some sports announcing along with other duties, such as reading hourly news reports or performing as a DJ. If you succeed, you may move into full-time sports reporting and play-by-play announcing. Another career path is to move to a larger-market station or, perhaps, to move from radio to television.

If you're successful in becoming a full-time sports professional for the electronic media, your work schedule and job description might well conform to one of the following models.

Sports Reporter for an All-News Network-Affiliated Radio Station in a Major Market. You're responsible for eight to ten live reports each day and three carted reports to be played after you've left the station. In addition, your popularity has opened up supplemental jobs that don't conflict with your station work: you do football play-by-play for a major university; you announce play-by-play during the football preseason for a professional team in your area; and you record commercials for a variety of clients, including a chain of sporting goods stores. Occasionally, when an important news story involves athletes or teams in your area, you prepare a report for your network.

Your work schedule is extremely demanding. Aside from the effort of working a six- to seven-day week, you must constantly keep up with developments in all major sports at amateur and professional levels. You spend hours each week reading several newspapers, *Sporting News, Sports Illustrated,* and other specialized publications. You're also asked to speak at team receptions and banquets, news conferences, and civic functions. You schedule yourself to cover as many sports events as possible. You do postgame interviews for use on your daily sports reports, and you deliver some of these actualities live to your station shortly after a game has ended. You record interviews with the star (or, occasionally, the goat) of a game on a small, portable recorder and insert them into your report. You also make notes as you watch the game so you can give a firsthand review, complete with actualities recorded in the locker room, on the following day's reports.

Sports Director for a Network Owned and Operated (O & O) Television Station. As sports director for an O & O television station, you prepare sports news for the daily 6:00 P.M. and 10:00 P.M., or 11:00 P.M., newscasts.[2] You view and edit tapes of sports action, select sports photos sent

---

[2]*O & O* is broadcast jargon for a station that is *owned and operated* by a parent network.

Figure 12.2

Sports play-by-play announcer Ted Robinson calls nearly 200 baseball games a season, starting in spring training and—if the San Francisco Giants are successful on the field—through the postseason. It takes a healthy vocal mechanism to sustain such a challenge. *Courtesy of Ted Robinson and the San Francisco Giants, San Francisco, California.*

by wire services, and write two, three- to five-minute segments for daily newscasts. You spend much of your time attending sports events with an ENG operator. Pregame and postgame interviews with players and coaches compose a good portion of your nightly sportscast. On some weekends, you spend hours at the station watching games on network television. You select key plays that you may want to use on the air and have them dubbed off. A three-hour game may provide you with as much as thirty minutes of dubbed action from which you'll choose a maximum of three minutes for each of your two sports segments.

Your day's work leaves little time for moonlighting. You attend three to five sports events each week to see nontelevised events firsthand and to record interviews. You regularly spend early afternoons covering sports stories, accompanied by an ENG operator.[3] You arrive at the station at 3:00 P.M., which leaves you less than three hours in which to view or review all available tape, to make selections, to review sports news from the wire services, to write your script, and to prepare for on-air performance during the 6:00 P.M. news. Between the 6:00 P.M. and the

---

[3]At some small-market stations, you may work without an ENG operator; therefore, you must set up your lightweight camera on a tripod, start the camera, and perform stand-ups and interviews without assistance.

late-night newscast, you eat dinner, prepare for your second sportscast, and review sports scores as they come in from the wire services. Your workday ends after the late-night news, but it begins early the next day. You spend mornings arranging interviews, reading several sports magazines and the sports sections of newspapers, and, perhaps, answering requests for information about the life of a sports reporter sent by high school and college students who would like to have your job.

Sports Director for a Medium-Market Radio Station. You focus on high school, college, and minor-league sports events. You work for the station and for the AA baseball team whose games are broadcast over a three-station network. When not on the road with the team, you do play-by-play descriptions of the most important high school football and basketball games. You work with a group of students you've recruited and trained to phone in ongoing scores of the games not being broadcast. You do play-by-play announcing of home football games for a nearby university. You provide several brief sports reports each day for the hourly five-minute newscasts. You act as spotter for play-by-play sportscasters when university sports events are regionally telecast. And, as time allows, you do play-by-play reports of newsworthy local sports events such as tennis and golf tournaments; hockey and soccer championship playoffs; Little League, Babe Ruth, and Pop Warner championships; and track and field meets.

Sportscaster for a Television Network. You owe no allegiance to owners, managers, teams, or players. Your responsibility is to your viewers, and they expect accurate, balanced, and entertaining reports of the games they watch. Because your continued success depends on perfection, you limit moonlighting and other commitments that might cut down on the hours of careful preparation necessary for a first-rate sportscast. Your schedule requires play-by-play work one day a week, which translates into a minimum of twenty-five baseball games during the season, plus preseason and postseason games, and sixteen professional football games, plus divisional playoff games and the Super Bowl.

This schedule adds up to nearly one game a week for the calendar year, depending on the duration of the playoffs. It's manageable because you're able to spend several days each week memorizing players by appearance, number, and position and you're able to rely on a professional support staff that includes a play and game analyst, a statistician, and (in the case of football) spotters. Your travel schedule is demanding, but you're able to return home for at least a portion of each week. Your high salary increases the number of hungry sportscasters coveting your job. This competition alone is reason enough for you to apply yourself constantly to perfecting and maintaining your skills.

Sportscaster for a Cable Sports Channel. Your work is similar to that of a network sportscaster, but you call far more games each season. As is true of most sports announcers, you shift from one sport to another as seasons change. You do play-by-play for as many as forty-five home games of a major-league baseball team, and another fourteen when traveling with the team on road trips. During the winter you call college football games. You work with a former star appropriate to the sport being covered who adds "color" and interpretations and explanations of strategies. When calling baseball games, your partner calls three innings of each game.

Play-by-Play Announcer for a Professional Major-League Baseball Team. You're employed jointly by a baseball organization and a radio station. In many respects, you lead a life similar to that of the athletes. You travel with the team and don't have to make your own arrangements for transportation or lodging. A traveling secretary handles all details; this eases the stress of travel considerably. Throughout the season you broadcast on a regional radio network of as many as ten stations.

Including spring practice games and games rained out before the end of the fifth inning, but not including divisional playoffs or World Series games, you call about one hundred and seventy games during the season. You work with a partner who calls between two and three innings and provides anecdotal and statistical information throughout the game.

Play-by-Play Announcer for a Minor-League Professional Baseball Team. You call fewer games each season than your major-league counterpart, but both travel and play-by-play announcing are more rigorous. One of the ways underfunded minor-league teams manage to survive is by economizing on travel. Buses are used for travel whenever possible. The team remains in each town for five or six days, and you must call six games during the five-day visit.

Play-by-Play Announcer for a Professional Football Team. Your working life is quite different from that of a baseball, basketball, or hockey announcer. Not counting preseason and postseason games, your team plays sixteen games each season, usually a week apart. You broadcast mainly on radio except when games are carried by a regional television network or by a cable sports network.

Play-by-Play Announcer for a University Football Team. You call about eleven games each season, assuming that funds make it possible for you to go on road trips with the team. Most universities offer free transportation to away games on charter flights but don't furnish per diem money. If a radio station, the university, and one or more advertisers put together a commercial package for broadcasting an entire season, your full travel expenses are met.

Play-by-Play Announcer for a Professional Basketball Team. You're part of a four-person announcing staff. You and a partner do television play-by-play, while radio coverage is provided by the two other members of the team's broadcasting staff.[4]

Play-by-Play Announcer for a Professional Hockey Team. Your traveling and broadcasting schedule is nearly identical to that of your basketball counterpart. Your team plays eighty games, not counting preseason and playoff games. A typical road trip involves five matches in five cities spread over twelve days. Your friends who do play-by-play for minor-league hockey teams call fewer games each season, but they must cope with more demanding travel schedules.

Interviewing Athletes

Interviews are an important resource for nearly all sports reporters. Chapter 8 will help you develop a general approach to interviewing. This section offers additional comments directed at sports reporting.

As a sports announcer, you'll generally interview players, coaches, managers, trainers, and owners. Your interviews will usually take place at a sports event or at a news conference. Pregame and postgame interviews are common to all sports. As you prepare for interviews, keep some of these questions in mind.

---

[4]Professional basketball announcing staffs range from four members to one member. Typically two announcers work together during radio-only broadcasts, and announcers work separately when a game is covered by both radio and television.

- What is the overriding significance of the game to be played or just concluded?
- Is there an interesting one-on-one player matchup?
- Is there something unique in the playing ability or game strategy of the person you interview?
- Has an athlete been on a hot or cold streak?
- Is there an unusually important or interesting game coming up?
- Is there any information about trades or free agents that might be newsworthy?

Interviews with athletes can sometimes be frustrating. The code of the locker room seems to demand that athletes—other than wrestlers, boxers, and some professional tennis players—be modest about their own accomplishments and praise their teammates or opponents, regardless of the facts. Moreover, athletes are preoccupied before a game and exhausted afterward. Finally, the noise and confusion in dugouts and locker rooms and on the playing field can make sensible, coherent conversation difficult.

When interviewing sports stars, keep the following points in mind:

Assume That Your Audience Is Interested In and Capable of Understanding Complex, Precise Discussions About Training and Technique. Avoid asking superficial, predictable questions. Your audience probably already knows a lot about the sport and the athlete and wants to find out more. Followers of tennis, golf, and Olympic performances such as gymnastics, diving, and equestrian events are less tolerant of superficial interviews than are most other sports fans. They've come to expect precise analytical comments, and they feel cheated if interviews with participants don't add to their understanding of complexities and strategies. Basketball and football have developed increasingly complex offenses and defenses, and fans have been educated to understand and appreciate detailed information about them. Baseball, one of the most subtly complex of all major sports, is seldom explained or discussed in an enlightened fashion through interviews, but you should not be discouraged from reaching for answers to complex questions.

Work up to Controversial or Critical Questions with Care. If you ask a big question without any preliminaries, you're likely to get a routine statement "for the record" from athletes and coaches. Sports figures are interviewed so often that most of them can supply the questions as well as the answers. They tend to rely on safe explanations for most common questions. If you want more, lead up to big questions with a sequence of less controversial ones. If you begin an interview with a football coach by asking whether the coach approves of a trade recently made by the club's owners, the coach is naturally going to say "yes" and avoid elaborating. Begin instead by talking about the team and its strengths and weaknesses. Move to a question about the playing abilities of the traded player. Ask specific questions about the player's strong and weak points. Finally, ask the coach to explain how the loss of this player will affect the team. A coach will seldom criticize the decisions of the club's owners, but you'll have a better chance of getting more than a vague response if you don't ask the big question straight out. Give your guest a chance to comment informatively as well as loyally.

A warning: don't use a roundabout approach to the big question if your intent is (or appears to be) entrapment. It could be more difficult to obtain cooperation in the future.

Get to Know the Athletes You Are Likely to Be Interviewing. Knowing the athletes you interview will help you to assess the kinds of questions they can and can't handle. Many sportscasters and some reporters travel with teams, visit locker rooms, and are invited to opening-day parties, victory celebrations, and promotional luncheons. If you have such opportunities, use them to become acquainted with the athletes who attend.

Listen to Conversations Among Athletes and Coaches. A good way to discover what athletes and coaches think is timely and important is simply to listen to their conversations. Though time pressures sometimes require you to enter into these conversations to come up with a story or anecdote for your program, you can often learn more by listening. If you're lucky enough to have meals with athletes and be accepted in clubhouses or locker rooms, try to be a silent observer. You'll be amazed at the spontaneous insights that will emerge.

Again, a warning: don't use your familiarity of friendships with sports figures to warp your judgment or betray a trust. In other words, don't make excuses for the poor play of an athlete because you have a warm relationship and don't report things said to you or overheard by you that should remain confidential.

Editing Considerations

When interviewing for later editing into actualities, know in advance whether your questions will remain on the recording. This consideration is important because the questions you ask and the answers you receive must be guided by the way you'll later edit them. The following question and answer would be difficult to use if the question were not included in the actuality when broadcast:

QUESTION:

You were in foul trouble early tonight. Do you think the refs were blowing a quick whistle?

ANSWER:

Well, I guess we had a little difference of opinion on that. I thought they were overeager. Talk of the possibility of some revenge for the last game probably had them uptight.

Without the question, the answer makes little sense. Of course, you could cut the question and write a lead-in that serves the same purpose:

LEAD-IN:

I asked Matty if he thought his early fouls came because the refs were blowing a quick whistle.

This approach works, but it would've been better if you and Matty had understood at the outset of the interview that you wanted complete statements that could stand alone without your question. In that event Matty's response might have begun like this:

MATTY:

I got into foul trouble early, and I think the reason might have been . . .

Figure 12.3

Sports reporter Steve Bitker delivers his reports ad lib, working from notes jotted down just prior to airtime. Steve studied journalism at San Diego State University, and later received a degree in sociology at the University of California, Berkeley. *Courtesy of Steve Bitker and KCBS, San Francisco, California.*

Sports Reporting

At some smaller radio and television stations, the title *sports reporter* is synonymous with *sports director.* Only prosperous stations can afford the services of more than one sports specialist. Radio station sports directors are usually responsible for both live and taped reports. They also prepare guidelines to be followed by news anchors who report in-progress scores and final results.

Television sports reporters are less likely to do double duty as reporter and director than are their radio counterparts. It's common to find three or more sports specialists at television stations: a sports director, who may or may not appear before cameras, and two or more reporters who prepare and deliver sports reports during regular newscasts. Typically, one sports reporter does the Monday-through-Friday newscasts, and the second reporter works weekends. Both cover sports events with ENG operators and prepare recorded material for the sports segments of the station's newscasts.

The Television Sports Reporter

As a sports reporter for a local television station, you may find yourself preparing and delivering three sports features daily—for the 5:00 P.M., 6:00 P.M., and 10:00 P.M. or 11:00 P.M. newscasts—plus a taped feature for weekend broadcast. In another common arrangement, one reporter performs for the 5:00 P.M. news and the second is featured on the 6:00 P.M. and the late-night newscasts. The first reporter does weekend sports.

As a sports reporter for a medium- or major-market television station, you can expect to have these resources available to you.[5]

- An ENG operator for taping sports action and pregame and postgame interviews
- Tapes of complete sports events
- Taped sports highlights from a parent network
- Taped stories from a nearby television station with which you have a reciprocal agreement
- Tapes and slides from professional and university athletic organizations
- Sports news, photos, and slides from the Associated Press (AP) or ESPN
- Sports magazines and the sports section of newspapers
- Press information kits and media guides from all major professional and university athletic organizations
- A telephone–audio recorder setup that allows you to make audio recordings of telephone interviews

The Associated Press, SportsTicker, and other services provide extensive material for sports reporters, including sports news items and up-to-the-minute scores. Throughout the year, special reports provide extensive information about the sport of the moment—the Kentucky Derby, football bowl games, the World Series, the Superbowl, the PGA Tournament, the NBA All-Star Game, the Stanley Cup, and so on.

The Associated Press provides nonstop coverage of sports, including detailed information on major-league baseball (MLB); the NFL, NBA, and NHL; all major college sports; the Olympics; professional golf and tennis; and everything from Alpine skiing to wrestling and bowling.[6]

---

[5]The term *tapes* is used here even though in many operations recorded sports material is dubbed from a digital video camera directly to a mass storage hard drive at a station, from which it is then edited for broadcast.

[6]In addition to the abbreviation *MLB* for major-league baseball, sports reporting organizations use *NHL* for the National Hockey League, *NBA* for the National Basketball Association, *WNBA* for the Women's National Basketball Association, *NFC* for the National Football Conference, *AFC* for the American Football Conference, *NFL* for the National Football League, *PGA* for the Professional Golfer's Association, and *LPGA* for the Ladies' Professional Golfers' Association.

The AP also supplies "Morning and Afternoon Sportswatch" as well as several "SportsMinutes" and headlines of sports stories of major importance. The AP calls its individual sports stories **separates**. These single-event stories are written for all MLB, NFL, NBA, NHL, and WNBA games, as well as college bowl games, basketball tournament games, and major breaking stories that involve any sport, team, or athlete.

In addition to regularly scheduled features, the Associated Press issues both bulletins and urgents. Examples of **bulletins** are blockbuster trades, deaths of noteworthy athletes, and pennant and World Series clinchers. **Urgents** include no-hitters, major firings of coaches and managers, and important breaking stories.

Team media guides are the best sources of detailed information. The guides outline in detail each player's sports career; give statistics for individuals, the team, and the team's opponents; and include each player's photograph to make recognition easier. The won–lost records of every coach or manager who ever served the team and the performance leaders through the years who lead the team in many different categories are also noted. Both statistics and significant facts are provided to help give your narrative a sense of authority.

Your job consists mainly of collecting, selecting, editing, and organizing the materials available to you into a cohesive, action-oriented package for each of the evening's newscasts, and of writing an entertaining and informative script. One of your tasks is to log significant plays as you watch games on television. The log is later used to edit the major plays for your reports.

Using essentially the same visual materials and sports news items, you must prepare as many as three different sports reports each day. The trick is to organize and write your reports to avoid unnecessary repetitions. Many of your viewers will see two of your nightly reports, and a few will see all three, so all reports must provide fresh information for addicted fans. (Of course, a truly spectacular play may be shown on all three reports; die-hard sports fans may actually stay up late to see it *one more time!*)

You'll be under constant pressure from your sports director to make your reports more *visual*. Because you're reporting on television, they'll obviously be "visual." What the director wants is a great deal of illustrative material (taped inserts, even still photos) to avoid using the kind of shots some television producers sarcastically refer to as **talking heads**. You may feel that a series of taped shots may be more confusing than enlightening or that some important stories should be narrated directly into a taking camera, but your judgment isn't the deciding factor.

When writing voice-over copy to accompany taped "play action," you must try always to match words and pictures cohesively. On television, when words and pictures don't reinforce one another, the sound tends to fade from the viewer's awareness. Confine your remarks to the few essential comments needed to enhance understanding of what the viewers are seeing.

The Radio Sports Director

As sports director for a medium- or major-market radio station, you'll have many of the same responsibilities as your television counterpart. You'll produce several fast-moving sports reports each day, you'll generate material to be broadcast after you've left the station, and you'll establish and supervise station policy concerning sports. This last responsibility includes preparing an instruction sheet or manual for use by general or staff announcers. In the manual you'll indicate how sports bulletins are to be handled, how the sports news section of general newscasts is to be structured, and the order and the manner of reporting scores and the outcomes of games.

Depending on your geographical region, you might ask that a certain sport be given priority in reporting. In the Northeast, hockey often comes before basketball; in Indiana, basketball usually comes before baseball; and in Chicago, baseball almost always comes before tennis. If your town has a minor-league baseball team, you might ask that its scores be given priority over major-league results.

As a radio sports director, you're likely to use the following resources:

- A high-quality audio recorder on which you record interviews and news conferences for delivery during a live report. The recordings are also used for later editing and broadcasting on your regular sports reports. Digital audiotape (DAT) recorders may be used to record and edit audiotapes at the station, but they're not rugged enough to withstand the punishment they'd receive in the field.
- Sports news and scores from the news wire services. (See a listing of offerings from the Associated Press in the preceding section.)
- Audio feeds from the wire services and perhaps from a parent network.
- Special wire-service sports features (listed earlier in this chapter).

- A specially adapted telephone for recording phone interviews.
- Press books and other sources of factual information from professional and university sports organizations.
- A variety of newspapers and magazines to which your station subscribes.

One of your most time-consuming jobs will be preparing the audio inserts for your broadcasts. This job includes gathering the recorded material, determining the items you'll use, writing a script to accompany the inserts, editing the excerpts, and dubbing the selected actualities to a storage system. Because modern radio practice demands extensive use of actualities, the procedures followed by one outstanding sports director, Hal Ramey of KCBS, San Francisco, California, are outlined here.

Hal Ramey records his interviews without assistance. He attends many sports events and news conferences, and carries with him at all times a top-of-the-line audio recorder with a high-quality external microphone. During day baseball games, he presents his twice-an-hour sports reports live from the press box of the stadium, often incorporating actualities recorded prior to game time. His voiced reports are transmitted to his radio station digitally over an ISDN (Integrated Services Digital Network) phone line of a telephone company.

When working at the station, Ramey arrives an hour or so before his first on-air report. He checks the sports wire and Internet sites to obtain information on games in progress, league standings, and other information appropriate to a given sport season. He then checks the notes he made following his locker room interviews of the previous day. His notes list the following information for each interview:

- Digital counter number where each actuality begins
- Name of the person being interviewed
- The in cue
- The out cue
- Length of the actuality
- A brief indication of the topic of the comments

Here's a typical note:

121 Fred Williams "I think we can" "be close" 15 secs "Win the pennant"

When preparing sports reports at the station, in addition to his own recorded interviews, Ramey uses audio feeds from CBS Radio Sports (SportsFeed) and the Associated Press as well as scores and sports reports sent to a desktop computer by the AP. A typical CBS SportsFeed menu will outline twelve to twenty-five available cuts. Each cut is identified by number, the name of the speaker, the general subject of the comments, the length of the cut, and the out cue. Cuts are brief, averaging about fifteen seconds. Newsroom staff members receive and record all reports, so it's a simple matter for Ramey to review them and make selections for inclusion in one of his ten live sports reports.

Ramey listens to the actualities, decides which ones to use, and moves to a small editing booth where he dubs the actualities from cassette to tape carts. He labels the carts and returns to his office to sketch a script for the actualities he's chosen and dubbed. At precisely fifteen and forty-five minutes past the hour he goes on the air in the studio/ announce booth to make his sports reports, usually incorporating up to four actualities in each.

Hal Ramey does ten live reports daily and records three more for later playing. Each report lasts two minutes. He is responsible for twenty-six to thirty minutes of broadcast material each day, for which he spends a minimum of eight hours preparing.

The Play-by-Play Announcer

Play-by-play coverage of football, basketball, hockey, and baseball games accounts for most of the many hours of sports reporting on radio and television. Other events that receive coverage are important golf and tennis tournaments, soccer matches, several popular horse racing events each year, auto racing, both the summer and winter Olympics, and some unusual sports such as wrist wrestling, "hot dog" skiing, and lumberjack championships. The person who calls the game, race, match, or event is known as the **play-by-play announcer**, even though sports such as track and field have no actual "plays." For many types of sports events, the play-by-play announcer works with a play or game analyst, whose role is described in the next section.

Working Conditions

If you're a sportscaster for a team that plays many games during a long season, you'll easily acquire the kind of information you need for intelligent ad-libbed commentary. Your association with league players will make player identification routine, and your exclusive involvement with a single sport should give you plenty of material for illuminating analyses and game trends.

At the highest levels of professional sports broadcasting, you'll have help from a broadcast staff and team management. Each broadcast day you'll be given a press information kit updating all relevant statistics. During the game, a sports wire such as SportsTicker, Inc., will give you the scores and details of other games.[7] Perhaps a full-time statistician will work with you, unearthing and bringing to your attention significant records or events you can incorporate into your running commentary. You may also have an engineer to continuously balance your voice with crowd sounds to add drama to your narrative. If you telecast a game, you'll have instant replay to enrich the coverage. Even when doing radio play-by-play, watching a television replay will give you the

Figure 12.4

SportsTicker displays a menu listing several categories of sports information available to announcers during a game. Categories include Headlines, Schedules, Previews, Standings, and Scoreboard. *Courtesy of SportsTicker, Inc.*

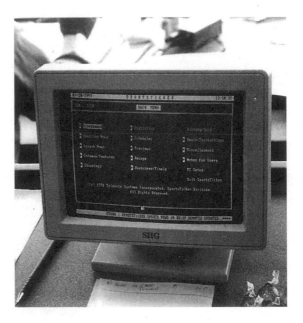

[7]SportsTicker, Inc., provides a computerized sports information system. A menu lists categories such as Scoreboard, League News, Standings, History/Quiz, Schedules, Statistics, and Deals/Transactions. When one of these is selected, the information appears on the computer screen. A hard copy of selected information can be made for use by the announcers.

information you need to tell your listeners that the game officials made a good, a questionable, or an incorrect call.

A famous athlete or former manager may be at your side giving evaluations and predictions that add another dimension to the broadcast. It's demanding work, but you have budget, personnel, and working conditions in your favor. However, overlapping and ever-expanding seasons, as well as competition from single-sport specialists, will require you to focus on no more than two, or possibly three, major sports.

If you work for a smaller station and announce a wide variety of games—ranging from high school to college and semipro—your job will be much more difficult. You can expect to cover all sports. Rules of play may not be standardized, you may not know the players, and press information kits may not exist. You can expect little help and a meager budget.

The booth setup will vary with the sport. Football usually demands the services of a team of four: a play-by-play announcer, a play analyst, and two spotters. If you're doing play-by-play, you'll sit between the two spotters, and the analyst will sit next to one of the spotters. For high school, college, and some professional games, the analyst is likely to be quite familiar with the home team; the analyst's proper position is next to the spotter who points for the visiting team.

Spotting charts list both offensive and defensive players, but because football, especially at the professional level, is an extremely complex game, spotting charts lack adequate flexibility to cover offensive and defensive realignments. As the play-by-play announcer, you'll be concentrating on the handling of the football. Spotters are responsible for showing changes in the lineups. For example, the defense spotter will hold up five fingers to indicate a nickel defense, or the offensive spotter will hold up three fingers to indicate three wide receivers in the game. In general, you should use spotters for actions you can't see for yourself. It's your job to follow the football, so leave other details of each play up to your spotters.

The booth setup for baseball can be as simple as one play-by-play announcer sitting with a remote mixer, a microphone, and an array of information sheets and scoring charts. Some radio and most television broadcasts are enhanced by adding two others to the announcing team: a second play-by-play announcer and a game analyst who also may serve as statistician. The three-person team is positioned with the statistician to the left of the two play-by-play announcers. Typically, one announcer will call six innings, and the other will call three. Before them are at least three cards or sheets of paper: two diagrams of the

Figure 12.5

San Francisco Giants radio producer and engineer Lee Jones records, edits, and logs game highlights on this tapeless audio unit manufactured by 360 Systems. Selected game highlights are played during the postgame recap. *Courtesy of Lee Jones and the San Francisco Giants, San Francisco, California.*

baseball field with the names of the defensive players of each team written in, and two score sheets, one for each team.

Another setup for baseball broadcasts calls for two announcers who take turns doing play-by-play and analysis, plus an audio engineer. The engineer serves as booth producer of the broadcast and adjusts the volume on the remote mixer, gives cues signaling "station break," feeds the on-air signal to the announcers' headphones toward the end of a commercial break so they know when to pick up their narrative, and operates the SportsTicker. The audio engineer also records the entire game on an audio recorder, makes a notation of important plays, and cues the cuts so they can be played in sequence during the play-by-play announcer's postgame wrap-up.

Basketball and hockey move so fast and have so few players that announcers have neither time nor need for spotters. A name and position chart with pins indicating the players in the game at any given moment may be helpful at times, but, in general, there's little time to refer to it. On two-person announcing teams, the second announcer provides analysis (or analysis and color, on radio).

Boxing, golf, tennis, speed and figure skating, skiing, ski jumping, and gymnastics present no problems of competitor recognition. Spotting is unnecessary, and many of the complexities that make football, basketball, and hockey difficult to call, such as multiple players, complex offenses and defenses, and speed of action, aren't factors. However, all of these sports require in-depth knowledge, and fans expect reporters to have outstanding comprehension and judgment. It's standard practice for sports generalists to introduce, talk around, and summarize gymnastics, skiing, and skating, with the actual "play-by-play" provided by a former participant of the sport. Boxing, golf, and tennis are covered by announcers who may or may not have competed in those sports, but who've made long and intense study of them. Announce booths may be lacking altogether at the sites of these sports; remote trailers take their place. At the opposite extreme, most notably for the Olympic Games, a highly sophisticated electronic center houses media coverage.

Practicing Play-by-Play Announcing

As a beginner, you should practice play-by-play announcing at every opportunity. Attend every sports event you can, not only the major sports, but tennis, track and field, gymnastics, and skiing—anything that's recognized as a sport and is the subject of radio or television coverage. Practice calling games or events into the mic of a battery-operated audio recorder. Set your work aside until your memory of the game has faded; then listen to it to see whether it paints a clear picture of the game. Make note of any instances in which you find your reporting incomplete, inaccurate, tedious, or marred by numerous corrections, and work to eliminate the flaws. In particular, *note any improvement.* Improvement builds confidence, and confidence guarantees further improvement.

As a play-by-play announcer for baseball, you must be able to score a game accurately and quickly. Indications of outs, scoring, and other basic information are essential when recapping game action.

It's difficult for a student of sports announcing to practice play-by-play for television. Practicing with an audio recorder will help prepare you for telecasting, but there are important differences in style, quantity of information given, nature of information provided, and availability of resources, including instant replay. Your apprenticeship for the challenge of televised play-by-play will probably be served by observing others as they call games. If you can, obtain permission to be a silent and unobtrusive witness in announce booths during the telecasts of games in your area. If you can't be in the booth, begin to view games on television with a critical eye and ear. Tape broadcasts of entire sports events. As you review them, make notes of your observations. Analyze moments of exceptionally competent as well as incompetent play-by-play narrative. Decide for yourself how much description is illuminating, and learn to sense the moment at which announce booth chatter begins to reduce your enjoyment of the game. Note especially those times when an announcing team is so carried away with descriptions of sea-gulls overhead or an amusing anecdote about a player that its members fail to give you an important detail such as whether or not a first down was made on the last play. Too often, television play-by-play broadcast-ers assume that viewers have seen and understood what occurred, even when the needed information wasn't seen by a camera. Most profes-sional play-by-play announcers maintain voluminous notebooks full of facts about players and teams from which they can enrich the listener's experience with interesting or informative comments. Too often those comments take away from the ongoing contest, rather than add to it.

Brief biographies of sports play-by-play announcers, commen-tators, program hosts, reporters, and play analysts may be found on the Internet. Try these URLs; then search for more:[8]

abcsports.go.com/announcers/index.html

espn.go.com/espninc/personalities/index.html

For a complete, updated list of URLs for this textbook, please see the text home site available at *www.hmco.com/college.*

Preparing for Play-by-Play Announcing

Preparation is the key to successful sportscasting. Don Klein, former voice of the San Francisco 49ers, says: "The two to three hours spent in calling a game is the easiest part of a play-by-play announcer's work. Preparation for most major sportscasts requires up to twenty hours of study." This comment, of course, refers to contests between teams that

---

[8]The Internet is changing constantly as new web sites are added and old web sites are abandoned. The URL listings in this textbook should be regarded as samples of the kinds of material available rather than as a stable index. If you seek a web site using one of these URLs and cannot connect, enter the key words for the topic into a search en-gine to find a site that may provide the information you want.

are unknown or only slightly known to the announcer. Less preparation of a different kind is appropriate for play-by-play announcers who work for teams that play the same opponent as many as thirteen times in a season—as in major-league baseball and basketball. When the problem of player recognition is minimized, preparation focuses on making each sportscast unique.

CHECKLIST

QUESTIONS
TO ASK
YOURSELF
BEFORE YOU
ENTER AN
ANNOUNCE
BOOTH TO
CALL A GAME

1. Is there anything unusual about this game?
2. Is either team or any player on a streak of any sort?
3. Are there any interesting rivalries in this matchup?
4. How might the weather affect the game?
5. Is there a home-team advantage?
6. How have these teams fared during the season and during the past few years?

Reflecting on these and similar questions should make you ready to call an interesting game.

In preparing to cover a game when at least one of the teams is unknown to you, begin your preparation as far in advance as possible. Your resources are team media guides, press information kits, official yearbooks, newspaper stories and columns, wire-service reports, and specialized sports magazines. Preparation includes memorizing all players by name and position and, if possible, appearance. In football, players' numbers are often important because, given the extensive covering of head and body by clothing and helmet, most players are unrecognizable from a distance. Preparation includes making notes, usually on three-by-five-inch file cards, of information that might prove useful during the game. Preparation also requires spotting charts, scoring sheets, and any other materials appropriate to the sport.

Arrive early the day of the game. Check starting lineups. If in doubt, check the pronunciation of players' names with press information personnel, assistant managers, or team captains. If possible, spend time with the players before the game; your effectiveness in describing the game will be enhanced by understanding how the players feel. Enter the booth long before game time. Lay out your spotting charts, scoring sheets, file cards of statistical and anecdotal information, and whatever notebooks or other materials you plan to use during the game. Examine your broadcast equipment. For both radio and television sportscasts, commercials, station promotions, and promotions of ticket sales are likely to be recorded before game time. This reduces pressure during the game and gives you many moments when you can take off your headset and make or read notes.

Plan ahead. Think about everything you'll need and make sure you have it with you when you arrive at the booth. Aside from the spotting charts, scoring sheets, and information cards, you'll need pencils, a pencil sharpener, erasers, pins for the chart, water or some other beverage, binoculars, and perhaps even an electric heater to keep your teeth from chattering!

 Although they don't "broadcast" games, public address (PA) stadium announcers are very much a part of sports announcing. To obtain a perspective on the work of a stadium PA announcer, go to the web site of Ed Brickley, booth announcer for the Boston Red Sox:

library.advanced.org/11902/booth/booth.html

For a complete, updated list of URLs for this textbook, please see the text home site available at *www.hmco.com/college.*

Figure 12.6

Sherry Davis, the first woman stadium announcer in major-league baseball history, announces lineups, batters, pinch hitters, pinch runners, substitutions, and other items of interest to crowds at the ballpark. *Courtesy of Sherry Davis and the San Francisco Giants, San Francisco, California.*

Calling the Game

In covering any sport as a member of a two-person team, it's helpful to develop and use simple nonverbal signals to avoid confusion. A sportscast can be deadly for listeners if you and your partner continually interrupt one another or start to speak at the same time. The general rule is that the play-by-play announcer is the booth director. As play-by-play announcer, you'll do all the talking except when you invite your play analyst or statistician to contribute. Play analysts indicate that they have a comment to make by raising a hand or slipping you a note. If you decide to allow the comment, you throw a cue by pointing an index finger when you come to the end of your own remarks. Analysts must always complete their remarks well ahead of the moment when you must again pick up the play-by-play. As you might imagine, hand signals (except for "you're on" cues) are unnecessary when sportscasters have worked together for long periods of time and sense when it's safe to interject a comment.

When calling a football game, many announcers stand rather than sit because it increases energy and frees them to move as needed to relate to the field, the television monitor, spotter's charts, and the play analyst.

When you call any game, keep several important principles in mind. First, truly believe that your chief responsibility is to your viewers or listeners. This translates into being completely honest in reports of the games you call. This belief will be difficult to hold to at times. Unreasonable owners, outraged players, and others who have a stake in your broadcasts may make irrational demands. In the long run, though, you'll prosper best if you have a loyal following of viewers or listeners who have faith in your integrity.

Second, remember that it's your responsibility to *report, entertain,* and *sell*. Your reporting must be accurate and fair. As an entertainer, you must attract and hold the fans' attention for up to three hours at a time. Selling means selling the sport more than the team. It means selling yourself as a credible reporter, who communicates natural energy and objectivity but avoids forced enthusiasm.

Finally, avoid home-team bias. **Homers** aren't unknown to sportscasting, and some play-by-play announcers are famous for their lack of objectivity. The most important reason to avoid home-team bias is that it will blind you to the actual events taking place. Regardless of affiliation or loyalties, it's your responsibility to provide fans with a clear, accurate, and fair account of the game. This responsibility is more apparent if you do play-by-play for radio. Television fans can compare your work with what they see, but when you serve as the eyes of radio listeners, you have an obligation to report with objectivity since your account is almost the listeners' total exposure to the event.

Additional Tips on Sportscasting

Some of these suggestions are appropriate to all sports; others apply to one or two:

Communicate the Important Events in a Game and Provide Interpretation When Appropriate. A game is more than a series of individual plays or events. Plays are part of a process that adds up to an overall pattern. If you're perceptive and deeply involved in the event, you'll be able to point out crucial plays and turning points immediately after they occur. It's your responsibility to grasp the significance of plays or incidents and then to communicate your awareness to viewers or listeners. You will transmit the significance not only by what you say but also by how you say it. Some critical situations will be apparent to any reasonably sophisticated fan, but at times you must be so tuned in to the game that your interpretation surpasses common knowledge.

When Doing Play-by-Play on Radio, Provide Listeners with Relatively More Information Than Is Necessary for a Telecast. Listeners need to know, for example, what the weather is like, how the stadium or court looks, how the fans are behaving, whether players are right- or left-handed, the wind strength and direction, who's on first, how many yards for a first down, how many outs or minutes left in the game, and whether a particular play was routine or outstanding. Most important of all: *repeat the score often, and always before going to a commercial and immediately after a commercial break.* You can't overdo this. Some sports announcers use a three-minute egg timer to remind them to mention the score (and other basic information) every time the sand has run through the glass.

When Doing Baseball Play-by-Play, Always Be Ready to Talk Intelligently and Entertainingly During Rain Delays. Baseball fans love baseball lore, and well-prepared announcers who can discuss historical aspects of the sport and provide a wealth of amusing or amazing anecdotes can make a rain delay a highlight of a game.

Never Make Events in a Game Seem More Important Than They Are. A dull game creates a natural temptation to entertain by exaggerating. Avoid this tendency.

Don't Overuse Sports Clichés. You can't avoid sports clichés entirely; there are a limited number of ways of describing things that happen over and over in a game. But unless frequent use of sports clichés is a part of your announcing persona, be conscious of clichés and try to avoid their overuse. Here are several overused sports expressions:

- in tonight's action
- over in the NBA
- over in the American League
- all the action is under the lights
- was in complete charge
- he got all of it
- he was taking all the way
- odds-on favorite
- off to a running start
- off to a shaky start
- sparked the win
- suffered a sixth setback
- raised her record to
- went the distance

Some familiar sports expressions are clear, direct, and uncomplicated and hardly can be improved on: *loaded the bases, gave up a walk, got the hat trick, was sacked, finished within one stroke of,* and *lost the decision.* In general, although you can't—and shouldn't—completely avoid clichés, improve the variety of your play-by-play delivery by using several ways of naming the same events or incidents.

Have Statistics in Front of You or Firmly in Mind Before You Start to Talk About Them. If you make an error, you can correct it, of course: "That's the fourth walk allowed by Rollins—hold it; it's the *third* walk." There's nothing wrong with making an occasional correction. If you repeatedly make corrections however, it becomes annoying.

On Television, Concentrate on Interpreting the Events and Adding Comments About Action not Clearly Shown by the Camera. Television viewers don't necessarily see everything that a trained observer sees. Your commentary and instant replay can provide viewers with specific details that illuminate, instruct, and entertain.

When Doing Play-by-Play on Television, Avoid the Extremes of Too Much or Too Little Commentary. Avoid extraneous chatter that confuses and distracts viewers.[9] On the other hand, don't go to the opposite extreme and assume that viewers have been with you throughout the entire game and therefore know everything important that's occurred. From time to time, review key plays, injuries, and other pertinent facts.

When a Player Is Injured, Never Guess About the Nature or Severity of the Injury. If you consider it important to report on the details of the injury, send an assistant to the team trainer or physician. Inaccurate information about an injury can cause unnecessary worry for friends and family.

Don't Ignore Fights, but Don't Sensationalize Them. Hockey and football are often violent, and fights between players aren't uncommon. If you dwell on them, you may provoke both aggression by fans (thrown bottles, for example) and attempts by players to exact revenge.

If You're Not Sure About Information, Don't Guess. Wait as long as necessary to give official verdicts on whether or not a ball was fair or foul, a goal was scored, or a first down was made. Constant corrections of such errors are annoying to the fans.

Tell a baseball audience what inning it is as you give the score. Tell football, basketball, and hockey audiences which quarter or period it is and how much time is left. Football audiences need to be reminded frequently of who has the ball, where the ball is, and what down is coming up. It's all but impossible to give such information too often.

---

[9]An exception to this generally sound point: Some sports broadcasts, especially those on network television, are meant to appeal to a wide range of viewers, including many who care little about the teams in the game being covered. Announcers are encouraged to be amusing, even when their comments have nothing to do with the game. Their "storytelling" often distracts them from providing essential information about the ongoing game.

Give Scores of Other Games, but Never Allow Them to Interfere with the Game at Hand. When telecasting, remember that your viewers are being bombarded with information not only from you, the play analyst, and the camera coverage of the game, but also from written information superimposed on the screen at the request of the director to show statistics, to promote an upcoming program, or to "tease" an after-game feature, such as "In the Clubhouse," or "The Fifth Quarter." Because of this overload, be careful not to further distract viewers from the game they're watching. Give scores of other games, but be discreet.

Take Care of First Things First. Provide essential information before going into an analysis of the action. On radio, don't describe the double play until you've told the fans whether or not the player on third scored. In football, don't start talking about key blocks or sensational catches until you've indicated whether or not a first down was made on the play.

Don't Keep Telling Your Audience How Great the Game Is. If it is a great game, the events and the way you report them will speak for themselves. If it isn't a great game, no amount of wishful thinking will make it exciting. At the same time, as an unusually exciting game winds down, it is appropriate to express your honest emotions about the suspense of the game or the victory of an underdog.

If You Can't Immediately Identify a Player, Cover the Play Without Mentioning Names and Give the Name When You're Sure of It. Here's a poor example of identifying players:

ANNCR:

The ball is taken by Richards . . . He's back in the pocket to pass. . . . He's being rushed. . . . He barely gets it away and it's intercepted by Pappas . . . no, I think it's Harrison. . . . He has it on the twenty-five, the thirty, the thirty-five and he's brought down on the thirty-seven. Yes, that was Pappas, the all-American defensive back.

This is a better example:

ANNCR:

The ball is taken by Richards. . . . He's back in the pocket
to pass. . . . He's being rushed. . . . He barely gets it away
and it's intercepted on the twenty . . . back to the thirty, the
thirty-five, and all the way to the thirty-seven. A beautiful
interception by Charley Pappas, the all-American defensive
back.

Learn Where to Look for the Information You Need. In baseball, watch
the outfielders instead of a fly ball to see whether the ball will be caught,
fielded, or lost over the fence. Watch line umpires to see whether a ball
is fair or foul. In football, watch the quarterback unless you clearly see
a hand-off or a pass; then watch the ball. Let your spotters or analyst
watch the defense and the offensive ends.

Don't Rely on Scoreboard Information. Keep your own notebook and
record the data appropriate to the sport you're covering. For football,
note the time when possession begins, the location of the ball after each
play, the nature of each play, and the manner in which the drive ends.
These notes will help you summarize each drive and will single out the
most important plays. For baseball, keep a regular scoring chart and
learn to read it quickly and accurately. For basketball, hockey, and soccer, rely on a statistician for data such as goals attempted and fouls and
penalties assessed.

Give Statistics and Records. Baseball fans are always interested in bat-
ting and earned-run averages, fielding percentages, strikeout records,
and comparative statistics. Track and field followers are obsessed with
distance and speed records. Statistics are only slightly less important to
followers of football, basketball, soccer, hockey, and golf. Remember,
though, that *some* statistics are of little value or interest, as in: "That was
the seventh time this season that the Hornets were the first to score in
the third quarter!"

Avoid Adopting Meaningless Catch Phrases. Perhaps the most prevalent and annoying habit of sports announcers is the interjection of the phrase *of course* into statements when the information being given isn't necessarily common knowledge, as in "Wilson, of course, has run for over a hundred yards in each of his past seven games." Even when the information is widely known, *of course* adds nothing to most statements: "Mark McGwire, of course, was Rookie of the Year in 1987."

Eliminate or Control the Use of the Word Situation. With some sports announcers, nearly everything is a situation: "It's a passing situation," "It's a bunting situation." "It's a third-and-three situation." Constant repetition of this word can become tiresome.

Use Background Sounds to Your Advantage. Most sports have moments of action that bring about an enthusiastic response from the crowd. The sounds of cheering fans can enhance your game coverage. Don't be afraid to remain silent at key times while the fans carry the excitement of the game for you.

When Working with a Play Analyst, Make Sure You and Your Partner Agree on the Pronunciation of Names That Could Be Pronounced in Different Ways. During a professional football telecast, the play-by-play announcer and play analyst pronounced the names of three players in different ways:

McMahon:	(muk-MAN) versus (muk-MAY-un)
Lippett:	(LIP-ut) versus (lih-PET)
Clayborn:	(KLAY-born) versus (KLY-born)

These differences probably went unnoticed by most listeners, but as a professional you should first *hear* such differences and then discuss them with your partners with the hope of reaching an agreement. Although this is not a major point, to truly be the best in your field demands that you correct even minor inaccuracies.

CHECKLIST

BECOMING A
BETTER PLAY-
BY-PLAY
ANNOUNCER

1. Communicate the important events in a game and provide interpretation when appropriate.
2. Provide a radio audience with more information than you would a television audience.
3. Be prepared to talk intelligently and entertainingly during rain delays.
4. Never make events in a game seem more important than they are.
5. Don't overuse sports clichés unless you use them as an important part of your on-air personality.
6. Don't talk about statistics unless you have them in front of you or firmly in mind.
7. On television, concentrate on interpreting the events and adding comments about events not clearly shown by the cameras.
8. When doing television play-by-play, avoid the extremes of too much or too little commentary.
9. When a player is injured, never guess about the nature or severity of the injury.
10. Don't ignore fights, but don't sensationalize them.
11. If you're not sure about information, don't guess.
12. Repeat the score at frequent intervals.
13. Give scores of other games without interfering with the announcing of the game at hand.
14. Provide essential information, such as yards gained or runs scored, before going into an analysis of the action.
15. Don't keep telling the audience how great the game is.
16. If you can't immediately identify a player, cover the play without mentioning names and give the name when you're sure of it.
17. Learn where to look for the information you need.
18. Don't rely on scoreboard information.
19. Give statistics and records.
20. Avoid adopting meaningless catch phrases.
21. Avoid overuse of the word *situation*.
22. Use background sounds to your advantage.
23. When working with a play analyst, reach an agreement on the pronunciation of names.

SPOTLIGHT

Plea to Radio Sportscasters: Give Us the Details

By Glenn Dickey

When the Raiders returned to Oakland, many of their fans hoped—in vain—that Bill King would return to the radio announce booth.

No wonder. There seems to be nobody like Bill King left.

Listening to King do a football game on radio was almost like watching it on television. Before each play, he'd tell listeners who was lining up for the Raiders at the skill positions, and who'd be defending against them on the other side of the ball.

A typical King call went something like this: "Stabler fakes to Hubbard and fades back. Upshaw levels Buchanan with a block. Stabler throws downfield to Biletnikoff, working against Thomas. Freddy makes the catch at the 35, spins to the 31 for another first down. Holy Toledo!"

But since then, a whole generation of announcers has grown up watching television, and they don't realize that, when calling games on radio, they have the responsibility for telling listeners what's happening.

Nobody is quite as bad as one former Giants announcer, who'd often say (remember, this was on radio) "Did you see that?" Too many radio play-by-play announcers fail to realize that they have to give listeners details, not just a broad impression. One announcer I know prepares assiduously for games, memorizing names, learning about players on opposing teams as well as the home team.

Yet little of that comes across to listeners because of his faulty technique. A typical call might go something like this: "Barnes is back to pass and . . . Can you believe that? . . . The receiver had to reach behind him, but he made the catch. What a bonanza!" Experienced listeners know that, if they're patient, he'll eventually tell them who the receiver was, where the ball is, and if it's a first down. Hopefully before the next play starts.

In the past, that type of thing was typical of older announcers whose eyesight wasn't good enough for them to keep up. Lindsay Nelson, a legend in the business, had that problem when he came to the Giants; his trademark phrase became, "Let's recap that play."

Growing Up on Televised Games

But now, it's common for younger radio announcers to give few details of the action on the field; they don't even realize that they're not doing their job, because they grew up watching televised games where a full description is unnecessary.

On television, a play-by-play announcer doesn't need to say very much. Ray Scott was the best of the early announcers because he recognized that. A typical Scott call would be, "Starr . . . Dowler . . . first down on the 30." He knew that viewers didn't need to be told that Starr was fading back and passing because they could see that.

Dick Enberg is probably the best example of that kind of announcer today. Enberg gives all the important facts without wasting words, and he's also superb at setting up comments for his color announcer. Al Michaels is also very good, even though he has the added challenge of getting his message through in a three-man booth.

For a color announcer, the requirements are different. Personality is very important. John Madden became a big star while Bill Walsh quit and Hank Stram has slowly faded into a lesser role—even though Walsh and Stram gave viewers far more information and insight than Madden ever could.

But there are at least some young announcers coming up who have learned the trick of giving significant information very concisely in the short time between plays.

Matt Millen is probably the best in the business right now because he gives viewers an insight beyond what is obvious in the play-by-play. Phil Simms has also been very good. He knows the rules better than most announcers, too, and he's a perfect balance for the colorful Paul Maguire.

Radio's Requirements

Radio, though, is still a much different medium with much different requirements.

The best radio announcers are still on baseball games, partly because radio coverage is much more important for baseball than it is for football. Announcers like Hank Greenwald and Lon Simmons have always had a feel for the rhythm of the game. They have been able to slip stories and humorous comments into the broadcast without losing the thread of the description.

Unfortunately, there no longer seem to be announcers who can give comparable descriptions of football games.

Maybe Bill King should send some of his old tapes to broadcasting schools.

Reprinted with permission from the San Francisco Chronicle.

The Play Analyst

Play analysts interpret individual plays and overall strategies. They also provide information that helps listeners and viewers learn the finer points of a sport. Analysts are, without significant exception, former athletes or coaches of the sports they describe. Their in-depth knowledge gives penetrating analyses of on-going sportscasts. Play and game analysis is highly specialized, and effective preparation requires considerable devotion to the sport itself.

Play analysts provide information and interpretation that complement rather than duplicate what's offered by the play-by-play announcer. As an analyst, you must have clear instructions about what to look for and how to report it. In football, you look for key blocks, tackles, and similar events of importance. In baseball, hockey, and basketball, you usually serve as a statistician and analyze the whole game rather than individual plays. In these sports, you'll see little or nothing that isn't seen by the play-by-play announcer, so you contribute information such as this:

> That was Ponce's twenty-first inning without giving up a
> walk.

> Garrett's forty-one points are a season high for him, but
> they're a long way from the record set by Wilt Chamberlain—
> he scored one hundred points in a game in 1962.

Hockey and basketball move so fast that opportunities for play analysis are limited. If interesting points are brought up at all, the play-by-play announcer usually introduces them. On the other hand, events in a baseball game proceed more slowly, allowing opportunities for analysts to explain the finer points of the sport.

The educational function of a play analyst is of great importance to those who care deeply about the sport being broadcast. In televised football games, play analysts use electronic "chalkboards" to draw the action and movements of a recently completed play. After viewing it and listening to the explanation, a reshowing of the play often helps us see things that we hadn't noticed during "real-time" action. In the process we learn a bit more about the subtleties of the sport.

A baseball analyst—most often a former pitcher, catcher, or manager—can teach us much about the game of baseball. Two examples:

ANALYST:

Jones just asked for a new ball. Not all baseballs are the
same, and some just don't "feel right" to a pitcher. However,

with two outs and the tying run on second, Jones most likely wants to throw a curve or a slider, and the ball he tossed back had flat seams. It's easy to throw a fastball with any baseball, but you want a ball with raised seams to help you throw a curve. And, of course, Chavez being a veteran, most likely knows that the next pitch he'll see will be a ball with a lot of motion on it. There's one complicating factor, though: Jones could have decoyed Chavez into assuming that a curve was coming by asking for a new ball.

ANALYST:

Notice how, with runners on base, second baseman Washington will move right behind second base after every pitch. He wants to make sure that the return throw from the catcher to the pitcher doesn't go into center field. A bad return throw from a big-league catcher to his pitcher is a rarity, but first-rate ball players leave nothing to chance.

Gymnastics, figure skating, ice dancing, diving, and similar sports of a strongly aesthetic nature are almost always described by experts in the event. Analysis is the primary responsibility of the people who cover sports in which points are assigned by judges, because the vast majority of viewers have little precise knowledge of the pluses and the minuses of individual performances.

Here are a few tips on play and game analysis:

- Never repeat either exactly or by paraphrase what the play-by-play announcer has just said.
- Don't feel compelled to comment after every play of a football game or after every pitch of a baseball game. If you have nothing significant to report, remain silent.
- Be precise in the comments you make. "What a great catch" is neither useful nor informative. "Frick has just gone over the one

hundred-yard mark for the eighth time this season" is precise and useful.

- Do your homework on both teams. The play-by-play announcer will also have prepared, but in the heat of the game it may fall to you to remember facts or statistics forgotten by your partner. Make notes of key moments of the game.

- Your major contribution is to see the game with an objectivity not always possible for a play-by-play announcer. Look for the dramatic structure of the contest and report it when appropriate. Don't overdramatize, however.

- Never correct the play-by-play announcer on the air. If an important mistake has been made, write and pass a note. Listeners and viewers become uncomfortable when they sense conflict between members of an announcing team.

- A discussion between play-by-play announcer and analyst in which different points of view are expressed can be useful to fans. As long as the discussion is friendly—perhaps even amusing—there's no reason to avoid or prematurely terminate it.

- Be careful what questions you ask of your partner. Even the most competent veteran can draw a blank when concentrating on a game.

- Follow the rules set down by your play-by-play partner. You may have to ask for an opportunity to speak and then do so only when your partner gives you your cue. If your agreement with the play-by-play announcer calls for it, be prepared to make intelligent comments during time-outs and intermissions in basketball and hockey contests.

- Always be sure to end your comments before the next play begins.

- It may be difficult to maintain harmonious relations with your partner, but it's imperative. Fans appreciate listening to announcing teams that complement each other and work together to present the sports experience competently and completely.

- If you hope to become a professional sports announcer of any kind—reporter, play-by-play, analyst—you should build your own sports library and become knowledgeable about as many sports as possible. And remember—there's no substitute for practicing your skills!

PRACTICE

Play-by-Play Announcing

Using a battery-operated audio recorder, do play-by-play announcing for a baseball, football, basketball, or hockey game (or any other sport you prefer). Put the tape aside for a week or two and then listen to it critically. Are you able to visualize the game from the words you spoke and recorded?

PRACTICE

Getting Athletes' Names Right

Prior to an amateur sports event of any kind, obtain a list of players' names. Mark any whose pronunciation isn't obvious: you may be sure of the pronunciation of *Smith* but not of the preferred pronunciation of *Smythe*. Depending on where you're allowed access, visit the locker room, the dugout, or other area where team executives may be found, and ask for the pronunciation of names in question. As you're given the information, use your favored system of phonetic transcription (wire service, diacritics, or IPA) to denote correct pronunciation of names on the list.

CHAPTER 13

Starting Your Announcing Career

CHAPTER OUTLINE

- Preparing for Your Career
- Job-Hunting Tools
  Résumés
  Types of Résumés
  Some Tips on Preparation
  Photographs
  The Cover Letter
  Audition or Résumé Tapes
  Answering Machines, Cellular
    Phones, and Pagers
  Mailing Address and Phone
    Number

- Finding Job Openings
- SPOTLIGHT: Surviving Career
  Changes
- Applying for a Position at a Radio
  Station
- Interviewing for a Job
- Joining a Union
- Going Where Your Career Takes
  You
- Preparing a Scannable Résumé for
  Today's Standards

THIS CHAPTER IS OFFERED TO HELP MEET THE NEEDS OF THOSE WITH little or no paid experience as an announcer but who feel they're ready for professional employment. Most of this information is also applicable to those with some professional experience and those who received their training in workshops or through self-study.

This chapter assumes you're looking for a job as an announcer in one or more of these categories:

- Popular music announcing (DJ)
- News reporting
- News anchor work
- News-related announcing as an environmental, consumer information, or entertainment news reporter
- Radio or television talk-show hosting
- Sports reporting and play-by-play announcing
- Weather reporting for either radio or television
- Radio commercial announcing as a freelance performer
- On-camera television commercial performance

- Voice-over television work for commercials, documentaries, or training tapes

Despite the focus on these specific career opportunities, your education also is appropriate to businesses or industries not directly related to broadcasting or cable. With the knowledge you've acquired in completing a liberal arts education, together with your focus on media performance, you should perform well in any number of careers that call for articulate, confident communication abilities. Each year, for example, many graduates from electronic communications programs obtain jobs in corporate media. They use their announcing abilities in making tapes for employee training, such as demonstrating or explaining new products or technologies to salespersons, or for other "in-house" uses.

This chapter assumes that you've become capable, though not necessarily completely proficient, in the announcing specialization of your choice. As indicated in Chapter 1, merely taking a course or two in broadcast performance can't make you a competent journalist, sports reporter, or talk-show host. The information that follows assumes that you've supported your education with practice, that you've completed course work in the area of your specialization, and—ideally—that you've completed one or more internships.

Preparing for Your Career

If you're convinced that you want to be an announcer, you undoubtedly have many positive reasons. Being an announcer is an important job. Broadcasting and cable are exciting and dynamic fields. Electronic communication will unquestionably become more and more influential in coming years. Noteworthy rewards of fame and wealth await those who make it to—or near—the top of this profession. Finally, the opportunity to inform or entertain vast numbers of people is surely a powerful motivating force.

Before committing yourself to a career as an announcer, it's important that you make an honest assessment of yourself—of your strengths, your skills, your areas of specialized knowledge, your interests, and your values. No one else can do this for you, but it's important that you make such an evaluation. It should help clarify a number of things: what type of job or freelance work corresponds with your career interests and abilities; what type of work you're equipped to perform; what kinds of working conditions are necessary for you to receive job satisfaction; what salary you'll need to support yourself; and where would you be willing or unwilling to live. Also ask yourself if you'll be comfortable in a field that offers little job security.

The checklist presented on page 370 will help you assess your potential for success. It consists of questions that only you can answer. These questions are personal, but you needn't share them with others. For this self-assessment to be of value, it's imperative that you dig deeply and not settle for superficial answers. Undertake this self-assessment at various points during your student years, and realize your most valid answers will come at or near the end of your studies. And, don't be unreasonably negative. No one expects a beginner to perform at the level of a veteran!

The time to begin preparing for that first job is while you're still in school. This is the time to start making connections that may someday pay off. As suggested in Chapter 1, you should join broadcast-related organizations such as *College Students in Broadcasting,* and the *Association for Women in Communication, Inc.* (AWC), the *International Radio and Television Society-Alpha Epsilon Rho,* and the *National Black Media Coalition.* Students with a broadcast journalism emphasis may become members of the *Radio-Television Journalism* division of the *Association for Education in Journalism and Mass Communication.* Membership in the student category of the *Radio and Television News Directors Association* (RTNDA) is also available to you.

Information about reaching these organizations through the Internet is provided in Chapter 1, page 16.

For a complete, updated list of URLs for this textbook, please see the text home site available at *www.hmco.com/college.*

During your final two semesters in college, serve internships at the kinds of stations or other communication-related organizations where you'd like to work. *Important:* Ask for an internship only when you're ready to make a contribution at a particular firm; otherwise, you'll likely wind up stuffing envelopes or answering phones. Because you may have little job-related knowledge to offer early in your educational program,

Figure 13.1

Established news anchor Frank Somerville began his career while he was a student. In his senior year at San Francisco State University, Frank's internship at a small market station turned into a paying position as a reporter and anchor. After two other jobs in larger markets, he became morning and noontime anchor on KTVU, Oakland, California. He is seen here checking a monitor for details of a breaking story on CNN. His immediate job is to size up the story and write appropriate lead-ins. *Courtesy of Frank Somerville and KTVU, Oakland, California.*

you may also make an unfavorable impression on those who may be in a position to hire you at a later time. On the other hand, when you're ready to help a business in some significant way, go for it, and give it all you have—your internship could very well turn into a job!

CHECKLIST

ASSESSING YOUR CAREER POTENTIAL

As a Communicator in the Electronic Media

1. Do I truly have talent as a performer?
2. Is my voice adequate for the career I seek? If not, is it improvable through exercises and practice? Am I prepared to work until the improvement has occurred?
3. (*For television performance*) Is my physical appearance appropriate for the kinds of positions I seek? If it is not, can my appearance be made acceptable or adequate through hair styling, makeup, and so forth?
4. Do I have an on-air personality that's engaging and unique?
5. What is there about me that makes me feel that I can succeed as an announcer?

CHECKLIST

ASSESSING
YOUR
CAREER
POTENTIAL
(cont.)

As a Radio or Television Announcer

1. Am I willing to start at the very bottom of the ladder?
2. Am I willing to work for low wages?
3. Am I prepared to move anywhere at any time to further my career?
4. Can I live with the fact that any change in ratings, ownership, or format could cost me my job?
5. Do I perform well under pressure?
6. Does mic or camera fright currently interfere with my performance? If so, what are the chances that I can eventually bring it under control?
7. (*For radio*) Do I possess the technical skills necessary to operate audio equipment in an effortless and error-free manner?

As a Voice-Over Announcer for Commercials, Industrials, and Documentaries

1. Do I take direction well and respond quickly and sensitively to instructions?
2. Do I perform effectively under pressure?
3. Can I do a professional job of interpreting copy that requires accents, dialects, or character voices?
4. Am I prepared to live on an absolutely unpredictable and uncertain income?

As a Reporter or Anchor for Radio or Television News

1. Am I a quick judge of the newsworthiness of events as they happen?
2. Have I properly prepared myself to work as a journalist?
3. Can I remain reasonably detached at the scene of a wreck, fire, or other catastrophe in which people have been badly injured or killed?
4. Can I maintain my composure and deliver a coherent live report on location despite many ongoing distractions?
5. Have I adequately learned to operate basic items of audio and video equipment that I'll most likely use on the job?

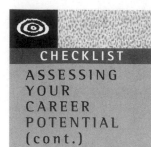

As a Sports Reporter or Play-by-Play Announcer

1. Do I have a thorough grounding in all of the major sports, or am I a single-sport devotee?
2. Do I love sports enough to commit myself to becoming a sports announcer despite the scarcity of jobs and the stiff competition?
3. Am I willing to spend years of frequent travel, often being away from family and friends for weeks at a time?

Job-Hunting Tools

For most announcing jobs, you'll look for employment at radio or television stations or with independent production companies, including those associated with cable networks. If you're interested in commercial announcing and narrating, you'll probably need to work through a talent agency. Whether you approach a station or talent agency, you'll need two things: a résumé with a cover letter and an audition tape.

Résumés

Your **résumé** is indispensable when you apply for a job in any announcing specialization. It lists in an abbreviated manner the most relevant facts about you. Employers can tell, almost at a glance, if you're appropriate for a vacancy or, at least, worthy of an interview. With so much at stake, the preparation of an attractive, factual, and to-the-point résumé is essential. Note, however, that *even the best résumé can't help you get a job unless you're truly capable, dependable, punctual, and an asset to any employer.* The suggestions that follow assume that you have these qualities and that you deserve a position in broadcasting.

Before starting to prepare your résumé, visit the nearest career guidance or job counseling center. If you're a student, you'll probably find such an office right on campus. If you're not attending school, you can still get help from the job center at almost any community college or four-year school. Some schools offer résumé-writing clinics regularly, sometimes for a small registration fee. Many college placement offices have free handouts on résumé writing. Arm yourself with as much information as you can find.

Although campus placement offices can help you with useful information on résumés, cover letters, and interviews, don't expect personnel in these offices to have all the answers. The field of broadcast performance is so specialized and so out of the ordinary that few career guidance counselors have firsthand in-depth knowledge of it.

Types of Résumés

Résumés come in two general types, and in a third type that's a hybrid of those two.[1] All provide some common items of information, including name, address, phone number, formal education, and references, but they differ in some important respects. The first type, the **chronological résumé**, lists relevant employment in reverse chronological order. The second type, the **competency-based**, or **functional résumé**, lists the applicant's areas of competency. The **hybrid**, or **combination résumé**, as the name indicates, combines features of both the chronological and the competency-based résumés.

The chronological résumé is used by anyone with some professional experience. A sample of this type of résumé is shown in Figure 13.2 (page 374).

The competency-based or functional résumé is your best choice if you're nearing graduation and looking for your first announcing job. Many graduating seniors can point only to the knowledge they've acquired in school, which includes skills learned on college radio and television stations or through internships at public-access cable companies and commercial or public broadcasting stations. A chronological listing of part-time jobs held while in school, such as busing dishes or working in a car wash, isn't likely to impress a prospective employer. However, if you earned half or more of your living expenses while in school, state this, together with a brief list of jobs held. This tells a prospective employer that you're an industrious person who made a sacrifice to gain your education. If you've had bookkeeping, accounting, or sales experience, or if you're fluent in a language other than English, say so.

More important, point out that you can perform the duties required of a person in a particular announcing position. Specify, for instance,

---

[1]The advice on résumé writing, and the sample résumés, are appropriate for most purposes. However, if you're applying to a large firm, you may want to find out (perhaps from a receptionist) if they want **scannable résumés**, and, if so, follow the advice given by Cisco Systems, included in this chapter (page 399).

Figure 13.2

A chronological résumé lists employment information in reverse chronological order.

Mary Ann Williams
586 Poplar Avenue
Huntington, Kentucky 25704
(304) 555-6572

EMPLOYMENT

1997–Present   News reporter, WBRE-AM, Mount Embree, Kentucky. Cover local stories. Report live from the field. Produce news packages. Specialize in education and the environment.

1994–1996   Paid news intern, WBRE-AM, Mount Embree, Kentucky. Collected and edited wire-service copy. Rewrote news stories. Maintained files. Performed as weekend news anchor.

1993–1994   Volunteer reporter at local National Public Radio station. Wrote and voiced reports on school board meetings, local election issues, and the impact of growth on the local community.

HONORS

Dean's list, all semesters in college
President, College Students in Broadcasting, 1996
Adam Marshall Scholarship, 1997
Albert Johnson Award, outstanding graduating senior, 1997
Graduated cum laude, 1997

EDUCATION

Kimball University, Hays, Kentucky
B.A., Radio and Television, 1997
Course work: news gathering, depth reporting, legal aspects of journalism, newswriting, and radio news performance.
Performed as news reporter and anchor on campus radio station for three years.

REFERENCES

Dr. Alice Barnes, Kimball University, 133 Campus Drive, Hays, Kentucky
Mr. Fred Morales, General Manager, WBRE, 1600 Morris Blvd., Mount Embree, Kentucky
Dr. Hamid Khani, Kimball University, 133 Grove Drive, Hays, Kentucky

that you can operate all standard control room or video equipment, that you can do audio or video editing, or that you can operate studio cameras and switchers. These and similar competencies serve as basic qualifications for an entry-level position. This is the thrust of a competency-based résumé, as the example in Figure 13.3 (page 376) illustrates.

It's appropriate on a competency-based résumé to list positions you've held as a member of a college radio or television station staff and to provide information about work you've done as an intern. But it's *crucial* that you identify such work clearly. Applicants who make positions held on a campus radio station appear to have been held at a commercial station will be seen as misrepresenting their backgrounds. And those who try to pass off an internship as paid professional experience are written off immediately. No prospective employer would likely schedule an interview or review an aircheck with an applicant who seemed to be providing misleading information.

The hybrid résumé is useful for students who've had some professional experience either before or during school years and who've acquired knowledge and competencies also as a student. An example of a hybrid résumé is shown in Figure 13.4 (page 377).

Some Tips on Preparation

With the flexibility offered by word processors it's easy to prepare more than one résumé, each with a different slant. For instance, as a graduate of a department of radio and television, you may want to apply for positions in both radio and television. The same résumé wouldn't be ideal for both. If you have two basic résumés—one for radio and one for television—you can further tailor each résumé to match your background and your interests with the requirements stated for the positions to which you're applying.

In most instances, résumés should be one page only. Although you may believe you have more than a page of information to disclose, prospective employers want to see your qualifications in the briefest form possible.

Most word-processing programs allow you to choose line spacing other than the traditional single, double, or triple spacing.[2] For a résumé, single spacing is too dense and double spacing is too wasteful of page space. After creating your résumés as single-spaced documents,

---

[2]If you're not sure how to adjust line spacing, look for help at a campus computer lab.

Figure 13.3

A competency-based, or functional, résumé presents the applicant's areas of competence.

Charles Gonzalez
1616 South M Street
Callison, New Jersey 08110
(609) 555-5456

EXPERIENCE

Intern at WBCD-AM and FM, an MOR station.
Produced jingles and station IDs. Timed music cuts and produced file cards of basic information.
Three years' experience as a DJ on the campus radio station featuring CHR and AOR music. Managed the station senior year. Served two years as the station's music director.
Worked two years as a stand-up comic at a local comedy club.

EMPLOYMENT

Manager of Callison Comedy Club, 1996–1997
Part-time sales associate, MusicLand, Callison, New Jersey, 1993–1994
Audio engineer at Genessee University student union for various performing groups, 1995–1997

EDUCATION

B.A. in Mass Communications, Genessee University, Fountain, New Jersey, 1998
Graduated with honors

REFERENCES

Ms. Gerri Boyd, Manager, Callison Comedy Club, Callison, New Jersey
Mr. Harry Freund, Manager, MusicLand, Callison, New Jersey
Professor Arthur Simons, Genessee University, Fountain, New Jersey

Figure 13.4

A hybrid, or combination, résumé gives both professional and academic achievements.

Ralph Wente
435 Livingston Street
Tacoma, Washington 98499
(206) 555-3790

OBJECTIVE

Entry-level position in television sports department

COMPETENCIES

Sports Knowledge — Thorough knowledge of sports officiating and scoring of gymnastics, diving, and other competitive sports. Six years' experience scoring baseball. Knowledge of football and basketball strategies.

Sports Experience — Played baseball (second base and shortstop), three years in high school and four years in college. Played football (running back) three years in college. Served as manager of the college basketball team for two years.

Other Competencies — Expert at both still and video camera work. Considerable skill in both on- and off-line videotape editing. Two years' experience in writing copy for sports newscasts on campus television station. Bilingual in English and Spanish.

AWARDS AND HONORS

Dean's list, 1996–1998
Member and president of University Block T Club (Sports Honor Society)
Valedictorian

EDUCATION

University of Tacoma, Washington, 1999, B.A., Broadcasting Specialized in television performance, production, and writing for sports broadcasts.

REFERENCES

Professor Ray Marucci, Varsity Coach, University of Tacoma, Washington
Dr. Joyce Ntare, University of Tacoma, Washington
Dr. Bruce O'Hare, University of Tacoma, Washington

you should convert to a line spacing that makes the best visual impression and fits comfortably on a single sheet of paper.

In preparing your résumés, it's wise to make drafts and then ask a qualified person—a teacher of broadcasting, a person working in a career-guidance or job-placement center, or a broadcaster—to review and comment on it.

Omit from your résumés all of the following:

- *Height, weight, hair color, and eye color*— unless you're applying for an on-air television position or a job as an on-camera commercial performer for which your physical features are of importance. In this case, supply all pertinent physical information and include photographs.
- *Hobbies*—unless they add to your qualifications. Listing your collection of 1960s and 1970s Top 40 albums could be important if you're applying for a position as a DJ on a station featuring hits of the past. Noting that you enjoy skateboarding or hiking is irrelevant.
- *Race, ethnic or national origin, gender, and physical condition*—It's against the law for employers to discriminate against job applicants on the basis of any of these facts or conditions. However, if you have a disabling physical condition that calls for special facilities or other considerations, mention this in your cover letter.
- *Your high school or college academic transcript*—unless it's requested. You may be asked to provide a list of courses you've taken that relate directly to a specific job, so keep your own list of courses you have taken, arranged by category.

Include information about the following in your résumés:

- *Your student record if it was exceptional*—For example, you may note that you were on the dean's list six semesters, that you graduated cum laude, or that you earned a 3.87 grade point average during your last sixty units.
- *Supplementary abilities that might be put to use at the station*— Include experience in sales, electronics, data processing, and audio production of commercials and features (including writing, recording, editing, and mixing). List the hardware (for example, Macintosh or PC) you can operate and the operating systems you're qualified to use.

- *Leadership positions*—such as student body officer, class president, commencement speaker, and so on.
- *Memberships in national associations that relate to broadcasting*—such as College Students in Broadcasting, the Association for Women in Communication, Inc. (AWC), the International Radio and Television Society-Alpha Epsilon Rho, the National Academy of Recording Arts and Sciences, the Radio-Television Journalism division of the Association for Education in Journalism and Mass Communication, and student membership in the Radio-Television News Directors Association (RTNDA).
- *Contributions to your community*—such as Little League coaching, charitable fundraising, and similar activities.
- *The ability to speak or read one or more languages*—with an indication of the degree of your proficiency (bilingual, fluent, or passable).

Career advisers are divided on the subject of references. Some suggest that you list four to six names, complete with titles and mailing addresses, others prefer a statement at the bottom, "References available on request." If you're applying to numerous potential employers, giving the same names could inundate those who are providing you with recommendations, so be selective. Choose your references wisely: avoid close friends and family members. Use employers only if the employment was related to the job you're seeking and the former employer can verify your dependability, punctuality, honesty, or other qualities that would make you a good employee. Your best references will come from teachers and those who supervised your work in an internship or a paying job at a broadcast station. *Always obtain permission before listing anyone as a reference.* And, when you do ask recommenders to send letters to potential employers, *always supply stamped and addressed envelopes.*

Your final draft should be printed, error-free, using a high-quality printer. Use a standard type font, such as Times, Helvetica (extended), or Geneva. Don't use a novelty font of any kind. Print size should be twelve point, unless your résumé will spill over onto two pages and you can find no information to shorten or eliminate. In this case, you may want to use ten- or eleven-point size type. Try different fonts and different point sizes. With most fonts and word-processing programs, you can select any point size you wish.

Your résumé will be more attractive if you print it on a laser printer or ink-jet printer. Any copying service equipped with word processors can use a floppy disk that includes your résumé to make excellent prints. Make certain, though, that the word-processing program you've used (Microsoft Word, MacWrite II, WriteNow, ClarisWorks) is installed on their computers. From each high-quality original you can use a copying machine to make an unlimited number of prints on twenty-pound bond paper. Have your résumés duplicated on white, off-white, or buff paper, and use matching envelopes. Avoid garish or weird colors.

Finally, despite all of these suggestions about what to put in your résumé, if you find that you can't comfortably fit your information on one page, omit the least important points. If you must omit such items as community service, membership in organizations, leadership positions, or academic honors, you may put these on a supplemental résumé, included as a second sheet.

Photographs

It's unwise to include a photograph when you apply for a position at a radio station or as a freelance voice-over performer. The physical appearance of those who do radio or voice-over work is totally irrelevant. The *sound* of the voice is all-important. A photograph adds nothing; it can in fact work against you if a potential employer thinks you don't "look like you sound."

On the other hand, photographs are essential when you apply for an on-air position in television. Even if you're sending an audition or résumé videotape, it's important to also send still photos. Send two or three photos that show you in different work environments. Photos may be black and white or in color, and should be either five by seven inches or eight by ten inches. Don't send "artsy" photos, provocative poses, or graduation photos. The best photos are those taken of you while performing as a reporter, anchor, program host, or other on-air role. You needn't spend a great deal of money on photos; producers and agents can see what they need to know by looking at high-quality snapshots. However, your photo's composition and what is depicted in it should have a professional look.

The Cover Letter

All résumés should be accompanied by a **cover letter.** This letter is perhaps as important as your résumé. It gives you an opportunity to stress some accomplishment or quality that makes you uniquely qualified for the job. It also allows you to say why you're interested in a particular station. The function of the cover letter is to persuade a prospective employer to read your résumé. The objective of the résumé is to influence the employer to listen to or to view your audition tape. The goal of the tape is to gain an interview. The anticipated outcome of the interview is to obtain that job!

The nature of the cover letter will differ depending on whether you're applying for station employment or looking for an agent. Keep cover letters to station managers brief and to the point. Most such letters should contain four short paragraphs. The first tells what position you're applying for and why you're applying to this particular station. The second paragraph gives brief details of your qualifications. The third refers to the accompanying résumé and audition tape, and underscores the most significant points. The fourth paragraph requests an interview and states when you'll call to request it.

You can keep cover letters to agents quite brief because the audition tape counts for nearly everything. An opening statement of your qualifications and aspirations, a request that your tape be reviewed, and information as to how you may be reached are all you need to include. Cover letters should be an honest expression of *your* feelings; don't look for a model cover letter to copy. If you can't clearly and effectively state your case in a cover letter, you may need to attend a résumé-writing workshop in which cover letters are also discussed.

Never send a cover letter that's been duplicated by a copy machine. Résumés may be duplicated, but always create a separate cover letter for each person to whom you're sending a résumé. Compose your letter on a computer and have it printed by a letter-quality printer. Poor-quality computer-generated letters give the impression that they're being produced in quantity. When composing your letter on a word processor, use a ragged, not justified, right margin. Personalize each letter so that you don't inadvertently give the impression that your applications are blanketing the nation. Personalize letters by addressing the employer by name and title and by mentioning call letters, music format, news policy, or whatever is appropriate. Such details tell the reader that the letter in hand is the only one of its kind. Above all, your letter should be neat. Proofread your letters carefully.

Audition or Résumé Tapes

A tape recording is a must for anyone seeking work as an announcer, whether at a station or as a freelance voice-over performer.

Producing Tapes for Employment at a Broadcast Station. If you're seeking station employment, you may send a **presentation tape** or an **aircheck.** Strictly speaking, the term *aircheck* refers to an edited recording of an on-air performance. This is usually the best kind of **audition tape.** Actually being on the air—even if it's a local cable company's public access television channel, a cable company's radio channel, or a "carrier-current" campus setup—gives you a level of energy and a sound that's difficult to duplicate when recording for audition purposes.

Students often compile tapes from radio or television performances in media performance classes or on news, entertainment, and information programs that their college department has supplied to local broad-

Figure 13.5

Student Jennie Jones, a broadcast and electronic communication arts major, introduces the music she plays on the campus radio station. The station, staffed and managed by students, features an alternative rock format. As Jennie opens her announce mic to comment on the music or promote a contest, a recorder is activated that produces a "skimmed aircheck"—a tape that records only her comments, which she may use later when she applies for a DJ position. Other students at this station create sound stories, radio dramas, public-service announcements, campus newscasts, KSFS radio sweepers, station IDs, and show promos. *Courtesy of Jennie Jones, and KSFS, San Francisco State University, San Francisco, California.*

casters or cable companies. Some departments of broadcasting make resources available to students to edit, assemble, and duplicate their presentation tapes. If you have a good collection of videotaped performances, you can select eight to ten minutes of your best work. For radio performance, limit the tape's length to no more than three minutes. And, because some station managers or news directors won't listen for the full three minutes, make sure you put your best work first on the tape.

Radio tapes are inexpensive to produce. The audio recording equipment available in most college departments of broadcasting is adequate for this purpose. A typical three-minute audiotape for a position as a DJ will feature five or six different pieces:

1. A series of ad-libbed music intros (or back announcing of a music set)
2. Ten seconds of an upbeat commercial
3. An ad-libbed comment on some amusing event of the day
4. A piece teasing a contest or some similar station promotion
5. Ten seconds of an intimate and subdued commercial
6. A brief news story, read at a rapid rate
7. One or two, ten-second PSAs

The most practical format for audiotapes is a good-quality thirty- or sixty-minute cassette. If you have a shorter tape—ten or fifteen minutes—use it. A Type II cassette will give you better quality than will a cheaper tape. Avoid one-hundred-and-twenty-minute tapes because they may stretch and distort your voice.

Like résumés, audition tapes for popular-music radio work are both simple and inexpensive to make, so it's important to make more than one tape. Each music radio station has an established sound, an overall mood and spirit. If you're applying for an announcing position at a station that expects its announcers to display wit, warmth, and congeniality, the material on your tape will be quite different from that prepared for a station whose announcers are instructed to keep their comments brief and matter-of-fact. Also, a given Country-music station may have a sound that differs considerably from a Top 40 station in the same market. Study the sounds of the stations in which you're interested and individualize your audition tapes accordingly.

If your audiotape is going to an all-news station, it should present several short news stories of varying moods, plus at least one fifteen- or thirty-second commercial. A presentation tape for a position in sports should include samples of sports reporting, play-by-play, and play analysis. Gear your tapes as specifically as possible to the stations at which you'd like to work. If time permits, use the actual call letters of the station to which you're applying.

If you can't use school equipment to record and edit your audiotape, find a recording studio that provides a taping service. Audio recording studios are generally found only in or near larger cities, so you may have to travel to one if you live in a smaller community. The business listings in telephone directories include recording studios. Obtain price quotations from at least three studios before choosing one.

Independent video production companies may be found in every medium-to-major market. Some produce only studio-based audition tapes. Others will go into the field with you to cover some planned news event, such as a parade, a picket line, or a marathon. If you have a choice of production companies, try to find and select one that will include field reporting that's ad libbed or ad libbed from notes. Most production companies will provide some guidance, including suggestions for improving your appearance or your performance. Production companies usually charge by the day, with a one-day minimum, plus extra charges for editing the tape and making copies. You can expect to pay between five hundred dollars and fifteen hundred dollars for a complete video presentation tape.

Producing Tapes for Review by a Talent Agent. Talent agencies require a different kind of tape. Most of the voice work you'll obtain through agencies is for these specializations:

- Radio commercials
- Voice-over narration for television commercials (both radio and television commercials are called **voice-overs** by freelancers)
- Corporate videos (also called **industrials**)
- Documentary narration, promos for stations, and promos for radio and television specials
- Cartoon voicing
- Looping

Looping is also called dubbing (short for *postproduction synchronous dubbing*). In this procedure, a person's voice is dubbed onto a tape or film soundtrack to match the lip movements and the emotions of another person acting in the film. The most common use of looping in the United States is in the dubbing of non-English-language films to English. At times, however, a producer will become dissatisfied with the voice or the acting ability of a performer and hire a voice-over professional to dub, and thereby replace, the words spoken by the performer who is seen by the audience.

To become a feelance performer, you almost certainly will need an agent. Agents notify their clients when work that suits their talent is available. Agents help their clients prepare and tape the audition for a specific job, and negotiate payments with potential employers. Agents collect ten percent of all payments earned, but effective agents more than earn their fee. If you decide to seek an agent, plan your first audition tape to persuade an agent to "take you on."

The presentation tape required for freelance work is different from that for radio station employment. Most important is that you demonstrate your ability to interpret copy. Unless you're convinced that your future lies in doing character voices or accents and dialects, you should concentrate on performing high-quality, imaginative, but basically standard, commercial copy. Select pieces that demonstrate a range of approaches—*thoughtful, concerned, upbeat, sultry, excited, laid back,* and so on. Do only ten to fifteen seconds of each. As you assemble the bits, arrange them in a sequence that shows contrast; begin with a soft sell, follow with a hard sell, and continue with samples of your entire range. The entire audition tape should run no longer than three minutes.

 It is helpful to listen to audition tapes of successful voice-over announcers. You can find such performances on the Internet. Enter this URL on a New Web Browser[3]:

www.provoice.com

More details about using this URL may be found in Chapter 2.

For a complete, updated list of URLs for this textbook please see the text home site available at *www.hmco.com/college*.

---

[3]The Internet is changing constantly as new web sites are added and old web sites are abandoned. The URL listings in this textbook should be regarded as samples of the kinds of material available rather than as a stable index. If you seek a web site using one of these URLs and cannot connect, enter the key words for the topic into a search engine to find a site that may provide the information you want.

If you want to do character voices and your repertoire includes foreign accents or regional dialects, use samples of these in carefully selected bits of commercials. Put on your tape only those voices or accents that you perform extremely well. Confine your voiced bits to ten to fifteen seconds each; take somewhat longer—for example, twenty to thirty seconds—to demonstrate your ability to do straight narration for industrials. In short, provide the agent with as great a range of vocal competencies as possible. Some freelance performers prepare as many as three different tapes: one of straight commercial announcing, one of characters and cartoon voices, and another of narration for industrials.

If you're serious about a career as a freelance announcer, consider taking a workshop given by a professional performer. Many reputable freelance performers conduct workshops with small groups of students that focus on developing the skills needed for this work. Workshops sometimes cover only one or two weekends and usually culminate in the production and packaging of a presentation tape. To identify a potential coach, ask your instructors as well as professional announcers for suggestions. When contacting those who offer courses, ask for permission to sit in on a session before enrolling in a course. If you're satisfied that the instructor is capable, that the workshop is compatible with your needs, and that the cost isn't excessive, you could wind up with greatly enhanced performing abilities, as well as a professionally produced audition tape.

Other Tips Concerning Presentation Tapes. Almost anyone can make an impressive audition tape if enough time and effort is spent preparing it. Working at it for several days, doing take after take, and then selecting only the best bits of your work and assembling them can result in a high-quality product. However this approach is unrealistic because it's too time consuming and may present a distorted image of your abilities. It might create an additional problem: if it's your tape that gets you an agent or a job, you'll have to live up to its quality consistently. Make certain that your tape truly reflects what you can do under actual recording circumstances.

Don't send out tapes that are hastily made, that are made with inferior equipment, or that you made before you attained your present level of ability. Poorly performed tapes can prejudice potential employers or agents against you.

Duplicate audition tapes for voice performance, whether for radio station or freelance employment, on new audiocassettes. Never record or duplicate on a used tape. Be sure to listen to every dub you make, and listen all the way through; often stations receive tapes with inaudible or distorted sections. Type your identification neatly both on the cassette itself and on its plastic box.

Answering Machines, Cellular Phones, and Pagers

A survey of broadcast announcers asked how they got their first job. More than 85 percent responded that they happened to be "in the right place at the right time." In other words, they were immediately available when an opening arose. You can't, of course, be at several radio or television stations at the same time, but you can be available by telephone at all hours—if you have a cellular phone, an answering machine, an answering service, a fax machine, an e-mail address, or a pager.

Cell phones are the most desirable of these communication devices, but they also are the most costly. Before deciding on a phone and a cellular telephone service, ask around to learn what advice users may offer you.

If you invest in an answering machine, make certain that the machine you buy allows you to pick up messages on it by calling from another phone. Also, make sure that you have a businesslike message on your tape. A prospective employer will be turned off by a raucous, bawdy, or childish message. Don't use an answering system that requires callers to punch numbers according to a programmed series of choices—"If you want to leave a message for Allison, press 1 now," and the like.

Pagers are small, relatively inexpensive devices that signal you whenever a telephone call is made to your home telephone number. The calling person is asked to leave either a numeric or a voice page. If a numeric page is left, a phone number appears on the pager's display, and you can return the call within minutes.

E-mail and faxed messages, including requests for information not on your résumé, can be received by fax/modem for later printing. If possible, have a dedicated line installed for your fax/modem. If you use the same telephone line for phone calls and incoming faxes, you won't receive the fax when you're using the telephone.

Mailing Address and Phone Number

Because you may be away at school and therefore without a permanent address, you should give some thought to the address and to the phone number you list on your résumé. For most job seekers, it's best to list only one address, one that will remain accurate for some time (that of your parents, perhaps). The telephone number given should be for the phone you use every day.

Finding Job Openings

Colleges and universities are sites of intensive recruiting activity every spring semester. That's the good news. The bad news is that broadcasters almost never appear on college campuses to interview prospective employees. However, this fact shouldn't discourage you. Media executives don't like to advertise job openings beyond the requirements of law. They are busy people, and they don't want to schedule interviews with dozens of job applicants. Many station executives, particularly those at smaller-market stations, make vacancies known to faculty members in college and university departments of broadcasting and request that no more than three to five students be told of each opening. If you've gained the confidence and respect of a faculty member, ask to be notified of job openings in your field of interest.

Also, remember that jobs are available if you're willing to move to a small market, to accept an entry-level position, and to work for a subsistence salary. This is called *paying your dues*.

The long-established and accepted practice of underpaying and overworking novices in the field of broadcasting is deplorable; however, the fact remains that this is the way it was, is, and (most likely) always will be. If you're committed to becoming a successful radio or television announcer, chances are that you'll have to begin at the proverbial bottom and gradually work yourself into better and higher-paying positions.

Announcements of job openings are published in trade magazines including *Broadcasting & Cable* and *Radio & Records (R & R)*. To find your first job, however, don't limit yourself to responding to ads for announcers. Most stations that advertise either can't find anyone willing to work at their station or are looking for people with at least a few years of appropriate experience. Announcing position vacancies occur regularly at most stations, so you should apply to every station you consider to be a good starting point or a second step for you. Begin with stations in your own area, unless you have compelling reasons to leave.

You can perform job searches on the Internet. Broadcast Employment Services offers a number of services under such categories as Master Station Index, Index, E-Resume Database, Freelance Directory, TV Forum, Situations Wanted, and Internship Database. Jobs in radio, television, cable, and film are included. URL:

www.tvjobs.com/index_a.htm

For a complete, updated list of URLs for this textbook, please see the text home site available at *www.hmco.com/college*.

SPOTLIGHT

Surviving Career Changes

Fred LaCosse is a media performer whose career demonstrates the twists, turns, frustrations, and successes that are common to most people who spend years in broadcasting. Fred earned his undergraduate degree in humanities at a small liberal arts college in Indiana. He then went to graduate school at Northwestern University and majored in broadcasting. The university guaranteed him thirty hours a week on the air with the local educational television station. His response: "A dollar an hour! Wow! It was great experience. It was in the third market in the country!" Here is Fred's story:

Everything was live—it was before videotape. Fantastic experience! We were live from 4:00 P.M. to 7:30 P.M., back-to-back programs, three studios. I did that for two years while I was getting my master's degree. Then I got a job in Columbus, Ohio, at the NBC station as studio supervisor.

After two years in the army (Korean War), Fred got a job as stage manager at Channel 11 in San Jose, California. After two years, he was promoted to the job of announcer–director:

I didn't want to do any air work, but I studied about six months—started doing voice-overs, reading anything into a tape recorder in an old shed. And I would go out there every morning for an hour or so and slooow-ly, slooow-ly, get better, al-most tolerable. After about six months, I started improving, and I mean it was fi-nally air-able.

After I was there about a year, they made me production manager. We finally got videotape, and every used-car dealer in the Valley wanted to cut commercials on videotape so he could sit there on Thursday, Friday, or Saturday night and watch himself on television.

During my time there, I would fill in on occasion when some of the anchors would go on vacation. At that time we had a three-person news department. We had two people who could shoot and report, and one guy in Monterey who would set the tripod, start the camera, go around the other side, and give his report. And he did wonderful stuff.

On the average day there, I'd go in about 11:00 A.M., play with the budget, meet with the boss, be concerned with union hassles. Then I'd produce the early newscast, go home and grab a quick bite, say "Hi" to my wife and kids. Come back and do the late newscast, then hang around 'til maybe 12:30 A.M. or so to finish up some paperwork. Those were long, long days. And that lasted for four years. Then KRON called and asked, "Would you consider coming to San Francisco to an-chor the news?" I wasn't sure, but I was willing to take a look. I was doing pretty well in San Jose at the same time, making decent dollars as a department head, but I decided to audition.

And what an audition! I auditioned with Jerry [an ongoing anchor]. I'd read a story, he'd read a story, I'd read a story, he'd read a story, and then we'd rap, ad-lib for thirty seconds just to see how the rapport was, how we'd jell. Jerry would bring up something, and I'd respond. Because that's what they wanted to find out—whether or not I could think on my feet, and how it worked, how it jelled. I was offered the weekend job, but it was $9,000 a year less than I was making in San Jose, and I couldn't do it. A lot of decisions you'll make along the line in your career make you wonder later: "What would have happened if?"

After four years in news in San Jose, I got another nod to come to San Fran-cisco to audition. They set me up in the newsroom, and said: "Why don't you just prepare about three minutes' worth of copy." I thought, "Great—I can at least read my own stuff." It's a lot easier to read your own stuff. So I wrote up about three minutes' worth of copy, maybe six or seven different stories, and went down to the studio with a stage manager and a camera operator. The stage manager cued me and I read the copy and signed off and just sat there wondering what was go-ing on. After about five minutes, the news director came in and said: "The station manager would like you to just sit there and talk about yourself, and how you feel about the news business for maybe five minutes or so."

Now, that's kind of interesting. That's when you learn whether or not you have that ability to keep it going. To think, to plan, and at the same time be talking. If you can develop that skill, if you happen to have it, it's amazing how much that will help you when you finally get into a situation when a heavy news story comes down and you've got to be out there at the anchor desk for an hour or two or three coordinating, gathering information, and trying to make it sound very smooth. That is not easy to do. Especially if you have the wrong producer telling you stupid things in your ear! So I talked for five minutes, telling how I felt about various things, and then I sat for about another ten minutes. Then the news director came down and said: "The manager would like to see you in his office."

I thought I'd probably blown the audition. As soon as I sat down, he said, "LaCosse, we'd like you to come to work for us." He could be a tough cookie, and I think in this first meeting he was establishing our relationship right then.

I spent the next four years anchoring the news. It was the most boring job I ever had in my life. The most boring job! I was in the fourth-largest market in the country. I'd come out of a situation where I was working twelve hours a day consistently. Working my head off but totally immersed in it. Now I come up here—fourth market—and all they'd let me do is anchor. And that is the most boring job in the business. It pays you five times as much money as any other job in the business, but it's boring.

Your primary job as an anchor is to be a journalist. The first hour and a half when I got to the station, I'd spend reading wire-service copy. I read about five different newspapers. You have to know what's going on. You have to read a lot, and you have to know how to spot the salient points. I took a speed-reading course in college, and it was invaluable to me.

After four years, the news director was replaced and another person took over and replaced me with "his man." Two years later, I replaced him. That's how this silly business works.

A few years earlier, during a strike, I had started a business. I coached business people on how to get their points across on television. Eventually it became so successful that I gave up anchoring altogether. After two years I was approached by a San Francisco television station to be a co-host on a morning talk and interview show. I did that for five years until a new owner cut the budget by fifty percent, fired half the producers and, at contract renewal time, reduced talent salaries by fifty percent. I went back to my business and lived happily ever after.

Figure 13.6

Broadcast major Doug Brown stands as he reads the news on KSFS, San Francisco State University, a student radio station. The station sends its signal throughout campus and, via cable, to the city of San Francisco. The radio station has digital postproduction editing systems, Sony digital audiotape players, digital special effects units, and other current broadcast equipment. You can access the campus radio station at this web site: *ksfs.sfsu.edu. Courtesy of Doug Brown and KSFS, San Francisco State University, San Francisco, California.*

Applying for a Position at a Radio Station[4]

With a completed résumé and presentation tape—and, of course, your education and college broadcasting experience—you're ready to apply for an announcing job. This section is appropriate for those applying for DJ work, Classical-music announcing, radio news reporting and anchoring, and sports reporting. Most first-time applicants for announcing positions should be able to follow these recommendations easily.

To apply for a job, obtain the names of the program directors of those radio stations where you'd like to work. Names of key station personnel are listed in *Broadcasting & Cable Yearbook,* which can be found at many libraries and at nearly every radio and television station. Before writing to a program director, however, telephone the station to confirm that the person listed is still with the station and in the same position. There's a great deal of movement of executives in the broadcasting industry.

---

[4]This text doesn't offer suggestions for applying at television stations because television stations hire relatively fewer announcers, and most are in a single specialization—news reporting and anchoring. However, some of the suggestions offered in this section may be applied to a television job search.

Send a brief letter, a résumé, and your presentation tape to each program director. In your letter, state that you'll call in a week to see if an interview can be arranged. Follow through with the telephone call but don't be discouraged if few or none of the station managers express interest in you. Even though announcing jobs are available, the number of persons applying for them far exceeds available positions. Perseverance is the most important quality a prospective announcer can possess.

If you live in a major or secondary market, it's unlikely that you'll be hired straight out of college as an on-air announcer. Therefore, be prepared to look for work in a smaller market. *Broadcasting & Cable Yearbook* can help you locate stations to which you can apply. It lists every radio station in the United States and Canada, indicates its signal strength (a clue to its audience size and therefore its economic standing), gives names of chief administrative personnel, and, for music stations, indicates the music format.

In addition to obtaining as much information as you can about a station to which you're applying, make sure you've actually listened to it. It will be very awkward for you if you have to admit that you know little or nothing about the station. If a station to which you're applying is so far away from your home that you can't receive its signal, you may be able to listen to it over the Internet. It will be to your advantage if you can intelligently discuss details of the station's programming. If applying to a popular-music station, for instance, you should know its music format, the nature of the DJ's chatter (if any), and so on. When listening to a music station, make notes as to how the news is handled—whether there are network cut-ins, an audio news service such as AP Network News that is responsible for reading the news, and so on. News reading may be a part of your air shift as a DJ. When applying to a news station, find out such basic details as these: What is the typical length of a report from the field? Does the station work with a single anchor or co-anchors? What news features (weather, traffic, skiing conditions, sports reports, business reports, and such) does the station provide?

Interviewing for a Job

The job interview is critical in your pursuit of a position as a radio or television station performer. A general manager, station manager, or program director may be impressed with your credentials, your tape, and your résumé, but an interview is usually the final test that puts you to work—or sends you away.

Before seriously seeking a job, you may want to discuss career possibilities and job seeking with an executive at a station where you're not applying for work. This is called an **informational interview.** Almost any college teacher of broadcasting can guide you to someone (perhaps a former student) who'll be happy to spend time exploring your employment prospects. Ask the professional to review your résumé and to discuss strategies for finding employment.

The suggestions and comments that follow are based on several assumptions: *that you truly are ready for the position you seek, that you'll honestly state your capabilities and competencies, and that you'll be able to back up your statements by performing effectively.*

Before you appear for an interview, practice being interviewed. A friend or an instructor may be willing to assist you and then to critique your performance. Remember that an interview is not acting, but it *is* a type of performance.

When confirming an appointment for an interview by phone, don't ask how to find the station or where to park. To ask such questions is to give the impression that you can't find your way around.

Before going to another town for a job interview, take time to learn something about that community. The *Places Rated Almanac,* published by Macmillan, and *Cities of the United States,* published by Gale Research in four volumes—*South, West, Midwest,* and *Northeast*—are convenient sources of information about nearly every town and city in the United States.

When you go to an interview have with you all pertinent information about yourself that you might need to complete an application

To find and print a map showing the location of a particular station or other business, use this URL to open the BigBook directory:

www.bigbook.com/

Enter the call letters and the city and state, and you'll receive both a map and driving directions.

For a compete, updated list of URLs for this textbook, please see the text home site available at *www.hmco.com/college.*

form. This includes your social security number, driver's license number, dates of graduation, dates of starting and ending various jobs, previous addresses, and so forth. Also bring a list of references in case you're asked for it.

Always be early for an interview but not too early; five to ten minutes ahead of your appointment is just about right. If you're being interviewed in an unfamiliar city or town, drive past the station sometime before the interview—preferably the day before and at the same time of day as your appointment. Not only will you learn the way to the station, but you'll also see how busy traffic is at that time of day and where to park.

Dress neatly and conservatively for your interview. Although some on-air radio performers dress casually, they're established, and you're not. You'll probably be interviewed by a person who is essentially a business person, not a performer. Suits, sport coats, and ties are appropriate dress for men for interviews. Conservative dresses or suits are appropriate for women.

Be yourself. Don't try to act the part of the person you assume the interviewer is looking for.

Be frank about your strengths and accomplishments but take care not to come across as boastful.

Figure 13.7

When keeping an appointment for a job interview, present yourself in the most attractive manner possible. Dress neatly and conservatively for an interview. Although some on-air radio performers dress casually, they're established and you're not. © *Hazel Hankin/Stock Boston.*

Match your eye contact with the interviewer's. Most interviewers maintain strong eye contact, but if you meet one who doesn't, act accordingly. Eye contact isn't the same thing as staring. Take your cue from the interviewer. If the interviewer looks you in the eye, try to reciprocate.

Don't take chances by making small talk that might reveal ignorance. For instance, don't ask what tune is being played—it might be number one in that community. Don't venture opinions about broadcasting in general unless they're important to the point of the interview. You can hurt your cause by stepping on the toes of your interviewer.

Be careful to avoid traps. Some interviewers will lead job applicants along and make somewhat outrageous suggestions to see if the applicant is an unprincipled "yes" person. Don't be argumentative but think carefully before you respond to questions that seem "off the wall."

Don't misrepresent yourself or your abilities in any way! Even if you obtained a job through an exaggeration of your capabilities, you wouldn't have it for long.

Stay away from politics, religion, and sex. If the interviewer tries to lead you into any of these areas, politely avoid them.

The law forbids discrimination on certain grounds. Interviewers can't require you to reveal information such as your national origin, religion, and physical condition. If you refuse to divulge such information, do it as tactfully as possible.

Although you're under pressure during a job interview, try to be relaxed, warm, open, and relatively energetic. Help the interviewer to enjoy spending time with you. Don't however, try to entertain by taking over the interview by telling stories, anecdotes, or jokes.

Be ready to answer any questions the interviewer may have regarding your résumé. Also, be prepared to tell your life story—in an abbreviated form, of course. This might include where you were born, where you grew up, schools attended, significant travel, relevant job experience, and where you're headed in your career.

During an interview, find opportunities to ask questions. Most people like to believe they have something of value to communicate. If you feel comfortable doing so, ask the interviewer for advice. You may or may not get the job, but you'll certainly get some tips from an experienced person and make that person feel your respect.

Mention your favorable opinions about the station, its sound, and its on-air personnel. This isn't the time to tell the interviewer what you don't like about the station or any plans you may have for changing things.

Never try to gain the sympathy of the person interviewing you by complaining about your problems. People will hire you for one or more of these reasons: (1) they believe you can help them or make them look good; (2) they believe you can make money for them; (3) they need someone and think that you're the best applicant. You'll never be hired because a station executive feels sorry for you.

You may be asked to do an audition after an initial interview. You've already sent in an aircheck or audition tape, but this is an on-the-spot, under-pressure audition, and it can be nerve-wracking and threatening. If you're truly prepared and well suited for an on-air position, this is your opportunity to really show off! The important point is that you should go into each job interview with the attitude that you *will* succeed. If you do, you'll always be prepared for an on-the-spot audition.

If you're asked to audition, you may be given scripts full of words that are difficult to pronounce, sentences that feature plosive and sibilant sounds, announcements that contain foreign words and names, or pieces that require you to read one-hundred-and-ninety to two-hundred words a minute. Practice in advance of job interviews for these and similar possibilities.

If you're taken on a tour of the station, make note of the equipment being used and be prepared to state whether or not you can operate it. When you're introduced to engineers, people in sales and traffic, on-air announcers, and others, show genuine interest in them and what they're doing. If you feel no such interest, you're probably applying to the wrong station.

If you smoke, avoid it totally while you are at the station. Even if your host is a smoker, others who are influential at the station may take offense. It's all right to accept an offer of coffee, tea, or a soft drink, but under no circumstances should you accept an offer of an alcoholic beverage.

Toward the end of the interview—especially if it's gone well—look for an opportunity to ask about salary and fringe benefits. A good interviewer will generally bring this up without your asking, but you can't count on it. Almost without exception, the salary of a first-time station employee will be abysmally low, so be prepared for that. At the same time, it's important for you to know whether health, dental, and vision plans are offered and how long you must be employed before they take effect.

Joining a Union

To work at a unionized station or to perform freelance at a high professional level, you'll be obliged to join a union. The two unions for performers are the **American Federation of Television and Radio Artists** (**AFTRA**) and the **Screen Actors Guild** (**SAG**). Generally speaking, AFTRA represents performers who work live on radio or television or whose performances are recorded on an electronic storage medium: audiotape, videotape, or mass storage hard disk. SAG represents those who perform on film. Radio and television station and network announcers usually belong to AFTRA. Freelance performers as a rule belong to both.

Joining a performers' union can be tricky. Acceptance by SAG requires that you've worked as a film performer; the catch is that you aren't likely to be employed as a film performer unless you already belong to SAG! A way around this dilemma is to join AFTRA, which doesn't require previous professional employment. After you've gained experience as a member of AFTRA, you'll be eligible for membership in SAG.

Going Where Your Career Takes You

If you live in a major or secondary market, you may have to leave for a smaller market to obtain that first job—unless, of course, you're willing to accept an entry-level job as a receptionist, a courier, or a clerk in the mail room. A few graduating seniors are so talented that they move directly from school to on-air positions at medium-market or even major-market stations. For most, though, a career begins by moving to a smaller market where there's less competition and, usually, lower pay. Most radio and television stations in markets of more than two hundred thousand hire only on-air performers who've gained experience and moved up through the ranks in smaller markets.

"Going to the sticks" is a negative and self-defeating phrase for gaining initial employment in a smaller market. It implies that moving to and working in a small town is an *unfortunate* necessity for most beginning broadcast performers. This attitude carries with it a feeling of contempt for life and work in markets outside of major metropolitan areas. It also implies that, after suffering for several years in some sort of rural purgatory, all will be well if the individual is able to "move up" to a larger market. There are several good reasons for shunning this attitude.

First, by starting your career in a smaller market you can begin your on-air work at once, thereby accelerating your growth as a performer. Unlike those who start at a major-market station as a receptionist or a runner, you don't have to wait for that break that may never come.

Second, life as a broadcaster in a small town can be deeply fulfilling. Knowing that you're able to help your community in significant ways through public-service work can be rewarding. Putting down roots, becoming a contributing member of society, and participating in town events can regularly confirm the fact that you do make a difference!

Salaries do tend to be lower in smaller markets, and many stations are nonunion but the cost of living is lower, and your standard of living might be higher in a small town than in a large city.

A final reason for avoiding a negative attitude about a small market is that people who do the hiring are quick to spot condescension. Would you hire applicants who acted as though they were making a sacrifice to come to work for you?

This chapter was designed to help you find entry-level employment at a radio or television station. Most of the suggestions are applicable to other kinds of employment—doing voice-overs, industrials, and other freelance work, for example. However, there are several things this chapter can't provide. It can't give you talent, good work habits, or the perseverance required for success in the world of broadcasting. Remember that the jobs are out there, and you can obtain one if you have performance skills, if you're a reliable and hardworking person, and if you have a strong drive to succeed.

Preparing a Scannable Résumé for Today's Standards[5]

Prepare a résumé that's consistent with today's technology and a job could be just a mouse-click away. Many leading businesses now use **electronic applicant tracking systems** that scan résumés into a computer system that searches for and extracts important information necessary to qualify you for a job. Knowing this can help you prepare a résumé that computers can scan and read. Landing the job of your life could be a résumé away!

A **scannable résumé** has standard fonts and crisp and dark type, and offers plenty of facts for the artificial intelligence to extract: the more skills and facts you provide, the more opportunities you have for your skills to match available positions. A scannable résumé is like a traditional résumé: you focus on format and content. When preparing your résumé, use the tips in the following checklist.

---

[5]Courtesy of Cisco Systems of San Jose, California. Cisco is a worldwide leader in networking for the Internet. News and information about Cisco are available at *www.cisco.com.*

**FORMAT
TIPS TO
MAXIMIZE
YOUR
VISIBILITY**

1. Submit a clean original and use a standard-style résumé.
2. An unusual format such as a newsletter layout, adjusted spacing, small font sizes, graphics or lines, type that's too light, or paper that's too dark make it difficult for the computer to read your résumé.

Tips to Maximize the Scannability of Your Résumé

1. Use white or light-colored paper printed only on one side.
2. Provide a laser print original.
3. Use standard typefaces (for example, Times, Helvetica, Geneva).
4. Use a font size of twelve to fourteen points.
5. Avoid fancy treatments.
6. Avoid vertical and horizontal lines, graphics, and boxes.
7. Avoid two-column formats that look like newspapers or newsletters.

Content Tips to Maximize "Hits"

1. Use enough key words to define your skill, experience, education, professional affiliations, and so forth.
2. Describe your experience with concrete words rather than vague descriptions.
3. Use more than one page if necessary.[6]
4. Use jargon and acronyms specific to your industry.

Additional Tips

1. When sending a résumé, use e-mail if possible because it always produces the best quality. In addition, when you send your résumé via e-mail, use plain text in ASCII (American Standard Code for Information Interchange) format.
2. When faxing, to make a better quality copy, set the fax to "fine mode."

---

[6]Scannable résumés aren't seen by an employer unless they pass a scanning test that notes key terms, called "hits." The more hits on the résumé, the more likely it will be selected and forwarded to the employer, even if it is longer than a single page.

PRACTICE

Drafting Your Résumé

Write a résumé following the guidelines and examples given in this chapter. Bring copies for your instructor and each class member to discuss and compare.

 PRACTICE

Checking Out the Job Scene

Visit your nearest career-guidance center and obtain any available handouts on résumés, job interviews, and other information that may help you find that first job. Find a current issue of *Broadcasting & Cable* magazine and compile a list of advertised job openings for on-air talent. Note the geographical areas in which the greatest number of openings exist, and note the areas of specialization most in demand.

APPENDIXES

References for
Broadcast Performers

APPENDIX A

Scripts to Develop Performance Skills

APPENDIX OUTLINE

- Solo Narrative Scripts
  - Essays
  - Impressions
  - Commentaries
- Radio Commercials
  - Scripts for Solo Delivery
- Dramatized Radio Commercials
- Character Voices and Accents
  - The Pitch "Artist"
  - Low-Pitched Voice
  - High-Pitched Voice
  - British Accent (Oxford)
  - Transylvanian Accent
  - Spanish Pronunciation
  - German Accent
- Public-Service Announcements (PSAs)
- Television Commercials

THIS APPENDIX IS MADE UP CHIEFLY OF RADIO AND TELEVISION COMMERCIALS and public-service announcements (PSAs). Other script types are included, specifically essays, "impressions" (a type of essay), sports analysis, and commentaries.

There are more commercials and PSAs in this appendix than the other categories combined. The reason? Aside from commercials and PSAs, all other types of scripts may be found on the Internet, so a near-endless supply of them is available for daily practice.

Aside from being readily available, there are other good reasons for finding and working with scripts found on the Internet. You can choose only copy that excites you and that serves your particular needs. After locating several essays, for example, you can print, read, and record your favorites. And, with a system such as RealAudio, you can *listen* to scripts read by their authors. Check out these sample essays, commentaries, and other scripts, and use them as models of material to find and retrieve from the Internet.

Solo Narrative Scripts

Essays

Radio and television essays are *personal statements* that represent the feelings or opinions of their authors, and they most often are narrated by their creators. Generally speaking, essays don't deal with "hard news," and they need not be "timely." The purpose of most essays is to explore a situation, a tradition, or a movement, and to present it with analysis and a personal point of view. Essays may be serious, tongue-in-cheek-humorous, or anger driven. Here's an essay, written with obvious disgust, in which the writer pulls no punches.

Talk-Show Trash[1]
Ayrien Houchin

Tonight, I want to get right down to business. I want to know what the hell has happened to daytime television? Have we totally lost it? I mean come on people—have we no shame? I'm beginning to think we don't. I'm specifically referring to talk shows, or rather talk-show *trash:*

It's disheartening to find that happy talk and variety shows have been replaced by fists fights and name calling. And it's not just one or two shows a day. They start at 9:00 A.M. and run throughout the night. Contemporary talk shows of the nineties have expanded enough to turn daytime TV into a garbage site of abnormality and amorality. With topics such as, "Women Raped and Pregnant," "I Married My Grandfather," or "My Mother Dresses Like a Slut," it's no wonder people watch out of sheer disbelief!!!

I've heard talk-show hosts say they serve a valuable role in educating the public about such things as rape, incest, and domestic

---

[1]Reprinted with permission of the author, Ayrien Houchin.

violence; what they *should* tell us is that these shows are done purely for entertainment, which translates into "generating money."

I wonder if so much deviance on the airwaves is causing viewers to become desensitized to their surroundings? I mean, there was a time when incest and devil worship were topics that made one feel disgusted, not intrigued. I know this sounds extreme, but think about it: are people really interested because they *care,* or because they think it's so *bizarre?*

It's more and more apparent to me that talk-show hosts are so devoted to portraying deviant, bizarre, and unusual behavior that their millions of daily viewers are becoming confused as to what's normal and abnormal in society. With so many people watching such trash, and the content becoming increasingly bizarre, it's certain to be causing problems for viewers. No matter how their apologists rationalize them, talk shows give legitimacy to behaviors once rightly labeled as abnormal or destructive, and the more attention given to people committing these acts, the harder it is to make them feel ashamed.

Talk shows portray many of their guests as victims who aren't responsible for their actions. Rather than being mortified, ashamed, or trying to hide their stigma, guests willingly and eagerly discuss their child molestation, sexual quirks, and criminal records in an effort to seek understanding for their so-called disease. And, there's inevitably an "expert" present to lend an aura of respectability to the discussion. It's obvious to me that the trend of "pointing fingers" at others and not taking responsibility for one's actions will eventually play a role in the breakdown of American culture. In my opinion, trash talk shows are promoting such behavior and profiting from what I believe to be irresponsible broadcasting.

Impressions

An impression is an essay that explores inner feelings, and is quite personal. While it differs from other essays only in its degree of "shared privacy," it's useful to consider separately because the mood conveyed, and the degree of self-involvement are of a different order. One way of expressing this is to say that, while all impressions are essays, not all essays are impressions.

Well-written "impressions" will help you appreciate the rich (and seldom used) potential of the aural medium of radio. The only broadcast service through which you're likely to hear such a piece is noncommercial radio. Here's an impression by a Japanese visitor, living for a time in the United States.

About the Rooms[2]
Midei Toriyama

On a rainy, quiet afternoon, I leave the window slightly open to allow the air to stream into the room. I hold a cup of hot raspberry tea in my hands, feeling the warmth and enjoying the aroma. I feel the movement of air on my cheek—the combination of the cold air from the outside and the warm steam rising from the tea cup. I am completely relaxed in this comfortable room where silence gently lies. With a sense of great appreciation, I lie down in the heart of solitude, thinking how lucky I am to be the resident of a room with such good vibrations.

Every room has a different atmosphere that cannot be seen, but only sensed with the surface of my skin; they call this "intuition." When I look for a place to live, the room has to have some kind of impression or impulse that welcomes me. I don't know if there are many people who share this feeling; however, I feel it when my

---

[2]Reprinted with permission of the author, Midei Toriyama.

senses respond to the frequency of the room—the vibration of the molecules of the airwaves. I believe there is a congeniality between the room and the resident. I can feel it when the room likes me. When I don't feel it in a room, I will not be living there for long.

I once had a room with no feeling of the vibration. At that time I was forced to find a place to live as quickly as possible. I was visiting here from another city to look for a place, but I did not have much time. All I had was a couple of days, which was not sufficient to find the best place. After miles of walking to look at many different places, I finally ended up with a two-bedroom flat near the Geary Theatre. However, although the place was nice and actually pretty, with a huge living room and a high ceiling, a spacious kitchen, and cozy bedrooms, I did not receive the feeling. I compromised because of the limited time that I could spend.

I moved in, but lived there just for a few weeks. Something did not feel right, and I was again thrown into the middle of town to look for "room to rent" signs.

Fortunately it did not take me long to find the next place. That time I knew I was getting the place even before I got to the door of the room; I could feel it while I was going to the stairs. I remember I was so excited to open the door that my hand was shaking. The room did welcome me in an obvious way. I heard every part of the room—the ceiling, the walls, the windows, and the floors—all giving a shout of joy to have me in. As soon as I opened the door I felt a big pressure of air on my whole body. The room was full of wind; there was a whirlpool of air and I was wrapped within it. It felt as though invisible tentacles were crawling over my body to identify me. I was welcomed.

I lived there for a whole year. When I moved out of the room I left a little wish for the next resident-to-be for their good time in this room where I packed pounds of memory in numbers of boxes. I loved the room, and I could tell the room as well appreciated my residency.

Then I was drawn to this present place nearby the ocean. It may be just a sentiment of my own; however, I think the space or rooms can sense the resident's feelings. I do not know how and why, but for some reason I hear something that space radiates. And it does change its atmosphere. After the absence of a few days, I can always tell the change in the air. It smells different. To me, it seems like it is complaining of my absence.

The space is alive, I believe, and it needs to be communicated with in some way. We are likely to be insensitive to this kind of matter, and treat it without respect. What if there is a spiritual thing involved? We don't know, but how can we be so sure that no such thing is present?

On a rainy day, on such a quiet afternoon, I comfortably sit in the room with a cup of tea in my hands. I hear the silence with my eyes closed. Slowly, the aroma of raspberry tea expands in the room. I open my eyes and smile, experiencing the same feeling of tentacles which crawled on me in that old room with the feeling of the wind. It was also a rainy, quiet day, just like this.

Commentaries

Commentaries are position statements, made by persons accepted as qualified to conceive and express them. They often address political or social issues, and their authors usually both write and voice the statements.

Sports Commentary and Analysis. Joan Ryan writes commentaries for the *San Francisco Chronicle.* Among her interests are events in the world of sports that teach valuable lessons about human frailties. Her sports commentaries are far more substantial than narrowly focused "sports reports." In this article—an essay, really—she finds lessons for all of us in a case of failed effort.

Our Weird Fascination with Colossal Failure[3]
Joan Ryan

In blowing a six-stroke lead, Greg Norman turned the Masters into the most compelling show on TV on Sunday. Watching his total collapse in the final round was, some say, like watching a car wreck. You wanted to shield your eyes; instead, a stronger impulse riveted you to the wreckage.

What is it that makes choking so fascinating to watch? It's one reason the Olympics is always dramatic. Olympians choke all the time: Debi Thomas, Jim Ryun, Kim Zmeskal, to name a few. Dan Jansen choked in both the 1992 and 1994 Winter Olympics—before finally winning—and became more famous than if he had won every race.

But perhaps no sport is more prone to choking than golf. Choking is a self-inflicted defeat. You aren't beaten when you choke; you bring about your own demise through a debilitating crisis of confidence. In golf, more than most sports, the game is so slow that a player's inner demons have plenty of time to feast.

"We all choke," Tom Watson once said. "You just try to choke last."

I have never much enjoyed watching golf on TV, though I occasionally find it a wonderful sedative on a lazy weekend afternoon. The drama of a collapse like Norman's, however, turns golf into theater. There's something fascinating and satisfying in seeing rich, gifted, famous athletes completely unravel before our eyes. For a viewer, the slow pace offers hope that the choking player will right himself. Any moment now he'll snap to. So you keep watching as he crumbles, hole by hole.

---

[3]© The *San Francisco Chronicle*. Reprinted with Permission.

"It's like you're walking down the fairway naked," Hale Irwin has said. "The gallery knows what you've done; every other player knows, and, worst of all, you know. That's when you find out if you're a competitor. The longer you play, the more certain you are that a man's performance is the outward manifestation of who, in his heart, he really thinks he is."

Other than cheating, choking is considered the greatest sin in sports. The challenge of sports is not simply to perform well but to perform well when the pressure is highest. Some, like Joe Montana, find pressure invigorating, a challenge to be met. It brings out their best because they feel most alive when they're risking everything and pushing themselves to the edge of their capabilities.

For most of us, like Norman, pressure is an enemy to be feared and beaten back. Though some might feel contempt for Norman for buckling the way he did, I think more empathized. Like golf, most of life is you against yourself. Just when you think you've got everything under control—*kablooey!* You go blank in a presentation to the board of directors. You freeze on deadline. You forget your spouse's name when the boss stops by your dinner table to say hello.

Everyone loses, everyone suffers public humiliation, but sometimes it seems as if it's only you. So it's strangely encouraging to watch someone else, such as Greg Norman, choke so spectacularly.

This kind of "tragedy," brought about by one's own character flaws, has always appealed to audiences. Our attraction to Norman's defeat is not so different from the ancient Greeks' attraction to *Medea,* the Elizabethans' to *Macbeth,* and today's audiences' to any soap opera on any channel on any afternoon.

We share in the anguish of every wrong move because, on some level, we've been there. We know what it's like to expect one outcome and watch in horror as something terribly different un-folds. We know about defeat, disillusionment, and unfulfillment, and so we can identify with the fallen hero perhaps more than the triumphant one. I have noticed that players we don't much like as winners seem more appealing once they lose.

We watch, too, to see how the fallen hero copes with failure. Will it destroy him? Will he face it with humor and dignity? Or with anger and self-pity? To paraphrase Irwin, a player's performance re-veals who he is. If Norman's collapse revealed something of his character, so, too, did his good-humored response to it.

That, I think is the ultimate heroism: accepting one's fate with grace.

 Now that you've seen a few examples, you're encouraged to use the Internet to find other narrative scripts to use for further de-velopment of your interpretive abilities. Richard Rodriguez, Clarence Thomas, Anne Taylor Fleming, and Roger Rosenblatt are highly respected commentators, and their works can be ac-cessed and printed through the PBS web site[4]:

www.pbs.org/newshour/essays–dialogues.html

For a complete, updated list of URLs for this textbook, please see the text home site available at *www.hmco.com/college*.

---

[4]The Internet is changing constantly as new web sites are added and old web sites are abandoned. The URL listings in this textbook should be regarded as samples of the kinds of material available rather than as a stable index. If you seek a web site using one of these URLs and cannot connect, enter the key words for the topic into a search en-gine to find a site that may provide the information you want.

Radio Commercials

Scripts for Solo Delivery

These commercials were written for delivery by a single performer. Nearly all can be performed effectively by persons of either gender and of any age. In some, an introduction, tag, or other addition is made by a second voice, but the main message of each commercial is delivered by one performer.

AGENCY:	Donn Resnick Advertising
CLIENT:	Lincoln Health Source
:	60 Radio
TITLE:	"Take Charge"
MUSIC:	LINCOLN HEALTH MUSIC

ANNCR: How long are you going to live?

How *well* are you going to live?

Knowing which habits and behaviors can hurt your health,

and making a few changes for the better can make a real

difference.

    For instance, lifestyle choices like smoking, unhealthy diet, lack

of exercise and alcohol abuse can lead to serious illness. Yet all

these factors are under your control. So, by making a few

changes—by taking charge—you can lead a healthier, happier life.

The Health Source, John C. Lincoln Hospital's resource center, has

the latest information on how your lifestyle affects your health,

and the important changes you can make. We're easier than a

library, give you more information than a magazine, and

we're free.

The Health Source is one more way Lincoln Health is making a difference in people's lives. To take charge of *your* lifestyle, call me, at 555–6356. That's 555–6356.

LINCOLN MUSIC ENDS

AGENCY: Annette Lai Creative Services
CLIENT: Celebration Coffee
LENGTH: 60 seconds
MUSIC: "CELEBRATION" BY KOOL AND THE GANG—INSTRUMENTAL

ANNCR: Tired of the same weak coffee every morning, America? Well, wake up to *CELEBRATION!* The new freeze-dried instant from International Cuisines. Made from the choicest Celebes (SELL-uh-beez) beans from Indonesia. A unique roasting process allows the beans to retain their rich and natural taste. Because of *CELEBRATION'S* deep flavor, you use less. An eight-ounce jar makes twice as many cups as the same-sized jar of the leading brand. With the fast-paced life you lead, CELEBRATION gives you the freshly brewed taste of coffee without the wait. And, it's not just for mornings—CELEBRATE all day with *CELEBRATION*. Made from the finest Celebes beans, and deep-roasted to perfection, perfectly brewed, and quickly freeze-dried to retain their priceless flavor. That's the secret of *CELEBRATION*. And, for those who like a deep-flavored coffee without caffeine, try ninety-seven percent caffeine-free

CELEBRATION. Come on, America—it's time to *CELEBRATE!*

AGENCY: Millar Advertising, Inc.
CLIENT: Andre's International Bakery
LENGTH: 60 Seconds

ANNCR: Hot, fresh, breakfast rolls, glistening with melting butter! Croissants (krah-SAHNTS) and cafe au lait (kahf-AY-oh-LAY). Raisin bran muffins to go with your poached eggs. Andre's has these delicacies, and they're waiting for you now. For afternoon tea, Andre suggests English crumpets, served with lemon curd. Or scones and pomegranate jam. For after-dinner desserts, how about baklava (bahk-lah-VAH), the Persian delicacy made with dozens of layers of paper-thin pastry, honey, and chopped walnuts? Or, if your taste runs to chocolate, a German torte (TOR-tuh)? These and dozens of other international delights are created daily by Andre and his staff. Made only of pure and natural ingredients—Grade A cream and butter, natural unrefined sugar, pure chocolate and cocoa, and imported spices. For mouthwatering pastries, it's Andre's International Bakery. We bring you the best from the gourmet capitals of the world. Visit Andre's today! In the Corte Madera Shopping Center. Andre's!

Dramatized Radio Commercials

Several commercials for two performers are presented here to help you work on characterization, teamwork, and timing. All of these spots are humorous, and their comic effectiveness is dependent on your ability to simultaneously project an "off-the-wall" delivery while remaining completely believable to your listeners. Slight exaggeration is called for in most instances, but avoid becoming too extreme or farcical. If listeners feel that you're "play-acting," you'll fail to communicate such subtle qualities as gullibility ("Research Lab") and slight annoyance and petulance ("Mona Lisa").

Eric Poole, writer-producer of the first spots in this section, describes himself as "head creative guy of Splash Radio, a commercial production company with nearly 50 Clio, Sunny, New York Festival, and London International Festival awards." These commercials demonstrate his understanding of the "Theatre of the Mind" potential of radio, as well as a wild but disciplined sense of humor.

AGENCY:	Splash Radio
CLIENT:	Frosty Paws
PRODUCT:	Intro
TITLE:	"Research Lab," as produced

SFX: FOOTSTEPS

MAN: And this is our motivational research center . . .

GUY: Wow . . .

MAN: Where we do all our doggie treat research.

GUY: Doggie treat?

MAN: Yeah, dogs are capable of much more than you think.

GUY: Really?

MAN: Oh, yes. They've just never had the right motivation.

GUY: Oh.

MAN: What does your dog do?

GUY: Well, he rolls over, plays dead . . .

MAN: Exactly. Now in here . . .

SFX: DOOR OPEN, PIANO, TAP DANCING

VOICE: Okay, girls, big finish!

GUY: Dogs tap dancing?

MAN: Yeah, they want the new frozen treat for dogs, Frosty Paws.

GUY: Frosty Paws?

MAN: It's like ice cream for your dog. Now in here . . .

SFX: DOOR OPEN, JAZZ COMBO PLAYING

GUY: A jazz quartet!

MAN: You should hear Muffin's tenor sax solo.

GUY: Wow.

MAN: We've found dogs will do anything for Frosty Paws. And over here . . .

SFX: DOOR OPEN, TYPEWRITERS

GUY: Secretarial school?

MAN: Typing, dictation, and shortpaw.

ANNCR: Unleash your dog's potential with Frosty Paws, the world's first frozen treat for dogs. There's never been anything like it. It's full of protein, vitamins, and minerals. And unlike real ice cream, it won't upset your dog's stomach.

SFX: DOOR OPEN, MUSIC UP

MAN: And this is our malt shop.

GUY: Lotta dogs eating Frosty Paws.

MAN: Uh huh. Smart as they are, they still think it's ice cream.

ANNCR: Frosty Paws, the world's first frozen treat for dogs. New in your grocer's ice-cream freezer. Go fetch some today.

AGENCY: Splash Radio
CLIENT: Wisconsin Dental Association
PRODUCT: Check-ups
TITLE: "Mona Lisa," as produced
MUSIC: ITALIAN CLASSICAL THEME UNDER

MONA: Gee, Leonardo, I'm really excited about you painting my portrait.

LEONARDO: So am I, Mona. You're gonna make me famous.

MONA: Ah, you DaVinci boys, such flatterers.

LEONARDO: Okay, sit down on this marble slab and smile.

MONA: Okay.

LEONARDO: (A BEAT) Mona . . .

MONA: Yeah?

LEONARDO: You're not smiling.

MONA: I know.

LEONARDO: I can't paint a world-famous portrait that'll hang in the Louvre if you don't put on a happy face.

MONA: This is as happy as it gets.

LEONARDO: Look, just say "cheese."

MONA: I can't.

LEONARDO: What do you mean, you can't? I got a career riding on this picture.

MONA: It's my teeth.

LEONARDO: Your teeth?

MONA: I didn't get regular checkups as a kid, so now I'm paying for it.

LEONARDO: Let me see.

MONA: No!

LEONARDO: Open your mouth.

MONA: Lay off, DaVinci, or I'm calling Mister Lisa.

LEONARDO: Maybe you oughta call a dentist.

MONA: Maybe I oughta call Van Gogh.

LEONARDO: Not with those ears.

ANNCR: Today's dentistry is more than just filling cavities. Your regular dentist cares about your teeth for the long term, too. And keeping your teeth healthy now can save you lots of money down the road. Get the picture?

MONA: Can't you just pretend I'm smiling and draw in some teeth later?

LEONARDO: Oh, forget it. Just sit there with that dumb blank expression.

MONA: It's mysterious.

LEONARDO: Yeah, who's gonna buy that?

ANNCR: Call your regular dentist for your six-month checkup now. A reminder from the Wisconsin Dental Association. And smile.

CREATION AND
PRODUCTION: Chuck Blore & Don Richman, Inc.
CLIENT: AT & T
LENGTH: 60 seconds

CATHIANNE: (ON PHONE) Hello.

DANNY: Uh, hi. You probably still remember me. Edward introduced us at the seminar . . .

CATHIANNE: Oh, the guy with the nice beard.

DANNY: I don't know whether it's nice . . .

CATHIANNE: It's a gorgeous beard.

DANNY: Well, thank you, uh, listen. I'm gonna, uh, be in the city next Tuesday and I was, y'know, wondering if we could sorta, y'know, get together for lunch?

CATHIANNE: How 'bout dinner?

DANNY: Dinner? Dinner! Dinner's a better idea. You could pick your favorite restaurant and . . .

CATHIANNE: How bout my place? I'm my favorite cook.

DANNY: Uh, your place. Right. Sure. That's great to me.

CATHIANNE: Me too. It'll be fun.

DANNY: Yeah . . . listen. I'll bring the wine.

CATHIANNE: Perfect. I'll drink it.

BOTH: (LAUGH)

DANNY: Well, OK, then, I guess it's a date. I'll see you Tuesday.

CATHIANNE: Tuesday. Great.

DANNY: Actually, I just, uh, I called to see how you were and y'know, Tuesday sounds fine!

SOUND: PHONE HANGS UP

(YELLING) Tuesday . . . AHHHA . . . she's gonna see me Tuesday.

(FADE)

SUNG: *REACH OUT, REACH OUT AND TOUCH SOMEONE*

AGENCY: Cunningham & Walsh, Inc.
CLIENT: Schieffelin & Co.
LENGTH: 60 Seconds

ANNCR: Once again, Stiller and Meara for Blue Nun.

ANNE: Hello, I'm Frieda Beidermyer, your interior decorator.

JERRY: Oh, yes, come in. This is my apartment.

ANNE: Don't apologize.

JERRY: Huh?

ANNE: They didn't tell me you were color-blind. Plaid windows?

JERRY: I want decor that makes a statement about me, that exudes confidence, savoya fair. Where do we begin?

ANNE: The Last Chance Thrift Shop. Everything's gotta go.

JERRY: Everything?

ANNE: Everything.

JERRY: These are mementos my parents brought back from their honeymoon.

ANNE: They honeymooned in Tijuana?

JERRY: You noticed the terra-cotta donkey?

ANNE: I noticed. Out.

JERRY: So, where do we start?

ANNE: We start with a little Blue Nun.

JERRY: I want my apartment converted, not me.

ANNE: No, Blue Nun white wine. It'll lend you some style.

JERRY: I never tried Blue Nun.

ANNE: You have so much to learn, my naive nudnick. Blue Nun tastes terrific.

JERRY: I *want* good taste.

ANNE: That's why you can get Blue Nun by the glass or by the bottle at swank bars and restaurants.

JERRY: Gee, style, confidence, and taste. Will Blue Nun do all that for me?

ANNE: It's a bottle of wine, honey, not a miracle worker.

ANNCR: By the glass or by the bottle, there's a lot of good taste in Blue Nun. Imported by Schieffelin (SHIFF-uh-lin) & Company, New York.

CREATION AND
PRODUCTION: Chuck Blore & Don Richman, Inc.
     CLIENT: Campbell Soup
    LENGTH: 30 seconds

DON: You're eating chunky chicken soup with a fork?

JOHN: Well, you've got to spear the chicken to get it into your mouth. Look at that. Look at the size of that. You gotta use a spoon for the noodles.

DON: You got some noodles on your fork.

JOHN: Yeah, but they slide through.

DON: Well, you use the spoon, you use the fork.

JOHN: That's right.

DON: Is chunky chicken a soup or a meal?

JOHN: I leave that up to the experts, but I personally . . .

DON: (OVER LAUGH) Why'd you say that?

JOHN: I know, but I mean, you know, I'm not a connoisseur in the food department but I would say it's a meal.

DON: But it's a soup.

JOHN: It's a meal within a soup can. Let's put it that way.

DON: Campbell's Chunky Chicken . . . it's the soup that eats like a meal.

Character Voices and Accents

No suggestions on how to affect accents or develop unusual character voices are given because written instructions are of little help. Audio recordings of professional announcers performing all sorts of character roles are available on the Internet and may be obtained through a program such as RealAudio. Some audiovisual departments and learning resource centers have recorded performances that may guide your efforts.

As you work with these scripts, make recordings and listen critically to the results. *If you aren't truly outstanding at doing a particular voice, abandon it in favor of others you can do with authority.*

The Pitch "Artist"

The commercial that follows is an example of a type of commercial that is, fortunately, rarely heard. Nevertheless, it will afford you an opportunity to see if you can perform it in sixty seconds without slurring or stumbling. The commercial contains 221 words.

AGENCY: Client's Copy
CLIENT: Compesi's Meat Locker
LENGTH: 60 Seconds

ANNCR: How would you like to save dollars, while serving your family the best in beef, pork, chicken, and lamb? Sounds impossible? Well, it isn't, if you own a home freezer and buy your meats wholesale at Compesi's Meat Locker. Hundreds of families have discovered that it actually costs less to serve prime rib, steaks, and chops than it does to scrimp along on bargain hamburger and tough cuts. The secret? Buy your meat in quantity from Compesi's. Imagine—one hundred pounds of prime beef steaks and roasts for less than $3.00 a pound! Save even more by purchasing a quarter of a side. With every side of beef, Compesi's throws in twenty pounds of chicken, ten pounds of bacon, and a leg of spring lamb—absolutely free! If you don't own a freezer, Compesi's will get you started in style. Buy any of their 300-pound freezers, and Compesi's will give you a freezer full of frozen food free! Meat, vegetables, even frozen gourmet casseroles, all free with the purchase of a new freezer. Prices for freezers start at $299, and terms can be arranged. Beat the high cost of living! Come into Compesi's and see which plan is best for your family. Compesi's has two locations—in the Lakeport Shopping Center, and downtown at 1338 Fifth Street.

Low-Pitched Voice

IN-HOUSE: KGO-TV
TITLE: 3:30 Movie, Creepy Creature Tease
MUSIC: "THE DAY TIME ENDED"

ANNCR: (STING ON "NIGHT") Hello. Afraid of those creepy things that go bump in the night? Well, I wouldn't watch Channel 7's "3:30 Movie," because we've got a whole week of creepy creatures.

SFX: LOUD FROG

Monday, it's Ray Milland and his giant (SFX) *Frogs.* (SLIGHT PAUSE) Tuesday, Hank Fonda is all wrapped up in *Tentacles.*

SFX: MALE SCREAM

Wednesday, it's back to those old days, with prehistoric creatures in *The People Time Forgot.*

SFX: ELEPHANT TRUMPET, BACKWARD

Thursday, little gnomes (NOMES) are after a luscious young wife in *Don't Be Afraid of the Dark,* (**SFX:** WOLF HOWL) Finally, Friday—if you haven't had enough—it's a submarine full of snakes in *Fer-de-Lance.* Creepy Creatures starts Monday on Channel 7's "3:30 Movie."

SFX: WOLF HOWL

High-Pitched Voice

AGENCY: Annette Lai Creative Services
CLIENT: Allison's Pet Center
LENGTH: 60 seconds
MUSIC: INSTRUMENTAL VERSION OF "RUDOLPH, THE RED-NOSED REINDEER" UP AND UNDER TO CLOSE

ANNCR: (HIGH PITCHED AND ELFLIKE) Hi! I'm Herman, one of Santa's helpers. Rudolph would have been here, too, but he's getting the light bulb in his nose replaced right now. We're inviting you to Allison's Pet Center for their annual and spectacular Christmas sale! Every year, kids send letters to Santa asking for puppies and kittens, monkeys and mice—and, to top it off, some ask for aquariums, too! Can you imagine what the back of Santa's sleigh looks like? Come on, give Santa a break! I don't want to baby-sit all those animals and fishes until Christmas Eve—I want to go back to building dollhouses! Come to Allison's, and save on household pets and presents for your pets. Get a head start on your Christmas shopping. The sale starts on Saturday and runs through Christmas Eve. Allison's is located at the corner of Fulton and North Streets, in Petaluma. And, a Meow-y Christmas and a Happy New Year from Allison's Pet Center!

British Accent (Oxford)

AGENCY: Ammirati & Puris, Inc.
CLIENT: Schweppes Mixers
LENGTH: 60 seconds

SFX: WINTER SOUNDS (RAIN, SLUSH, ETC.)

BRITISH VO: Leave it to American ingenuity to take a rather bleak time of year and transform it into a season full of quaint but cheerful holiday traditions.

SFX: HOLIDAY MUSIC

And leave it to British ingenuity to impart a rare sparkle to these festivities—Schweppes.

For example, when feasting until immobilized on an oversized bird, Schweppes Club Soda, bursting with Schweppervescence, makes a lively dinner companion. Your ritual of cramming as many people as possible into a department store elevator, meanwhile, inspires a thirst only Schweppes Ginger Ale with real Jamaican ginger can quench. And while transfixed to the telly watching a group of massive, helmeted chaps smash into one another, what could be more civilized than Schweppes Tonic Water with essence of lime and Seville oranges? And while many of your holiday traditions seem quite curious to us, we certainly toast their spirit. And suggest you do the same, with the purchase of Schweppes. The Great British Bubbly.

Transylvanian Accent

AGENCY: Scott Singer
CLIENT: Partytime Novelties
LENGTH: 30 seconds

ANNCR: (SCARY MUSIC) (BELA LUGOSI IMITATION) Good evening. You are probably expecting me to say that my name is Count Dracula, and that I am a vampire. Do you know what makes a vampire? Do you really? It's not the hair—bah! greasy kid's stuff! It's not the cape, made from your sister's satin bedsheets. No! It's the fangs that make the vampire. Now, you too can have the fangs. Dress up for parties—frighten the trick-or-treaters on Halloween. These plastic marvels fit over your regular teeth, but once there—you'll be the hit of the party. Amaze and delight your ghoul friend. It is so much fun! I know. So, send for your fangs today. Send $2.98 to FANG, Box 1001, Central City, Tennessee. Or dial toll-free: 800–DRA–CULA. Order before midnight tonight. That's an order!

Spanish Pronunciation

AGENCY: Smith and Steiner, Advertising
CLIENT: Su Casa
LENGTH: 60 seconds

MUSIC: MEXICAN HARP, UPBEAT TEMPO, IN AND UNDER TO CLOSE

ANNCR: Ole, Amigos! (oh-LAY ah-MEE-gos) Su Casa (soo-KAH-sah) means
"your home," and that's how Ramona wants you to feel when you
visit her at San Antonio's most elegant Mexican restaurant, Su Casa.
Ramona features the most popular dishes from Mexico, including
enchiladas verdes or rancheros (en-chil-AH-das VEHR-days or
rahn-CHAIR-ohs), chile con queso (CHEE-lay kahn KAY-so), and
chimichangos (chee-mee-CHANG-gos). But, Ramona also has special
family recipes that you won't find anywhere else. Try pescado en
concha (pess-KAH-do en COHN-chah), chunks of sole in rich cream
and cheddar cheese sauce, served in scallop shells. Or scallops La
Jolla (lah-HOY-uh), prepared with wine, lemon juice, and three kinds
of cheeses. Or baked swordfish manzanillo (mahn-zah-NEE-oh). See
Ramona today, where her home is *your home. Su Casa!*

German Accent

The two award-winning commercials that follow feature Dieter (DEET-
er), a German, imported-car salesman. These commercials were impro-
vised, so the scripts were actually typed after the fact.[5]

---

[5]The following two Lincoln-Mercury commercials were supplied by their creators, John
Crawford of John Crawford Radio and Gene Chaput of Young & Rubicam.

AGENCY: Young & Rubicam
CLIENT: Lincoln-Mercury Dealers
LENGTH: 60 seconds
TITLE: "Dieter 5"

DIETER: Pull over and help me, please, my car is . . .

WEAVER: Hi, Dieter.

DIETER: Hello, Mr. Weaver.

WEAVER: Having a little trouble with that fine European sedan, huh?

DIETER: Having a little lunch.

WEAVER: Yeah, the hood's up.

DIETER: Heating my bratwurst on the engine block.

WEAVER: It must be done; it's smoking.

DIETER: It's smoked bratwurst.

WEAVER: Hmm, some kind of hot purple liquid's dripping out of there.

DIETER: Smoked fruit punch.

WEAVER: Uh huh, you know I haven't had any trouble since I traded in that car you sold me for this Mercury Cougar, Dieter.

DIETER: Mercury Cougar, it's a very fine car.

WEAVER: Oh, it's a lovely car, Dieter.

DIETER: Could you give me a ride in the Mercury Cougar to the mechanical?

WEAVER: Oh, I want to give you more than a ride, Dieter. I want to give you a push.

DIETER: I don't want a push.

WEAVER: Get in the car, Dieter.

DIETER: My car is moving.

WEAVER: Turn the flashers on. I want people to see this.

DIETER: Let me get in there.

WEAVER: Clear the way.

DIETER: (LOUDLY OUT THE CAR WINDOW) He's not pushing me; I'm pulling him!

ANNCR: The Mercury Cougar. Compare the performance with luxury European imports. Compare the styling with the luxury European imports. Even before you compare the price.

WEAVER: Okay, Dieter, you're on your own.

DIETER: Wait, this isn't a service station; it's a Lincoln-Mercury dealership.

WEAVER: Think about it, Dieter.

ANNCR: The Mercury Cougar. See your Lincoln-Mercury dealer today, at the sign of the cat.

AGENCY: Young & Rubicam
CLIENT: Lincoln-Mercury Dealers
LENGTH: 30 seconds
TITLE: "Dieter/Law"

DIETER: Mr. Weaver. I have something for you.

WEAVER: What is this, Dieter, a flyer? Are you having a sale?

DIETER: It's a subpoena. I'm suing you.

WEAVER: Suing me? For what?

DIETER: I'm no longer just Dieter Eidotter, car salesman. You're dealing with Dieter Eidotter, third week law student.

WEAVER: What is this? "Defamation of car"?

DIETER: You told people that Mercury Cougar was better looking than the car I sell.

WEAVER: It's a fact.

DIETER: It's an opinion.

WEAVER: "Alienation of affection?"

DIETER: Well, the people who found out that the Mercury Cougar costs one-half as much as the car I sell don't come into the showroom anymore.

WEAVER: You're blowing more smoke than one of those diesels you sell.

DIETER: Oh, now you're into the murky legal area of libel, and slander, and torts.

WEAVER: What's a tort?

DIETER: Well, right now, it's a chocolate cake. But when I find out what it is . . .

WEAVER: You're not even a real lawyer. I don't have to put up with this. Here is what I think of this thing, right back at you!

DIETER: This could be second-degree littering, Mister.

ANNCR: The Mercury advantage. Compared to the imports, Mercury gives you more style, more features, more for your money. See your Lincoln-Mercury dealer.

Public-Service Announcements (PSAs)

The first two sets of PSA campaigns, "Child Abuse" and "Buy Recycled," were created by advertising agencies as *pro bono* contributions to the National Committee to Prevent Child Abuse and to the Environmental Defense Fund. These and many other PSA campaigns are coordinated, produced, and distributed by the Advertising Council, a private, non-profit organization of volunteers. Since 1942, the Ad Council has been the leading producer of public service advertising in the United States. In 1996, it generated more than $700 million worth of free advertising time.

The Advertising Council, Inc.
CHILD ABUSE PREVENTION CAMPAIGN
For: National Committee to Prevent Child Abuse
:30 LIVE RADIO COPY—"Before It Starts"

For years, child abuse has been a problem to which there were few
answers. But now, there's an innovative new program that can help
stop the abuse before it starts. A program that reaches new parents
early on, teaching them to cope with the stresses that lead to
abuse. It's already achieving unprecedented results. To learn how
you can help where you live, call 1–800–CHILDREN. Because the
more you help, the less they hurt. Call 1–800–CHILDREN today. A
public-service message from the National Committee to Prevent
Child Abuse and the Ad Council.

CHILD ABUSE PREVENTION CAMPAIGN
"Testimony" :30
MUSIC UNDER ENTIRE SPOT

WOMAN: I first met Jane right after Jonah was born.

ANNCR: Now there's a revolutionary new approach to stopping child abuse
before it can start.

WOMAN: She said it was normal for new mothers to get frustrated. She
taught me when to take a minute for myself.

ANNCR: By reaching new families early on, this program teaches them how to cope with the stresses that lead to abuse. But we need your help where you live. Call 1–800–CHILDREN, 1–800–CHILDREN.

A public-service announcement brought to you by the National Committee to Prevent Child Abuse and the Ad Council.

The Advertising Council, Inc.
BUY RECYCLED CAMPAIGN—for the Environmental
Defense Fund[6]
"Circle" :60

ANNCR: Hi, I'm Joanne Woodward. Ever notice how many things in life happen in a circle? The seasons. Revolving credit. Hula hoops. The spinning of the circle we call Earth. And recycling. Together we've already made a difference. Sorting—glass, plastic. Separating cans. Stacking newspapers. Now, there are lots of products made from things we've already recycled. A paper clip? In a more daring life, a '56 convertible. A cereal box? Once your Sunday paper. It all goes back to the circle. It starts when we recycle trash at home and at work. It's completed when we buy products made from recycled materials. How do you know the difference? Check the label for something called Post-Consumer Recycled Content. Then buy the

---

[6]As indicated, this spot was voiced by actress Joanne Woodward. When performing this PSA, you may, of course, substitute your own name. Ms. Woodward is one of many performers who has contributed time and talent to causes she supports.

highest percentage of it you can find. You'll save a tree, you'll save energy, and in your own way, you'll help save the world. Complete the circle.

ANNCR: For your free BUY RECYCLED SHOPPING GUIDE, call 1–800–CALL–EDF. Brought to You by the Ad Council and EDF, the Environmental Defense Fund.

CLIENT: Amigos de las Americas
LENGTH: 60 seconds

ANNCR: Are you a teenager, sixteen years or older? Are you looking for the adventure of a lifetime? Why not check out Amigos de las Americas? Amigos is a nonprofit organization, with chapters in cities all over America. Amigos spend the school year studying Spanish and paramedic work, and spend the summer working in a Latin American country. What do Amigos do? Well, last year Amigos administered over 230,000 dental treatments to 60,000 children. They gave over 90,000 immunizations for polio and other diseases. And, they tested over 22,000 people for tuberculosis. Amigos work in rural areas and big city slums. They are not on vacation. Assignments in Panama, Ecuador, Paraguay, and the Dominican Republic, among others, call for dedicated, caring young people. If you think Amigos is for you, write for information.

The address is: 5618 Star Lane, Houston, Texas 77057. Or, use the

toll-free number: 1–800–555–7796. Amigos!

Television Commercials

Only a handful of television commercials are provided here. Nearly all television commercials, whether produced by large advertising agencies or small market stations, require special effects, animation, or elaborate sets, which generally are unavailable to students. Computerized digital-effects equipment manipulates images in a number of dazzling ways, and announcers, aside from those in dramatized sketches, are limited most often to voice-over delivery. In many commercials, an announcer may be seen briefly at the outset, and then performs as an unseen voice-over narrator. To practice television commercial delivery, you may want to adapt some of the radio commercials for direct, on-camera presentation.

AGENCY: Ketchum Advertising
CLIENT: Safeway Stores, Inc.
LENGTH: 30 seconds

VIDEO	AUDIO
OPEN ON SAFEWAY LOGO. MOVE IN UNTIL ENTIRE SCREEN IS RED. DISS[7] TO WHEEL OF WISCONSIN CHEDDAR WITH CRACKERS ON TOP AND PIECE OF BUNTING ON SIDE.	SFX: MUSIC UNDER. MALE VO: Safeway's international cheese experts invite your taste buds and your taste budget to enjoy some of the world's finest cheeses. So we

---

[7]DISS is an abbreviation for *dissolve*; "dissolve to" means to replace one picture with another.

DISS TO LARGE SLICE OF DUTCH
GOUDA WITH DUTCH FLAG.

feature them at low Safeway
prices.

DISS TO SLICES OF HAVARTI
AND CRACKERS WITH HAVARTI
ON THEM. DANISH FLAG IS
STUCK IN ONE SLICE OF CHEESE.

A deliciously economical world

DISS TO SLICE OF JARLSBERG
ON CUTTING BOARD, WHEEL OF
JARLSBERG IS IN BACKGROUND.
WOMAN'S HAND PLACES
NORWEGIAN FLAG ON SLICE OF
JARLSBERG.

taste tour that you can enjoy
now.

DISS TO SQUARE OF SWISS
CHEESE WITH SWISS FLAG.
SMALL PIECES OF CHEESE ARE
ON CUTTING BOARD.

Quality world cheeses. Low
Safeway prices. No passport
required: just an appetite.

WOMAN'S HAND LIFTS PIECE OF
CHEESE.

SFX: MUSIC ENDS.

DISS TO CU MAN BEING FED
SWISS CHEESE BY WOMAN'S
HAND.

MAN: Mmmmm.

DISS TO SAFEWAY LOGO.

LOGO: Safeway. Everything you
want from a store and a little
bit more.

AGENCY: Backer & Spielvogel, Inc.
CLIENT: Quaker
PRODUCT: Celeste Pizza
LENGTH: 30 seconds

SUPER: Guiseppe Celeste (Fictitious Little Brother)

GUISEPPE: I need your help. My big sister, Mama Celeste, she make a great crust for her pizza. But was Guiseppe's idea. I say, "Mama, you make perfect sauce, perfect toppings, make a perfect crust." She do it. But I think it. So my picture should be on the box, too, no? Which you like? (HOLDS UP PICTURES) Happy—"Hey, I think of great crust!"? Or serious—"Yes, I think of great crust"? Or it could be bigger? (HOLDS UP HUGE PICTURE)

ANNCR VO: Celeste Pizza. Delicious crust makes it great from top to bottom.

CLIENT: Herald Sewing Machines
TITLE: Preholiday Sale
LENGTH: 60 seconds

VIDEO	AUDIO
OPEN ON SHOT OF ANNCR SEATED BEHIND SEWING MACHINE CONSOLE. ZOOM IN ON MACHINE, AND FOLLOW	ANNCR: This is the famous Herald sewing machine. Notice the free arm, perfectly designed to allow you to sew

SEQUENCE OF SHOTS INDICATED BY ANNCR.	sleeves, cuffs, and hems. Note, too, the stitch regulator dial.
ANNCR DEMONSTRATES THE REGULATOR DIAL.	You move easily and instantly to stretch stitch, embroider, or zigzag stitches.
	The Herald has a drop feed for darning, appliquéing, and monogramming.
ANNCR DEMONSTRATES.	This advanced machine has a self-stop bobbin winder. Other standard features include a built-in light, a thread tension dial, and a snap-on extension dial for flat-bed sewing.
ZOOM BACK TO MEDIUM SHOT OF ANNCR AND MACHINE.	Yes, there isn't a better or more versatile sewing machine available today.
ANNCR STANDS, AND WALKS AROUND MACHINE AND TOWARD CAMERA.	But, I've saved the best for last. The Herald Star model sewing machine is now on sale at dealers everywhere. The Star, the most advanced model Herald makes,

ANNCR HOLDS UP SALE SIGN, WITH $349 CROSSED OUT AND $299 WRITTEN IN.	is regularly priced at three hundred and forty-nine dollars. During this month, you can buy the Star for only two hundred ninety-nine dollars—a savings of fifty dollars. You can't beat a deal like this, so visit your Herald dealer soon, while you still have your choice of color. Check the Yellow Pages for the dealers in your area.

AGENCY: In-house
CLIENT: Madera Foods
LENGTH: 60 seconds

VIDEO	AUDIO
OPEN ON ANNCR STANDING BEFORE CHECKOUT STAND.	ANNCR: I'm here at Madera Foods checking up on the specials you'll find here this weekend.
CUT TO PRODUCE SECTION. ANNCR WALKS INTO FRAME.	There are excellent buys this weekend in fresh fruits and

ANNCR PICKS UP A GRAPEFRUIT.	vegetables. Like extra fancy Indian River ruby red grapefruit, three for ninety-nine cents. Or
ANNCR POINTS TO LETTUCE.	iceberg lettuce, two heads for seventy-nine cents. And, don't overlook the relishes—green onions or radishes, two bunches for twenty-nine cents.
CUT TO MEAT DEPARTMENT. ANNCR WALKS INTO FRAME.	Meat specials include rib roast at two sixty-nine a pound, all lean center cut pork chops at two seventy-nine a pound, and lean ground chuck at only one thirty-nine a pound.
CUT BACK TO CHECKOUT STAND.	And, here I am, back at the checkout stand. Here's where you'll really come to appreciate Madera Foods. Their low, low prices add up to a total bill that
CUT TO ANNCR OUTSIDE FRONT ENTRANCE.	winds down the cost of living. So, pay a visit to Madera Foods this weekend. Specials are

<table>
<tr><td></td><td>offered from Friday opening to closing on Sunday night. Madera Foods is located in the Madera Plaza Shopping Center. Hours are from 9:00 A.M. 'till 10:00 P.M., seven days a week.</td></tr>
<tr><td>DISS TO MADERA FOODS LOGO SLIDE. HOLD UNTIL CLOSE.</td><td>See you at Madera Foods.</td></tr>
</table>

AGENCY: Sherman Associates, Inc.
CLIENT: Bayview Health Club
LENGTH: 60 seconds

VIDEO	**AUDIO**
OPEN ON MCU OF TALENT.	Get ready! Swimsuit season is almost here! Now is the time to shed those excess pounds and achieve the body you know is hidden somewhere within you.
ZOOM OUT TO MEDIUM SHOT.	The Bayview Health Club will help you find the possible you. Bayview is a complete fitness

CUT TO STILL PHOTOS OF EACH FEATURE AS IT IS MENTIONED.	club. We offer day and evening classes in weight training, aerobic and jazzercise dance, full Nautilus equipment, tanning, Jacuzzi, and sauna facilities.
CUT TO MCU OF TALENT.	In addition, we sponsor weight reduction clinics, jogging and running programs, and health
CUT TO MCU OF TALENT.	and beauty seminars, with a supportive staff to coach you in every facet of personal health care. Bayview is tailored for you—the modern man or woman—and, for this month only, we're offering new members an introductory price to join: Just half price! That's right, a 50 percent reduction during the month of April.
CUT TO MCU OF TALENT.	So, call now for a tour of our facilities. Meet the staff, and chat with satisfied members.

MATTE IN ADDRESS AND PHONE NUMBER.

Bayview Health Club, in downtown Portland. Join now. Don't lose time—instead, lose that waist, with a 50 percent reduction in membership costs. Find the hidden you, and be ready for the beach! Bayview Health Club: we're ready when you are!

APPENDIX B

Phonetic Transcription

AS AN ANNOUNCER, YOU FACE UNIQUE AND CHALLENGING PROBLEMS IN pronunciation. In reading news, commercials, and Classical-music copy, frequently you'll encounter words of foreign origin, and you'll be expected to read them fluently and correctly. As a newscaster, you'll be expected not only to pronounce foreign words and names with accuracy and authority but also to know when and how to Americanize many of them. Although British announcers are allowed to Anglicize categorically, you would be seen as odd or incompetent if you said *don KWIKS-oat* for *Don Quixote* or *don JEW-un* for *Don Juan,* as they do.

Because English pronunciation is subject to few general rules, English is one of the most difficult languages to learn. In Spanish the letters *ch* are always pronounced as in the name *Charles*; in American English *ch* may be pronounced in the following ways:

sh as in *Cheyenne*

tch as in *champion*

k as in *chemist*

two separate sounds, as in the name *MacHeath*

There are many other examples. In the sentence "I usually used to use this," the letter *s* is sounded differently in the words *usually, used,* and *use.* The letter *a* is pronounced differently in the words *cap, father, mate, care, call, boat,* and *about.* Similar variations are seen for all other vowel sounds and most consonants as well. For example, *th* is pronounced differently in *Thomas, thought,* and *then; r* is pronounced differently in *run, fire,* and *boor.* Letters may at times be silent, as in *mnemonic, Worcester,* and *Wednesday.* At other times, and for no logical reason, a word is pronounced correctly only when all letters in it receive some value, as in *misunderstood* and *circumstances.* The letters *ie* are sometimes pronounced "eye," as in *pie,* and sometimes "*ee,*" as in *piece.* Two words with almost identical spellings, such as *said* and *maid,* can have quite different pronunciations. In short, the only constant in spoken American English is variation.

The whole problem of English pronunciation was reduced to its most obvious absurdity by George Bernard Shaw, who wrote *ghoti* and asked how this manufactured word was to be pronounced. After all attempts had failed, Shaw revealed that it was to be pronounced "fish": the *gh* to be pronounced "f" as in *enough,* the *o* to be pronounced "ih" as in *women,* and the *ti* to be pronounced "sh" as in *motion.*

Of course, common words don't cause pronunciation problems. But try to determine the correct pronunciation of the following words—some quite familiar, others less so—according to your knowledge of language and any rules of pronunciation you may have learned:

quay	flaccid
dais	mortgage
interstices	gunwale
medieval	forecastle
brooch	egregious
cliché	phthisic

Now look up the correct pronunciation of these words in any standard dictionary. After checking the pronunciation, you'll agree certainly that no amount of puzzling over them, and no rules of pronunciation, would have helped.

Correct American and Canadian pronunciation of English not only is inherently illogical but also changes with time and common usage, generally tending toward simpler forms. It is becoming more and more acceptable, for example, to pronounce *clothes* as KLOZ, to leave the first *r* out of *February,* and to slide over the slight "y" sound in *news* so that it becomes NOOZ.

If you have difficulty pronouncing words whose spelling offers little help, you may be perplexed doubly by American personal names and place names that are derived from foreign originals. As a sportscaster, for example, you cannot assume that a player named Braun gives his own name the correct German pronunciation, "Brown," but he may pronounce it "Brawn" or "Brahn." If, as a sportcaster, you tried to pronounce every foreign-derived name as it would be pronounced in the country of origin, your audience would wince every time you failed to use the established pronunciation.

American place names present the same problem. In Nebraska, *Beatrice* is pronounced bee-AT-riss. In South Dakota, *Pierre* is pronounced PEER. In California, *Delano* is pronounced duh-LAY-no. In Kentucky, *Versailles* is pronounced ver-SALES. In Georgia, *Vienna* is pronounced vy-EN-uh. In the Southwest, Spanish place names are pronounced conventionally neither as the Spanish original nor as they seem to be spelled. For example, in California, the *San* in *San Jose* is pronounced as in *sand* rather than as Spanish speakers would pronounce it (as in *sonnet*), and ho-ZAY is used rather than the Americanized jo-ZAY or the Spanish ho-SAY.

Because the only standard for pronouncing place names is the common practice of the natives of the region, you must be on guard to avoid error. All American and Canadian communities have special and capricious ways of pronouncing the names of streets, suburbs, nearby towns, and geographic landmarks. Radio and television announcers who are new to an area and offend listeners consistently with mispronunciations may not be around long enough to learn regional preferences. Los Angelenos pronounce *Cahuenga* as kuh-WENG-uh, and in San Francisco, *Gough* Street is pronounced GOFF. In Arkansas, *Nevada* County is pronounced nuh-VAY-duh. In Georgia, *Taliaferro* County is pronounced TAHL-uh-ver. Bostonians may not care if you mispronounce *Pago Pago* (correctly pronounced PAHNG-go PAHNG-go), but they will be annoyed if you pronounce *Quincy* as KWIN-see rather than KWINZ-ee.

It's not surprising that the problems inherent in the pronunciation of American English have given rise to various systems of phonetic transcription. Two of these systems are outlined here, and the third—the International Phonetic Alphabet—is discussed at length.

Wire-Service Phonetics

Several news agencies provide radio and television stations with news stories, sending the stories via satellite and telephone lines to computer terminals. When a word or a name that might cause pronunciation problems is transmitted, that word often is phoneticized—given a **pronouncer**—as in the following example.

(Sydney, Australia) The island nation of Vanuatu (Vahn-oo-AH-too)—formerly the New Herbrides (HEB-rih-deez)—was hit today by a strong earthquake.

Pronouncers are useful, but you shouldn't rely on them completely. They're sometimes ambiguous and occasionally inaccurate. A few sounds defy accurate transcription. Wherever possible, check pronunciations in dictionaries, atlases, or other appropriate sources.

All of the symbols of wire-service phonetics appear in Table B.1, arranged in the same order in which they appear in the International Phonetic Alphabet. (Because we are dealing with speech sounds, alphabetic arrangement has no relevance.) Key words have been chosen for clarity; therefore, most are commonplace. Two symbols are sometimes given for a single sound. For example, for the second vowel sound listed, I, works well for the word *impel*, but IH works better for *bituminous*. If this word were transcribed as bi-TOO-muh-nus instead of bih-TOO-muh-nus, a reader might pronounce the first syllable as the English word *by*.

| TABLE B.1 | SYMBOLS OF WIRE-SERVICE PHONETICS |

Symbol	Key Word	Phonetic Transcription
Vowels		
EE	*believe*	(bih-LEEV)
I or IH	*impel, bituminous*	(im-PELL), (bih-TOO-muh-nus)
AY	*bait*	(BAYT)
E or EH	*pester, beret*	(PEST-er), (beh-RAY)
A	*can*	(KAN)
AH	*comma*	(KAH-muh)
AW	*lost*	(LAWST)
O	*host*	(HOST)
OO	*Moorhead*	(MOOR-hed)
OO	*pool*	(POOL)
ER	*early*	(ER-lee)
UH	*sofa*	(SO-fuh)
Diphthongs		
Y	*lighting*	(LYT-ing)
AU	*grouse*	(GRAUSS)

TABLE B.1	SYMBOLS OF WIRE-SERVICE PHONETICS (*Cont.*)

Symbol	Key Word	Phonetic Transcription
OY	*oiling*	(OY-ling)
YU	*using*	(YUZ-ing)
Consonants*		
TH	*think*	(THINGK)
TH	*then*	(THEN)
SH	*clash*	(KLASH)
ZH	*measure*	(MEZH-er)
CH	*church*	(CHERCH)
J	*adjust*	(uh-JUST)
NG	*singing*	(SING-ing)
Y	*yeoman*	(YO-mun)

*The consonants P, B, T, D, K, G, F, V, S, Z, H, M, N, L, W, and R are pronounced as in English and therefore are not listed. The symbol G is always as in *green*, never as in *Gene*.

With a little practice—and some ingenuity—you can make wire-service phonetics into a useful tool. The consonants are easiest to learn because most of them represent only one sound; the symbols T, D, S, Z, and M, for instance, can hardly cause confusion. Other consonant sounds need two letters to represent them: for example, TH (THIN), CH (CHAT), and SH (SHOP). One symbol, Y, is used for two sounds: one a consonant and the other a diphthong. As a consonant, it appears in the word *yeoman* (YO-mun); as a diphthong, it represents an entirely different sound, as in *sleight* (SLYT). The symbol TH is the most troublesome, for it represents the initial sounds in *think* and *then*. Context can help in some instances, but not all. It works for *hearth* (HAHRTH), but not *calisthenics*. Anyone seeing KAL-is-THEN-iks might read THEN as the common English word, and this is not the correct sound.

Some vowel sounds are a bit troublesome, but they can be differentiated usually by their contexts. The letters OO, for example, stand for vowel sounds in *food* and *poor*, which are not, of course, the same. Here is how context can help distinguish between them:

buoy (BOO-ee)   boorish (BOOR-ish)

In these examples, the words *boo* and *boor* tell which sound to give OO.

It is not for common words that wire-service phonetics were developed. Here are some typical words that might be given pronouncers by a wire service:

Beirut (bay-ROOT)	Sidon (SYD-un)
Bayreuth (BY-royt)	Coelho (KWAY-lo)
Clio (KLY-oh)	Ojai (O-hy)
Schuylkill (SKUHL-kill)	Yosemite (yo-SEM-ih-tee)
Faneuil (FAN-uhl)	Hamtramck (ham-TRAM-ik)

Obviously, your use of such phonetic transcription will be reserved for the few names and words in your copy that require you to turn to a dictionary, gazetteer, or similar reference work. Table B.2 offers suggested sources for correct pronunciations in several different problem categories.

TABLE B.2   SOURCES FOR CORRECT PRONUNCIATION OF PERSONAL NAMES AND PLACE NAMES

Category	Source
Names of persons	The individual featured in the story; failing that, members of the family or associates
Foreign names	Appropriate embassy or consulate
Foreign place names	*American Heritage Dictionary*
State or regional place names	State or regional historical societies or the state police or highway patrol
Names of members of legislatures	Clerk of the legislature

At times you'll have to read a news story for which no pronouncers are given. When time permits, you should look up difficult or unfamiliar words in a dictionary, and do your own transcribing of them as in this example—done easily and quickly on a word processor:

(Nashville, Tennessee) Medical researchers today revealed a study showing that as few as two cups of coffee can cut the blood flow to your brain by 10 to 20 percent. Dr. William Wilson, assistant professor of psychiatry at Vanderbilt

University, and co-author of the study, said: "While the blood-flow reduction does not seem severe enough to cause problems in normal individuals, it is unclear whether it may increase the risk of transient ischemic (iz-KEE-mik) attacks and cerebral infarctions (seh-REE-bruhl in-FAHRK-shunz) in high-risk individuals or those recovering from cerebrovascular (seh-REE-bro-VAS-kyu-ler) accidents." Caffeine could also magnify the effects of certain drugs, such as the diet drug phenylpropanolamine (FEN-uhl-pro-pan-OHL-uh-meen), which already contains caffeine.

Wire-service phonetics work well in this example, but there are times when the system will not work. There is simply no foolproof way to use the twenty-six letters of the English language to represent more than forty speech sounds. Furthermore, the wire-service system doesn't include symbols for most foreign speech sounds that don't occur in English. Until a few years ago, teletype machines were limited to the same symbols found on an ordinary typewriter. Today's computers, however, could be programmed to reproduce any symbol desired, so the time may come when additional pronunciation symbols will be added to the twenty-six letters now in use. A good starting point would be to add these symbols from the International Phonetic Alphabet:

[ð] for the initial sound in *then*
[ʊ] for the vowel sound in *good*

Diacritical Marks

Dictionaries use a system of phonetic transcription that features small marks placed above the vowels a, e, i, o, and u, along with a few additional symbols for sounds such as th in *thin* and zh in *vision*. The *American Heritage Dictionary* uses these symbols:

ă	pat	ā	pay	âr	care	ä	father	oi	boy
ĕ	pet	ē	be					ou	out
ĭ	pit	ī	pie	îr	pier			hw	which
ŏ	pot	ō	toe	ô	paw				

o͝o	took	o͞o	boot
th	thin	*th*	this
ŭ	cut	ûr	urge
zh	vision		
ə	about		

Diacritical marks are not standardized completely; there are variations from dictionary to dictionary. The *American Heritage Dictionary* uses seventeen symbols to indicate the vowel sounds of the English language. *Webster's Collegiate Dictionary,* on the other hand, uses more than twenty. If you decide to use diacritical marks to indicate correct pronunciation on your scripts, it is important to adopt one system of marks and stick with it. Going from one dictionary system to another could be very confusing.

The system of phonetic transcription used in dictionaries has at least three important limitations. First, diacritical marks are rather difficult to learn and to remember. The publishers of most English-language dictionaries recognize this fact and place a guide to pronunciation on pages throughout the book. A second disadvantage is that diacritical marks were not designed for use by oral readers. The marks are small and vary only slightly in their configurations. When accuracy under pressure is demanded, diacritical marks often fail to meet the test. A final limitation of the method of transcription used in dictionaries is that the key words used may vary in pronunciation from area to area. To learn that *fog* is pronounced as *dog* may tell some Texans that "fawg" rhymes with "dawg" and a Rhode Islander that "fahg" rhymes with "dahg."

Some modern dictionary publishers have developed rather sophisticated pronunciation guides. They have eliminated some ambiguity through the use of more standardized key words. Fairly extensive discussions of pronunciation, symbols to indicate foreign speech sounds not heard in the English language, and a few symbols from more sophisticated systems of phonetic transcription have been added.

The International Phonetic Alphabet

The International Phonetic Alphabet (IPA) was devised to overcome the ambiguities of earlier systems of speech transcription. Like any other system that attempts to transcribe sounds into written symbols, it is not totally accurate. It does, however, come closer to perfection than any other system. Like diacritics, the IPA uses key words to indicate pronunciation, so if you speak with a regional accent (other than so-called standard broadcast speech), you may have difficulty making the IPA work for you.

The International Phonetic Association has assigned individual written symbols to all of the speech sounds of the major languages of the world. Whether the language is French, German, or English, the symbol [e] is always pronounced "ay" as in *bait*. Speech sounds not found in English have distinct symbols: for example, [x] represents the sound *ch* in the German word *ach,* and [y] represents the sound *u* in the French word *lune.*

The IPA is not difficult to learn, but few professional announcers use or have even heard of it. Most broadcast announcers get by with wire-service phonetics or diacritics, but those who want to excel in certain areas of news or sports announcing (international coverage or competitions) should learn and continue to practice with the IPA. Announcers at the Winter Olympics in Lillehammer, Norway, for example, were asked to pronounce the names of competitors from a great many nations, including Wang Xlulan of China, Ivar Michal Ulekleiv of Norway, Bernhard Gstrein of Austria, Mitja Kunc of Slovenia, and Eva Twardokens of the United States. It is unlikely that any announcer present knew the rules of pronunciation for all languages represented, so a good ear and an efficient system of phonetic transcription were necessities. The need for an effective system of transcription is also important for Classical-music announcers.

This appendix presents a detailed exposition of the IPA. With the help of the IPA, you can learn the principles of French, German, Spanish, and Italian pronunciation.

The IPA is a system for encoding the correct pronunciation of problem words, allowing efficient and accurate retrieval. The IPA may seem formidable at first, but it is actually easier to learn than the system of diacritical markings used in dictionaries. You will find many uses for the IPA, and if you intend to enter the field of broadcast performance, you should make a sincere effort to learn it. Because spoken language is the communication medium used by announcers, mastery of any aspect of human speech will benefit your work.

Although it is true that only a small number of professional announcers are familiar with the IPA, all would benefit from knowing and using it. Those who do not know the IPA usually follow the principles of wire-service phonetics, adding symbols of their own as necessity demands. Such a system is capable of handling most of the pronunciation problems that arise in a day's work, but it fails often enough to warrant being replaced by a more refined and accurate system.

The IPA has several advantages:

- It is an unvarying system of transcription in which one symbol represents only one speech sound.
- Every sound in any language, however subtle it may be, is given a distinctive symbol.
- Once the correct pronunciation of each sound is learned, there is almost no possibility of error because of regional dialect.
- The IPA is the most nearly perfect system of describing human speech sounds yet devised.

The IPA is used by music departments to teach lyric diction, both for English and foreign languages; speech departments use the IPA to teach dialects. Unfortunately, the IPA is seldom taught to those intending to become broadcast announcers, even though a knowledge of the IPA could spare announcers many embarrassing moments.

The *NBC Handbook of Pronunciation* (New York: Harper & Row, 1984) transcribes names of persons and places using IPA symbols. Many foreign language dictionaries and texts use the IPA to indicate correct pronunciation. *A Pronouncing Dictionary of American English,* by John S. Kenyon and Thomas Knott (Springfield, Mass.: G. & C. Merriam, 1953), transcribes exclusively into the symbols of the IPA. Both it and the *NBC Handbook of Pronunciation* are excellent sources of correct pronunciation of American and foreign place names and the names of famous composers, authors, artists, scientists, and political figures.

As is true of any system that connects speech sounds to symbols, the IPA defines each sound in terms of its use in a particular word. For example, the sound of the IPA symbol [i] is pronounced like the vowel sound of the word *bee.* This poses no problem in instances in which the key word is pronounced uniformly throughout the United States and Canada, but a distinct problem arises when there are regional variations in the pronunciation of a key word.

In learning the IPA, keep in mind that the speech sounds and the key words used in describing them are as in "Standard American" or "standard broadcast" speech. As stated in Chapter 4, deviations from this style of speaking are not substandard *unless* speech sounds are so distorted as to make comprehension a problem. While this chapter does not put forth "Standard American" as the only or best way to pronounce American English, it is necessary to use it to teach the IPA system of transcription. The system developed by the International Phonetic Association is based on speech sounds as formed by those who speak "what is vaguely called standard speech" (Kenyon and Knott, in *A Pronouncing Dictionary of American English*). The authors make it clear that "standard speech" is that spoken by most network announcers. If you live in a region of the United States or Canada where Standard American is not spoken, you may experience some difficulty in learning the IPA symbols. If, for example, you live in the southeastern United States, and you pronounce the word *bait* as most Americans pronounce *bite,* then the key words used to explain the IPA may confuse you.

Use of the IPA will be reserved for the occasional word in your copy with which you're unfamiliar. After determining pronunciation by referring to a source—one suggested in Table B.2, or by other means that work for you—you can render it into IPA symbols directly above the unfamiliar word in your script. With practice, you should be able to read your script, problem word and all, with little chance of stumbling.

Here's an illustration of how this appears on a script:

The mayor of the small North Carolina town of

[ˈkɪmbl̩tən]

Kimbolton said today that he is skeptical about reports of

flying saucers above his community.

A glance at *A Pronouncing Dictionary of American English* shows that Kimbolton is pronounced Kim-BOLT-un [kimˈboltn̩] in the Ohio community of that name, but in the town of the same name in North Carolina it is pronounced KIM-bul-tun [ˈkɪmbl̩tən]. The correct pronunciation of the name of a town may seem of slight importance to some, but to a professional announcer it is a matter of pride to be as accurate as time and resources permit.

IPA symbols represent vowel sounds, diphthongs or glides, and consonants. This appendix covers only the sounds in American speech.

Remember that IPA is used to transcribe *sounds.* Pronounce the word as you transcribe it, breaking it down into its component sounds. In transcribing the word *broken,* for example, say to yourself the first sound, "b," then add the second, making "br," then the third, forming "bro," and so on. Because one sound in a word may condition the sound that precedes or follows it, you should use an additive system, rather than one that isolates each sound from all others. Note, however, that this advice is meant for those in the early stages of learning to use the IPA. With practice and growing proficiency, you will be able to transcribe almost without conscious effort.

TABLE B.3	IPA SYMBOLS FOR THE FRONT VOWELS		
Vowel Sound	IPA Symbol	Key Word	IPA Transcription of Key Word
"ee"	[i]	*beet*	[bit]
"ih"	[ɪ]	*bit*	[bɪt]
"ay"	[e]	*bait*	[bet]
"eh"	[ɛ]	*bet*	[bɛt]
"ah"	[æ]	*bat*	[bæt]
"aah"	[a]	*bath*	[baɵ]*

*Eastern United States and British pronunciation only

Vowel Sounds

Vowel sounds are classified as front vowels and back vowels, depending on where they are formed in the mouth. The front vowels are produced through vibrations of the vocal folds in the throat and are articulated by the tongue and teeth near the front of the mouth. The back vowels are produced in the same manner but are articulated by the tongue and the opening in the rear of the mouth.

The Front Vowels. The front vowels are summarized in Table B.3. Note that [a] is pronounced "aah," as in the word *bath* as pronounced in parts of the northeastern United States. This sound is not usually heard in Standard American speech, but the symbol must be learned because it is a part of two diphthongs to be considered later.

If you pronounce each of these key words in turn, beginning at the top of the table and running to the bottom, you will find your mouth opening wider as you move from one sound to the next. As your mouth opens, your tongue is lowered and becomes increasingly relaxed.

The two front vowels [i] and [ɪ] require some elaboration. If you look in some American dictionaries, you may be surprised to discover that the final sounds of words such as *busy* and *worry* are given the pronunciation [ɪ], as in *ill*. Now there can be no doubt that in Standard American, as well as in the speech of most other sections of the country, these words have a distinct "ee" sound. Kenyon and Knott, in *A Pronouncing Dictionary of American English,* take note of this fact but indicate that minor variations in the pronunciation of this sound are too complex to pin down. Like many other American dictionaries, Kenyon and Knott's work uses the symbol [ɪ] for words in which the sound may actually be either [ɪ] or [i]. Thus they arrive at the pronunciation [ˈsɪtɪ] (SIH-tih) for *city*. Though it is doubtful that many Americans actually pronounce the word in this manner, most Americans do pronounce the final sound in the word somewhere between a distinct [ɪ] and a distinct [i].

It is worth repeating at this point that the essential purpose of IPA is to help you transcribe words whose pronunciation may be unknown to you. The examples used here and throughout this chapter are included to make the IPA clearer to you, not because of any assumption that you actually have problems pronouncing words such as *busy* or *city*.

The Back Vowels. Table B.4 presents the back vowels.[1] If you pronounce each of these vowel sounds in turn, you will find your mouth closing more and more and the sound being controlled at a progressively forward position in your mouth.

The Vowel Sounds "er" and "uh." Only two other vowel sounds remain, "er" and "uh," that cause some trouble for students of phonetics. Consider the two words *further* and *above.* In *further,* two "er" sounds appear. Pronounce this word aloud and you will detect that, because of a stress on the first syllable, the two "ers" sound slightly different. The same is true of the two "uh" sounds in *above.* Because the first syllable of this word is unstressed and the second is stressed, there is a slight but definite difference between the two sounds. The IPA makes allowances for these differences by assigning two symbols each to the "er" and "uh" sounds:

TABLE B.4	IPA SYMBOLS FOR THE BACK VOWELS		
Vowel Sound	IPA Symbol	Key Word	IPA Transcription of Key Word
"ah"	[ɑ]	*bomb*	[bɑm]
"aw"	[ɔ]	*bought*	[bɔt]
"oh"	[o]	*boat*	[bot]
"ooh"	[ʊ]	*book*	[bʊt]
"oo"	[u]	*boot*	[but]

---

[1]The English language has many words with unsounded letters, such as the final *b* in the key word *bomb* in Table B.4. You may experience an unconscious tendency to include these in phonetic transcriptions. You should remember, however, that you are transcribing *sounds,* not letters, and should disregard all letters not sounded in a word.

[ɝ] for a stressed "er," as in the *first* syllable of *further* [fɝ·ð'ɚ]

[ɚ] for an unstressed "er," as in the *second* syllable of *further* [fɝ·ðɚ]

[ʌ] for a stressed "uh," as in the *second* syllable of *above* [əbʌv]

[ə] for an unstressed "uh," as in the *first* syllable of *above* [əbʌv]

The unstressed "uh" sound is given a special symbol and name— [ə], the **schwa vowel.** Naturally, in a one-syllable word with an "uh" or an "er" sound, the sound is stressed. For this reason, in all one-syllable words, both "er" and "uh" are represented by their stressed symbols:

bird [bɝd]   church [tʃɝtʃ]   sun [sʌn]   come [kʌm]

Certain combinations of sounds may be transcribed in two ways, either of which is as accurate as the other. The word flattery, for example, may be transcribed either [ˈflætɚi] or [ˈflætəri]. The difference in the way [ɚ] and [ər] are pronounced is imperceptible to most ears.

Diphthongs. A diphthong is a combination of two vowel sounds, pronounced with a smooth glide from one sound to the other. If you say the "ow" of *how,* you will notice that it cannot be completed without moving the lips. There is no way of holding the sound of the entire diphthong;

TABLE B.5   IPA TRANSCRIPTIONS FOR AMERICAN ENGLISH DIPHTHONGS

Diphthong	Pronunciation*	Key Word	IPA Transcription of Key Word
[aɪ]	A rapid combination of the two vowels [a] and [ɪ]	*bite*	[baɪt]
[aʊ]	A rapid combination of the two vowels [a] and [ʊ]	*how*	[haʊ]
[ɔɪ]	A rapid combination of the two vowels [ɔ] and [ɪ]	*toy*	[tɔɪ]
[ju]	A rapid combination of the two vowels [j] and [u]	*using*	[juzɪŋ]
[ɪu]	A rapid combination of [ɪ] and [u]	*fuse*	[fɪuz]
[eɪ]	A glide from [e] to [ɪ]	*say*	[seɪ]

*Note the subtle difference in the sounds of the diphthongs [ju] and [ɪu].

you can hold only the last of the two vowels of which it is formed. The diphthong in *now* is actually a rapid movement from the vowel [a] to the vowel [ʊ].

The diphthongs of American English are summarized in Table B.5. Note that the vowel [e], as in *bait,* is actually a diphthong, because its pronunciation in a word such as *say* involves a glide from [e] to [ɪ]. In other instances—in the word *fate,* for example—the [e] is cropped off more closely. Because it changes according to the context, the [e] sound may be transcribed either as a pure vowel, [e], or as a diphthong, [eɪ]. It will be found both ways in various dictionaries and other works using the IPA.

Consonants

With only seven exceptions, the IPA symbols for consonant sounds are the same as the lowercase letters of the English alphabet. The consonants are therefore fairly easy to learn.

In general, consonants may be classified as either voiced or unvoiced. If you say aloud the letters *b* and *p,* adding the vowel sound "uh," to produce "buh" and "puh," you will notice that each is produced in exactly the same way, except that *b* involves **phonation** (a vibration of the vocal folds) and *p* is merely exploded air, with no phonation at all. Because most consonants are related this way, they are listed here in their voiced-unvoiced paired relationships rather than alphabetically:

[p] is exploded air with no phonation, as in *poor* [pʊr].

[b] is a phonated explosion, as in *boor* [bʊr].

[t] is exploded air with no phonation, as in *time* [taɪm].

[d] is a phonated explosion, as in *dime* [daɪm].

[k] is exploded air with no phonation, as in *kite* [kaɪt].

[g] is a phonated explosion, as in *guide* [gaɪd].

[f] is escaping air with no phonation, as in *few* [fɪu].

[v] is escaping air with phonation, as in *view* [vɪu].

[θ] is escaping air with no phonation, as in *thigh* [θaɪ]. It is similar to the consonant [f] but has a different placement of the tongue and lips. The Greek letter theta is its symbol.

[ð] is escaping air but with phonation, as in *thy* [ðaɪ].

[s] is escaping air without phonation, as in *sing* [sɪŋ].

[z] is escaping air with phonation, as in *zing* [zɪŋ].

[ʃ] is escaping air without phonation, as in *shock* [ʃak].

[ʒ] is escaping air with phonation, as in *Jacques* (French) [ʒak].

[tʃ] is an unvoiced, or unphonated, combination of [t] and [ʃ]. It is pronounced as one sound, as in *chest* [tʃɛst].

[dʒ] is a voiced, or phonated, combination of [d] and [ʒ]. It is pronounced as one sound, as in *jest* [dʒɛst].

The following consonants have no pairings:

[h] is an unvoiced sound, as in *how* [haʊ].

[hw] is an unvoiced sound, as in *when* [hwɛn].

[m] is a voiced sound, as in *mom* [mɑm].

[n] is a voiced sound, as in *noun* [naʊn].

[ŋ] is a voiced sound, as in *sing* [sɪŋ].

[l] is a voiced sound, as in *love* [lʌv].

[w] is a voiced sound, as in *watch* [wɑtʃ].

[j] is a voiced sound, as in *yellow* [ˈjɛlo].

[r] is a voiced sound, as in *run* [rʌn].

Some Common Consonant Transcription Problems. A few consonants are potential sources of confusion and deserve special consideration.

The word *fire* is pronounced usually [faɪɚ] in the United States and Canada but is transcribed frequently as [fír] by the authors of dictionaries and phonetics texts. The problem here is that the "r" sound in a word such as *run* is really quite different from the "r" sound in the word *fire*; that is, the "r" sound differs depending on its position in a word. There is another difference: the *r* in *boor* is different from the *r* in *fire*, even though both are in the same position in the word and follow a vowel sound. This difference stems from the fact that it is easy to produce [r] after the vowel [ʊ] but difficult to produce [r] after the diphthong [aɪ]. If you transcribe *fire* in the conventional manner as a one-syllable word—(fír)/FYR/[faɪr]—you must be careful, because the word can be spoken only with two syllables—/FY/ and /ER/ (fī) and (er) [fai] and [ɚ].

Another potential source of trouble is the plural ending. Years of conditioning have taught us that most plurals end in an "s," though in actuality nearly all end in a "z" sound—*brushes, masters, dozens, kittens,* and so on. Make certain, when transcribing into IPA, that you do not confuse the two symbols [s] and [z].

The common construction *-ing* tends to make one think of a combination of [n] and [g] when transcribing a word like *singing.* Some students mistakenly transcribe this as [ˈsɪŋ͵gɪŋ]. In IPA a distinct symbol, [ŋ], is used for the "ng" sound. The correct transcription of *singing* is [ˈsɪŋɪŋ]. Another common error is to add [g] after [ŋ]. To do so is incorrect.

The symbol [j] is never used to transcribe a word like *jump.* The symbol [dʒ] is used for the sound of the letter *j.* The symbol [j] is always pronounced as in *young* [jʌŋ], *yes* [jɛs], and *William* [ˈwiljəm].

Note that many of the consonants change their sounds as they change their positions in words or are combined with different vowel sounds. You have already seen how the "r" sound does so. A similar change takes place in the "d" sound. Notice it in the first syllable of the word *dazed.* Because the initial *d* is followed by a vowel sound, [e], the *d* is sounded. But when the *d* appears in the final position of the word, it is merely exploded air and is only slightly different from the sound a *t* would make in the same position. The only way the final *d* could be sounded would be if a slight schwa sound were added.

Syllabic Consonants. Three of the consonants, [m], [n], and [l], can be sounded as separate syllables without a vowel sound before or after them. Though the word *button* may be pronounced [bʌtən], in colloquial speech the [ə] sound is often missing, and the word is represented [bʌtn̩]. In such a transcription, the **syllabic consonant** is represented by a short line under the symbol. Here are transcriptions for a few other words using syllabic consonants:

hokum [ˈhokm̩]   saddle [ˈsædl̩]   apple [ˈæpl̩]

Accent Marks

Polysyllabic words transcribed into IPA symbols must have accent marks to indicate the relative emphasis to be placed on the various syllables. The word *familiar* has three syllables, [fə], [mɪl], and [jɚ]. In Standard American the first of these syllables receives little emphasis, or stress, the second receives the primary emphasis; the third receives about the same degree of emphasis as the first.

The IPA indication of primary stress in a word is a mark ['] *before* the syllable being stressed.[2] In the word *facing* ['fesɪŋ], the mark indicates that the first syllable is to receive the **primary stress**. If the mark is placed below and before a syllable, as in *farewell* [ˌfɛrˈwɛl], it indicates that the syllable is to receive **secondary stress**. A third degree of stress is possible, but no mark is provided—this is an unstressed sound.

The word *satisfaction* will clarify the stressing of syllables. A continuous line drawn under the word indicates the degrees of stress placed on the syllables when uttering them:

sæt   ɪs   fæk   ʃən

It can be seen that there are three rather distinct degrees of emphasis in the word. This word would be transcribed [ˌsætɪsˈfækʃən]. The primary mark is used for the syllable [fæk] and the secondary mark for the syllable [sæt]; there is no mark on the two unstressed syllables, [ɪs] and [ʃən]. Because secondary stress varies from slightly less than primary stress to slightly more than the unstressed syllables in a word, the secondary accent mark is used for a wide range of emphases, although it is used only once per polysyllabic word.

The following list of related words (related either in meaning or in spelling) shows how accent marks are used in IPA transcriptions to assist in representing the correct pronunciation:

consequence ['kɑnsəˌkwɛns]	*consequential* [ˌkɑnsəˈkwɛnʃəl]
overalls ['ovɚˌɔlz]	*overwhelm* [ˌovɚˈhwɛlm]
interim ['ɪntɚɪm]	*interior* [ɪnˈtɪriɚ]
mainspring ['menˌsprɪŋ]	*maintain* [menˈtaɪn]
contest (n.) ['kɑntɛst]	*contest* (v) [kənˈtɛst]
Oliver ['alɪvɚ]	*Olivia* [oˈlɪviə]
invalid (sick person) ['invəlɪd]	*invalid* (not valid) [ɪnˈvælɪd]

Because the schwa vowel, [ə], and the vowel [ɚ] are by definition unstressed, they need no further mark to indicate stress. Because the vowel sounds [ʌ] and [ɝ] are by definition stressed, they, too, need no additional mark when they appear in a transcribed word. For example, the words *lover* [lʌvɚ] and *earnest* [ɝnəst] are transcribed without accent marks of any kind.

---

[2]Note that this practice is the opposite of dictionary phonetic transcription, in which the stress mark comes at the end of the stressed syllable.

PRACTICE

Phonetic Transcription

For additional practice, transcribe any of the passages of this book into IPA symbols. When you have acquired some degree of proficiency with the IPA, begin transcribing from the daily news any names and words with which you are unfamiliar. Gazetteers and dictionaries will give you correct pronunciations of unfamiliar words. To find the correct IPA transcriptions of unfamiliar words, use *A Pronouncing Dictionary of American English* or the *NBC Handbook of Pronunciation*.

Summary of the IPA

For handy reference, all of the IPA symbols used to transcribe Standard American speech are listed in Table B.6. Examples of words whose phonetic transcriptions contain each symbol are also given in the table.

TABLE B.6	IPA SYMBOLS FOR SOUNDS OF STANDARD AMERICAN	
IPA Symbol Vowels	**Key Word**	**Other Words**
[i]	*beet* [bit]	*free* [fri] *peace* [pis] *leaf* [lif] *misdeed* [mɪsˈdid] *evening* [ˈivn̩iŋ]
[ɪ]	*bit* [bɪt]	*wither* [ˈwɪðɚ] *pilgrim* [ˈpɪlgrɪm] *kilowatt* [ˈkɪləwat] *ethnic* [ˈɛθnɪk] *lift* [lɪft]
[e]	*bait* [bet]	*late* [let] *complain* [kəmˈplen] *La Mesa* [ˌlɑˈmesə] *coupé* [kuˈpe] *phase* [fez]

TABLE B.6	IPA SYMBOLS FOR SOUNDS OF STANDARD AMERICAN (*Cont.*)

IPA Symbol Vowels (cont.)	Key Word	Other Words
[ɛ]	*bet* [bɛt]	*phlegm* [flɛm] *scherzo* [ˈskɛrtso] *Nez Perce* [ˈnɛzˈpɚs] *pelican* [ˈpɛlɪkən] *bellicose* [ˈbɛlə,kos]
[æ]	*bat* [bæt]	*satellite* [ˈsætḷaɪt] *baggage* [ˈbægɪdʒ] *campfire* [ˈkæmp,faɪr] *Alabama* [,ælə'bæmə] *rang* [ræŋ]
[ɝ]	*bird* [bɝd]	*absurd* [əbsɝd] *early* [ɝli] *curfew* [kɝfju] *ergo* [ɝgo] *hurdle* [hɝdḷ]
[ɚ]	*bitter* [bɪtɚ]	*hanger* [hæŋɚ] *certificate* [sɚ'tɪfə,kɪt] *Berlin* [bɚ'lɪn] *flabbergast* [ˈflæbɚ,gæst]
[ɑ]	*bomb* [bɑm]	*body* [ˈbɑdi] *collar* [ˈkɑlɚ] *pardon* [ˈpɑrdn̩] *padre* [ˈpɑdre] *lollipop* [ˈlɑli,pɑp]
[ɔ]	*bought* [bɔt]	*fought* [fɔt] *longwinded* [ˈlɔŋˈwɪndɪd] *rawhide* [ˈrɔhaɪd] *Kennesaw* [ˈkɛnə,sɔ] *awful* [ˈɔfḷ]
[o]	*boat* [bot]	*closing* [ˈklozɪŋ] *Singapore* [ˈsɪŋgəpor] *tremolo* [ˈtrɛməlo] *odor* [ˈodɚ] *Pueblo* [ˈpwɛb,lo]

TABLE B.6	IPA SYMBOLS FOR SOUNDS OF STANDARD AMERICAN (*Cont.*)

IPA Symbol Vowels (cont.)	Key Word	Other Words
[ʊ]	*book* [bʊk]	*looking* [ˈlʊkɪŋ] *pull* [pʊl] *took* [tʊk] *tourniquet* [ˈtʊrnɪ‚kɛt] *hoodwink* [ˈhʊd‚wɪŋk]
[u]	*boot* [but]	*Lucifer* [ˈlusɪfɚ] *cuckoo* [ˈku‚ku] *losing* [ˈluzɪŋ] *nouveau riche* [nuvoˈriʃ]
[ʌ]	*sun* [sʌn]	*lovelorn* [ˈlʌvlɔrn] *recover* [‚rɪkʌvɚ] *chubby* [ˈtʃʌbi] *Prussia* [ˈprʌʃə] *hulled* [ˈhʌld]
[ə]	*sofa* [sofə]	*lettuce* [ˈlɛtəs] *above* [əbʌv] *metropolis* [‚məˈtrapl̩ɪs] *arena* [əˈrinə] *diffidence* [ˈdɪfədəns]
Diphthongs		
[aɪ]	*bite* [baɪt]	*dime* [daɪm] *lifelong* [ˈlaɪfˈlɔŋ] *leviathan* [ləˈvaɪəθən] *bicycle* [ˈbaɪ‚sɪkl̩] *imply* [‚ɪmˈplaɪ]
[aʊ]	*how* [haʊ]	*plowing* [ˈplaʊ‚ɪŋ] *endow* [‚ɛnˈdaʊ] *autobahn* [ˈaʊto‚ban] *council* [ˈkaʊnsl̩] *housefly* [ˈhaʊs‚flaɪ]
[ɔɪ]	*toy* [tɔɪ]	*toiling* [ˈtɔɪlɪŋ] *oyster* [ˈɔɪstɚ] *loyalty* [ˈlɔɪl̩ti]

TABLE B.6	IPA SYMBOLS FOR SOUNDS OF STANDARD AMERICAN (*Cont.*)

IPA Symbol Diphthongs (cont.)	Key Word	Other Words
		annoy [əˈnɔɪ] *poison* [ˈpɔɪzn̩]
[ju]	*using* [ˈjuzɪŋ]	*universal* [junəˈvɝsl̩] *euphemism* [ˈjufəmɪzm̩] *feud* [fjud] *refuse* [rɪˈfjuz] *spew* [spju]
[ɪu]	*fuse* [fɪuz]	
[eɪ]	*say* [seɪ]	

Consonants

IPA Symbol	Key Word	Other Words
[p]	*poor* [pʊr]	*place* [ples] *applaud* [əˈplɔd] *slap* [slæp]
[b]	*boor* [bʊr]	*break* [brek] *about* [əˈbaʊt] *club* [klʌb]
[t]	*time* [taɪm]	*trend* [trɛnd] *attire* [əˈtaɪr] *blast* [blæst]
[d]	*dime* [daɪm]	*differ* [ˈdɪfɚ] *addenda* [əˈdɛndə] *closed* [klozd]
[k]	*kite* [kaɪt]	*careful* [ˈkɛrfəl] *accord* [əˈkɔrd] *attack* [əˈtæk]
[g]	*guide* [gaɪd]	*grand* [grænd] *aggressor* [əˈgrɛsɚ] *eggnog* [ˈɛgˌnɔg]
[f]	*few* [fɪu]	*finally* [ˈfaɪnl̩i] *affront* [əˈfrʌnt] *aloof* [əˈluf]
[v]	*view* [vɪu]	*velocity* [vəˈlɑsəti] *aver* [əˈvɚ] *love* [lʌv]

| TABLE B.6 | IPA SYMBOLS FOR SOUNDS OF STANDARD AMERICAN (*Cont.*) |

IPA Symbol Consonants (cont.)	Key Word	Other Words
[θ]	thigh [θaɪ]	thrifty [ˈθrɪfti] athwart [əˈθwɔrt] myth [mɪθ]
[ð]	thy [ðaɪ]	these [ðiz] although [ˌɔlˈðo] breathe [brið]
[s]	sing [sɪŋ]	simple [ˈsɪmpl̩] lastly [ˈlæstˌli] ships [ʃɪps]
[z]	zing [zɪŋ]	xylophone [ˈzaɪləˌfon] loses [ˈluzɪz] dreams [drimz]
[ʃ]	shock [ʃak]	ashen [æʃən] trash [træʃ]
[ʒ]	Jacques [ʒak]	gendarme [ˈʒanˈdarm] measure [ˈmɛʒɚ] beige [beʒ]
[tʃ]	chest [tʃɛst]	checkers [ˈtʃɛkɚz] riches [ˈrɪtʃiz] attach [əˈtætʃ]
[dʒ]	jest [dʒɛst]	juggle [dʒʌgl̩] adjudicate [əˈdʒudɪˌket] adjudge [əˈdʒʌdʒ]
[h]	how [haʊ]	heaven [ˈhɛvən] El Cajon [ˌɛlˌkəˈhon] cahoots [ˌkəˈhuts]
[hw]	when [hwɛn]	Joaquin [hwɑˈkin] whimsical [ˈhwɪmzɪkl̩]
[m]	mom [mɑm]	militant [ˈmɪlətənt] amusing [əˈmjuzɪŋ] spume [spjum]
[n]	noun [naʊn]	nevermore [ˌnɛvɚˈmɔr] announcer [əˈnaʊnsɚ] sturgeon [ˈstɚˈdʒən]

TABLE B.6	IPA SYMBOLS FOR SOUNDS OF STANDARD AMERICAN (*Cont.*)

IPA Symbol Consonants (cont.)	Key Word	Other Words
[ŋ]	*sing* [sɪŋ]	*English* [ˈɪŋglɪʃ] *language* [ˈlæŋgwɪdʒ] *pang* [pæŋ]
[l]	*love* [lʌv]	*lavender* [ˈlævəndɚ] *illusion* [ɪˈluʒən] *medial* [ˈmidiḷ]
[w]	*watch* [wɑtʃ]	*wash* [wɑʃ] *aware* [əˈwɛr] *equestrian* [ɪˈkwɛstriən]
[j]	*yellow* [ˈjɛlo]	*William* [ˈwɪljəm] *Yukon* [ˈjukɑn]
[r]	*run* [rʌn]	*Wrigley* [ˈrɪgli] *martial* [ˈmarʃəl] *appear* [əˈpɪr]

APPENDIX C

American English Usage

TO BE AN ANNOUNCER IS TO BE A USER OF WORDS, AND SERIOUS students of announcing will undertake a careful study of their language—English for most in the United States; English and French for Canadians; and Spanish, Chinese, German, Polish, Russian, or Tagalog, for instance, for those who intend to broadcast in a non-English language. Learning about language means engaging in several different but related studies. It means making a lifelong habit of using dictionaries. It means becoming sensitized to nuances of language and seeking the precise, rather than the approximate, word; changing your vocabulary as changes in our language occur; cultivating and practicing the art of plain talk. And it means perfecting your pronunciation.

This appendix is designed for those who will speak on English-language stations, and it considers usage from the standpoint of the broadcast announcer.

Top professional announcers use words with precision and manage to sound conversational while honoring the rules of grammar. Regrettably, though, some broadcast announcers are far from perfect and commit errors in usage daily. During a two-week period, the following mistakes were made by broadcast announcers:

- "The power is out, traffic lights aren't working, and traffic is snarling." Dogs sometimes snarl; congested traffic is said to be *snarled*. With the traffic snarled, though, some drivers may have been snarling at one another.
- "That's like shooting ducks in a barrel." The announcer has mixed together two clichés—"shooting fish in a barrel," and "shooting sitting ducks."

473

- ". . . and this poor old guy was trodding along the street, looking for aluminum cans." The word is *trudging,* and is the past participle of *trudge.* The announcer may have meant *plodding.*
- "And, while Debbie's marriage was floundering on the rocks, . . ." To flounder is to stumble or lurch. The correct word is *founder,* a term used for a ship in danger of sinking.
- "And _____ is the latest state to reintroduce corpulent punishment." *Corpulent* means "excessively fat." The announcer meant *corporal* punishment, a euphemism for the death penalty. Even a skinny person might receive corporal punishment.
- "The secretary of state reportedly will visit South America late this summer." There are many kinds of visits—long visits, brief visits, surreptitious visits—but no one can make a *reported* visit. The announcer meant "It is reported that the secretary of state . . ."
- "Coach Washington has done a great job of gerrymandering his team in light of its injuries." The sports reporter meant *jury-rigging,* a term for coping with problems by improvising temporary solutions. To *gerrymander* is to draw voting district boundaries in such a way as to give an advantage to the political party that drew them.
- "The jury's verdict culminated a case that had dragged along for seven months." The verdict may have *concluded* the case, but the case *culminated* in a verdict.
- "And the Oakland A's are on a pace to set a new, all-time record!" By definition, when a record is set it is both new and "all-time." This is a rare case of *double* redundancy.
- "The violinist transcended the audience to a state of rapture." The announcer meant *transported,* not *transcended.*

American English is a dynamic, ever-changing language. Although change is slow during periods of relative stability, it never ceases. During times of upheaval, whether political, economic, or social, changes in our language take place rapidly. World War II, for example, created many new words, among them *blitz, fellow traveler, fifth column, radar,* and *quisling.* Operation Desert Storm brought us *SCUDS, Stealth bombers,* and *smart bombs.* Many terms from the world of computers have been added to our language, including *byte, modem, RAM, ROM,* and *hacker.* Professional announcers must be alert when reading and listening in order to keep up with our changing language.

Usage Guidelines

Jargon and Vogue Words

Every profession and social group has a private or semiprivate vocabulary, and some words and phrases from such groups enter the mainstream of public communication. It is useful and enriching when expressions such as *gridlock, agribusiness, software,* or *hostile takeover* (the world of business) are added to the general vocabulary. As an announcer, you should guard against picking up and overusing expressions that are trite, precious, deliberately distorting, or pretentious. Here are a few recent vogue words and phrases with translations into plain English (slightly facetious in some cases).

From the Military

de-escalate	To give up on a lost war
balance of power	A dangerous standoff
nuclear deterrent	The means by which war can be deterred when antagonistic nations possess enough nuclear weapons to destroy the world
debrief	To ask questions of someone
collateral damage	Dead civilians
friendly fire	The accidental killing of soldiers by their comrades

From Government

at home and abroad	Everywhere
nonproliferation	Monopolization of nuclear weapons
disadvantaged	Poor people
Department of Human Resources Development	The unemployment office
decriminalize	To make legal
dehire	To fire an employee

From Academe	
quantum leap	A breakthrough
de-aestheticize	To take the beauty out of art
dishabituate	To break a bad habit
microencapsulate	To put into a small capsule
found art	Someone else's junk
megastructure	A large building

One of the most offensive speech habits of recent years is tacking the suffix *-wise* onto nouns that create awkward words:

- Culturewise, the people are . . .
- Foodwise, your best buy is . . .
- National-security-wise, we should . . .

Such clumsy errors are made by those who don't know any better and by others who've found such usage an easy way to avoid more complex sentence structure. The suffix *-wise* does, of course, have a proper use in words such as *lengthwise* and *counterclockwise*.

Redundancies

To be **redundant** is to be repetitive. Redundancy can be a useful tool for reinforcing or driving home a point, but most often redundancy is needless repetition. *Close proximity* is redundant because *close* and *proximity* (or *proximate*) mean the same thing. A *necessary requisite* is redundant because *requisite* contains the meaning of *necessary*. Spoken English is plagued with unnecessary redundancy, so be on guard, and use repetition only when it serves a purpose.

Here are some redundancies heard far too often on radio and television:

Phrase	Why It's Redundant
an old antique	There can be no such thing as a new antique.
both alike, both at once, both equal	*Both* refers to two people or things, and *alike, at once,* and *equal* all imply some kind of duality.

completely surround, completely abandon, completely eliminate	To *surround*, to *abandon*, and to *eliminate* are done completely if they're done at all.
cooperate together	To *cooperate* means that two or more operate *to-gether.*
divide up, end up, finish up, rest up, pay up, settle up	All of these are burdened by unnecessary *ups.*
equally as expensive	If something costs what another thing does, then inevitably their costs are equal. (The correct form is *equally expensive* or *as expensive as.*)
exchanged with each other	An exchange is necessarily between one and another.
general consensus	*Consensus* means "general agreement."
I thought to myself	Barring telepathy, there is no one else one can think to.
joint partnership	*Partnership* includes the concept of *joint.*
knots per hour	A *knot* is a nautical mile per hour, so *per hour* is redundant.
more preferable	Use this phrase only if you're comparing two preferences.
most outstanding, most perfect, most unique	A thing is outstanding, perfect, or unique, or it isn't. There are no degrees of any of these qualities.
Sahara Desert	*Sahara* means "desert."
serious crisis	It's not a crisis unless it's already become serious.
set a new record	All records are new when they're set.

Sierra Nevada mountains	*Sierra* means "rugged mountains."
still remains	If something *remains,* it must be there still.
totally annihilated	*Annihilate* means "to destroy totally."
true facts	There can be no untrue facts.
visible to the eye	There's no other way a thing can be visible.

Develop a keen ear for redundancies. Recognizing errors in usage is the first step toward avoiding them.

Clichés

A **cliché** is an overused expression or idea. Many clichés are **similes**, a figure of speech in which two essentially unlike things are compared—"Frank was strong as a bull." Other clichés are merely overused expressions, such as "without further ado" or "none the worse for wear." It's important to detect trite catch phrases or overused similes that may have invaded your vocabulary and then to eliminate them. Memorable speakers and writers are noted for the avoidance of commonplace expressions, as well as for their language skills in evoking the mood, character, or the ambiance of a particular place.

Most popular clichés were once innovative and effective. They became clichés by being overused and, in many instances, misapplied by people who weren't aware of their original meanings. In a recent postgame interview, a sports reporter made this comment: "With Pete having a sprained ankle, and you playing with a broken toe, it seems that you guys played the game with your hearts on your sleeves." The term, *hearts on your sleeves,* is a cliché, but that's not the only problem. The phrase is from the days of chivalry (knighthood) and means "openly showing your love" for a lady. The reporter apparently intended to say something like this, "You guys are all heart." (Another cliché, by the way. . . . !)

Many clichés reflect our rural past. We say he was "mad as a wet hen," "fat as a pig," "stubborn as a mule," "silly as a goose," "strong as an ox," and similar expressions. Though not all clichés are similes, most similes in common use are clichés. Most of these animal similes have been learned by rote and are used by people who've never associated with creatures of the barnyard. Most of us should replace these expressions with similes that reflect our own experiences.

Good use of language demands that we think before we fall back on the first cliché that comes to mind. Commonly used clichés include these:

- *hustle and bustle*
- *first and foremost*
- *at any rate*
- *at this point in time*
- *to make a long story short*
- *stop on a dime*
- *by and large*
- *the phone was ringing off the hook* (few of today's telephones have *hooks*)
- *hurly-burly*
- *quick as a flash* or *quick as a wink*
- *quiet as a grave* or *quiet as a tomb*
- *dead as a doornail*
- *dry as a bone*
- *as cool as a cucumber*
- *as hungry as a bear*
- *fresh as a daisy*

The effectiveness of these clichés and dozens more like them has simply been eroded by endless repetition. Good broadcast speech isn't measured by the ability to produce new and more effective images, but quite often creative expression can make for memorable communication. See what a little thought and time can do to help you use language creatively. How would you complete the following similes to make novel and effective images?

as awkward as _____

as barren as _____

as deceptive as _____

as friendly as _____

as quiet as _____

as strange as _____

In addition to overworked similes, many other words and phrases have become hackneyed through overuse. Many clichés can be heard on daily newscasts. If you intend to become a news reporter or newscaster, you should make a careful and constant study of words that have become meaningless and replace them with meaningful synonyms.

Many speakers and writers use clichés without knowing their precise meaning. In doing so, it is easy to fall into error. For example, the adjectives *jerrybuilt* and *jury-rigged* sometimes become "jerry-rigged" or "jury-built" when used by people unaware that the first adjective means "shoddily built" and the second is a nautical term meaning "rigged for emergency use."

It's also important to avoid incorrect quotations from or allusions to works of literature. Here are a few examples of this type of mistake.

- The phrase "suffer, little children" or "suffer the little children" has been used recently to mean "let the little children suffer." The original expression, in the King James Bible version of Mark 10:14, is "Suffer the little children to come unto me." In this context *suffer* means "allow": "Allow the little children to come unto me."

- "Alas, poor Yorick, I knew him well." This is both corrupt and incomplete. The line from *Hamlet,* Act V, scene i, reads: "Alas, poor Yorick! I knew him, Horatio: a fellow of infinite jest."

- The misquotation "Music hath charms to soothe the savage beast" is an inelegant version of a line from the play *The Mourning Bride* by William Congreve. The original version is "Music hath charms to soothe the savage *breast*."

- The all-too-familiar question "Wherefore art thou Romeo?" is consistently misused by people who think that *wherefore* means "where." It means "why." The question asks "*Why* are you Romeo?" not "*Where* are you, Romeo?"

- "I have nothing to offer but blood, sweat, and tears." Winston Churchill really said, "I have nothing to offer but blood, toil, tears, and sweat."

These are but a few of the many common misquotations. As a broadcast announcer, you should check original sources routinely. Excellent sources for checking the accuracy of quoted phrases are *Bartlett's Familiar Quotations* and the *Merriam-Webster Book of Quotations,* available in print and also on compact disc. Use a quotation if it truly belongs in your work. When in doubt, skip the cliché—even correctly cited clichés are still clichés.

Latin and Greek Plurals

When you discuss media, a term that includes broadcasting, cable, and print media, be meticulous in using *medium* for the singular and *media* for the plural. Radio is a *medium*. Radio and television are *media*. We can speak of the *news media* but not of *television news media*. If people who work in broadcast media don't practice correct usage, no one else will, and the incorrectly used plural *media* will take over for the singular form.

Data is another Latin plural that is misused commonly as the singular, as in "What is your data?" This sentence should be "What *are* your data?" The sentence "What is your *datum?*" is correct if the singular is intended.

Many other words of Latin and Greek origin are subject to similar misuse. Here are some of the more important of these (note that in the singular form the Greek words end in *-on* and the Latin words end in *-um*):

Singular	Plural
addendum	*addenda*
criterion	*criteria*
memorandum	*memoranda*
phenomenon	*phenomena*
stratum	*strata*
syllabus	*syllabi*

Words that refer to graduates of schools are a more complicated matter, for both gender and number must be considered:

- Female singular—*alumna:* "She is an alumna of State College."
- Female plural—*alumnae:* pronounced (uh-LUM-nee). "These women are alumnae of State College."
- Male singular—*alumnus:* "He is an alumnus of State College."
- Male plural—*alumni:* pronounced (uh-LUM-ny). "These men are alumni of State College."
- Male and female plural—*alumni,* pronounced the same as the male plural: "These women and men are alumni of State College."

Solecisms

A **solecism** is a nonstandard or ungrammatical usage. It's related to a **barbarism** (a word or phrase not in accepted use), and both should be avoided by broadcast announcers. Surely you don't need to be told that *ain't* is unacceptable or that educated speakers don't use *anywheres*. In early childhood we all pick up substandard words and phrases, but they survive to plague us if we don't become aware of them. These include the following:

- *Foot* for *feet*, as in "She was five foot tall." Five is more than one, and it demands the plural *feet*: "She was five feet tall." (No one would say that a person is "five foot, six inch tall.")
- *Enthused over* for *was enthusiastic* about.
- *Guess* as a substitute for *think* or *suppose*, as in "I guess I'd better read a commercial."
- *Expect* for *suppose* or *assume*, as in "I expect he's on the scene by now."
- *Try and* for *try to*, as in "She's going to try and break the record."
- *Unloosen* for *loosen*, as in "He unloosened the knot."
- *Hung* for *hanged*, as in "The lynch mob hung the cattle rustler." *Hung* is the past tense of *hang* in every meaning other than as applied to a human being. Correct usages are "I hung my coat on the hook" and "He was hanged in 1884."
- *Outside of* for *aside from*, as in "Outside of that, I enjoyed the movie."
- *Real* for *really*, as in "I was real pleased."
- *Lay* and *lie* are problem words for some speakers of English. *Lie* is an intransitive verb (it does not require a direct object) meaning "to recline." It's used correctly in the following examples:

    Present tense: "I lie down."

    Past tense: "I lay down."

    Past participle: "I had lain down."

- *Lay* is a transitive verb (requiring a direct object) that means "to place."

    Present tense: "I lay it down."

    Past tense: "I laid it down."

    Past participle: "I had laid it down."

Hens *lay* eggs, but they also *lie* down from time to time. A parent can *lay* a baby on a blanket and then *lie* next to her.

Words Often Misused

Hopefully, reportedly, and *allegedly* are among several adverbs misused so pervasively and for so long that some modern dictionaries now accept their misuse. Adverbs modify verbs, adjectives, and other adverbs. In other words, adverbs tell us how something happened. In the sentence "He runs rapidly," *rapidly* is the adverb, and it *modifies* the verb *runs*. The adverb tells how he ran.

Hopefully means "with hope" or "in a hopeful manner." To say "Hopefully, we will win" is not the same as saying "We hope we will win." The former implies that *hope* is the means by which we'll win. *Hopefully* is used correctly in these sentences: "She entered college hopefully"; "He approached the customer hopefully."

There is no proper use of *reportedly*. This quasi-adverb is of recent origin and doesn't stand up to linguistic logic because there's no way to do something *in a reported manner.* To say "He was reportedly killed at the scene" isn't the same thing as saying "It's reported that he was killed at the scene." "He was reportedly killed" means that he was killed *in a reported manner.*

The adverb *allegedly* is misused widely, and a detailed discussion of its misuse may be found in Chapter 9, "Radio News."

Adverbs such as *hopefully, reportedly,* and *allegedly* represent a special problem to announcers. Should you go along with conventional misuse? One argument in favor of doing so is that everyone understands what's meant. An argument against it is that widespread misuse of adverbs undermines the entire structure of grammar, making it increasingly difficult for us to think through grammatical problems. Because any sentence can be spoken conversationally without misusing adverbs, it's to be hoped that you'll use adverbs correctly.

Other words often misused are discussed in the following paragraphs:

Don't say *anxious* when you mean *eager. Anxious* means "worried" or "strained" and is associated with anxiety.

Connive, conspire, and *contrive* are sometimes confused. To *connive* is to "cooperate secretly in an illegal or wrongful action. To *conspire* is to "plan together secretly"; one person cannot conspire, because a conspiracy is an agreement between two or more persons. To *contrive* is to "scheme or plot with evil intent"; one person is capable of contriving.

Contemptible is sometimes confused with *contemptuous.* Contemptible is an adjective meaning "despicable." *Contemptuous* is an adjective meaning "scornful" or "disdainful." You may say "The killer is contemptible" or "He is contemptuous of the rights of others."

Continual and *continuous* are used by many speakers as interchangeable synonyms, but their meanings aren't the same. *Continual* means "repeatedly regularly and frequently"; *continuous* means "prolonged without interruption or cessation." A foghorn may sound continually; it doesn't sound continuously unless it's broken. A siren may sound continuously, but it does not sound continually unless it's going off every five minutes (or every half-hour or every hour).

Convince and *persuade* are used interchangeably by many announcers. In some constructions either word will do. A problem arises when *convince* is linked with *to,* as in this incorrect sentence: "He believes that he can convince the Smithsonian directors to give him the collection." The correct word to use in this sentence is *persuade. Convince* is to be followed by *of* or a clause beginning with *that,* as in "I could not convince him of my sincerity" or "I could not convince him that I was honest." The sentence "I could not convince him to trust me" is incorrect. In the following sentence, heard on a network newscast, *persuade* should have been used: "He did not know whether or not the president could convince them to change their minds."

Distinct and *distinctive* are not interchangeable. *Distinct* means "not identical" or "different"; *distinctive* means "distinguishing" or "characteristic." A distinct odor is one that cannot be overlooked; a distinctive odor is one that can be identified.

Emanate means to "come forth," "proceed," or "issue." You may say "The light emanated from a hole in the drape." Note that only light, air, aromas, ideas, and other such phenomena can emanate. Objects such as rivers, automobiles, or peaches cannot emanate from mountains, a factory, or an orchard.

Farther and *farthest* are used for literal distance, as in "The tree is farther away than the mailbox." But *further* and *furthest* are used for figurative distance, as in "further in debt."

Feasible often is used interchangeably with five other words: *possible, practical, practicable, workable,* and *viable.* These words should be differentiated by people who want to be precise in their use of American English.

- *Feasible* means "clearly possible or applicable": "The plan was feasible" or "Her excuse was feasible."

- *Possible* means "capable of happening": "It is possible that the plan will work."
- *Practical* refers to the prudence, efficiency, or economy of an act or thing: "This is a practical plan" or "He is a practical person."
- *Practicable* means "capable of being done": "The plan is hardly practicable at this time." Note that *practicable* never refers to persons.
- *Workable* means "capable of being worked or dealt with": "The plan is workable." Note that *workable* implies a future act.
- *Viable* means "capable of living, growing, or developing": "That is a viable tomato plant." Recently, *viable* has replaced *feasible* in many applications. You should avoid using this overworked word. If you remember that it's derived from the Old French *vie* and the Latin *vita,* both of which mean "life," it's unlikely that you will speak of "viable plans."

Flaunt and *flout* often are used interchangeably and therefore incorrectly. To *flaunt* is to "exhibit ostentatiously" or to "show off." To *flout* is to "show contempt for" or to "scorn." You may say "He flaunted his coat of arms" or "He flouted the officials."

Implicit means "implied" or "understood"; *explicit* means "expressed with precision" or "specific." "He made an implicit promise" means that the promise was understood but was not actually stated. "His promise was explicit" means that the promise was stated very clearly.

To *imply* is to "suggest by logical necessity" or to "intimate"; to *infer* is to "draw a conclusion based on facts or indications." You may say "Her grades imply a fine mind" or "From examining her grades, I infer that she has a fine mind." Avoid the common practice of using one of these words to mean the other.

Libel meant originally "any written, printed, or pictorial statement that damages by defaming character or by exposing a person to ridicule," but libel includes also words spoken over the air, especially when read from a script. *Slander* means "the utterance of defamatory statements injurious to the reputation of a person." *Defamation* is a more general term meaning both libel and slander.

A *loan* is "anything lent for temporary use"; to *lend* is to "give out or allow the temporary use of something." *Loan* is a noun, and *lend* is a verb. You may say "She applied for a loan" or "He lent me his rake" or "Don't lend money to friends." Avoid using loan as a verb, as in "Don't loan money to friends."

Oral means "spoken." *Verbal* means "of, pertaining to, or associated with words." *Aural* means "of, pertaining to, or perceived by the ear." *Verbal* is less precise than *oral,* because it can mean spoken or written. For this reason, the phrase "oral agreement" rather than "verbal agreement" should be used if the meaning is that the agreement wasn't written. Although *oral* and *aural* are pronounced the same, they're used in different senses: "She taught oral interpretation" but "He had diminished aural perception."

People (not *persons*) should be used in referring to a large group: "People should vote in every election." *Persons* and *person* should be used for small groups and for individuals: "Five persons were involved" and "The person spoke on the telephone." A *personage* is an important or noteworthy person. A *personality* is a pattern of behavior. It's technically incorrect to call a disc jockey a **personality**, even though the term has wide acceptance.

Most dictionaries indicate that *prison* and *jail* can be used interchangeably, but strictly speaking, a jail is maintained by a town, city, or county, whereas prisons are maintained by states and the federal government. Jails generally confine prisoners for periods of less than a year; prisons or penitentiaries are for people with longer sentences.

Repulsion is the act of driving back or repelling; *revulsion* is a feeling of disgust or loathing. Do not say, "His breath repelled me," unless you mean that his breath physically forced you backward.

Reticent means "silent"; *reluctant* means "unwilling." Don't say "She was reticent to leave" when you mean "She was reluctant to leave."

Rhetoric is the art of oratory or the study of the language elements used in literature and public speaking. Rhetoric isn't a synonym for *bombast, cant,* or *harangue. Rhetoric* is a neutral term and should not be used in a negative sense to mean empty and threatening speech.

A *robber* unlawfully takes by violence or intimidation something belonging to another; a *burglar* breaks into a house or store to steal valuable goods. Although both actions are felonies, they're different crimes, so *robber* and *burglar* shouldn't be used interchangeably.

Xerox is the trademark of a corporation that makes copying machines. The company specifies that *Xerox* is the name of the company or, if followed by a model number, a specific machine. A photocopy made by that or any other machine is not "a Xerox."

This review of common usage errors is necessarily limited, but it may be adequate to alert you to the problem. If you habitually make errors such as those described here, you should undertake a study of English usage.

Deliberate Misuse of Language

As an announcer, you'll at times have to read copy that's ungrammatical, includes poor usage, or requires deliberate mispronunciation. Here are a few examples: "So, buy _____! There's no toothpaste like it!" If there is no toothpaste like it, the advertised product itself doesn't exist. The correct expression is "There's no *other* toothpaste like it." In "So, gift her with flowers on Mother's Day!" the word *gift*, which is a noun, has been used ungrammatically as a transitive verb. You can *give* her flowers on Mother's Day, but unless all standards of grammar are abandoned, you can't *gift* her. When you are asked to commit these and other errors as an announcer, what should you do?

You may resent the advertising agency that asks you to foist poor examples of American speech or pronunciation on the public. Although some errors in usage are made by copywriters through ignorance, don't assume that all copywriters are unaware of correct standards of grammar or pronunciation. Many of the mistakes in their copy are deliberate. Poor grammar, many advertising copywriters believe, is more colloquial and less stilted than correct grammar. Poor usage causes controversy, and to attract attention is to succeed in the primary objective of any commercial message.

You may be obliged to make deliberate mistakes when they're requested of you, and this is a problem because your audience will assume either that the mistake is yours or that the poor usage or mispronunciation actually is correct! You should use language properly in all broadcast circumstances that you control. When you're asked to read ungrammatical copy exactly as it is written, you should, if possible, ask the writer or the agency if it can be changed.

This appendix ends as it began, with a brief compilation of some usage errors heard on radio and television. The sentences that follow have one thing in common—all are incorrect:

- "The owner of the destroyed house was nonplused about it." This would seem okay except that in the accompanying sound bite the owner said, "Well, it could've been worse." The owner, then, actually was *nonchalant,* rather than *nonplused.*
- "So much for the wisdom of political pundents." This blunder was heard several times during a recent political campaign. The correct word is *pundit,* derived from the Hindi "pandit," meaning a learned person.

- "The Bears were hoping to cash in on their field position, but that point is now mute." The word is *moot,* which, in this usage, would mean "irrelevant."
- ". . . and, for music lovers, this Saturday night at 8:00 the Opera Guild stages the Mozart opera, *The Marriage of Figuroa.*" "Figuroa" is a major thoroughfare in Los Angeles, named after an early Californian. The announcer meant *The Marriage of Figaro.*
- ". . . and, when the storm came in, it rained unrelentlessly for the next eight hours." The unnecessary *un* canceled out *relentlessly,* so according to the reporter, it didn't rain much at all! (Beware of unnecessary *uns* that literally say the opposite of what was intended, as in "unloosen the knot.")
- ". . . so, it's important for the inspectors to sift through the chafe." The announcer meant *chaff,* a word referring to the outer coating of grains removed during threshing. To *chafe* is to "irritate by rubbing."
- "A barge with a large wench is on its way to the scene of the accident." It's is unlikely that even a *huge* wench could lift a truck from the bay. The word the announcer meant is *winch,* a stationary hoisting or hauling machine.
- "They [the 49ers] have been top-heavy, passwise to runwise." This statement, made during a football broadcast, combined jargon (tacking "wise" onto nouns) with an expression ("top-heavy") that isn't a good substitute for "lopsided," "unbalanced," or "disproportionate."

This list of errors in usage is brief, but it illustrates the kinds of mistakes made by professional speakers who should be providing models of correct speech. If you make mistakes such as these or if you confuse *who* and *whom, shall* and *will, like* and *as,* and *which* and *that,* this appendix should serve as notice that you should undertake a serious study of American English. The suggested resources in Appendix D include several works on American English usage that should be a part of every announcer's library.

APPENDIX D

Suggested Resources

IN THE BROAD FIELD OF ELECTRONIC COMMUNICATION SOME PRACTICES undergo constant change, while others are more permanent. Production and programming are the most vulnerable to change; voice improvement, for example, is far less transient. Accordingly, this bibliography lists many books that discuss recent developments in the field of electronic communication, as well as other works that treat less short-lived aspects of our field. To bring this down to specifics, a ten-year-old book on television lighting is not listed here because the move from camera pickup tubes to digital signal processing has changed lighting requirements dramatically. On the other hand, twenty-year-old texts on voice improvement, articulation, interpretation, and interviewing are listed because the information contained in them is not time bound. Although a number of the latter are no longer in print, they're likely to be found in your school's library, because many are timeless classics.

In addition to the works listed here, check Appendix E for web sites that lead to many sources of information and practice material. Remember, however, that the Internet undergoes change daily, with new web sites being added, and others being deleted.

Chapter 1: Announcing for the Electronic Media

Rivers, William L., Wilbur Schramm, and Clifford G. Christian. *Responsibility in Mass Communication*, 3d ed. New York: Harper & Row, 1980. (out of print)

U.S. Department of Labor. *Occupational Outlook Handbook*. Published periodically. Available at U.S. Government bookstores and most college libraries.

Chapter 2: The Announcer As Communicator

Blythin, Evan, and Larry A. Samovar. *Communicating Effectively on Television*. Belmont, CA: Wadsworth, 1985. (out of print)

Duerr, Edwin. *Radio and Television Acting: Criticism, Theory and Practice.* Westport, CT: Greenwood Press, 1972.

Follett, Wilson. *Modern American Usage: A Guide.* Edited by Jacques Barzun. New York: Hill & Wang, 1998.

Newman, Edwin. *Strictly Speaking.* New York: Warner Books, 1983.

Chapter 3: Voice Analysis and Improvement
Chapter 4: Pronunciation and Articulation

Anderson, Virgil A. *Training the Speaking Voice,* 3d ed. New York: Oxford University Press, 1977.

Cooper, Morton. *Change Your Voice, Change Your Life.* North Hollywood, CA: Wilshire Book Co., 1996.

Keith, Michael C. *Broadcast Voice Performance.* Stoneham, MA: Focal Press, 1988. (out of print)

McCallion, Michael, et al. *The Voice Book.* New York: Theatre Arts Books, 1988.

Modisett, Noah F., and James G. Luter, Jr. *Speaking Clearly: The Basics of Voice and Articulation,* 4th ed. Edina, MN: Burgess, 1998.

Morrison, Malcolm. *Clear Speech: Practical Speech Correction and Voice Improvement,* 3d ed. Stoneham, MA: Heinemann, 1997.

Rizzo, Raymond. *The Voice As an Instrument,* 2d ed. New York: Odyssey Press, 1978. (out of print)

Sprague, Jo, and Douglas Stuart. *The Speaker's Handbook,* 5th ed. San Diego: Harcourt Brace Jovanovich, 1999.

Stone, Janet, and Jane Bachner. *Speaking Up: A Book for Every Woman Who Talks.* New York: Carroll & Graf, 1994.

Uris, Dorothy. *A Woman's Voice: A Handbook to Successful Public and Private Speaking.* Chelsea, MD: Scarborough House, 1974. (out of print)

Utterback, Ann S. *Broadcast Voice Handbook: How to Polish Your On-Air Delivery,* 2d ed. Chicago: Bonus Books, 1995.

———. *Vocal Expressiveness.* Chicago: Broadcast Voice Series, Bonus Books, 1992.

Chapter 5: Audio Performance
Chapter 6: Video Performance

Ehrlich, Eugene H., and Raymond Hand, Jr. *NBC Handbook of Pronunciation,* 4th ed. New York: HarperCollins, 1991. (out of print)

Hawes, William. *Television Performing: News and Information.* Stoneham, MA: Focal Press, 1991.

Malandro, Loretta A., et al. *Nonverbal Communication,* 2d ed. New York: McGraw Hill, 1989.

McConkey, Wilfred J. *Klee As in Clay,* 3d rev. ed. Lanham, MD: Madison Books, 1992. (out of print)

Chapter 7: Commercials and Public-Service Announcements

Alburger, James R. *The Art of Voice Acting: The Craft and Business of Performing for Voice-Over.* Woburn, MA: Butterworth-Heinemann, 1998.

Apple, Terri, and Gary Owens. *Making Money in Voice-Overs: Winning Strategies to a Successful Career in TV, Commercials, Radio, and Animation.* Los Angeles: Lone Eagle Publications, 1998.

Baker, Georgette. *You Too Can Be in TV Commercials.* Diamond Bar, CA: Talented, 1988.

Beardsley, Elaine Keller. *Working in Commercials.* Boston: Focal Press, 1992. (out of print)

Berland, Terry, and Deborah Ouellette. *Breaking Into Commercials: The Complete Guide to Marketing Yourself, Auditioning to Win, and Getting the Job.* New York: Dutton/Plume, 1997.

Blu, Susan, and Molly Ann Mullin. *Word of Mouth: A Guide to Commercial Voice-Over Excellence,* rev. ed. Los Angeles: Pomegranate Press, 1996.

Blythin, Evan, and Larry A. Samovar. *Communicating Effectively on Television.* Belmont, CA: Wadsworth, 1985. (out of print)

Clark, Elaine A. *There's Money Where Your Mouth Is: An Insider's Guide to a Career in Voice-Overs.* New York: Back Stage Books, 1995.

Cronauer, Adrian. *How to Read Copy: Professionals' Guide to Delivering Voice-Overs and Broadcast Commercials.* Chicago: Bonus Books, 1990.

Douthitt, Chris. *Voice-Overs: Putting Your Mouth Where the Money Is.* Portland, OR: Grey Heron Books, 1976.

Fridell, Squire. *Acting in Television Commercials for Fun and Profit,* updated ed. New York: Crown, 1995.

Peacock, James. *How to Audition for Television Commercials and Get Them.* Chicago: Contemporary Books, 1982. (out of print)

Quinn, Sunny. *Put Your Mouth Where the Money Is: How to Build a Successful Radio and TV Voice-Over Business.* Jupiter, FL: Airwave Publications, 1998.

Searle, Judith. *Getting the Part: Thirty-Three Professional Casting Directors Tell You How to Get Work in Theater, Film, Commercials, and Television.* New York: Limelight Editions, 1995.

See, Joan. *Acting in Commercials,* 2d ed. New York: Watson-Guptill Publications, 1998.

Chapter 8: Interview and Talk Programs

Brady, John Joseph. *The Craft of Interviewing.* New York: Random House, 1997.

Cohen, Akiba A. *The Television News Interview.* Newbury Park, CA: Sage Publications, 1987. (out of print)

Chapter 9: Radio News
Chapter 10: Television News

Cremer, Charles F., Phillip O. Keirstead, and Richard D. Yoakam. *ENG: Television News (McGraw-Hill Series in Mass Communication),* 3d ed. New York: McGraw-Hill, 1995.

Fang, Irving. *Television News, Radio News,* 4th rev. ed. St. Paul, MN: Rada Press, 1985. (out of print)

Goldstein, Norm, ed. *The Associated Press Stylebook and Libel Manual,* rev. ed. New York: Dell Publishing, 2000.

Gans, Herbert J. *Deciding What's News: A Study of CBS Evening News, NBC Nightly News, Newsweek and Time.* New York: Random House, 1989.

Graber, Doris A. *Processing the News,* 2d ed. Lanham MD: University Press of America, 1994. (out of print)

Hewitt, John. *Air Words: Writing for Broadcast News,* 2d ed. Mountain View, CA: Mayfield, 1994.

Killenberg, George M., and Rob Anderson. *Before the Story: Interviewing and Communication Skills for Journalists.* New York: St. Martin's Press, 1989.

Shipley, Kenneth G., and Julie McNulty Wood. *The Elements of Interviewing.* San Diego, CA: Singular Publishing Group, 1997.

MacDonald, R. H. *A Broadcast News Manual of Style,* 2d ed. New York: Longman, 1994.

Chapter 11: Music Announcing

Apel, Willi. *Harvard Dictionary of Music,* 2d ed. Cambridge, MA: Belknap Press, 1969.

Crofton, Ian, and Donald Fraser. *A Dictionary of Musical Quotations*. New York: Schirmer Books, 1989.

Cross, Milton. *New Milton Cross' Stories of the Great Operas*. New York: Doubleday, 1955. (out of print)

Keith, Michael C. *The Radio Station,* 4th ed. Stoneham, MA: Focal Press, 1996.

Lieberman, Philip A. *Radio's Morning Show Personalities: Early Hour Broadcasters and Deejays from the 1920s to the 1990s*. Jefferson, NC: McFarland & Co., 1996.

Weigant, Chris. *Careers As a Disc Jockey*. New York: Rosen Group, 1997.

Chapter 12: Sports Announcing

Gunther, Marc, and Bill Carter. *Monday Night Mayhem: The Inside Story of ABC's Monday Night Football*. New York: William Morrow, 1988. (out of print)

Madden, John. *One Size Doesn't Fit All and Other Thoughts from the Road*. New York: Villard Books, 1988.

Smith, Curt. *The Storytellers: From Mel Allen to Bob Costas: Sixty Years of Baseball Tales from the Broadcast Booth*. Foster City, CA: IDG Books, 1995.

———. *Voices of the Game: The First Full-Scale Overview of Baseball Broadcasting,* updated ed. New York: Simon and Schuster, 1992. (out of print)

Chapter 13: Starting Your Announcing Career

Ellis, Elmo I. *Opportunities in Broadcasting Careers,* rev. ed. Lincolnwood, IL: Vgm Career Horizons, 1998.

Pearlman, Donn. *Breaking into Broadcasting*. Chicago: Bonus Books, 1986.

Reed, Maxine K., and Robert M. Reed. *Career Opportunities in Television, Cable, and Video,* 4th rev. ed. New York: Facts on File, 1991.

APPENDIX E

Suggested
Internet Resources

THE INTERNET IS CHANGING CONSTANTLY AS NEW WEB SITES ARE ADDED and old web sites are abandoned. The URL listings in this textbook should be regarded as samples of the kinds of material available rather than as a stable index. If you seek a web site using one of these URLs and cannot connect, enter the key words for the topic into a search engine to find a site that may provide the information you want.

The Houghton Mifflin Company site for Hyde, *Television and Radio Announcing*, Ninth Edition:
www.hmco.com/college

Chapter 1
Announcing for the Electronic Media

United States Bureau of Labor Statistics:
stats.bls.gov/oes/national/oes34017.htm

Talent agencies:
www.cybershowbiz.com/ncopm/member_1.html
www.pozproductions.com/agtmainp.htm

United States and Canadian institutional members of the Broadcast Education Association:
www.beaweb.org/inst1.html

The Association for Women in Communication, Inc.:
www.womcom.org/

International Radio and Television Society-Alpha Epsilon Rho:
www.onu.edu/org/nbs/

The Radio and Television News Directors Association (RTNDA):
www.rtnda.org/join/index.htm

The National Black Media Coalition:
www.nbmc.org/index.html

The Radio-Television Journalism Division of the Association for Education in Journalism and Mass Communication:
www2.drury.edu/rtvj/rtvjl.html

Codes that pertain to the Radio and Television News Directors Association (RTNDA):
www.rtnda.org/rtnda/index.htm

The American Society of Newspaper Editors (ASNE) Statement of Principles:
www.asne.org/kiosk/archive/principl.htm

Chapter 2
The Announcer As Communicator

Audition performances by professional announcers can be accessed via:
www.provoice.com

News scripts for realistic and up-to-date practice sessions*may be obtained by opening Yahoo, and clicking on "full coverage" under "News and Media."

Near-instantaneous information on usage and grammar, as well as specific rules for punctuation:
www.yourdictionary.com/

Chapter 3
Voice Analysis and Improvement

Chapter 4
Pronunciation and Articulation

Alderman Center Library at the University of Virginia. Contains a vast collection of the works of major British and American poets:
etext.lib.virginia.edu/britpo.html

---

*Note: You may use these scripts and transcripts for practice, but *you must not use them for any on-air performance, as they are copyright protected.*

Chapter 5
Audio Performance

Radio essay and commentary scripts from National Public Radio's *NewsHour with Jim Lehrer**:
www.pbs.org/newshour/essays–dialogues.html

Chapter 6
Video Performance

Drew's Script-o-Rama. Contains scripts of complete television dramas, both serious and comic*:
www.script–o–rama.com/tv/tvscript.shtml

The Television Transcript Project. Includes commercial scripts arranged by category: for instance, headache remedies and restaurants*:
www.tvtp.simplenet.com/

The Chicago Tribune. This site will lead you to scripts of many kinds*:
www.chicagotribune.com/news/columnists/zorn/feature/
  0,1438,9554–9554,00.html

Chapter 7
Commercials and Public–Service Announcements

Advertising Age magazine. Includes insightful reviews of current commercials:
www.adage.com/news_and_features/ad_review/index.html

The Houghton Mifflin Company web site for this text provides information on character voices. In addition, it contains practice copy*:
www.hmco.com/college/communication/index.htm

---

*Note: You may use these scripts and transcripts for practice, but *you must not use them for any on-air performance, as they are copyright protected.*

Chapter 8
Interview and Talk Programs

Web Sites for Students. Contains biographical sketches of thousands of people under such categories as African Americans, Artists, Astronauts, Authors, General Biographies, Government and History, Mathematicians, Miscellaneous, Musicians, Scientists, and Women:
www.ad12.k12.co.us/northglennhigh/nghs/bio.html

CNN. Contains transcripts of interviews by such people as Larry King and Jesse Jackson, as well as transcripts of programs such as *TalkBack Live, Crossfire, Burden of Proof, Reliable Sources,* and *CNN & Company**:
www.cnn.com/TRANSCRIPTS/

Chapter 9
Radio News

Chapter 10
Television News

To obtain printouts of up-to-the-minute news copy* go to
fullcoverage.yahoo.com/

Chapter 11
Music Announcing

To learn more about club or mobile DJs, visit the following three web sites:
search.yahoo.com/bin/search?p=mobile+disc+jockeys
**www.altavista.com/cgi-bin/query?pg=q&what=web&q=Disc+Jockeys
 &user=yahoo**
www.realnames.com/Resolver.dll?provider=1&realName=disc+jockeys+

To learn more about show preparation for music announcers, visit the following two web sites:
dir.yahoo.com/News_and_Media/Radio/Show_Preparation/
www.almostradio.com/

---

*Note: You may use these scripts and transcripts for practice, but *you must not use them for any on-air performance, as they are copyright protected.*

Chapter 12
Sports Announcing

Brief biographies of sports play-by-play announcers, commentators, program hosts, reporters, and play analysts may be found by visiting the following two web sites:
abcsports.go.com/announcers/index.html
espn.go.com/espninc/personalities/index.html

To obtain a perspective of the work of a stadium public address announcer, visit the web site of Ed Brickley, booth announcer for the Boston Red Sox:
library.advanced.org/11902/booth/booth.html

Chapter 13
Starting Your Announcing Career

You can perform job searches on the Internet. Broadcast Employment Services offers a number of services under such categories as Master Station Index, Index, E-Resume Database, Freelance Directory, TV Forum, Situations Wanted, and Internship Database. Jobs in radio, television, cable, and film are included:
www.tvjobs.com/index_a.htm

To find and print a map showing the location of a particular radio or television station, or other business, access the Big Book Directory:
www.bigbook.com/

Appendix A
Scripts to Develop Performance Skills

To further develop your interpretive skills, you can access, through the PBS web site, essays and dialogues of Richard Rodriguez, Clarence Thomas, Anne Taylor Fleming, and Roger Rosenblatt, all highly respected commentators*:
www.pbs.org/newshour/essays–dialogues.html

---

*Note: You may use these scripts and transcripts for practice, but *you must not use them for any on-air performance, as they are copyright protected.*

CREDITS

GLOSSARY

Terms are defined here only as they are used in this book. Many of the terms have additional uses and meanings not explained here.

A/C or AC   Abbreviation for *Adult Contemporary,* a popular music category.

abstraction ladder   S.I. Hayakawa's term for the fact that several terms usually are available for the same phenomenon, some precise and some abstract.

accent   The way words are pronounced, usually determined by the regional or national background of the speaker. Everyone has an "accent," because the term simply means the way we sound words.

account executive   A person who sells broadcast time for a radio station or an agency.

actuality   A term used in radio news to refer to a report featuring someone other than broadcast personnel (politician, police inspector, athlete, or eyewitness) who provides an actual statement rather than one paraphrased and spoken by a reporter.

ad-lib (noun, verb, or adj.) and ad lib (adverb)   To improvise and deliver spontaneously.

Adult Alternative   A radio station format that plays Eclectic Rock with wide variations in musical style.

Adult Contemporary   Descriptive of a format or type of music played on some radio stations, consisting of soft-to-moderate rock, ballads, and current hits.

Adult Contemporary Hit Radio   A radio station format that features more up-tempo Contemporary hits with no Hard Rock or Rap.

Adult Standards   A radio station format featuring standards and older non-Rock popular music.

affricates   Speech sounds that combine a plosive (release of air as in saying the letter *p*) with a fricative (friction of air through a restricted air passage as in saying the letter *s*); an example is the "ch" sound in *loose*.

501

AFTRA   Abbreviation for American Federation of Television and Radio Artists, the union made up of radio and television announcers whose work is either live or taped.

AGC   Abbreviation for *automatic gain control.*

AH   Abbreviation for *Adult Hits,* or *Hot Adult Contemporary,* a popular-music category.

aircheck   An audition tape, usually a portion of an actual broadcast.

Album Rock   A format descriptive of a radio station that features mainstream Rock 'n Roll.

allusion   An indirect but pointed, or meaningful, reference: "he is as subtle as Dirty Harry" is an allusion.

alveolus   The upper gum ridge.

ambient noise   Unwanted sounds in an acoustical environment (such as air conditioners, traffic noises, airplanes).

ambient sounds   Normal background sounds that do not detract from the recording or the program and may even add to the excitement of the broadcast (such as crowd sounds at a sports event).

amplitude   The strength of a radio wave.

anchor   The chief newscaster on a radio or television news broadcast.

announcer   Anyone who speaks to an audience through an electronic medium: radio or television transmission over the public airways, cable or other closed-circuit audio or video distribution, or electronic amplification, as in an auditorium or a theater. Announcers include newscasters, reporters, commentators, sportscasters, narrators, "personalities," disc jockeys, program hosts, and people who deliver commercial messages (as contrasted with those who act in dramatized commercials).

AP   Abbreviation for *Adult Alternative,* a popular-music category.

AR   Abbreviation for *Album Rock,* a popular-music category.

articulation   The physical formation of spoken words by means of teeth, tongue, and lips working together with the soft palate, gum ridges, and each other to break up phonated sounds into articulate (or even inarticulate) speech sounds.

AS   Abbreviation for *Adult Standard,* a popular-music category.

ASNE   Abbreviation for American Society of Newspaper Editors.

aspirate To release a puff of breath, as in sounding the word *unhitch*. Over-aspiration results in a popping sound when sitting or standing close to a microphone.

attenuator A volume control on an audio console

attitude An announcer's position or bearing, made up of mindset, stance, point of view, and beliefs; similar to mood, but going deeper and connoting a relationship between the announcer and persons being addressed.

audience demographics See *demographics.*

audience rapport A bond between performer and audience, based on a feeling of mutual respect and trust.

audio console The control board that receives, mixes, amplifies, and sends audio signals to a recorder or a transmitter.

audiotape cartridge A cartridge of 1/4-inch audiotape that plays, rewinds, and cues itself.

audition tape An audio or videotaped collection of performances by an announcer, used to accompany a job application.

automatic gain control A device that automatically regulates the volume to maintain a consistent level.

AWRT Abbreviation of American Women in Radio and Television.

back-announce To identify songs and artists after the music has been played.

barbarism A blunder in speech; similar to a solecism.

barter The exchange of airtime for goods or services.

BB Script symbol for *billboard,* used to indicate to an announcer that an upcoming feature or event should be promoted.

BEA Abbreviation for Broadcast Education Association.

beat check Using a telephone to search for and tape news stories from a list of agencies, including the FBI, police and fire departments, local hospitals, the weather bureau, and airport control towers; also called the *phone beat.*

bed See *music bed.*

beeper Electronic beeping tones placed on the audio track of a videotape for cuing. Eight beeps are laid down, one second apart. The last two seconds of the electronic leader are silent, and the director, responding to the rhythm of the eight beeps, allows two more seconds to elapse before giving the next instruction to the technical director.

beeper reports   News reports, either recorded or live, telephoned to a station, during which an electronic beep is sounded to let the person speaking know that a recording is being made. The beep is not used when station personnel are recorded and need not be used for others if they are told that they are being recorded or being broadcast.

bending the needle   Causing the swinging needle of a VU or VI meter or an audio console to hit the extreme right of its calibrated scale, indicating to the operator that the volume of the sound being sent through the console is too high.

best time available   A radio station advertising package that schedules commercials at the station's discretion, with a promise to broadcast them at the best available time slots.

BG   Abbreviation for *Black Gospel,* a popular-music category.

BG   Script symbol for "background," referring most often to background music.

bidirectional   The pickup pattern of a microphone that accepts sounds from two of its sides.

bilabial   Sounds articulated primarily by both lips, for example, the consonants *p* and *w*; also called *labial.*

billboard   To promote an upcoming feature or event on the air.

billing log   The name given by the sales and business departments to a radio station's program log, a listing, in sequence, of each element of the broadcast day, including commercials.

Black Gospel   A radio station format that features religious music in the Gospel tradition.

blocking   Instructing performers in a television production as to when and where to stand, walk, and so on.

board   In radio, an audio console; in television news operations, a large Plexiglas sheet on which the elements of a newscast are entered throughout the day.

board fade   A lowering of the volume on an audio console, usually to the point of losing the sound altogether.

boom   Short for "audio boom," a device for moving a microphone without allowing either its operator or the mic to be seen on the television screen. Most booms are mounted on movable dollies and have controls for moving the microphone in or out, up or down, or sideways. Television camera cranes are sometimes called booms.

boosting   Strengthening an audio signal by means of an amplifier.

box graphic   Pictures and words, contained in a rectangle, that symbolize a news story being delivered. The graphic usually is seen in the upper right or upper left of the television screen.

brain   The computer used to program an automated radio station; also called a *controller.*

BTA   Abbreviation for *best time available.*

bulletin   Sports news stories issued by the Associated Press. Bulletins include blockbuster trades, deaths of noteworthy athletes, and pennant and World Series clinchers.

bulletin font   The oversized type produced by a printer or typewriter that prints scripts for television news broadcasts.

bumper   The device used to move a television program from one element to another, as in a transition from the program to a commercial or from one segment of the program to another.

buttons   Allow you to open and close your announcer mic, to open and close the intercom or talk-back mic, and to open a mic in the newsroom for feeding out a news bulletin.

calling the game   Giving a play-by-play description of a sports event.

camera consciousness   The awareness on the part of a performer of the capabilities and limitations of the television cameras.

cardioid   A type of microphone pickup pattern that is heart-shaped.

cart   Short for "audiotape cartridge"; a loop of tape encased in a plug-in cartridge that automatically recues.

cart machine   An electronic audio device that records and plays back (or sometimes only plays back) material for broadcast.

cart with live tag   A commercial that begins with a recorded announcement, often with musical background, and ends with a live closing by a local announcer.

carted commercials   Commercials dubbed to audiotape cartridges.

carted music   Music selections transferred to audiotape cartridges. Most music stations have switched to digitally recorded play machines.

carting   The act of dubbing, or recording on, an audiotape cartridge.

CD   Abbreviation for *compact disc.*

CG   Abbreviation for *character generator.*

chain   A group of broadcast stations owned by one company or by a network.

channel selector switch   A control on an audio console that enables the operator to select from two or more inputs.

character generator   An electronic device used for creating titles, bar graphs, and many other graphics for the television screen.

cheating to the camera   Positioning oneself to create the impression on screen of talking directly to another person, while presenting a favorable angle to the camera.

CHR or CH   Abbreviations for *Contemporary Hit Radio,* a popular-music category.

chroma-key   An electronic system that makes it possible for one television scene to be matted in behind another. Chroma-keying is used to show a slide or some other graphic aid behind a news anchor, for instance. Blue is generally used for chroma-key matting.

chronological résumé   A résumé that presents basic information on work experience in chronological order.

Classic Hits   A radio station format that features Classic Rock and Pop hits from the late 1960s through the early 1980s.

Classic Rock   A radio station format featuring Rock-oriented Oldies of the 1960s, 1970s, and 1980s.

clichés   Overused and worn-out expressions.

clock   See *hot clock.*

club DJs   DJs who perform live in dance halls, as well as at birthdays, company parties, weddings, reunions, and similar festive events. Club DJs represent a large and growing number of music announcers whose work is not broadcast.

cluster   Two or more radio commercials played without intervening comment or program material; also called *commercial cluster* or *spot set.*

CNN   Abbreviation of Cable News Network.

co-anchors   Two or more announcers who share the role of chief newscaster on a radio or television program.

cold copy   A script not seen by an announcer until the moment to read it has arrived.

color   Comments made by a member of an announcing team to add an extra dimension to a live broadcast, usually consisting of human-interest anecdotes and informative, amusing, or unusual facts.

combination résumé   A résumé that combines features of a competency-based and a chronological résumé; also called a *hybrid résumé.*

combo operator   A radio disc jockey who does his or her own engineering.

commercial cluster   See *cluster.*

commercial sweep   A series of radio commercials, played without intervening program material.

communicaster   Used by some radio stations to identify the host of a telephone call-in show.

community billboard, community bulletin board, community calendar   Representative names for segments of airtime devoted to brief public-service announcements.

compact disc or CD   A small optical disc, on which digitally recorded music is stored.

competency-based résumé   A résumé that stresses the skills an applicant possesses.

compressor   An electronic device that keeps a sound signal within a given dynamic range.

condenser microphone   A type of microphone that features a diaphragm and an electrode as a backplate.

console   An audio control board.

Contemporary Hit Radio   A radio station format that features the current top rock hits, sometimes interspersed with a few golden oldies; also known as *Top 40.*

continuity book   A loose-leaf compilation of radio commercials in the order they are to be read or introduced (if on tape) by the announcer on duty; sometimes called *copy book.*

continuity writers   Writers of broadcast scripts other than news scripts.

controller   The computer that controls the programming of an automated radio system; also called the *brain.*

cooperative commercials   Commercials used on both radio and television, whose cost is divided between a national and a local advertiser.

copy book   See *continuity book.*

copy sets   Multipart forms, complete with one-use carbon papers, used widely in television newsrooms to create as many as six duplicate scripts of a program.

corporate media   See *industrial media.*

correspondents Reporters stationed some distance away from their stations or network headquarters.

Country A format descriptive of a radio station featuring contemporary and traditional Country music.

cover letter The letter written to accompany a résumé or an audition tape.

cover shot A television shot that gives a picture of a medium-to-large area. On an interview set, a cover shot would include both interviewer and guest(s).

CR Abbreviation for *Classic Rock,* a popular-music category.

crank up the gain To increase the volume of sound going through an audio console.

crescendo An increase in the volume or intensity of an announcer's voice.

cross fade Manipulating the volume controls of an audio console so that one program sound fades out while another simultaneously fades in.

crossplug A pitch made by a disc jockey or talk program host to promote another program on the same station.

CU Television script symbol for *close-up.*

cue box Small speaker in an audio control room or on-air studio that allows an audio operator to hear program elements as they are being cued up or previewed; sometimes called a *cue speaker.*

cue cards Cards used in television to convey information or entire scripts to on-camera performers.

cumes Short for *cumulative ratings,* which indicate the number of people listening to or viewing a particular station at a given time.

cut sheet In radio, a listing that indicates how to edit one or more cuts from an audiotape to a tape cartridge; in television news operations, a form on which information about taped material is entered during editing by videotape engineers.

cutaway shots Reaction shots, usually of a reporter listening to a newsmaker, recorded at the time of an interview and later edited into a package to avoid jump cuts at points in the report where parts of the speaker's comments have been omitted.

CW or C/W Abbreviations for *Country,* a popular-music category. Despite the W, the format is referred to simply as "Country."

CZ Abbreviation for *Classic Hits,* a popular-music category.

DAT Abbreviation of *digitial audio tape.*

daypart   A term used by music radio stations to identify specific portions of the broadcast day, which may be *dayparted* into morning drive time, afternoon drive time, midday, nighttime, and overnight.

DCM   Abbreviation of *digital cartridge machine.*

debriefing log   A record kept by radio and television stations of information about the performance of guests and the degree of audience interest in them.

decrescendo   A decrease in the force or loudness of an announcer's voice.

de-essing   The process of using a compressor to reduce sibilance.

delegation switch   A switch on an audio console that allows its operator to send a signal to a selected channel.

demographics   The profile of an actual or intended audience, including information on age, sex, ethnic background, income, and other factors that might help a broadcaster attract or hold a particular audience.

denasality   A quality of the voice due to speaking without allowing air to pass through the nasal passage.

depth of field   The area in front of a camera lens in which everything is in focus.

design computer   A device for making television graphics. Most feature a keyboard, a monitor, an electronic tablet with stylus, and a menu of effects that it can produce.

Desk   A name used for the assignment editor in broadcast news operations.

diacritical marks   The marks used by dictionaries to indicate pronunciation.

diaphragm   The muscular membrane that separates the stomach from the lungs.

diction   Same as *articulation* and *enunciation.*

digital audio tape   One medium (a compact disc and a hard storage disc being others) for storing and later playing digitally recorded sound.

digital cartridge machine   A tape player that records and plays digitally recorded sound.

digital video effects (DVE)   Special effects produced by equipment that changes an analog video signal to digital, making it possible to manipulate images in many creative ways.

diphthongs   Speech sounds that consist of a glide from one vowel sound to another: for example, the "oy" sound in the word *joy.*

disc jockey   The person who identifies the music and provides pertinent comments on a popular-music radio station.

DJ   Abbreviation for disc jockey; sometimes spelled "deejay."

donut commercial   A commercial with a recorded beginning and end, and live material read by a local announcer in the middle.

double out   A term used in radio production to warn an engineer that a speaker repeats the out cue in a particular tape. A sports coach, for example, may say "early in the year" both in the body of his comments and at the end of the cut; the warning *double out* is given so that the engineer will not stop the cart prematurely.

drive time   Hours during which radio stations receive their highest audience ratings, usually 6–10 A.M. and 3–7 P.M.

drugola   The acceptance of illegal drugs in exchange for such favors as promoting a recording produced by the supplier of the drugs.

dubbing   Transferring audio- or videotaped program material to another tape; also, recording another person's voice onto the soundtrack to replace the voice of the person who is seen on the screen.

DVE   Abbreviation for *digital video effects*.

DVE machine   A device that can turn a video picture into a mosaic, swing it through space, make it shrink or grow in size, and achieve many other visually interesting effects.

dynamic microphone   A rugged, high-quality microphone that works well as an outdoor or hand-held mic; also known as a *pressure mic*.

earprompter   A small earpiece worn by a performer, used to receive instructions from a producer or director.

ear training   Developing a sensitivity to sounds, especially spoken words, and the ability to detect even slight variations from accepted standards of pronunciation, articulation, voice quality, and other aspects of human speech. Ear training is an essential part of voice improvement.

Easy Listening   A radio station format featuring primarily instrumental versions of popular songs.

easy listening formula   A system for judging the clarity of a script that is to be broadcast.

EFP   Abbreviation for *electronic field production*.

egg-on-face look   The strained look of a performer who is trying to hold a smile while waiting for the director to go to black.

elasped time clock   A clock that shows how much time has been used up, rather than time remaining, in a broadcast segment.

electronic applicant tracking systems   Systems that scan résumés into a computer system that searches for and extracts important information necessary to qualify you for a job.

electronic field production   Any kind of videotaping using minicams and portable recorders and done on location.

electronic news gathering   Producing news reports for television in the field, using the same kind of portable equipment employed in electronic field production.

electrostatic microphone   An alternative term for a *condenser mic.*

ELF   Abbreviation for *easy listening formula.*

ellipses   A series of three or four periods to indicate an omission of words.

Emergency Alert System   The FCC's replacement for the Emergency Broadcast System, a program that requires certain broadcast stations to notify the public in case of an emergency such as a tornado, forest fire, or toxic spill.

ENG   Abbreviation for *electronic news gathering.*

enunciation   Same as *articulation.*

equalizer   A system that automatically controls sound by selecting frequencies to emphasize or to eliminate.

equal time   A provision of the Communications Act that requires broadcast licensees in the United States to provide time on an equal basis for legally qualified candidates for office.

ESPN   Abbreviation of Entertainment and Sports Programming Network.

ET   A script symbol for "electrical transcription," which was an early term for a certain type of phonograph record, now used for any kind of disc recording.

extemporaneous   Comments prepared in advance but delivered without a script or notes.

EZ   Abbreviation for *Easy Listening,* a popular-music category.

FA   Abbreviation for *Fine Arts-Classical,* a Classical-music category.

fact sheet   An outline of information about a product or an event, from which a writer prepares a script for a commercial or public-service announcement.

fade out   Using a *fader* or *potentiometer* to gradually reduce the sound until it no longer can be heard. The same term is used for the fading to black of a video signal.

fader   A control on an audio console enabling an operator to increase or decrease the volume of sound going through the board.

fairness doctrine   A former policy of the FCC that required broadcast licensees to devote airtime to the discussion of public issues.

fax   Abbreviation of "facsimile," the transmission of images or printed matter by electronic means.

FCC   Abbreviation for *Federal Communications Commission.*

feature reporter   Reporter who writes, edits, and announces soft news stories that engage audiences with stories that move, entertain, amuse, and/or illuminate.

Federal Communications Commission   The governmental agency that oversees broadcasting and other telecommunications industries in the United States.

feedback   A howl or squeal created when a microphone picks up and reamplifies the sound from a nearby loudspeaker.

fidelity   Faithfulness to an original sound, as in a recording of a live music performance.

field reporter   A radio or television reporter who covers stories away from the station, as contrasted with anchors who perform on a news set.

field voicer   A report from the field, sent live to a station by a reporter.

Fine Arts-Classical   A radio station format featuring Classical music, opera, theatre, and culture-oriented news and talk.

flaring   Flashes on the television screen caused by reflection of studio lights or sunlight off some shiny object, such as jewelry.

format   (1) A type of script used in television, usually a bare script outline; (2) the type of programming provided by a radio station (for example, an MOR format); (3) the layout of a radio or television script, or the manner in which dialogue, sound effects, music, and other program elements are set forth on the page.

freelance   An announcer or other media performer who works without a contract or a long-term appointment.

freeze   To remain motionless, usually at the end of a television scene.

fricatives   Sounds created by the friction of air through a restricted air passage; an example is the sound of the letter *f*.

functional résumé   See *competency-based résumé.*

future file   A set of 31 folders (one for each day of the month) holding information about coming events so that they may be considered by an assignment editor for news coverage.

gaffer's tape　　The tape used to hold cables in place in television studios. (A *gaffer* is the chief electrician on a motion picture set.)

gain　　The degree of sound volume through an audio console.

gain control　　A sliding vertical fader or rotating knob used to regulate the volume of sound through an audio console.

General American　　The speech of educated citizens of the Midwest and Far West of the United States and of most of Canada; also called "broadcast speech" and "Standard American Speech."

general-assignment reporter　　A radio or television reporter who does not have a regular beat, or assignment.

glide　　In speech, a rapid movement or *glide* from one vowel sound to another, as in the "oy" sound in the word *joy*. Also called a *diphthong*, pronounced *dif-thong*.

glottal consonant　　The letter *h*, when uttered without vibration of the vocal folds.

glottal stop　　A speech sound produced by a momentary but complete closure of the throat passage, followed by an explosive release of air.

graveyard shift　　Working hours that extend from midnight until 6:00 A.M.

hand signals　　Signals developed to communicate instructions to performers without the use of spoken words.

happy talk　　A derogatory term for a newscast featuring news personnel who ad-lib, make jokes, and banter with one another.

hard copy　　The printed copy of the output of a computer or word processor.

hard news　　Important stories that are usually unanticipated by a broadcast news department.

hard sell commercial　　A commercial that is characterized by rapid vocal delivery, high volume, and excessive energy.

headline　　To *tease* upcoming music selections on a radio show.

headlines signal　　A hand signal given by an announcer to tell the engineer that headlines will follow the news item currently being read.

headphone jack　　A receptacle on a tape recorder or audio console for connecting a headset.

hemispheric　　The pickup pattern of a microphone that accepts sounds within a half globe.

hitting marks　　Moving to an exact spot in television performance, usually indicated by tape placed on the floor or the ground.

homers   Sports play-by-play announcers who show an obvious bias for the home team.

horizontal spots   Radio commercials scheduled at about the same time across the days of the week.

hot change   Words created by a character generator that jump from one word or phrase to another on the television screen.

hot clock   A wheel used by music, satellite, and news radio stations to schedule program elements. At popular-music stations, the hot clock indicates the types of music to be played during a typical broadcast hour (up tempo, golden oldie, current hit, etc.), and indicates precisely when local insertions (commercials, weather reports, or local news) may be made. News station hot clocks specify the timing of headlines, news stories, weather and traffic reports, commercials, and other program components; also called the *clock*.

hybrid résumé   A résumé that combines the features of a chronological and a competency-based résumé.

hypercardioid   A microphone pickup pattern.

I & I   Script symbol for "introduce and interview."

IDs   Brief musical passages used to identify an upcoming sports report, business report, or other feature; also called *sounders* or *logos*.

IFB   Abbreviation for *interruptable foldback*.

impromptu   A performance delivered with little or no preparation and without a script.

in cue   The recorded words that open a segment of an interview that will be dubbed and used as part of a report.

industrial media   Audiovisual presentations made for (and often by) corporations, government agencies, and similar entities and intended for internal use, usually for training purposes; usually referred to as "industrials."

industrials   See *industrial media*.

inflection   The variation of the pitch of a human voice.

infomercial   *Informercials* typically are half-hour television sales pitches, with two or more announcers demonstrating such products as exercise machines, hair restorer, cooking equipment, fishing equipment, and beauty aids.

informational interview   A conversation with an experienced broadcast executive for the purpose of gaining information about job-seeking.

input selector switch   Control on an audio console that allows more than one program input (several microphones, for example) to be fed selectively into the same preamp.

interdental   A speech sound made with the tongue between the upper and lower teeth: for example, the "th" sound in *thin*.

International Phonetic Alphabet   A system of phonetic transcription that employs special symbols to denote pronunciations.

interruptable foldback   A miniaturized earphone worn by news reporters, anchors, and sportscasters. Instructions and cues are given over the IFB by producers and directors.

in the mud   Expression used when the volume of sound going through an audio console is so weak that it barely moves the needle of the VU meter; the needle is said to be *in the mud*.

in the red   Opposite of in the mud, *in the red* is the term used to describe sounds that are too high in volume. Other terms for this are *bending the needle* and *spilling over.*

intro   Abbreviation of *introduction.*

IPA   Abbreviation for *International Phonetic Alphabet.*

jargon   The specialized vocabulary of a group such as computer technicians, athletes, military personnel, or a particular ethnic group.

Jazz   A radio station format featuring mostly instrumental traditional and smooth jazz.

jock   Short for *disc jockey.*

jump cut   A noticeable "jump" in the television picture when a portion of taped material has been edited out.

JZ   Abbreviation for *Jazz,* a popular-music category.

keys   Images, usually lettering, keyed into a background image by a *character generator.*

labial   A speech sound made primarily with the lips: for example, the sound of the letter *p.*

labiodental   A speech sound requiring the lower lip to be in proximity to the upper teeth. Labiodental sounds are associated with the letters *f* and *v.*

larynx   The part of the body connecting the trachea (or windpipe) and the pharynx (the area between the mouth and the nasal passages) and containing the vocal folds.

lavaliere microphone   A small microphone clipped to the dress, tie, or lapel of a performer.

lead-in   The opening phrases of a taped or live report or the words used by a reporter to introduce a taped actuality or voicer.

lead-out   The closing phrases of a taped or live report or the words used by a reporter in adding a conclusion to a taped actuality or voicer.

LED   Abbreviation for *light-emitting diode.*

level indicator   A device that shows graphically the amount of volume being sent through an audio console or to an audio- or videotape recorder.

libertarian theory   A theory concerning the media that maintains that except for defamation, obscenity, or wartime sedition there should be no censorship of the news whatsoever.

light-emitting diode   A device that indicates audio volume through the activation of a series of small lights.

limiter   In audio operations, a device that limits the output volume, regardless of the strength of the input volume.

liner notes   Notes prepared by a radio station executive, from which a disc jockey will promote a contest, an upcoming feature, or another disc jockey's show; sometimes called "liner cards."

lingua-alveolar   A speech sound made with the tip of the tongue (or lingua) placed against the upper gum ridge (or alveolus): for example, the sound of the letter *t.*

linguadental   A speech sound made with the tongue between the upper and lower teeth: for example, the initial sound in *thin.*

linguapalatal   A speech sound made with the tip of the tongue nearly touching the upper gum ridge: for example, the sound of the letter *r.*

linguavelar   A speech sound made when the rear of the tongue is raised against the soft palate (or velum) and the tip of the tongue is lowered to the bottom of the mouth, as in sounding the letter *k.*

lip synch   Matching, or synchronizing, the movement of the lips with the speech sounds of the performer. This is achieved automatically with video equipment, but is difficult when dubbing one performer's voice to the lip movements of another who is seen on-screen.

live coverage   Reporting on a story as it happens, most often from the scene of the event.

LMA   See *local marketing agreement.*

Local Marketing Agreement (LMA)   In this practice, two or more radio stations enter into an arrangement in which they share facilities, staff, and equipment and, in some instances, even a frequency.

logo   An aural or visual symbol used to identify a program, product, company, or similar entity. The famous CBS eye is the logo for that network. An aural logo is also called a *sounder.*

looping   The dubbing of one person's voice onto the soundtrack of a tape to replace the voice of the person who is seen on the screen.

MA   Abbreviation for *Modern Adult/Contemporary,* a popular-music category.

major market   A city or metropolitan area with a potential viewing or listening audience of more than 1,000,000.

market   The reception area of a radio or television station, classified as major, secondary, or smaller.

marking copy   Making notations on scripts as reminders of when to pause or to stress a word or phrase or to show phonetic transcriptions of difficult words.

marks   Positions for television performers, usually indicated by small pieces of gaffer's tape on the floor of the studio or the ground at an exterior location.

master pot   A control of an audio console, capable of raising and lowering simultaneously all sounds going through the board; *pot* is short for *potentiometer.*

matte in   To combine electronically two pictures on the television screen without superimposing one over the other; see also *chroma-key.*

menu   A listing of stored information available for retrieval through a computer workstation. Menus are tailored to the needs of news directors, reporters, play-by-play sports announcers, and talk-show hosts, among others.

MERPS   Abbreviation for "multievent recorder/player systems," which are audio/video electronic cart machines.

message design and testing   The process of determining in advance the objectives of a given program and then rating its degree of success after it is performed.

mic fright   A fear of performing in front of a microphone.

microcasting   Same as *narrowcasting.*

microphone consciousness   An awareness of the capabilities and shortcomings of microphones.

minicam   A small, lightweight, portable television camera and its associated equipment.

minidoc   A short documentary, usually produced as a series for a radio or television news program.

minus out   To eliminate the announcer's voice from the sound relayed back from a satellite to the announcer's IFB so that the 1½ second delay will not confuse the announcer.

mixer   An audio console.

MLB   Abbreviation for *Major-League Baseball*.

mobile DJs   DJs who perform live in dance halls, as well as at birthdays, company parties, weddings, reunions, and similar festive events. Mobile DJs represent a large and growing number of music announcers whose work is not broadcast.

Modern Adult/Contemporary   A radio station format featuring a softer spectrum of Modern Rock.

moiré effect   A wavering or shimmering of the picture on a television screen, due to patterns of small checks or narrow stripes on performers' clothing.

monaural   A sound system featuring only one loud speaker.

monitor pot   A control on an audio console enabling the operator to adjust the volume of sound coming from a monitor speaker without affecting the volume of sound being broadcast or recorded.

monitor select switch   A switch on an audio console used to selectively monitor program and audition outputs.

monitor speaker   A speaker in an audio control room that enables the operator to hear the material being broadcast or recorded.

mood   A state of mind or emotion projected by a performer. Some typical moods are gloomy, joyous, cynical, elated, and festive. See also *attitude*.

moonlighting   Working at odd jobs, usually at night, while holding down a permanent position.

morgue   A collection of magazine and newspaper clippings, organized by topic and used for gathering background information for news stories and interviews.

MOS   Script abbreviation for "man-on-the-street interview." (Despite efforts to avoid gender-specific references in broadcast terminology, this term is still used.)

multidirectional microphone   A microphone that can be adjusted to employ more than one pickup pattern.

multievent recorder/player systems (MERPS)   Audio/video computerized electronic cart machines. MERPS's memory and storage capacity permit it to perform a variety of functions once done by a cumbersome master reel.

multi-images   A digital video effects device that changes the video signal from analog to digital; one of many options that DVE equipment offers is that of *multi-imaging,* splitting the screen into sectors, with each section containing a different visual image, or repeating the same video information in each cell.

music bed   The musical background of a radio commercial, usually laid down before voices are added.

music sweep   Several music recordings played back-to-back without interruption or comment by the DJ.

musical IDs   Musical logos that identify a program or a program segment.

muting relays   Devices that automatically cut off the sound from a monitor speaker when an announce mic in the control room is opened.

NAB   Abbreviation for National Association of Broadcasters.

narrowcasting   Programs not intended for large, heterogeneous audiences.

nasality   A quality of the voice due to allowing air to exit through the nose, rather than the mouth, when speaking.

nasals   Speech sounds that employ nasal resonance, such as *m, n,* and *ng.*

National Public Radio   A network of noncommercial radio stations, established by the Corporation for Public Broadcasting.

NBA   Abbreviation for *National Basketball Association.*

New Rock   A radio station format that features Modern Rock.

news script   The copy from which news anchors work. News scripts may be seen by anchors as hard copy or as electronically generated copy seen on a prompter.

newswheel   News station *newswheels* or hot clocks specify the timing of headlines, news stories, weather and traffic reports, commercials, and other program components; also called the *clock.*

NFL   Abbreviation for *National Football League.*

NHL   Abbreviation for *National Hockey League.*

nonverbal communication   That part of a person's communication with others that does not involve speech, such as gestures, facial expressions, and so on.

NPR   Abbreviation for *National Public Radio*.

NR   Abbreviation for *New Rock,* a popular-music category.

O & O   Abbreviation for *owned and operated;* refers to radio or television stations owned and operated by a parent network.

off hours   The portion of a broadcast day, usually late night and very early morning, when the audience is least likely to be tuned in.

off mic   Persons are said to be *off mic* when they speak outside the ideal pickup pattern of a microphone.

OL   Abbreviation for *Oldies,* a popular-music category.

Oldies   A term used in popular-music radio programming to describe a genre of music. Comparable terms are *Golden Oldies, Rock 'n Roll Classics,* and *Solid Gold.*

omnidirectional   A microphone pickup pattern in which all sides will accept sound signals.

on-air studio   The studio in which radio DJs and news anchors perform.

on-air talent   Persons who perform on radio or television. The term usually is associated with music station announcing, but reporters, anchors, and voice-over performers also are *on-air talent.*

opening up to the camera   Positioning oneself at a slight angle from a second person to present a favorable appearance to the camera.

optimum pitch   The pitch at which a speaker feels most comfortable while producing the most pleasant speech sounds.

orbiting spots   See *rotating spots.*

out cue   The words that conclude a recorded and carted program segment, alerting an announcer that the carted segment has come to its conclusion. When editing audiotaped interviews or statements, an out cue indicates the final words spoken in a given segment, and tells the editor (usually the reporter) where to electronically or manually "cut" the tape.

outro   A lead-out at the end of a radio or television news report, such as an actuality or a wrap.

overmodulation   Excessive volume that distorts an audio signal.

package   (1) A complete news report prepared by a field or special-assignment reporter, needing only a lead-in by an anchor; (2) a series of programs marketed to television stations as a unit.

pan pot   Short for *panoramic potentiometer.*

panic button   A control that allows a producer to cut off obscene or defamatory comments by a caller on a telephone talk show.

panoramic potentiometer   A volume control that allows an operator to change the volume balance between two audio channels.

payola   The accepting of money in return for playing certain songs on the air.

pay-per view   Cable television offerings, such as new movies or sports events, for which viewers are charged a fee beyond their monthly cable service cost.

PC   Abbreviation for "politically correct" or *political correctness.*

peripheral vision   The ability to see out of the corners of the eyes, to see a hand signal, for example, without looking at the person giving it.

personal attack, personal attack rule   A *personal attack* is a verbal attack, made during a broadcast, on "the honesty, character, integrity or like personal qualities" of another person. The *rule,* set forth by the Federal Communications Commission, requires broadcast licensees to notify those who are attacked and to inform them as to the ways in which they may reply.

personality   A term sometimes used for a DJ, program host, or other popular entertainer.

pharynx   The area between the mouth and the nasal passages.

phonation   The utterance of speech sounds; articulation breaks up these sounds into recognizable speech.

phone beat   See *beat check.*

phone check   Using a telephone to search for and gather news stories from a list of agencies, including the FBI, police and fire departments, local hospitals, the weather bureau, and airport control towers; also called the *phone beat* and *beat check.*

phone screener   A person, usually a producer or assistant producer, who receives telephone calls from listeners or viewers who want to talk with a program host, and who attempts to eliminate calls from people who are obviously cranks or drunks or are too-frequent callers.

phoneme   The smallest unit of distinguishable speech sound.

pickup   The term *pickup* is used in at least three ways in voice-over recording work. If you stumble or slur a word, you are expected to pause, say "pickup," pause again, and begin reading from the beginning of the sentence in which you stumbled. A *pickup session* is a recording session in which specific lines, recorded at an earlier session, are deemed unusable and must be recorded again. *Pickup* also refers to picking up one's cue—in other words, speaking more closely on the heels of a line delivered by another performer.

pickup arm   The arm on a turntable that contains the stylus; also called the *tone arm*.

pickup cartridge   The pickup cartridge on an audio turntable contains a stylus and a mechanism that picks up vibrations on a phonograph record and transduces the vibrations into electrical energy.

pickup pattern   The three-dimensional area around a microphone from within which sound is transmitted most faithfully, also referred to as the *polar pattern*.

pickup session   See *pickup*.

pitch   The property of a tone that is determined by the frequency of vibration of the sound waves. For humans, the slower the vocal folds vibrate, the lower the pitch of the voice.

pitch "artist"   A type of announcer whose style is reminiscent of sideshow barkers and old-time medicine shows.

platform speech   An exaggerated style of speaking, featuring overly precise articulation and a distinct "British" sound.

play analyst   An announcer, usually a former star athlete, who works with a play-by-play announcer, providing insight and analysis of a game.

play-by-play announcer   A sportscaster who describes the action of a game.

playlist   Music approved by radio station management for playing at stipulated times.

plosive   A speech sound manufactured by the sudden release of blocked-off air. In English, the plosives are *p, b, t, d, k,* and *g*.

plugola   The free promotion of a product or service in which the announcer has a financial interest. (Reading or playing commercials that have been paid for is not illegal, even when the announcer has an interest in the product being advertised.)

polar pattern   See *pickup pattern*.

political correctness (PC)   A concept with a range of meanings but confined in this text to *language* that is sensitive and appropriate, as opposed to that which is hurtful or demeaning.

polydirectional   A pickup or polar pattern that can be adjusted to operate with more than one pickup pattern. Same as *multidirectional*.

popping   The sound made when a plosive is spoken too closely to a sensitive mic.

postmortem   A meeting held after a broadcast to discuss what worked, what did not, and why.

postproduction   Editing and other electronic manipulation of audio or videotapes after they have been recorded.

pot   Short for *potentiometer*.

potentiometer   A volume control on an audio console.

preamplifier   An electronic device that boosts the strength of an audio signal and sends it to the program amplifier; often shortened to "preamp."

presentation tape   An audition tape.

press kit   An organized body of printed information prepared by political parties, law enforcement agencies, or sports teams, among others, for reporters, sportscasters, and others who may find such kits useful as they plan their stories or prepare for play-by-play coverage.

pressure microphone   A rugged professional microphone that features a molded diaphragm and a wire coil suspended in a magnetic field; also called a *dynamic microphone*.

pressure zone microphone   A type of microphone that eliminates time lags between direct and reflected sounds.

Preteen   A radio station format featuring music, drama or readings that focus mostly on a preteen audience.

primary stress   The syllable in a spoken word that receives the emphasis. In the word *primary*, the first syllable receives the primary stress.

prime time   That part of the broadcast day during which the radio or television audience is most likely to be tuned in.

production console   An elaborate audio console with features not found (or needed) on on-air studio boards, including equalization and other signal processing options. A production console or board.

production studio   A radio studio in which music is dubbed from discs to carts or DAT, station promos are recorded, and other program elements requiring a sophisticated audio setup are produced.

program amplifier   An electronic device that collects, boosts, and sends sounds to a transmitter or tape recorder.

program log   A listing of all commercials, public-service announcements, and program material broadcast by a station.

promo   Short for "promotion"; any prepared spot that promotes viewing or listening to a station or a program broadcast by the station.

prompter   Any of several machines that display a script before a broadcast performer; also called "prompting devices" or "teleprompters" (however, TelePrompTer is the brand name of one prompting system).

pronouncer   The phoneticized pronunciation for a word or name included on wire-service copy.

pronunciation   A way of speaking words. The particular accent used by persons in sounding words.

prop   Short for "property"; any article other than sets or costumes used in a television production.

property   An object that a performer holds, displays, or points to.

PSA   Abbreviation for *public-service announcement.*

PT   Abbreviation for *Preteen,* a popular-music category.

public-service announcement   A radio or television announcement that promotes a charitable or nonprofit organization or cause.

PZM   Abbreviation for *pressure zone microphone.*

Q & A session   Question-and-answer session; a brief on-air discussion of a news story between an anchor and a reporter in the field.

raw sound   Recorded or live sounds from the site of news stories that add to the "reality" of reports. Raw sounds include those of foghorns, crickets chirping, jet aircraft flying overhead, people chanting, and the sound of marching bands at a parade.

RB   Abbreviation for *R&B/Urban,* a popular-music category.

R&B/Urban   A radio station format featuring a wide range of musical styles, often called *Urban Contemporary.*

RC   Abbreviation for *Religious/Contemporary,* a popular-music category.

real time   Whether live or recorded, *real time* refers to performances that are unedited and heard or seen by an audience exactly as they are or were performed.

recurrent   A term used in music radio to indicate selections that are just off the playlist.

redundancy   Repetition of ideas or words or phrases, which is sometimes appropriate, as in repeating a telephone number to be called, and sometimes excessive, as in the term "joint partnership."

Religious/Contemporary   A radio station format featuring Modern and Rock-based religious music.

reporter   A person who reports news stories that occur away from a radio or television station; some categories are *field, general-assignment,* and *special-assignment reporters.*

resonance   The intensification of vocal tones during speech as the result of vibrations in the nose and cheekbones.

résumé   A written statement that includes work experience, qualifications, educational background, and interest areas, often submitted with employment applications.

résumé tape   Same as *audition tape.*

reveal   Words or phrases produced by a character generator and "revealed" one at a time on the television screen to match the points being made by an announcer.

ribbon microphone   A sensitive, professional microphone that has a metallic ribbon suspended between the poles of a magnet; also referred to as a *velocity mic.*

rip and read   To take news copy directly from a wire-service and read it on the air without editing it, marking it, or prereading it.

robotic cameras   Television cameras programmed to move to predetermined positions without individual human operators.

roll   Words or phrases produced by a character generator and moved from bottom to top on the television screen.

ROS   Abbreviation for *run of station.*

rotating potentiometers   Knobs on an audio console that are turned clockwise or counterclockwise to raise or lower the volume of sound; see also *vertical fader.*

rotating spots   Commercial announcements whose time of broadcast varies throughout the week; also called *orbiting spots.*

rotating table   The "table" on a record player that holds a disc and spins while a pickup stylus transmits sound from its grooves to another destination, such as a speaker or an audio console.

RTNDA   Abbreviation for *Radio and Television News Directors Association.*

rule of three   A theory that the impact of a statement is diluted by going beyond three words or phrases in a sequence.

run of station   A system of scheduling radio commercials on a random basis at available times.

run sheet   A run sheet, or *running log,* follows the established format of a news radio station and indicates the times at which you will give headlines, features, time checks, commercials, and other newscast elements or the times at which they will be played. The log may be on sheets of paper, on a computer screen, or on both.

running log   A listing of the times at which every program element will be broadcast by a radio station.

SA   Abbreviation for *Soft Adult Contemporary,* a popular-music category.

SAG   Abbreviation for the Screen Actors Guild, the union for those actors and announcers whose work is filmed (as opposed to taped).

SAT PIC   Abbreviation for "satellite picture," a view of the earth's weather sent from a satellite.

SB   Abbreviation for *Soft Urban Contemporary,* a popular-music category.

scannable résumé   A résumé specially formatted for scanning by a potential employer.

scener   A live or taped radio news report on a breaking event.

schwa vowel   In phonetic transcription, the *schwa* vowel represents an unaccented "uh" sound, as the last syllable in *sofa.* It is transcribed as an inverted "e," depicted as [ə].

search engines   World Wide Web indexing and searching systems, such as Fast Search, Alta Vista, Yahoo!, Lycos, and Infoseek. Users select a search engine and enter a key word(s) to locate web sites with information they seek.

secondary market   An area with a potential broadcast audience of between 200,000 and 1,000,000 viewers or listeners.

secondary stress   Multisyllabic words usually have different degrees of stress, as in the word *secondary.* SEC receives primary stress, ON is unstressed, DAR receives secondary stress, and Y is unstressed.

segue   To broadcast two elements of a radio program back-to-back without overlap or pause. The first sound is faded out, and the second is immediately faded in.

semivowels   Speech sounds similar to true vowel sounds in their resonance patterns. The consonants *w, r,* and *Y* are the semivowels.

separates   The term used by the Associated Press for individual sports stories.

set   Two or more songs played back to back without intervening commentary by the DJ.

SFX   Script symbol for *sound effects.*

shopping channels   Television channels devoted to the showing and selling of products. Viewers may make purchases by telephone or email.

showprep   The abbreviation for *show preparation.*

sibilance   The sound made when pronouncing the fricatives *s, sh,* and sometimes *z.* Excessive sibilance is exaggerated by sensitive microphones.

signature   Same as a *logo* or *ID.*

simile   A figure of speech in which two essentially unlike things are compared, as in "a meal without salad is like a day without sunshine."

simulcast   The simultaneous broadcasting of the same program over an AM and an FM station, or over a radio and a television station.

situationer   In most television news operations, news directors, producers, reporters, directors, and other key members of the news team meet to discuss and plan upcoming newscasts. A list of available stories, called a situationer, is handed out, and the stories are discussed one by one as decisions are made as to what stories to cover, who is to gather each report, and the order in which the stories will be broadcast.

slate   An audio and/or visual identification of a taped television program segment that is included at the beginning of the tape and provides information about the segment—its title, the date of recording, the intended date of showing, and the number of the take.

slip start   A method of starting to play a cued-up phonograph record by allowing the turntable to rotate while the operator's hand holds the disc motionless and then releasing the disc.

slug commercial   A hard-hitting commercial, usually characterized by high volume, rapid reading, and frenetic delivery.

slug line   The shortened, or abbreviated, title given to a news event for identification purposes.

smaller market   An area with a potential audience of fewer than 200,000 viewers or listeners.

social responsibility theory   A theory concerning the media that charges journalists with considering the potential consequences of their coverage of the news.

Soft Adult/Contemporary   A radio station format featuring primarily non-current Soft Rock originals.

soft news   News stories about scheduled events, such as meetings, briefings, hearings, or news conferences, that lack the immediacy and urgency of hard news.

soft sell commercial   A commercial that features restrained announcer delivery and (usually) a melodious musical background.

Soft Urban Contemporary   A radio station format featuring soft R&B mixed with Smooth Jazz, and often heavy in Oldies.

solecism   A blunder in speech.

SOT   Script symbol for *sound on tape*.

sound bite   A brief statement made on-camera by someone other than station personnel; equivalent to an actuality on radio.

sounder   A short, recorded musical identification of a particular radio program element, such as a traffic, sports, or weather report; also referred to as an *ID* or *logo*.

sounds   Recorded statements introduced as part of radio news stories. Sounds include actualities, wraps, sceners, and voicers.

Spanish   A radio station format featuring music from Latin America.

special-assignment reporter   A radio or television reporter who specializes in one aspect of news gathering, such as crime reporting, politics, environmental issues, or news from a particular geographic area.

speech personality   The overall quality of a person's voice, which makes one instantly recognizable to friends when speaking on the telephone.

spilling over   Another expression for bending the needle.

spot   Another term for a commercial.

spot set   A cluster of commercials played one after the other.

SS   Abbreviation for *Spanish*, a popular-music category.

Standard American Speech (or Standard American Dialect)   That manner of pronouncing words used by educated persons in the Midwest and Far West of the United States and Canada.

stand-up   A direct address made to a camera by a television reporter at any time within a news package, but almost always for the closing comments.

stash   A term used for songs that are not on a radio station's current playlist but are occasionally played.

station ID   Short for *station identification.*

station logo   A symbol, either aural or visual, by which a station identifies itself.

status-conferral function   The concept that the media of radio and television confer exalted status to those who appear on them.

stereo   A two-or-more-speaker sound system. Abbreviation of "stereophonic."

sting   Abbreviation of "stinger," a sharp musical chord used to highlight a transition or draw attention.

stop set   A cluster of commercials played one after the other.

streaming audio   Playing and announcing music over the Internet.

streaming radio   Playing and announcing music over the Internet.

stringer   A free-lance reporter who is paid only for stories chosen and used by a station's news department.

studio cards   Cards used in television to convey information or entire scripts to on-camera performers.

stylus   Part of a tone arm pickup cartridge, the needle.

super   Short for *superimposition,* the showing of one picture over another on the television screen.

supercardioid   A microphone pickup pattern used chiefly in television boom mics. Also called *hypercardioid.*

sweep   The playing of several songs consecutively, without intervening comment by the DJ.

sweetening   Electronically treating music, during recording and in postproduction, to improve the sound quality.

switchable   A microphone that features a switch that changes the pickup pattern of the mic. Also called *multidirectional* and *polydirectional.*

switcher   (1) The video console that allows an operator to cut, dissolve, and perform other electronic functions; (2) the title given to the person who operates such a console.

switches   Allow you to open and close your announce mic, to open and close the intercom or talk-back mic, and to open a mic in the newsroom for feeding out a news bulletin.

syllabic consonant   The consonants *m*, *n*, and *l*, which can be sounded as separate syllables without a vowel sound preceding or following them. In phonetic transcription, the word *saddle* can be transcribed as [ˈsædl̩], with the line under the letter *l* indicating that it is sounded as a separate syllable.

tag   To make closing comments at the end of a scene or program segment.

takes   Any number of attempts to record a program segment successfully.

taking a level   A procedure in which performers, prior to going on the air or being recorded, speak into a microphone at the volume level they will use during the show. This enables an audio engineer to establish the optimal volume level.

taking camera   In a multi-camera television production, the camera that is "on" at a specific moment.

talk-back microphone   The mic located in a control room that allows the audio operator to speak to people in other production areas, such as studios or newsrooms.

talking head   A derogatory term for a television shot featuring a close-up of a speaker addressing the camera.

talk station   A radio station, usually an AM station, that features a number of talk and telephone call-in shows daily.

tally light   A red light mounted on the top of a television camera that, when lit, indicates the *taking camera.*

TAP   Abbreviation for *total audience plan.*

tape cart   A cartridge of 1/4-inch audiotape that rewinds and that recues itself.

tape cart players   Machines that play quarter-inch audiotapes that are looped inside a cartridge and that automatically rewind as they are played.

target audience   The intended audience for a program or a commercial.

tease   A brief promotion of a program or an upcoming segment of a program.

telegraphing a movement   A subtle indication by a television performer who is about to move, stand, or sit. Directors and camera operators need such warnings to follow movements effectively.

tempo   A speaker's rate of delivery.

tight shot   A close-up shot.

time code   A means of marking each frame of a videotape for later editing.

time-delay system A means of delaying material being broadcast live (such as a radio call-in talk show) to permit intervention if someone uses profanity or makes other unacceptable comments.

tone arm The device on a turntable that holds the pickup cartridge and its stylus. The stylus "rides" the grooves of a record and converts the vibrations into electrical energy.

Top 40 A radio station format that rotates the top hits of the day, usually interspersed with Golden Oldies; also called *Contemporary Hit Radio*.

toss To turn the program over to a co-anchor, a weather reporter, or another member of the broadcast team with a brief ad-libbed transitional statement.

total audience plan A system for distributing commercial messages over three or more dayparts.

trachea The windpipe.

traffic department The personnel at a broadcast station who schedule the placement of commercials.

transduction The conversion of sound waves into electrical energy.

trash television Television talk shows that regularly use intimidation, obscenity, vulgarity, and controversial and unsubstantiated statements to attract an audience that seeks cheap thrills.

turntable The "table" on a record player that holds a disc and spins while a pickup stylus transmits sound from its grooves to another destination, such as a speaker or an audio console.

unidirectional A microphone pickup pattern in which sound is accepted from only one direction.

unphonated Speech sounds that don't employ vibrations of the vocal folds, as in the plosive sounds p, b, t, k, and g.

unvoiced consonants The consonants of spoken English that do not involve the vibration of the vocal folds. Examples are p, t, k, and f.

uplink A transmitter that sends a signal to a satellite and is often part of a mobile van.

urgent Sports news story issued by the Associated Press. Urgents include no hitters, major firings of coaches and managers, and important breaking stories.

variable equalizer A filter that enables an audio console operator to eliminate undesirable frequencies, such as those associated with scratches on a record.

velocity microphone   See *ribbon microphone*.

velum   The soft palate.

vertical fader   A sliding lever on certain audio consoles that is moved up or down to raise or lower the volume of sound.

vertical spots   Radio commercials scheduled at various times on a given day.

videotape recorder   Any of several types of electronic recording devices that record and store picture and sound for later playback or editing.

VI meter   Short for *volume indicator meter,* which registers the volume of sounds through an audio console.

virgule   A slash, used by some announcers to indicate a pause when marking broadcast copy for delivery.

viscous damping   The tone arm of a record player uses a silicone fluid in a hydraulic mechanism to prevent it from making sharp or sudden movements. The fluid is *viscous* and the *damping* acts as a restraint.

vitality   The enthusiasm and high energy level of a performer.

vocal folds, vocal cords   A part of the speech mechanism that vibrates to generate sounds. The rate of vibration determines pitch, and the amount of energy behind the vibration determines the loudness of a sound produced.

vocalized pauses   Sounds, such as "er" or "uh," uttered by some speakers to cover what otherwise would be silence as they search for a word or a thought.

voice quality   The way your voice sounds, including such characteristics as resonance, thinness, timbre, nasality, huskiness, and tone.

voiced consonants   The consonants of spoken English that require the vibration of the vocal folds. Examples are *b, d, g,* and *v.*

voice-overs   Taped performances in which the announcer is not seen.

voicer   A carted report from a radio news reporter.

volume   In audio terms, *volume* or *amplitude* refers to the relative strength (magnitude) of a sound signal.

vowel   A pure phonated tone that can be held indefinitely without moving the articulators: for example, the sound "ah" in *father.*

vox pop   Abbreviation of *vox populi,* Latin for *voice of the people.* Newscasts often feature brief expressions of opinion elicited from passersby. The term *man on the street* (MOS) is seldom used for such collections of opinion because of its gender bias.

VTR   Abbreviation for *videotape recorder.*

VTR SOT Abbreviation for *videotape, sound on tape.*

VU meter Short for *volume unit meter,* a part of an audio console that shows, by means of a swinging needle, the volume of sound going through the board.

web browser A tool that allows users to find sites on the Internet. Popular browsers are Mosaic, Microsoft Internet Explorer, and Netscape Navigator.

wheel Another term for a *clock,* or *hot clock.*

wild spots Radio commercials guaranteed by a station to be played at some point within a designated block of time.

windpipe The windpipe, also called the *trachea,* is a tube, slightly longer than four inches, that extends from the larynx to the lungs.

wipe An electronic effect in which one picture appears to push another off the television screen.

wire-service phonetics Symbols used to illustrate sounds. They were designed at a time when teletype machines were limited to capital letters only. An apostrophe was used to indicate the syllable to be stressed, as in (SILL'-UH-BUHL).

WNBA Abbreviation for *Women's National Basketball Association.*

woodshedding The careful study, marking, and rehearsing of broadcast copy before performance.

working combo Performing both announcing and engineering functions for a radio broadcast.

wowing The distorted sound when a record or tape is run at an incorrect or inconsistent speed.

wrap A recorded report from the field in which a radio news reporter provides a lead-in and a lead-out, *wrapped around* an actuality; also called a *wrap-around.*

WX Script symbol for "weather report."

INDEX

Please note: An "n" following a page number indicates that the information is located in a footnote.